C0-ABL-105

The Adventurous Palate

HOUSTON

Kathi Mosbacher

Pennybacker Publishing

To Wally, with love and gratitude for sharing the adventure with me.

Copyright © 1998 by Kathi Mosbacher

All Rights Reserved. No part of this book may be reproduced in any manner without the express written consent of the publisher, except in cases of brief excerpts in critical reviews and articles. All inquiries should be addressed to:
Pennybacker Publishing, Inc.
712 Main Street
Suite 2200
Houston, TX 77002-3290

Design: Tony Meisel
Printed in the United States of America
ISBN 0-914373-45-5

Contents

Acknowledgements

Not only have my friends been an invaluable resource for my column, but have – often at a moment's notice – allowed themselves to be spirited off to the far corners of the city in pursuit of the unusual – sometimes the inedible. Their insight, boundless enthusiasm and healthy appetites have made my job a lot more fun than it has a right to be.

My heartfelt thanks to my editor (and boss) at the Houston Chronicle, Jane P. Marshall, for keeping me on track and always reminding me that I would not run out of restaurants.

To my family (especially my father) for their love and support.

To my husband, Wally Cox, who has navigated sometimes very foreign territory and matched me forkful for forkful on this great adventure.

And to Carol A. Waldrop – who has helped me with everything.

About The Author

The author is a free lance food editor who has studied with everyone from James Beard twenty years ago in Greenwich Village to Ken Lo at Memories of China in London. In Paris, she attended La Varenne École de La Cuisine and then graduated from Le Cordon Bleu. She has contributed a weekly column as The Adventurous Palate© mostly about restaurants outside the mainstream for the Houston Chronicle's Dining Guide since its inception two and a half years ago.

She is a native Houstonian and is married to Wally Cox.

Introduction

When did my research as The Adventurous Palate© begin? Did it begin in New Orleans where – as a twelve-year-old – my friend Allison and I would put on our Sunday best, carefully count our allowance, and ride the street car down St. Charles Avenue to the French Quarter to eat stuffed eggplant and crabmeat Yvonne at Galatoires?

Or maybe in New York City in the seventies when I would insist dates take me to the Spanish restaurant Café San Martin, instead of "21" when I knew they had fresh shipments of angulas (baby eels) in from Spain. I always preferred the rustic charm of a plate of sausage and peppers at La Luna in Little Italy to the prim elegance of Quo Vadis on the Upper East Side of Manhattan.

"How perfect!" my friends exclaimed when I was asked by the Houston Chronicle to contribute a weekly column about restaurants outside the mainstream. "A match made in heaven!"

So, the adventure began in earnest. There were no restaurants too small (or quirky) to qualify. I visited all restaurants anonymously. When I didn't like the food, I simply moved on.

When I did, I would visit a second time before introducing myself and arranging an interview with the owner and chef when they were not the same person. In the meantime, I would try to learn as much as possible about the culture and cuisine. What did I want to know about these restaurants? Everything.

What is this food? How do they eat it? Why do they eat it? What are its most distinctive characteristics? (i.e. what are you likely to eat here that you won't find anywhere else?) Are there any off-the-menu specialties that only regulars know about? What do they drink with it? And finally, always … what are they proudest of? If friends or family visited from – for instance – Hong Kong, what would you feed them?

I learned so much. I learned that when you ask someone what they do best, nine times out of ten, they are right.

When it was good old American food, I was interested in the origins of recipes; how and where people learned to cook.

My objective always was to demystify the unfamiliar. How often have you passed a Korean restaurant and wanted to try it, but not gone in because you didn't know what to order or how to eat it?

So, I set out to tell the story and – like one trusted food friend to another – pass on my (very specific) recommendations – what to eat and how to eat it.

These are obviously my opinions. There is probably no more subjective art than that of food editing. The information in this guide was both current and, to the best of my knowledge, accurate when this book was printed. But, as everyone knows, in the restaurant world things change . . . and not always for the best.

The last section, "Mainstream Choices of the Adventurous Palate," includes some oldies-but-goodies that everyone I know frequents, and a few new favorites (like Sabine and Mark's).

As The Adventurous Palate, it has also been my job (and great pleasure) to always sample the strange and unusual – things like blood sausage, sweet breads and tripe – "specialties" that I sometimes couldn't entreat my fellow diners to eat even in the name of research.

I'll tell you what I tell them.

Life is short. Try everything. Be adventurous.

Kathi Mosbacher

Locations

Map of Greater Houston

George Bush
ercontinental Aiport
Eastex Frwy
B
C
Hardy Tollway
59
90
10
East Frwy
F
Clinton
Federal Rd
225
610
Sam Houston Tollway
Hobby Aiport
Sam Houston Pkwy
H
I
Gulf Frwy
45
To Galveston

MAINSTREAM CHOICES OF THE ADVENTUROUS PALATE

(Initial after name indicates area of map)

Américas - E
Anthony's - E
Brennan's of Houston - E
Brenner's Steak House - D
Cadillac Bar - E
Café Annie - E
Café Caspian - D
The Capital Grille - E
Confederate House - E
Damians - E
Goode Company Seafood - E
Gugenheim's Delicatessen - E
Hunan - E
La Mora Cucina Toscana - E
La Réserve - D
Mark's - E
Maxim's - E
Nino's - E
Nit Noi Thai Restaurant - E
Ousie's Table - D
Palm Restaurant - D
Pappas Bros. Steakhouse - D
Pavani - D
Redwood Grill - E
Ruggles Grill - E
Ruth's Chris Steak House - D
Sabine - E
Tommy Mandola's Gulf Coast Kitchen - E
Tony's - E

THE ADVENTUROUS PALATE RESTAURANTS

(Initial after name indicates area of map)

AMERICAN-BURGERS, ETC.

Baba Yega - E
Barnaby's Café - E
Bubba's Sports Bar & Grill - E
Kenneally's Irish Pub - E
The King Biscuit Patio Café - E
Texas Borders Bar and Grill - D

AMERICAN-ECLECTIC

Anjou Café - D
Baich's Bar and Grille - E
Cosmos Café - E
Dixie's Roadhouse - D
The Hobbit Hole - E
Paulie's - E
The Sundance Grill - I
Super Steak and More - E
Tommy's Patio Café - I
The Village Brewery and Restaurant - E

AMERICAN-HOMESTYLE COOKING

Ducho's Steak House - E
Harry's Restaurant - E
Mom's Kitchen - E
This Is It - E
West Gray Café - E

ARGENTINEAN/URUGUAN

Chimi Churri's - D
Empanadas by Marini - D

BARBECUE

Gus' - I
Heights Camphouse Bar B Q - E
Hinze's Bar-B-Que-Sealy - D
Hinze's Bar-B-Que-Wharton - G
Lyndon's Pit Bar-B-Q - D
Pete's Fine Meats - D
Pizzitola's Bar-B-Cue - E
T-Bone Tom's Meat Market and Steakhouse Restaurant - I

CHILEAN

Don Pepe - D

CHINESE
Auntie Chang's Dumpling House - E
Daniel Wong's Kitchen - E
Empress - A
Fung's Kitchen - D
Golden Bo - D
Kam's - E
P.F. Chang's China Bistro - E
Van Loc Vietnamese and Chinese Restaurant - E

COLOMBIAN
La Fogata - G

CREOLE-CAJUN
Crazy Cajun Food Factory - I
Denis' Seafood Restaurant - D
Super Steak and More - E
Tommy's Patio Cafe - I
Zydeco Louisiana Diner - E

CUBAN
Café Piquet - D
El Meson - E
El Rey - E
Latina Café & Food Market - E

DELICATESSEN
Carter & Cooley - E
Nielsen's Delicatessen - E
Pete's Fine Meats - D

ETHIOPEAN
Queen of Sheba - E

EUROPEAN-STYLE CAFÉ
Epicure Bakery and Tea Room - E

FRENCH
Chez Georges - D

FUSION
Empress - A

GERMAN
What's Cookin' - I

GREEK
Athens Bar and Grill - F

GUATEMALAN
El Pueblito Place - E

INDIAN
Bombay Brasserie - E
Madras Pavilion - E
Taj Mahal - F

IRISH
The Claddagh Irish Pub and Grill - D
Kenneally's Irish Pub - E

ITALIAN
Cavatore - E
Claudio's Piano Bar Restaurant - I
Collina's Italian Café - E
Crapitto's - E
Josephine's Italian Ristorante - E
New York Pizzeria - E
Ugo's Italian Grill - D

JAMAICAN
Reggae Hut - E

JAPANESE
Café Japon - E
Coco's - D
Tomokazu - D

KOREAN
Korea Garden Restaurant - D
Seoul Garden - D

KOSHER
Madras Pavilion - E

MEXICAN
Bocados - E
El Meson - E
El Paraiso - E
El Pueblito Place - E
El Rey - E
La Jaliscience Taqueria Restaurant and Bar - E
La Mexicana - E
Lupe Tortilla's Restaurant - D
Tampico - E
Taqueria Cancun - D

PIZZA
Collina's Italian Cafe - E
Keneally's Irish Pub - E
New York Pizzeria - E

PUERTO RICAN
Tex-Chick - E

SALVADOREAN
Los Ranchitos - D

SEAFOOD
Clary's Restaurant - I
Crazy Cajun Food Factory - I
Denis' Seafood Restaurant - D
The Sundance Grill - I
Thai Seafood - I
Tommy's Patio Café - I
Zydeco Louisiana Diner - E

SPANISH
Tasca Kitchen and Wine Bar - E
Tio Pepe - D

STEAKS
Ducho's Steak House - E
Gus' - I
Lynn's Steakhouse - D
Super Steaks and More - E

SWISS
Roland's Swiss Pastry and Tea Room - D

TEX-MEX DINER
Andy's in the Heights - E
Cortes Restaurant - E
Lupe Tortilla's Restaurant - D

THAI
The Blue Orchid-Viet-Thai Restaurant - D
Sawadee Thai Restaurant - E
Thai Gourmet - D
Thai House - D
Thai Racha - D
Thai Seafood - I

VEGETARIAN
Baba Yega - E
The Hobbit Hole - E
Paulie's - E

VIETNAMESE
The Blue Orchid-Viet-Thai Restaurant - D
Miss Saigon - E
Nam - D
Pho Cong Ly - E
Van Loc Vietnamese and Chinese Restaurant - E

ANDY'S IN THE HEIGHTS

1115 East 11th Street
Houston, Texas 77009
713/861-9423

Type of Cuisine: Tex-Mex Diner
Bar: No
Dress: Casual
Entertainment: No
Payment: Cash Only
Entrée Range: $1.55-$7.99
Recommended Dishes:
  Breakfast Dishes: Hot Cakes
    Migas con Huevo ("a la Mexicana" with "Cheese on top")
    Chorizo con Huevo (Burrito)
    Pork Chops
  Entrées: Cheese and Onion Enchiladas
    Menudo
    Bacon Cheeseburger
    Bistec a la Mexicana
Hours: Open 24 hours, Seven days a week
  (Closed Christmas Day)
Reservations: Not Accepted

"'A Tex-Mex diner.' That's how I describe the place to friends!" says Andy Morales of Andy's in the Heights. "I mean, where else are you going to have cheese enchiladas and hot cakes at 3:00 in the morning?"

Morales says that when his parents, Jesse and Sadie, opened (then) Andy's Home Café in August of 1977, and named it after the youngest of their eleven children, menudo and migas shared equal billing with hot dogs, hot cakes and apple pie. "My dad's always been set on having a Mexican/American restaurant. So, we've always had Mexican breakfasts, and American breakfasts."

The hot dogs (and apple pie) are gone, but the hamburgers are superb – "a classic greasy spoon hamburger," as Morales says – and the hot cakes, divine.

"The idea was always to keep it simple – chili, cheese and onions – no complicated ingredients. My mother cooked originally. They are all her recipes, and she cooked (at Andy's) exactly the way she cooked at home for us. But remember, my parents are from El Campo. So, this isn't Mexican food and it isn't American food. At Andy's you'll find authentic Tex-Mex dishes."

As evidence he cites the spectacular cheese and onion enchiladas – "a real taste of Texas," he says. He's right. They are Tex-Mex bliss. Grated American cheese and chopped onion folded in a freshly made corn tortilla surrounded by what Morales calls "my mom's enchilada gravy," a well-guarded family secret, he says, with more American cheese melted over the top. This qualifies as genuine comfort food for anyone who grew up in this area.

For breakfast, fluffy, flawless hot cakes are as popular at 3:00 in the afternoon as they are at 3:00 in the morning. They went well with an order of thin, crisp curls of smoky bacon or juicy discs of pork sausage.

Another breakfast meat, pork chops, were succulent, simply-seasoned with salt and lots of black pepper and browned quickly on a hot grill. They are a reminder of how good pork chops can be when they are not cooked to the dried hockey puck stage. Morales says he has customers who come in exclusively for pork chops always, he says, ordered with Andy's meaty, freshly made French fries. They are good but, as Morales admits, "not always as crisp as we would like them to be."

Morales tells me that the motto on their menu in the eighties was "Andy's … where everything is made from scratch." The chorizo, flavored with garlic and vinegar, and scarlet with chili powder is a good example. A bit daunting on its own, it's best scrambled with eggs (Chorizo con Huevo), and tucked into a soft, warm flour tortilla as a Breakfast Burrito.

Still, the best of Andy's Breakfast Combos may be the Migas con Huevo. The migas or "crumbs" of tortilla chips and eggs are elevated to star status when scrambled with finely diced jalapeños, onions and tomatoes, "a la Mexicana," and better still with molten queso or American cheese melted on top.

Fajitas, also eaten with eggs or hot cakes at Andy's, are fabulous – a classic cut of skirt steak marinated in garlic, lime, salt and pepper overnight, and grilled. But my choice in the red meat genre – apart from their perfect bacon cheese burger – is the Bistec a la Mexicana. Listed under "Andy's Dinner Platters," lean strips of sirloin steak are browned quickly on the flat grill with chopped onion, jalapeños and tomatoes. It is served with satiny refried beans and nicely seasoned Mexican rice, a few French fries and warm tortillas.

"Tex-Mex beef tips and gravy" is how Morales describes the Carne Guisada. It is a soulful stew of bite size beef tips (of sirloin, again) sautéed with onion, bell peppers, garlic and tomatoes in classic brown, cumin-flavored flour gravy. For added impact, a little of one of the two salsas on the table – the green salsa – should be drizzled on top. It is a simple purée of fresh jalapeños, garlic and cumin.

For dipping or spooning on top of my cheese and onion

enchiladas (or anything else), I preferred the red salsa, a warm, tomatoey, Salsa Ranchera – good enough for regulars to take home by the pintful.

The mother of all stews – menudo – well earns its South Texas reputation as the "Breakfast of Champions" at Andy's. This tripe stew, a famous hangover cure, is available seven days a week and not just on weekends as is often the case elsewhere. Morales says they sell so much menudo – equally popular with Latino and Anglo customers – sometimes they have to make it twice a day. A pig's foot adds extra depth and harmony to their menudo. At dinner, I longed for a beer to wash down this heady brew. But, Andy's has never gotten a liquor license.

Depending on the time of day (or night) and what they're eating, most customers seemed perfectly content to drink orange juice, iced tea, hot (Mexican) chocolate or tart, freshly squeezed lemonade. Morales says that sometimes he wishes they served alcohol, but speculates that the fact that they don't probably contributes to they homeyness of the atmosphere. That, he says, and the fact that, although the Heights has changed since he was three when his parents opened Andy's, it still feels a bit like a sleepy, small town, "not a lot of rowdy drinking going on around here, you know."

There is a comfortable coziness about Andy's, "a little bit like stepping back in time," Morales adds. "Andy's is a real family owned place. One of us is always here."

ANJOU CAFÉ

966 S. Fry Road
Katy, Texas 77450
281/578-3959

Type of Cuisine: American/Eclectic
Bar: Wine and Beer
Dress: Casual
Entertainment: No
Payment: All Major Credit Cards
Entrée Range: $7.95-$21.95
Recommended Dishes:
Appetizers: Artichoke and Spinach Dip
Salmon Imperial
Fresh Basil Leaves
Tortilla Soup
Entrées: Mother's Baked Chicken
Ancho-Crusted Smoked Chicken Breast
Ribeye Strindberg
Rack of Lamb Provencal
Hours: Tuesday-Thursday, 11:00a.m.-3:00p.m., 5:00p.m.-9:00p.m.
Friday, 11:00a.m.-3:00p.m., 5:00p.m.-9:30p.m.
Saturday, 5:00p.m.-9:30p.m.
Sunday, 10:00a.m.-3:00p.m.
(Closed Monday)
Reservations: Accepted
Smoking: Not Permitted

What's the likelihood of finding matzo ball soup, Vietnamese spring rolls, and a great authentic-tasting, down and dirty "South Philly Sandwich" all under the same roof?

"Diversity. That's the way I went into this. I wanted variety," explains chef Ruskin Jackson, of the menu at his three year old neighborhood restaurant, Anjou Café. "I wanted people to feel that they were getting a little bit of different cultures. A little bit of Jewish. A little bit of Middle Eastern. A little bit of Italian and at the same time, a little bit of mother's home style cooking. But always with a twist."

Indeed, his mother is given credit for what I believe is the best dish on the menu. He calls it "Mother's Baked Chicken," which doesn't nearly do it justice. His mother did dry-season and marinate the chicken overnight before baking it. She did not, however, "toast" the seasonings – cumin, paprika and chili powder – in the oven first to open up the flavor as Jackson does. He then rubs them into, "every nook and cranny," and leaves them overnight. Then, and this is the best part, he bakes the chicken slowly in a clay smoker. The resulting fowl is crusty with spices on the outside, unbelievably moist, seasoned (and smoked) to the bone. As fabulous as it is hot, it has a little heart next to it on the menu advertising its "heart healthy" qualities. The half chicken is accompanied by an unimpressive mixture of crisp, but way under-seasoned steamed vegetables (my only complaint), and a couple of potato pancakes.

Like the matzo ball soup and his classic, absolutely perfect Reuben Sandwich, the potato pancakes are a legacy of Jackson's tenure as chef at a Jewish deli in Detroit, Michigan. There's nothing simpler or better than a little shredded potato, onion, seasoned simply, bound lightly with a little egg, and browned crisp on a flat grill. In keeping with the Jewish tradition, customers come in exclusively to eat an order of the pancakes with sour cream and apple sauce.

Another favorite entrée, the Ancho-Crusted Smoked Chicken Breast, also benefits from a visit to the clay smoker, or "big green egg," as Jackson calls it. The breast is black, sweet and smoky from being dusted with crushed ancho (dried poblano peppers). After smoking it briefly, he finishes it on a charcoal grill. Freshly-made jalapeño-flavored fettuccine with cumin-scented sauce shares the plate with the chicken breast (and again, steamed vegetables).

The robust blend of toasted "house spices" is also used to dress up the Gilled Snapper after he has marinated the filets in an olive oil-based mayonnaise for extra moistness.

Jackson worked for a year or so as a chef in Zurich, Switzerland, and takes from that experience – among other things – an affinity for France. He named the restaurant after Anjou, the historic province in Western France (now "Maine-Et-Loire").

A classic rendering of French Rack of Lamb Provencal is elevated a notch or two by luxuriating for twenty-four hours in a marinade of olive oil and oven-roasted garlic and rosemary. Three hefty chops arrive propped up in a brown sauce thinned with a homemade, vinegar-based mint sauce and garnished with fried balls of mashed potatoes flavored with Roquefort cheese. A nice touch.

Moist, brownish-yellow crusted diamonds of grilled polenta decorate the dish called Ribeye Strindberg. This may qualify as the rarest of all beasts – an original recipe. A six ounce lean ribeye is coated in black pepper, French course-grain mustard, and sweet, roasted minced shallots, and then gently cloaked in a thin veneer of cornmeal – on hand for the polenta – "to create a barrier between the pan and the wet stuff," Jackson explains. The cornmeal also helps it brown. The ribeye is also served with a rich brown sauce, this time accented by slices of sautéed domestic mushrooms. Very interesting.

While I'm on the subject, I also don't recall a previous encounter with Fried Basil Leaves coated with goat cheese. Jackson says he created the dish for New Year's Eve dinner ('96), and "we had to make them going upstream. We sold out." Now, he says they're his signature dish. He serves them with a helping of homey, long-simmered marinara sauce.

Other appetizers of note are Vietnamese-style spring rolls in delicate rice paper, filled with crunchy vegetables and flaked poached salmon, hence the name – Salmon Imperial – and that seventies favorite – Artichoke and Spinach Dip – hot and cheesy, served with warm tortilla chips.

The best way to start the meal may be with a cup or bowl of body-warming Tortilla Soup. Fiery with chili powder and cayenne, and fragrant with cilantro.

A fine meal could be made of a cup of Jackson's Tortilla Soup and one of my three favorite sandwiches. My theory is that you have to love sandwiches a lot to make a great one, and be willing to go to the trouble to make everything from scratch.

The South Philly Steak at the Anjou Café achieves nirvana because Jackson fills a warm, crusty French roll with shaved top round beef that he's studded generously with garlic cloves and roasted in a low oven for hours. Add green pepper, mushrooms and onions caramelized on the grill, melt some Monterrey Jack over the top and you have a sublime sandwich.

It's matched by the Reuben Sandwich. Good rye bread is spread with pink Russian dressing – the telltale sign of an authentic Reuben – and covered with salty ribbons of red corned beef and sauerkraut, both homemade.

Another winner, the California Club, is a departure from convention. The contents – ham, turkey, bacon, tomato, lettuce and guacamole – are rolled in a soft flour tortilla.

To finish, I liked the little individual pecan tortes warmed and topped with a scoop of vanilla ice cream. But, the best of the dessert entries was called Butterfinger Pie. The maple-syrupy filling of the pecan torte is covered in a layer of cream cheese and sour cream, and sprinkled with crushed Butterfinger candy bars.

There is a short, all-California wine list. No smoking is allowed in this small 50-seat restaurant unless they set up tables outside. The walls are lined with paintings for sale by local artists.

ATHENS BAR AND GRILL

8037 Clinton Drive
Houston, Texas 77029
713/675-1644

Type of Cuisine: Greek
Bar: Full
Dress: Casual
Entertainment: Thursday-Saturday
Greek Band 8:00p.m., Belly Dancer 9:00p.m.,
Greek Singer 9:00p.m. and 11:00p.m.
Payment: All Major Credit Cards
Entrée Range: $9.95-$18.75
Recommended Dishes:
Appetizers: Athens Saganaki (Flaming Cheese)
Feta Cheese with Olives
Keftedakia (Meatballs)
Calamari
Octopus
Entrées: Athens Combination Platter
Red Snapper
Baked Lamb
Pastitso
Musaka
Hours: Lunch: Monday-Friday, 10:00a.m.-2:00p.m.
Dinner: Wednesday-Saturday, 6:00p.m.-2:00a.m.
(Closed Sunday and Monday and Tuesday Dinner)
Reservations: Accepted

"Opa!" may officially replace "yee-hah!" in this Texan's vocabulary. Our waitress, Popi Karambinaki, says the two words are interchangeable and she should know. Not only is she from Crete originally, but she has worked at the Athens Bar and Grill for twenty-three years where there is plenty to say "opa!" about.

This Houston Ship Channel institution is every bit as much fun as I'd heard it was, but the big surprise for me was how wonderful the food is. The red snapper alone merits at least two opas! in my book.

Terry Margetusakis says the menu has changed little in thirty-six years, but he believes that the quality of the food and entertainment has improved. Also a native of Crete, Margetusakis bought the Athens Bar and Grill from the original owner, Steve Vionis, when he retired to his farm two years ago.

An ideal way to start – especially an evening meal – is with an assortment of appetizers. In Greece often an entire meal is made of mezedakia (hot and cold appetizers). Margetusakis says, "We eat a little bit of everything, you know.

We start with the appetizers so we can drink a little bit of wine."

Indeed, the mention of practically every appetizer prompted Margetusakis to note that, "ah yes, that's very good with wine." I found this to be particularly true of two of the appetizers that featured two different Greek cheeses: Athens Saganaki and Feta Cheese with Olives.

Also called flaming cheese, Athens Saganaki is a piece of hard, deliciously salty Greek cheese (called Kefalotyri) similar to Italian pecorino. It is broiled briefly just to melt the top of the cheese, ignited with dark 151 proof rum and arrives flaming at the table. ("Saganaki" is the name of the two-handled shallow pan in which the cheese was originally melted and served.)

Another excellent choice, a simple plate of feta, Greece's best known cheese, with olives. The oily, slightly pungent Kalamata black olives off-set the briny freshness of feta cheese, and the combination is wonderful when drizzled with a fragrant Greek olive oil and scattered with little crumbled oregano.

Admittedly an acquired taste, retsina, the Greek wine flavored with pine resin, is at it's best when paired with either of these cheese dishes. Two other Greek wines I can recommend without qualification are a dry, white wine called Kouros and a robust, red wine, Caliga Rubie, that suited the heartiness of the Greek style of cooking perfectly.

The Keftedakia (meatballs) were memorable – moist and well-seasoned finely minced beef with a subtle enhancement of fresh mint. Another favorite appetizer, paper thin, parchment-crisp phyllo dough is gently folded around a mixture of feta cheese, eggs and seasoning to create Tyropitakia (cheese puffs). The calamari is lightly coated with savory garlic-flavored flour then deep fried. They require little more than a good squeeze of lemon to make them perfect. But the appetizer of my dreams is the octopus.

If you like octopus, you'll love it here. If you don't, I implore you to try it. The succulent morsels are tender with mild flavor that in Greece is often compared in both texture and taste to lobster. Instead of pounding it against a rock as they do there to tenderize it, Josefina Peresteris, who has cooked at Athens Bar and Grill practically from the beginning, tells me that they first boil it, marinate it overnight in red wine vinegar, oregano and olive oil, and then "run it under the grill when it's ordered."

The only appetizer I would rather have missed was the fried liver which I found unpleasantly harsh with a preponderance of sage.

According to culinary lore, the Greeks were the first to

bake pasta dishes so it stands to reason that they have gotten really good at it. Both the musaka and the pastitsio are deeply satisfying, stick-to-your-ribs stuff. Lighter and better than the best lasagna, pastitsio is a tomatoey mixture of ground beef and Greek macaroni, topped with a rich, cheesy sauce, and baked until golden brown. Their musaka is equally good – made with ground beef instead of lamb and bite-sized chunks of eggplant, and treated to the same thick blanket of crusty cheese sauce.

Margetusakis tells me that an incredible 90% of both Greek and American customers order the Athens Combination Platter. It's easy to understand why. The plate includes two huge, impeccably fried shrimp ("We're kind of famous for our fried shrimp," he says); two dolmades – rice and beef rolled in grape leaves knapped with a little bechamel sauce; a piece of both musaka and pastitsio; two keftedakias (meatballs); a square of spanakopita – spinach and feta casserole surrounded on the top and bottom by phyllo dough; and two tyropitakias – a warm triangle of flaky phyllo with seasoned feta inside.

It is a generous plate at a terrific price, and has the added advantage of allowing the diner to sample most of the "Greek specialties." But you would be missing out on my two favorite dishes – the snapper and the baked lamb.

Although we enjoyed everything, the red snapper merited superlatives at our table. It is an excellent example of the deceptively simple practice in Mediterranean countries, of taking one perfect fish, adorning it with a little garlic, olive oil, lemon and a sprinkle of oregano and broiling it. Skillfully prepared and beautifully presented, it arrives whole. (Unless this happens to be your area of expertise, I would ask them to filet the fish there at the table for you.)

"The Greeks, they like lamb, you know." Margetusakis says the lamb undergoes a two day process of first being marinated in lemon, garlic and olive oil and then being baked slowly in a low oven until it falls off the bone. Offered with a choice of rice or French fries, I would ask instead for the Greek potatoes – lemony whole chunks of peeled, baked Idaho potatoes.

The kitchen concocts an exceptionally flaky baklava with a dense filling of toasted walnuts and bread crumbs and laces it with a sauce of honey flavored with cinnamon, cloves and lemon. Originally baklava was made with forty sheets of phyllo dough signifying the forty days of Lent. Athens Bar and Grill celebrates the end of the week-long fast at midnight the Saturday preceding Easter in the Greek Orthodox Church by serving margentsa – Easter lamb soup.

I wasn't living in Houston twenty years ago during the hey day of the Athens Bar and Grill, but I'd heard the stories.

Just the mention of the restaurant conjured images of celebratory plate smashing, ouzo drinking and belly dancing revelry – especially when a Greek ship was in dock.

While there is no plate smashing, four nights a week – Thursday, Friday, Saturday and Sunday nights – there is still infectious, wholesale whooping it up. There are five musicians, one female Greek singer and a belly dancer. I recommend going with a group. Everyone is encouraged to dance. When I asked Margetusakis if another waitress who danced with cheerful abandon back and forth from the kitchen to get her orders was Greek, he said, "No, but once you've been here for a little while, everyone is Greek!"

Two misconceptions I had: Athens Bar and Grill is across the street from the ship channel, so it is not actually on the water and it is closer and more accessible than I imagined it to be – it's probably seven minutes from the downtown area. The proximity to town and the reliable excellent food explain why it is a popular weekday destination for lunch and for those looking for earthy, gratifying Greek food in a cozy, grotto-like setting.

AUNTIE CHANG'S DUMPLING HOUSE

2621 S. Shepherd #290
Houston, Texas 77098
713/524-8410

Type of Cuisine: Chinese
Bar: Wine and Beer
Dress: Casual
Entertainment: No
Payment: All Major Credit Cards
Entrée Range: $6.96-$11.95
Recommended Dishes:
Appetizers: Dumplings-Pan-fried Pork and Beef
Moo Shu Pork
Honey Roasted Pork Ends
Entrées: Crispy Whole Fish in Spicy Sauce
General Tso's Chicken
Pork in Garlic Sauce
Mongolian Beef
Boneless Duck in Ground Pepper Sauce
Dessert: Fried Bananas with Vanilla Ice Cream
Hours: Monday-Thursday, 11:00a.m.-10:00p.m.
Friday, 11:00a.m. -10:30p.m.
Saturday, 11:30a.m.-10:30p.m.
Sunday, 11:30a.m.-10:00p.m.
Reservations: Accepted

Steven Chiang likes dumplings. A lot. The owner, along with his wife Cecilia, of Auntie Chang's Dumpling House likes to tell a story about the time he ate seventy-three dumplings in one sitting as a teenager in his native Taiwan.

"You know how in high school you can eat a lot. Well, my friends asked me how many dumplings I could eat at once and I ate seventy-three of them!" Did he win any kind of prize? "No, but they paid for my meal!" he laughs.

The dumplings he ate that day were the standard steamed pork dumplings common to "dumpling stores," as he calls them, in Taiwan almost always, he says, accompanied by steaming bowls of appetite-stimulating, "stomach-opening," hot and sour soup.

They were not, however, the dumplings of his youth that he speaks of so fondly. The dumplings made and enjoyed by the whole family around the kitchen table. Those were his mother's, Auntie Chang's dumplings.

Chiang named the restaurant for his mother whose maiden name was Chang because he says most of the dishes he serves are his mother's recipes.

"When we opened Auntie Chang's (in 1992), we wanted American people to taste real Chinese food, real Chinese flavors; the kind of food we ate at home." He stresses that this is one of the reasons the dumplings are so good. "Everything here is handmade." For instance, the dumpling skins – or "pei" in Chinese – are thinner and more delicate than the competition's because they are made by hand and not machine as Chiang says they are elsewhere.

The five different types of dumplings vary from the sensational to the merely so-so. As you might guess, the Chiang family recipe for the classic pork dumpling is superb, either steamed or pan-fried. (I tend to prefer the crisp under-belly of the pan-fried.) But, the best and most interesting dumplings of all are the aggressively-seasoned beef variety. This spicy meatball is a departure from tradition because, as Chiang points out, "China is a farmer's country and the cow works for us, so we eat much more pork than beef."

The mostly spinach filled vegetable dumplings are another (less successful) concession to his environs. He says he developed the recipe for his "Houston heart healthy" customers and that they are his second biggest sellers after the pork dumplings. They are my least favorite. I'd rather have one beef or pork dumpling than a full order of the less flavorful vegetable dumplings. But, see for yourself. By ordering the Assorted Dumplings, it's possible to sample two pork, two shrimp, two chicken (both good), and two vegetable. This excludes the stellar beef dumplings, though.

All four attending sauces are freshly-concocted by Chiang daily, he says, because "they are my recipes." There is chopped ginger in vegetable oil, a pungent sauce made from finely-minced jalapeños, "for Texans – we don't eat jalapeños in Taiwan"; and my two favorite sauces to combine with the dumplings – the ginger-flecked, oyster-sauce-flavored soy sauce, and the familiar incendiary sauce made from red peppers steeped in hot oil.

As far as I'm concerned, dumplings aren't even what Auntie Chiang's does best. The most unusual appetizer is the Honey Roast Pork Ends. Chiang thinks that the end is the best part of the roast pork and he hates to see it go to waste, so he stir fries it with a little honey. This gives the resulting dish a rich, almost maple syrupy flavor. It goes nicely with an order of simple Hot Oil Sesame Noodles. But, an order of Moo Shu Pork to split among fellow diners, is an even better way to start the meal. Chiang agrees, "Yes, this is how we eat moo shu pork in Taiwan – as an appetizer. Everyone gets one (filled) pancake. It's finger food." The pancakes are thin – made with impressive care – and the filling is a well-seasoned, soulful sauté of vegetables and shredded pork. Thick, sweet hoisin sauce brings out the flavor. This is Chinese comfort at its best.

My favorite dish of all may be the Crispy Whole Fish in Spicy Sauce. It is perfect. A whole red snapper is fried to a greaseless turn, and arrives supported by a dense pool of black sauce richly flavored with garlic, onions and Chinese rice wine. It is fileted for you at the table by Auntie Chang's exceptionally helpful and well-informed wait staff. Chiang tells me that in China they won't eat fish unless it is served with its head, "otherwise, you cannot see if the fish is fresh or not."

I thought the Sesame Chicken, listed as one of the Chef's Specials, was good until I tried General Tso's Chicken which, along with the fish, may be Auntie Chang's finest accomplishment. Strips of snow white chicken breasts are fried crisp and coated in a thick, brown, slightly-searing sauce spiked with plenty of red pepper flakes.

I liked the curry-flavored Singapore Noodles. The dainty, saffron-yellow rice noodles are especially good with shrimp. But, I find it difficult to pass up the heartier Lo Mein Noodles – stir-fried like the Singapore noodles, with a choice of chicken, pork, beef, shrimp or any combination of the four. I lean towards the Young Chow Lo Mein, which appears to be Chinese for "everything but the kitchen sink." Chiang says the name comes from the style of preparing fried rice in the city of Yangzhou, "with everything," he says. Like the Lo Mein, the Young Chow Fried Rice has that nice smoky flavor that Asian dishes get when they are cooked quickly in a very hot wok.

The Mongolian Beef, the best of the beef dishes, is the finest example of how this technique can render simple lean ribbons of beef and pieces of scallions earthy and satisfying.

The Dry Sautéed Green Beans are also skillfully seared in a hot wok so their natural sugars are allowed to caramelize on the outside, but stay appealingly crunchy on the inside. "This is traditionally Chinese food, you know," Chiang says. "The only difference is, in China we would sauté them with some ground pork."

Lustrous, slender Chinese Eggplant is the perfect foil for the strong but complementary flavors of the popular garlic sauce. Chiang says that most people just love his garlic sauce and attributes its particularly fine flavor to the expensive, slightly heavier brand of soy sauce he uses. The Shredded Pork in Garlic Sauce is an unqualified winner – match stick-sized shreds of pork, aromatic tree ear mushrooms – more for texture than flavor – and carrots, in a garlic-strewn sauce with plenty of sass.

It is exactly this bold, in-your-face style of cooking that appeals to me so much about Auntie Chang's. Chiang points out that it is the sturdy, "heavier flavors" of for instance, the wonderful Shrimp and Scallops in Hot Black Bean Sauce, that best characterize "the way we eat at home."

Duck devotées should enjoy the Boneless Duck in Ground Pepper Sauce. I loved the peppery pungency of the dark sauce with the richness of the succulent, crisp-skinned duck.

Auntie Chang's has an interesting little wine list that includes a Chilean white and red wine, as well as the usual suspects from California. If you time it right, this casual, clean-cut setting on the second floor of a Shepherd Square, which faces west, makes a nice spot to watch the sun set over the roof tops.

Sweet, crunchy discs of honey-coated fried banana with vanilla ice cream are a splendid (and soothing) coda to this wonderful, vibrantly-spicy meal.

BABA YEGA

2607 Grant Street
Houston, Texas 77006
713/522-0042

Type of Cuisine: American/Burgers/Vegetarian
Bar: Full
Dress: Casual
Entertainment: No
Payment: All Major Credit Cards
Entrée Range: $8.75-$11.95
Recommended Dishes:
Appetizers: Chilled Artichoke
Stuffed Mushrooms
Baked Brie
Entrées: Greek Salad
Bacon Burger
Potato Salad
French Fries
Reuben Sandwich
Hours: Sunday-Thursday, 11:00a.m.-10:00p.m.
Friday-Saturday, 11:00a.m.-11:00p.m.
Reservations: Accepted for Large Parties

Baba Yega, the devil's grandmother in Slavonic mythology, makes a cameo appearance in profile on the front of the menu and is defined on the back as "a thunder witch an ugly old woman with a monstrous nose, long teeth and disheveled hair who flies through the sky in an iron caldron and uses a broom to sweep her traces from the air."

Sidney Hakim, owner of Baba Yega Saloon and Cafe since 1975, says he took the name from an Emerson, Lake and Palmer song, "The Huts of Baba Yega" because when he first saw this charming, incredibly cozy 1930's Montrose house he thought it looked like the "old witches house made of chicken bones" on the album cover.

He bought the house in the shade of a sprawling oak tree with the intention of redoing it, but decided instead to open a "saloon/sandwich shop...just a place where people could stop in for a beer and maybe a sandwich." He opened in 1975 with six bar stools and not quite enough money to finish out the kitchen and serve food. After six months, he began preparing sandwiches and salads himself for his customers. Several of those sandwiches are still on the menu: "The Fantasy" – French bread served openface with ham, tomato, melted provolone cheese, topped with slices of avocado, still a bestseller he says; "The Bird" – unadorned, shredded baked chicken breast on French bread (a bit dry for my tastes); and the "California" – now listed under "Vegetarian's Delight" on the menu, but recommended to me by a nonvegetarian – avocado, provolone cheese, sliced tomato and sprouts served on very fresh tasting, nutty whole wheat bread.

Sidney says the menu has changed as food fashions have evolved over the past twenty-three years, adding some dishes, subtracting others, always improving recipes as he and the kitchen staff go along.

One important addition was the grill fifteen years ago. The moist, marinated grilled breast of chicken is wonderful as an entrée served with rice and skewered grilled vegetables, whole on a sandwich, or my personal favorite sliced and placed on top of the "Baba Yega Caesar". But, for a restaurant with as many as six vegetarian dishes to choose from, they grill one heck of a hamburger. All four burgers have a fresh, homemade quality with excellent ingredients and cheese melted over the top, and although they sell the most of the mushroom burgers topped with sautéed domestic mushrooms on a toasted bun, my siren's song is the bacon burger served with shimmering slabs of crunchy, smoky bacon on top, easily one of the best in town.

You're given the tough choice of either potato salad or French fries with all sandwiches and burgers. The potato salad is above reproach, made with fresh dill, chopped celery and the faintest whisper of an interesting dehydrated lime in powder form from the Middle East that they use in a lot of recipes. Sidney says the potato salad, made without mustard, is roughly based on a salad his mother used to make with peas and chopped chicken when he was a child.

As popular as the potato salad is, the French fries alone are worth the price of admission. Thin wedges of Idaho potatoes with their skins on are cloaked in a well-seasoned veil of batter thin enough to see the potato through, and fried briefly in vegetable oil.

We enjoyed the pizza of the day, a sauté of spinach with lots of fresh garlic on a crisp whole wheat crust topped with tart feta cheese.

My two favorite sandwiches are the classic Reuben made with very lean corned beef, sauerkraut and melted Swiss cheese on the traditional toasted rye bread, and a great rendition of that old standard club sandwich.

I've found all salads to be luminously fresh from the aforementioned Caesar, to the first-rate Greek salad. The spinach salad is a handsomely composed plate of fresh spinach leaves, avocado, tomato wedges, red onion, walnuts and strawberries. (I'd probably choose the house Italian dressing over the sweet honey-mustard vinaigrette next time.)

The restaurant has a particularly welcoming atmosphere. There is an enchanting patio/herb garden complete with a small pond and waterfall behind the restaurant that serves as overflow for the terraced party room upstairs.

Baba Yega seats seventy people inside and almost as many outside on both front and back patios. (Sidney says it's SRO when the weather is good!) Open seven days a week, the restaurant draws (among others) a number of business types from downtown at lunch and at night is a popular favorite of the local gay community.

While they have fresh squeezed juices including orange, grapefruit, carrot, carrot-celery, apple (and wheat grass!) and herbal teas, including the cleansing kombucha mushroom teas, they also have a full bar that serves a mean Bloody Mary with celery salt around the rim, and a great cup of espresso.

BAICH'S BAR AND GRILLE

2016 Main
Houston, Texas 77002
713/650-8830

Type of Cuisine: American/Eclectic
Bar: Full
Dress: Nice Casual
Entertainment: Jazz: Friday 6:00p.m.-10:00p.m.
Saturday 7:00p.m.-11:00p.m.
Payment: All Major Credit Cards
Entrée Range: $9.95-$24.95
Recommended Dishes:
Appetizers: Portobello Appetizer
Gnocchi Florentine
Chicken Quesadillas
Cajun Puffs Marinera
Entrées: Grilled Chicken Pizza
Redfish "Jackie"
Stuffed Chicken Jose
Crabmeat Enchiladas
Veal Chop
Rack of Lamb
Desserts: Apples Susan
Baich's Foster
Bayou Mudd Pie
Hours: Lunch: Monday-Friday, 11:00a.m.-2:00p.m.
Dinner: Monday-Thursday, 5:00p.m.-9:00p.m.
Friday, 5:00p.m.-10:00p.m.
Saturday, 6:00p.m.-11:00p.m.
(Closed Sunday)
Reservations: Not Accepted

Suit yourself. That's the theme of the nineties. There are no hard and fast rules in the worlds of food or fashion. Restauranteurs confidently design menus around a theme no more central than, "What do I like to eat?"

Baich's Bar and Grille embraces this free-wheeling notion and I love it. While the slightly grim, hotel-dining room décor doesn't scream with personality, the food certainly does.

"New American with a Southwest flair," is how owner Susan Hill describes the fare at Baich's. But that barely scratches the surface of the geography covered by even the "starters" on this wildly eclectic menu.

The list of the entrée-size appetizers (all ample enough to share) begins with Gnocchi Florentine. Delicate, melt-in-your-mouth pillows of potato gnocchi arrive laced with whole leaves of dark green spinach in a large shallow bowl, hot and cheesy in a tomato sauce thinned with cream and white wine.

An order of basil-fragrant toasted Garlic-Cheese Bread goes nicely with the Gnocchi.

Next, to Mexico for "Quesadillas 'a Signature Specialty,'" as it boasts on the menu. They are quesadillas in name only. Huge flour tortillas are folded over three different kinds of cheese – a mixture of mozzarella, Cheddar and a hot pepper cheese – whole strips of grilled chicken (my favorite of the possible fillings), roasted peppers and sautéed mushrooms. The "quesadillas" are first sautéed in clarified butter, then baked briefly in a hot oven. They come with a welcome scoop of very creamy guacamole and perfect, finely diced pico de gallo. (This might by a good time to mention that Hill's very talented chef, José Silva, is from Guadalajara, Mexico.)

The third listed appetizer is an item that Hill and her former partner, Ed Baich, had great success with in their catering business before they opened Baich's in 1992. Cajun Puffs Marinera are like savory beignets resting on a bed of the heady house marinera sauce. Puff pastry is folded neatly into squares around a handful of well-seasoned Italian sausage and deep fried until they expand and crisp.

The many regulars who frequent Baich's at lunch know to order the extraordinary off-the-menu specials. Hill has advised me that they will be added to a revised menu in the works. One of the best – the Portobello Appetizer – is a case of several of my favorite foods being combined on one plate.

Seasonal greens dressed lightly in Balsamic vinegar and a sprinkling of fresh herbs are allowed to wilt under the weight of a tangle of chili-flavored onion rings, strips of meaty, marinated then grilled portobello mushrooms, a generous dollop of fresh lump crabmeat, a few grilled shrimp and for the final coup de grace, a drizzling of creamy, white wine-flavored sauce.

Two other off-the-menu winners were the Dijon mustard crusted Rack of Lamb which came on a bed of barely-cooked spinach with a side order of horseradish-flavored mashed potatoes and a succulent 12-ounce veal chop, grilled to perfection, topped with strips of portobello mushrooms and served with a rich marsala and domestic mushroom sauce.

Back to the menu. The Grilled Chicken Pizza is a 12-inch pizza on a light, crisp, cheesy homemade crust piled high with chargrilled peppers, mushrooms, grilled chicken breast and their mixture of three cheeses. It's as fine as interpretation of gourmet pizza as you're likely to taste in town.

Again, we span the globe as we review my favorite entrées. Starting at the top (since they are all equally good) is Redfish "Jackie." Named for a one-time regular who had a good eye for combinations of ingredients, the nicely seasoned redfish is lightly striped on the grill, then loaded down with scallops, crabmeat, and shrimp sautéed with onions, mushrooms and peppers in a light olive oil, white wine and basil sauce.

Another favorite, Stuffed Chicken José is a breast of chicken rolled around a piece of proscuitto, provolone cheese, sautéed spinach, roasted peppers then, wrapped in bacon, tied and roasted in the oven. The lemon butter sauce is a nice complement to an already very fine dish.

The Crabmeat Enchiladas are equally popular at lunch and dinner. They are fabulous – a simple tribute to our glorious local lump crabmeat. Flour tortillas are filled with little more than lump crabmeat and sweet, chargrilled red and green peppers. The enchiladas are topped with tart tomatillo sauce then embellished further with a creamy alfredo lightened with a little white wine. They are accompanied appropriately by black beans and Mexican rice.

Parchment-thin scallops of veal are dusted with flour and pan-sautéed with Dijon mustard for the ambrosial Panned Veal with Tarragon Mustard. It is served alongside a heaping portion of cream-sauced capellini, which our animated and extremely attentive waitress, Deborah, correctly assessed, "just makes the dish!"

The most successful pairing of side dishes may just be the assertively-seasoned roasted corn salsa and the fabulous aforementioned chili-flavored onion rings that accompany the smoky Mesquite Grilled Ribeye.

The dessert selection is as interesting (and inventive) as the rest of the menu. Dainty puff pastry is skillfully used to hold vanilla ice cream topped with a sauté of cinnamon-scented apples and toasted pecans for the Apples Susan. Add bananas, and the same ingredients become Baich's Foster. The Bayou Mudd Pie is a dandy, decked out in dark cookie crust, mocha almond fudge ice cream covered in whipped cream with crunchy shavings of dark chocolate.

Hill claims they are getting famous for their martinis, "made like James Bond," she says, "shaken and not stirred." Chile, Italy, France and especially California are well-represented on the wine list. As an interesting promotional gesture, the wines are reasonably priced at 30% over retail.

The room is warmed by live jazz on Friday and Saturday nights.

BARNABY'S CAFE

604 Fairview
Houston, Texas 77006
713/522-0106

Type of Cuisine: American/Burgers
Bar: Wine and Beer
Dress: Casual
Entertainment: No
Payment: All Major Credit Cards
Entrée Range: $5.00-$10.50
Recommended Dishes:
Hawaiian Pork Chops
Burgers
Best French Fries
Hickory Smoked Pink Chicken
Meat Loaf
Lasagna
Hours: Sunday-Thursday. 11:00a.m.-10:00p.m.
Friday-Saturday, 11:00a.m.-11:00p.m.
Reservations: Not Accepted

My heart does a little dance when I see simple things done well – a perfect hamburger; flawless, crisp, golden French fries; a warm piece of the kind of apple pie you wish your mother used to to make – the unmistakable sign of someone who believes that the whole is only as good as the sum of its parts; an uncompromising attention to detail and insistence that every ingredient be the best quality available.

The first bit of whimsy you encounter upon entering Barnaby's is the shellacked dog biscuits artfully arranged on the lemon-yellow wall and English sheep dogs with wings painted among the clouds on the ceiling. "Well, Barnaby was my childhood pet dog. When I wanted to name the restaurant, I just thought of happy times, good times, memories, and the dog Barnaby, kind of came up."

I first visited Barnaby's on a stormy Monday night traditionally the slowest night in the restaurant trade and was amazed to see how busy they were. I couldn't help but wonder why all these hardy souls had braved the elements, including Harris County-wide tornado watches. Soon I learned what all my fellow diners seemed to know – the food is really good.

The menu is short and fairly conventional. There are no appetizers. Although the diner never feels rushed, Gale intended Barnaby's to be "the type of neighborhood place where you come to get a quick bite to eat and run to a movie or something. It is a classic coffee shop diner-type menu, but we make it a little healthier. We spend a little extra attention trying to make sure that there is a little less fat, and that you get the best version that's in town. Everything that we serve has a really strong flavor . . . and we like to think that if it's got a strong flavor, that people remember it and crave it."

The Hawaiian Pork Chops are a memory that lingers: succulent, centercut pork chops marinated for two days in a sweet teriyaki sauce of soy, garlic and ginger, are grilled over charcoal, glazed with more sauce and served with grilled wedges of fresh pineapple, a warm, cinnamon-flavored compote of apples and a generous mound of what may just be the best French fries in town.

Addictively delicious, they are long, thin sticks of what I think of as the original "French" fried potatoes – actual "pommes frites" or "pommes allumettes" (matchstick potatoes). Gale says that "the secret to Barnaby's fries is that they are prebaked which means they require less frying time than normal, so they don't absorb much oil. We add a kind of peppery salt to them."

Like everything else on the menu, a lot of thought has gone into the neatly-constructed burgers. "People do eat with their eyes," Gale points out. They manage to be both healthy and delicious particularly the one made from the naturally very lowfat ground buffalo meat. "Everyday we go to Whole Foods Market to pick up organic meats for our hamburgers, turkey burgers and buffalo burgers. It all comes from Coleman ranch in Colorado. The buns are called 'uptown buns.' They're whole wheat with seven or eight different organic grains in them. We use romaine lettuce instead of iceberg, thin overlapping layers of both red and white onions and slices of crunchy, cold Schwartz pickles from Chicago."

The Hickory Smoked "Pink" Chicken is slow-smoked in East Texas until the meat has a sweet, rosy hue. It is then treated to a coat of the house honey-based barbecue sauce and finished on the grill. The same moist, smokey chicken is shredded and used in the popular Smoked Chicken Tostados With Roasted Corn Salsa. Danish Baby Back Ribs are tender with little fat or gristle, brushed with barbecue sauce and scored on the grill.

Doctor Gale's Meatloaf is named for Gale's father, an optometrist in San Rafael, California. "It's an Italian-style meatloaf. We mix it with spicy pork sausage and the same hamburger meat we use for our burgers, add fennel to it, Italian seasonings then we top it with tomato sauce. It's really like a giant Italian meatball."

Also in the stick-to-the-ribs genre, both the spinach and the meat lasagnas are worth sampling. Compact and full of flavor with an appealing crust of crisped cheese on top, the meat variety is served with a freshly-made chunky tomato sauce which is thinned with a little cream when served with the spinach lasagna. Gale says they are both so popular that "people come to us and buy pans of it." (He says a pan feeds about twenty-five people.)

I also know who to call next time I need an apple pie; it is sublime. With a flaky, buttery crust, it is served in shallow, clear bowls so that a scoop of Amy's Mexican vanilla ice cream can collect in a pool around it as it melts over the warm butter cinnamon topping. They happened to be out of ice cream that first night we ate there so we had them melt a piece of good cheddar cheese over the top instead; an oldfashioned, but delicious practice. The three layer chocolate cake was equally good, moist and fudgy with a rich, dense icing. It is listed under sweets as "Chocolate Something" with the idea that they would have the flexibility to change the "something" occasionally, but Gale has assured me the cake is there to stay for now, anyway. I did not sample the carrot cake, but I have subsequently discovered that they are famous for it.

The service is fast and friendly. The employees are encouraged to play their favorite music and both times I was there it was classic Frank Sinatra. "The music adds a lot to the personality of a place."

His clientele is fairly eclectic. "You know, it is a neighborhood restaurant and it is in a gay neighborhood. But, it has grown outside of that spectrum. I get a tremendous lot of business from the gay community, but I get a tremendous amount of business from the straight community and from the main stream. We get people from River Oaks, students from Rice and St. Thomas, and we get artists, (as well as) downtown 'suits'. It is really a collective group of people. We give you good food at great prices and a fun atmosphere and I think that is part of the romance of Barnaby's that there are strange people sitting around you."

Baby Barnaby's next door serves a stellar breakfast seven days a week and is half the size of the cafe. It seats twenty people. I enjoyed everything on the short menu with the possible exception of the slightly gummy pancakes. Also, I wished the orange juice had been fresh, as advertised on the menu. The bacon and sausage were wonderful, however, and the huge freshly made biscuits and cream gravy are something to get out of bed for on a Saturday morning. Better make it early, though. Baby Barnaby's is busy, too.

THE BLUE ORCHID VIET-THAI RESTAURANT

14004 Memorial Drive
Houston, Texas 77079
281/870-8636

Type of Cuisine: Vietnamese/Thai
Bar: Wine and Beer
Dress: Casual
Entertainment: No
Payment: American Express, MasterCard, Visa
Entrée Range: $6.95-$12.95
Recommended Dishes:
Appetizers: Vietnamese Egg Rolls
Pork Summer Rolls
Crispy Shrimp
Entrées: Pork Caramel
Crispy Rice Noodle Plate
Oriental Bird Nest
Hearty Duck in Sesame Sauce
Dessert: Crispy Ice Cream Flambé
Hours: Lunch: Monday-Saturday, 11:00a.m-3:00p.m.
Dinner: Monday-Saturday, 5:00p.m.-10:00p.m.
(Closed Sunday)
Reservations: Accepted

Help! The Blue Orchid is having an identity crisis! Advertised as a "Viet-Thai Restaurant," is it "a Vietnamese restaurant serving Thai specialties" as Le Qui Lee, twenty-three year old son of chef and owners Nam and Anh Dao Lee claims; or is it "equal parts Vietnamese, French-influenced Thai-style cooking in a part-Asian, part-European atmosphere" as his parents maintain?

The truth is it's all of these things.

A handsome, youthful couple in their late forties, the Lees left Saigon City in 1982 to join his older brother, already a successful restauranteur in the little town of Fréjus between Nice and Cannes in the South of France. After first helping out at his brother's restaurant, the Lees soon opened a second Chez Lee in Draguinan not far from the original location and finally a third venue in the little village of Brignon.

It was at the second Chez Lee that Nam says he first learned to cook Thai food in his completely individual style with a bit of a French accent. In fact, both of the Lees say that it is the Thai dishes on the menu that they are proudest of many of which were originally conceived to serve a French clientele and evolved into an even more distinctive style when they created the menu for the Blue Orchid.

In 1992 when Le Qui applied and was accepted at the University of Houston for the fall term, they decided to leave all three Chez Lees in their brother and sister-in-law's hands and join Nam's mother and three older sisters already living here. They arrived August 6th and at breakneck speed, they found a location, purchased and renovated the building that housed an unsuccessful Chinese restaurant, developed an entirely different menu, this time adapting Nam's unique blend of influences to date to their new surroundings.

Since that moment both Lees have spent every day, lunch and dinner (except Sunday) in the kitchen, which explains why I needed an interpreter to conduct my interview. "We've been too busy to learn English!"

Ah, but what emanates from that kitchen is a sort of culinary slight-of-hand; a wonderful hybrid of subtle herbaceous Vietnamese offerings and more assertively-seasoned Thai and Thaistyle dishes.

Although the writing is barely legible, the first couple of pages of the menu just past the lunch specials are "house specialties" many of which are Nam's personal creations. I especially enjoyed the Hearty Duck in Sesame Sauce; the lighter, elegantly simple Oriental Bird Nest – a stirfry of chicken, shrimp, vegetables and squid, scored and sliced so that it's almost translucent, served in a crisped "nest" of shoestring potatoes (which should be broken up and eaten after it's had a chance to absorb the oniony garlic sauce); and the hauntingly aromatic, intensely-flavored Thai Seafood Hot Pot – seafood and herbs simmered and then served in the traditional clay pot.

This is where I part company with the Lees. As wonderful as all of the house specialties are, my very favorite dishes on the menu are those of Vietnamese origin. Practically considered the national dish of Vietnam, the Vietnamese egg rolls are spectacular – always eaten by placing the hot, crispy cylinders inside a cold piece of romaine lettuce, adding sprigs of both fresh mint and cilantro, a little julienned carrot, folding to form a little parcel and dipping them into a dish of light Vietnamese fish sauce called nuoc nam – producing a heavenly concert of contrasting tastes, textures and temperatures in your mouth.

Nuoc nam is the one constant presence that distinguishes Vietnamese cooking from its neighbors'. The sauce is actually tiny anchovies fermented in huge wooden barrels. With a reverence normally reserved for producing fine wine or olive oil, it is manufactured in several steps over the span of six months and is sold in varying grades or "pressings." The first syphoning is considered the highest quality and is used on the table as a dipping sauce. The second pressing is used as an all purpose ingredient, often imperceptibly, in most recipes, giving Vietnamese dishes a pleasant distant, but distinctive taste of the sea.

The Charcoaled Shrimp on Sugar Cane is probably the second-best known Vietnamese dish after the egg rolls. The shrimp are pounded to a paste, seasoned, molded to a succulent piece of sugar cane, grilled over charcoal and (like the egg rolls) eaten swaddled in lettuce with the attending garnishes, but with a sweet, dipping sauce of sugar cane juice, garlic, nuoc nam, chili and ground roasted peanuts.

Another sauce considered almost as valuable a staple in the Vietnamese kitchen as nuoc nam is a jar of homemade caramel sauce. While it's possible to have shrimp cooked this way, I recommend the ambrosial Pork Caramel – lean bitesize morsels of pork simmered (originally in the fields of Vietnam in a clay pot) in a bronze, nutty-sweet, black pepper-flecked sauce.

Of the noodle dishes, the Patt Thai was exemplary, but the Crispy Rice Noodle Plate offered the contrasting pleasure of crunchy rice noodles, a sauté of shrimp, squid, pork and vegetables supported by a bed of soft, warm vermicelli.

Don't leave without trying the Crispy Ice Cream Flambé, an elaborate confection invented by the chef. Vanilla ice cream is coated in shredded coconut, encased in batter, fried and dramatically flambéed at the table with first sake, and then rum.

The Blue Orchid also doesn't look like any other Asian restaurant that I know. This is the European influence. With light streaming through windows on three sides of the small dining room during the day, it has a bright casual elegance; but at night, the recessed lights are dimmed and tables are graced with votive candles and flower petals floating in water in shallow champagne glasses. Very romantic.

The Lees say that they're not sure why, but most Vietnamese who have lived here for a long time drink red wine with their meal, although it's much more common to drink beer. We preferred Hue, the lighter Vietnamese beer, to Singha, the more bitter choice from Thailand.

The Vietnamese coffee is a nice way to finish the meal – sweetened with condensed milk – with little individual drip filters placed on top of each cup.

BOCADOS

1312 West Alabama
Houston, Texas 77006
713/523-5230

Type of Cuisine: Mexican
Bar: Full Bar
Dress: Casual
Entertainment: No
Payment: All Major Credit Cards
Entrée Range: $8.95-$19.95
Recommended Dishes:
Appetizers: Bocaditos Sampler
Queso Flameado
Crabcakes con Salsa Tomatillo
Ceviche
Bocados House Salad
Entrées: Grilled Jumbo Shrimp
Carne Guisada
Grilled Red Snapper
Dessert: Trés Leches
Key Lime Pie
Hours: Tuesday-Thursday, 11:00a.m.-2:00p.m., 5:30p.m.-10:00p.m.
Friday, 11:00a.m.-2:00p.m., 5:30p.m.-11:00p.m.
Saturday, 5:30p.m.-11:00p.m.
Sunday, 12:00p.m.-9:00p.m.
(Closed Monday)
Reservations: Accepted

"Remember that expression, 'keep it simple, stupid?'" asks Terry Flores, co-owner of Bocados with Lily Hernandez. "That's what I was trying to do. I only chose dishes that I thought most people would ask for." This paired-down, minimalist approach applies not only to the short, plainly-stated menu, but also the cool, jazzy interior of this very welcome addition to Houston' contemporary Mexican food scene.

It is an elegantly simply approach – a recipe for a successful restaurant, circa 1998 – great food, an excellent bar (fabulous margaritas and sangria), starched white tablecloths and napkins, with a dash of salsa playing in the background. "I wanted people to feel at home," Flores explains.

Bocados' menu is the antidote to anyone – like Flores – who dislikes long, fussy menus with too much description. She tells me that, "Bocados means 'morsels' or 'little bites' in Spanish so I wanted to emphasize the appetizers, what we call 'Bocaditos.'"

The Bocados Sampler is a grazer's delight, a virtual smorgasbord of some of the kitchen's finest efforts assembled on one large plate, suitable for sharing as an appetizer (for a minimum of three people). Or, a fine meal could be made for one by ordering the sampler as an entrée rounded out maybe by the Bocados House Salad – a mound of seasonal greens dressed with the tart roasted garlic and balsamic vinaigrette.

This is what you get. One crescent-shaped chicken, cheese and mushroom-filled Empanadita de Pollo with and exceptionally flaky, buttery crust. Three Stuffed Jalapeños – manageably-mild pickled peppers packed with mostly shrimp and low-fat mozzarella – the cheese of choice at Bocados – very lightly coated with bread crumbs and deep-fried. (The Stuffed Jalapeños are memorable and were, at the time of my visits, the only "Bocadito" not available to order on their own. Flores says that they're very popular and that she plans to rectify this.) Three wedges of Quesadillas filled with strips of grilled chicken and mozzarella, which featured Bocados' delicate, handmade flour tortillas. The quesadilla is framed by a scoop of satiny, well-seasoned guacamole, "like everything else, made as ordered," as Flores says, and a pert, finely-diced pico de gallo.

A saucer of Ceviche rests in the center of the platter. It is refreshing – cool and pleasantly acidic with bite-sized chunks of shrimp, red snapper and salmon, and plenty of cilantro.

Saving the best for last, the sampler is rounded out by a lone Crabcake con Salsa Tomatillo. This is a very lightly-bound mixture of shrimp, crabmeat and a little salmon cloaked in a veneer of breadcrumbs fine enough to see through, and accompanied by an emerald-green citrusy-salty, garlic-flavored tomatillo sauce so good that one fellow diner was compelled to eat it by the spoonful.

Flores says she plans to serve the Salsa Tomatillo with the basket of thin, warm chips in addition to the also-excellent house red salsa – a smoky salsa cruda of roughly chopped onions, tomatoes and jalapeños with a faint, but welcome, reminder of chiles charred on the grill. Both salsas are so popular that they're selling them by the pint-full (16 ounces for $10.00).

The Queso Flameado is hand-folded for you tableside – a gracious practice that began at Armando's. (Flores worked collectively for about seven years as Armando's general manager and has smartly recreated some of the best features of Armando's in the early days.) The highlight of the Queso Flameado is the exceptional soft, fresh tortilla. "It is my mother, Rachel Flores' recipe (and technique)," Flores explains. "She came the first week of business, before we actually opened and trained the staff to hand roll the tortillas with a palote." I love that the thin, skillfully-prepared tortilla is filled with meaty strips of marinated and grilled portobello mushrooms as well as the usual sautéed onion rings and bell peppers and low-fat mozzarella.

Flores manages to successfully navigate the territory between old fashioned practices and new-fangled ingredients. For instance, an off-the-menu special was Portobello Mushroom Fajitas – served just as their beef or chicken fajitas are – on a sizzling platter with caramelized onions and bell peppers, but with brown rice and cumin-flavored black beans instead of the nutty, red-tinted Mexican rice and pinto beans that accompany the other fajitas.

The Beef Fajitas were good, notable for their tenderness and sliced razor-thin, but my favorite in the sizzling platter genre was the Grilled Jumbo Shrimp – six huge, outsized specimens doused in chopped garlic-flavored oil and seared quickly on the grill.

Flores says they are becoming known for their Grilled Salmon. It was napped with a delicate lemon-dill sauce. The Grilled Red Snapper was even better – topped with a buttery lime-flavored sauté of whole lump crabmeat and pico de gallo. Another off-the-menu winner, the Blackened Snapper was crusty and hot with blackened seasoning and (also) lagnaipped with the mildly-acerbic lime butter sauce.

A soulful beef stew, the Carne Guisada, was a favorite among the Platos Especiales. It is an old-fashioned recipe courtesy of Rachel Flores. But her best gift of all may be Bocados Frijoles Refritos. Rich with garlic and whole chunks of bacon, the flavor is gutsy and authentic, and I loved the half-creamy texture with broken chewy bits of pinto beans. This is a result of hand-mashing the beans in a bowl with a wooden palo. I prefer the Frijoles Refritos to the unmashed Frijoles de Ollo – a reference to the "ollo" or earthenware pot they were originally cooked in – or the aforementioned, also good, black beans – Frijoles Negros.

The "signature" margaritas were perfect – made from fresh limejuice and barrel-aged "gold" tequilla (best shaken and served "up"). Bocados Sangria went especially well with dinner. They're using a nice Cabernet, three different types of liquor and enough fruit to flavor it, but not sweeten it too much. Careful, it's a potent sangria and especially easy to drink on a summer's eve. (There were several attractive couples doing just this at the tables under red and blue San Pellegrino umbrellas on the small terrace in front of Bocados.)

The two best desserts are made in-house – a creamy Trés Leches that everyone fought over, and a pale-green, puckery Key Lime Pie.

Bocados features what they call a "Disco Brunch" on Sundays complete with 70's disco music and (presumably) John Travolta-style dancing. Flores laughs, "It's important to come up with new ideas to keep the customer interested!"

BOMBAY BRASSERIE

5160 Richmond
Houston, Texas 77056
713/355-2000

Type of Cuisine: Indian
Bar: Full
Dress: Casual
Entertainment: No
Payment: All Major Credit Cards Accepted
Entrée Range: $5.95-$19.95
Recommended Dishes:
Appetizers: Chicken Pakora
Reshemi Kabab
Entrées: The Viceroy of India Dinner for Two
Lamb Chop Kabab
All Tandoori Dishes, especially Tandoori Red Snapper
Mixed Grill Bombay
Chicken Tikka Masala
Saag Paneer (Spinach)
Bengan Bhartha
Vegetable Biryani
Breads: Kema Naan
Onion Kulcha
Dessert: Mango Kulfee
Kheer
Hours: Lunch (and Buffet): Monday-Sunday, 11:00a.m.-2:00p.m.
Dinner: Monday-Sunday, 5:30p.m.-10:30p.m.
Reservations: Accepted

The décor is warm and welcoming. The service, impeccable. And the food is the kind you sit bolt upright in the middle of the night with a craving for. Bombay Brasserie isn't just good by Indian food standards, this is a meal that compares favorably with any you are likely to eat in town.

Manager, Krishan Sardana, attributes their success to the combined talents of Amar Singh, a "bawarchi" or "master chef" – from Nepal originally – and Chander Bahadur, a luminary from the kitchen of the five-star Taj Mahal Hotel in New Delhi. "I've been in the restaurant business for twenty years and I strongly believe that our chefs aren't just the best, but The Best!" This is no idle boast. If you like Indian food, you will love Bombay Brasserie. If you think you don't like Indian food or haven't really tried it, this is your place.

The buffet at lunch, seven days a week, is a beehive of activity. It is a lavish spread of nineteen, well-labeled dishes for the (incredibly) reasonable price of $8.95 for all-you-can-eat. The composition varies daily, but there are several constants that might incite a riot if they were missing. They are Chicken

Tikka Masala, Saag Paneer and unbelievably succulent, red-fleshed quarters of Tandoori Chicken.

The Tandoori Chicken is divine. "The secret is the marination!" Sardana says. But, the Chicken Tikka Masala is addictively delicious – the sort of dish you continue eating long after you're full.

"Little pieces" or "tikkas" of chicken are marinated overnight, skewered and cooked instantly over charcoal in the vat-shaped tandoor ovens. The tikkas are then finished in a tomato-based sauce rich with the highly-prized ghee (clarified butter) and cream, and fragrant with freshly-chopped cilantro or coriander, as they call it.

Naan – the crusty, leavened bread that takes its distinctive tear drop shape from being cooked on the wall of the tandoor – makes a perfect edible scoop for chicken tikka masala when torn into bite-sized pieces.

A third staple of the buffet, Saag Paneer, is another must to try. It is an ambrosial mixture of soft, freshly-made white cheese (paneer), whipped cream and spinach. Think of this simply as the best creamed spinach you've ever tasted.

Two other vegetables to keep an eye out for are Okra Masala and the earthy, immensely-satisfying Eggplant Bhartha. Okra Masala is a crunchy sauté of sliced okra, garlic, onions and ginger, tinted yellow and perfumed by tumeric and mustard seeds. There is a chance this wonderful dish will be added to the menu, but Sardana says only if they can find okra fresh regularly at the Farmer's Market, as they refuse to use anything frozen. "No cutting corners here!" he says.

Happily, Eggplant Bhartha or "Bengan Bhartha" on the menu, is regularly available. It can (and should) be ordered any time. Whole eggplants are speared, lowered into the tandoor until their purple skins wrinkle and char, then mashed with tomatoes, garlic, matchstick-size slivers of ginger and enough cumin to remind you of a bowl of Texas chili. Bengan Bhartha is a fabulous dish.

At night, candlelight transforms Bombay Brasserie. As an added, civilized bonus, there is a full bar for anyone who cares for a cocktail before dinner. My idea of the perfect accompaniment for Indian cooking and its complexity is the Indian Kingfisher Beer – "Most thrilling chilled!" – as it says on the label.

Two sauces called "chutneys" and a basket of body-heating, black-pepper-studded papadums neatly folded in quarters are placed on the table once you're seated. Spoon a little imli – the syrupy, deep-red tamarind purée – and the tart, pale-green minced cilantro and mint ("mint chutney") on your plate for dipping. If the black pepper papadums are too intense, they have two tamer alternatives on hand and are happy to serve them – a cumin-flavored one and my personal favorite, garlic-flavored. While I always think of the thin, parchment-crisp papadums as the precursor to the main event, Sardana says that the Gujarati eat papadums throughout their meal. "They love that! For instance, when they are eating a naan or a Chicken Tikka Masala, they'll break a piece of papadum every minute and put it in their mouth to make the inside of their mouth crispy."

The Viceroy of India's Dinner for Two is a ten-dish blow-out fit for Lord Mountbatten himself. It covers all major points of interest on the Northern Indian or Punjabi culinary landscape: Tandoori Chicken, Boti Kabab (juicy chunks of marinated, tandoori-roasted lamb), a couple of large, cumin-scented shrimp (Tandoori Prawns), Seek Kabab (cigar-shaped sausagy pieces of minced lamb), as well as the aforementioned Chicken Tikka Masala and Saag Paneer. This all-out splurge is rounded out by a shrimp curry, Prawn "Bhuna" ("with onions"); a satiny Daal (black lentils and small red beans in a tomatoey cream sauce); a simple Pullao (saffron-flavored basmati rice with green peas); and two tandoori-roasted breads – Naan and Paratha.

When asked if the Viceroy of India Dinner is sometimes too much for two people, Sardana says, "Yes, occasionally. But, they love to take it home and have it for lunch the next day." He adds that another popular combination dinner, The Maharani of Jaipur's Pleasure, is perfect for one person who is game to sample a number of disparate dishes.

The various menus I would construct for friends (and for future visits myself) would include the following dishes. Among the appetizers, the Chicken Pakora drew raves at our table. They are alarming-looking, but delicious, fried bright orange-red wrinkles of minced chicken or "chicken fritters."

The Mixed Grill Bombay is the best way to sample an assortment of the "Tandoori Specialties." Let's face it, fellow Texans. This is barbecue and it's fabulous. Several spectacular dishes have recently been added to expand Bombay Brasserie's tandoori repertoire: Reshemi Kabab, Lamb Chop Kabab and Tandoori Red Snapper.

"Reshem" is the Hindi word for "silk" and these (always) marinated white chunks of chicken breasts have the distinctive taste of the tandoor and the advertised texture of silk. We actually ate the Reshemi Kabab pieces impaled with frilly toothpicks as hors d'oeuvres with our drinks, just as they would in India.

A huge Tandoori-roasted Red Snapper, served whole, was well worth the effort. The sweet, white chunks of well seasoned snapper practically swooned off the bones.

Best of all are the new Lamb Chop Kababs. Two-inch thick lamb chops the size of baseballs are encrusted with garam masala, the aromatic mixture of "hot spices" – cloves, cardamon, cinnamon, cumin and black pepper, to name a few – and cooked quickly in the tandoor. Crusty on the outside, juicy on the inside – they were perfect. Sardana believes that the appeal of the dish is that "the lamb is cooked on the bone. That's the best meat!" I quite agree.

The chunky lamb chops are served perched on a bed of basmati rice, but any of the other tandoori specialties would go nicely with Vegetable Biryani – an elegant, steamed casserole of layered basmati rice, vegetables, dried fruits and nuts – a triumph of flavors and textures.

I would add a whole or half order, depending on the size of your group, of saag paneer (great with everything, but especially the tandoori-roasted meats), Bengan Bhartha (eggplant) and the sumptuous, altogether poetic Malai Kofta Kashmiri (vegetable dumplings simmered in a creamy cilantro-flecked sauce).

Apart from the plain naan, two other breads not to miss are Kema Naan with ground lamb, fresh ginger and cilantro folded into the layers of dough, and Onion Kulcha, flavored with sweet caramelized pieces of onion.

I can't think of a better way to finish this feast of mind altering flavors than with an order of Mango Kulfee – the dense, deep orange palate-cleansing ice cream made from reduced milk and mango pulp.

Or Kheer – a heavenly rice pudding. Infinitely better than I remember it being elsewhere, their Kheer is studded with golden raisins, shelled pistachios and has a subtle, lingering aftertaste of rose water. As Sardana says when complimented on it, "I mean, if there is no flavor, then it is not dessert." My sentiments, exactly.

BUBBA'S SPORTS BAR &GRILL

6225 Washington
Houston, Texas 77007
713/861-7161

Type of Cuisine: American/Burgers
Bar: Full Bar
Dress: Casual
Entertainment: No
Payment: All Major Credit Cards
Prices: Daily Specials $6.95-$8.95
Sandwiches $3.95-$6.95
Recommended Dishes:
Chicken Fried Steak (Wednesday)
T-Bone Steak (Monday/Friday)
Home Run Burger
Home Run Chicken Sandwich
Breakfast Buffet (Saturday/Sunday)
Hours: Monday-Friday, 11:00a.m.-2:00a.m.(Kitchen closes at 10:00p.m.)
Saturday-Sunday, Breakfast: 8:00a.m-12:00p.m.
Full Menu: 12:00p.m.-6:00p.m.
Reservations: Not Accepted

In this politically correct-free zone, there is smoking. There is drinking. There is (some) cussing. There is conspicuous consumption of beef. But, there is no Bubba.

In fact, the fictionalized Bubba was conceived eighteen years ago, before "Bubba" had worked its way into our vernacular, by owner Tom Fore and his (then) partners, who used to greet each other as "Bubba!"

Fore thinks that one of the best things about Bubba's is how few fights they've had in eighteen years. ("Five. Not that a single fight is good. Mind ya!") I think one of the best things is the chicken fried steak.

Beaten, battered and fried, Bubba's Wednesday special (lunch and dinner) is a classic. As it should, it heaves over the side of the plate, barely makes room for a scoop of good, still-lumpy, homemade mashed potatoes, and strains under the considerable weight of thick, rich black-pepper-flecked cream-style gravy. Need I say more?

Fore says he prefers the Thursday special – chicken fried chicken – where a chicken breast receives the same abuse as a piece of round steak. It's served the same. But as a Texan, I've always thought that was sort of sacrilegious.

Another special that would gladden the heart of any cowboy is the Monday/Friday night steak special. The 12-ounce T-bone is marinated in a garlicky vinegar-oil-and-beer-basted-bath, basted with butter and nicely scored on the char-broiler. The other choice is an 8-ounce ribeye. Add a tossed salad, huge baked potato, and they are practically given away at $6.95 (Monday nights) or $8.95 (Fridays).

But best of all are "Bubba's Famous Burgers." Fore claims braggin' rights to what he believes is "one of the best hamburgers – if not the best hamburger – in Houston. There is an art to making a great hamburger, you know. More so certainly than I would have ever thought before going into the hamburger business." Originally inspired by the success of Roznoskey's, Bubba's has been under the recent tutelage of Cliff Cullen of Cliff's Hamburgers fame. The most notable improvement has been the chili. This also elevates the Low Ball Burger – a well-seasoned, perfectly grilled burger topped with chili, shredded Cheddar cheese and onions.

But the burger that will woo me back is The Home Run Burger. Good, smoky, scarlet-red hickory sauce is seared into the meat on the flat grill. It is topped with onions caramelized with a little Worcestershire Sauce, crisp, meaty bacon and American cheese. The bun is buttered and toasted lightly on the grill. Substitute a grilled chicken breast, toasted whole wheat bread for the bun and you have the delicious Home Run Chicken Sandwich.

The burgers and sandwiches are offered with French fries or cole slaw. The French fries are good. The cole slaw is better – finely chopped, lightly and not too-sweetly dressed.

The onion rings are the best of the "Appetizers and Munchies" I sampled. It is a well-seasoned, beer battered, "industry product" (read – frozen) as Fore says, "that we simply couldn't duplicate in our own kitchen." Of the other "industry products," the Buffalo wings are good-sized, meaty wings and drumettes. I don't mind this so much.

However, Bubba's nachos are an insult to nachos everywhere. I would direct Fore a scant block or two away to Cadillac Bar or even Leo's, where America's favorite snack food is made the way it should be – with crisp, warm chips covered in a bubbling, gooey mass of melted Monterrey Jack and/or Cheddar cheese. Bubba's are nachos you might expect to find at the Astrodome or maybe Cineplex Odeon – phony cheese and all.

The only other citation I would like to issue is for the mini-tubettes of fake butter or margarine on the otherwise authentic and especially good breakfast buffet offered from 8:00 a.m. – 12:00 noon, Saturday and Sunday. While the scrambled eggs and grits could have used a little more salt and pepper, it's a fine breakfast with thick, crisp bacon, sausage patties and – this was the best – doughy, homemade buttermilk biscuits. (That's what I needed the butter for. That, and the flawless pancakes!)

Fore says the recently added breakfast buffet "has become a phenomenal success. We stick out a bunch of newspapers and it is just kind of a nice, leisurely way (for people) to spend the weekend morning. It's especially popular with joggers and people from the nearby Memorial Park."

The best reason of all to visit Bubba's is that it just feels great to be there. There's a coziness that comes partially from the log cabin-like atmosphere and partially from the warmth of the wait staff. Fore thinks it feels the way it does because the residual spirit of a thousand good times lingers there. "I think the place takes on a personality, after all this time, of old friendships, a couple of Rocket championships and – I don't want to get too metaphysical here – of joy. I mean, there's been so much, so many big, good times at Bubba's." He may have something there.

CAFÉ JAPON

3915 Kirby Drive
Houston, Texas 77098
713/529-1668

Type of Cuisine: Japanese
Bar: Wine, Beer and Sake
Dress: Casual
Entertainment: No
Payment: All Major Credit Cards
Entrée Range: $9.00-$15.00
Recommended Dishes:
All Sushi: Especially "Special Rolls" or Handrolls:
Spider Roll
Yamaguchi (Cooked Tuna) Roll
Appetizers: Gyoza (Dumplings)
Uzura Teriyaki (Grilled Quail)
Geso Fry (Calamari)
Nasa Tempura (Shrimp and Eggplant Tempura)
Crab Puffs
Harumaki (Spring Rolls)
Entrées: Salmon Steak Salad
Nabeyaki Udon (Noodle Soup)
Hours: Monday-Thursday, 11:00a.m.-10:00 p.m.
Friday, 11:00a.m.-11:00p.m.
Saturday, 12:00p.m.-11:00p.m.
Sunday, 12:00p.m.-10:00p.m.
Reservations: Not Accepted

I'd like to round up all those who shudder at the notion of artfully arranged raw fish and find the Zen-like austerity of the average Japanese restaurant experience off-putting, and treat them to an evening at Café Japon.

We'd settle into one of the cushy, candlelit booths and I'd start by ordering a bowl of warmed Edamame Beans to enjoy with our hot sake and cold Japanese beer. As we pop these irresistible beans out of their pods into our mouths, I'd set about to do exactly what owners, brothers Denis and Kin Lui have almost inadvertently done – shatter the stereotype of Japanese dining.

I hardly know where to start, there are so many dishes to recommend on this menu.

For the squeamish, I can't think of a better introduction to sushi than any one of the nine house special rolls or twenty hand rolls, all very much geared to the Western palate and made almost exclusively with non-raw ingredients. The most popular is the Spider Roll – a symphony of textures and flavors – fried soft shell crab, cool cucumber, scallion and mayonnaise or Kin's favorite, the Yamaguchi Hand Roll with spicy (cooked) tuna and green onion, although both brothers say they're especially proud of the Café Japon Roll that "you can get nowhere else."

This time the spicy tuna is rolled with fresh salmon and avocado and of course, cooked vinegared short grain rice that is always used when making sushi. Any of these are good enough to inspire that Japanese phenomenon known as "sushi rapture," but the sushi is only part of the story at Café Japon.

There are as many as twenty-five appetizers, each better than the next, and since the portions are small, it is possible to sample several at a time or in fact, to make a meal of them. Starting at the very top of the list is the wonderful Negima – lean, thin strips of ribeye steak wrapped around a piece of green onion, basted in teriyaki sauce and broiled. Second is Gyoza – the pork-filled pan fried dumplings more delicate than Chinese dumplings. Another dish unique to Café Japon, Uzura Teriyaki – grilled quail – would go nicely with an order of Gomaae – fresh spinach leaves lightly dressed with sesame sauce. Next on the list is Geso Fry – fried calamari. It is Japanese calamari – more tender and flavorful than the variety that is ordinarily used – encased in a well-seasoned etherial layer of batter and fried quickly in vegetable oil.

Tempura, the deceptively simple practice of gently coating food with batter and frying it, is practically re-invented here. Theirs is exquisite, light as air and completely greaseless. Of course, the Ebi (shrimp) Tempura is fabulous, but I wouldn't miss ordering Kin's invention – Nasu Tempura, where shrimp is seasoned, ground with onion, wrapped in a sliver of egg plant, dipped in tempura batter and fried. It is excellent, but so is another original dish, brand spanking new on the menu, the Chicken California.

I challenge anyone to not be completely won over to this style of cooking by this intricate creation. Chicken breast, salmon, asparagus and carrot are rolled like sushi, but fried like tempura and sliced to reveal six slightly larger than bite-size pieces (or twelve for an entree-size order) in a kaleidoscope of gem-like colors. In true Japanese fashion, it is as beautiful as it is delicious.

The Crab Puffs are a divine, very un-Japanese mixture of cream cheese and crabmeat, fried and served with their version of sweet and sour sauce. The Harumaki (Japanese spring rolls) are another must to try.

Kin admits that "people associate spring rolls with Chinese food, but the Japanese eat them, too. They're quite different. The wrapper is thinner and crisper, and the contents are different. We use ground chicken and vegetables and they use pork, and we serve them with ponju (a citrusy, soy-based sauce) rather than sweet and sour sauce."

The Salmon Skin Salad is adapted from a dish Denis and Kin sampled on one of their tasting expeditions to the cutting edge Japanese restaurants of Los Angeles. Seasoned and well-crisped strips of salmon skin, ordinarily used exclusively in a hand roll, are placed on top of a mixture of seasonal greens and shredded carrots dressed with a tart, oil-free vinaigrette. The salad is superb and ample enough to share. Two of the other house dressings – ginger and especially creamy sesame – were good enough to drink.

The first entrée listed under "Dinner" is the Sesame Chicken. One of Kin's favorites, it is a slight variation from the traditional treatment as garlic, a stranger in the Japanese kitchen, is used ever so slightly in powder form to flavor the sauce. The chicken breast is pan fried, then left to simmer and absorb the sauce – a reduction of sake, soy sauce, mirin (sweet wine), beef broth and sesame seeds. Served with pieces of scored, grilled vegetables, the dish is a marvel of simplicity and full of flavor. Another excellent choice among the entrées is Tonkatsu – lean, tender slices of pork loin lightly battered in panko (Japanese bread crumbs) and deep fried.

This brings us to the piéce de résistance – Nabeyaki Udon. The best and most satisfying of all Japanese noodle dishes, Café Japon's obliterates the image of all those that have gone before it. Both brothers agree that there are several reasons theirs is so much better. First of all, unlike most other Japanese restaurants in town, they use freshly made frozen udon noodles (made from wheat and flour flown in from Chicago) and not dry noodles. Also, the broth is intensely flavored from hours of simmering on the stove. Elsewhere, they say it is often (incredibly) just seasoned water with the standard ingredients added. Intended for sharing, the large iron tureen arrives with shrimp tempura, chicken breast and nearly translucent slices of beef swimming in rich broth with long, firmly-textured udon noodles, and a poached egg. The diner breaks the egg, stirs the yolk and egg white into the soup and divides the contents between the little individual bowls. There are no fewer than seven other varieties of udon dishes to choose from (without the egg) including the unusual Duck Udon, but I recommend the nabeyaki udon. I think of this as Japanese comfort food.

For dessert, Café Japon is not content to stop with the standard offerings of either red bean or green tea Ice Cream that even I have not acquired a taste for. The choice is made nearly impossible by the addition of Banana Tempura and Ice Cream Tempura to the menu. The banana tempura is creamy chunks of banana dipped in batter, fried and served hot with a scoop of vanilla ice cream. One diner said that "it's better than banana's foster!" The second, equally good choice is a scoop of vanilla ice cream coated with a thin veneer of pound cake and re-frozen until it is ordered. The scoop of ice cream is then treated to a second coating of tempura batter, fried and served with the kind of sauce that you would normally find on strawberry shortcake. They're both sublime.

Café Japon is the young Lui brothers' third and most successful restaurant in the Houston area. With the help of their younger sister, Mona, these Hong Kong natives first opened the more traditional Japon ("Japan" in French) in 1990 near the corner of Westheimer and Fountainview. Then in June of 1995, they opened a second Japon on Times Boulevard in the Village. Next came Café Japon opening just a year ago in November, 1995. A second Café Japon serving the same menu has opened near the corner of Hays and Westheimer. It's a good thing because this one plays to a packed house. Since the service suffers a bit when they're busiest, to avoid the crowds Denis says it's best to come for lunch before 11:45 a.m. or after 1:30 p.m., and for dinner before 7:00 p.m. or after 9:00 p.m.

CAFÉ PIQUET

6053 Bissonnet
Houston, Texas 77081
713/664-1031

Type of Cuisine: Cuban
Bar: No (You can bring your own wine.)
Dress: Casual
Entertainment: No
Payment: Mastercard and Visa
Entrée Range: $6.95-$11.95
Recommended Dishes:
  Appetizers: Croquetas
    Empanadas
    Papas Rellenos
    Fried Yucca
  Entrées: Pan Con Bistec (Steak Sandwich)
    Grilled Chicken Breast
    Fried Pork Chunks
    Picadillo
    Ropa Vieja
    Fried Whole Red Snapper
    Yucca with Garlic Sauce
    Moros (Black Beans with Rice)
Hours: Tuesday-Thursday, 11:00a.m.-9:00p.m.
  Friday-Saturday, 11:00a.m.-10:00p.m.
  Sunday, 11:00a.m.-7:00p.m.
  (Closed Monday)
Reservations: Accepted

There is an old Creole saying popular with Cubans that, "Lo que bien se quiso nunca se olvida." (That which you greatly loved never is forgotten.)

Guido Piquet says the finest complement he is ever paid, is that his cooking tastes just like his Cuban customers' mothers'. Everything is handmade. Fresh garlic is crushed in a "mortero" (mortar and pestle) and the sofrito – the chopped onions, bell peppers, garlic and aji cachucha (incendiary Scotch bonnetlike Cuban peppers) – that is the very basis of almost all Cuban recipes is not made in bulk, but when the order is placed for the dish. The menu is short because he insists that everything be fresh and, "I want to keep all the plates good."

The cooking, in fact, did start with his mother. "My mother, my father, my two sisters and I left Cuba on October 22, 1962. It was the last flight that left Cuba during the missile crisis. We were fortunate to be in the United States. We landed in Miami and lived there about a year and four months. Miami was real tough at the time and we had some cousins in Los Angeles. So, we were on our way there on a Greyhound bus, and stopped in Houston to visit some other cousins who had been here about a year. We ended up staying. I was seven years old. I went to Pilgrim Elementary right there on Richmond Avenue.

"At first my father got a job working with one of my cousins. Then, in 1974, my dad started selling things like plantains, coffee, Cuban crackers you know, all the things Cuban people are very accustomed to having out of the garage of the house. He would deliver to people's homes in a Ford Fairlane. That's how we got started. He moved briefly to a little warehouse on Royalton. When I was about fifteen, I took D. E. (Distributive Education) and went to work for him half of the day. On June 1, 1976, we opened Piquet Market at 6619 Chimney Rock. It was a small grocery store that served the Cuban and Latin American community. We were there for twenty years."

It was at that location his mother began cooking in the back of the market for the family and employees. Piquet says, "Customers would come in, smell the food and ask, 'Hey, can I buy a plate of that?' That's how (the restaurant) got going. Cafe Piquet is a continuation of a tradition that we started at Piquet Market.

"When my parents decided to close Piquet Market, my wife and I decided it was important to keep the tradition alive. We wanted our own place, but just the restaurant no grocery store. We found this location at Bissonnet and Rampart and opened the doors October 4, 1996."

Stark white walls are covered in neatly framed and arranged photographs of European castles and 8 x 10 black and white glossies of people like baseball player José Cruz. It is a modest place where most of the atmosphere comes from the extraordinary exuberance of the cooking and the warmth of both Guido and his wife Nellie, who runs the show.

Cubans are great snackers and most of the appetizers are the sort of party dishes or snacks that might be found in Miami's Cuban bakeries; wonderful things like Croquetas (creamy, pinky-sized croquettes made with bechamel sauce and ground ham), and empanadas – their most popular appetizer.

The secret to the empanadas is that they are filled with the glorious, assertively-seasoned Picadillo – a sort of Cuban sloppy Joe. Piquet says they are handmade and labor intensive. Lean ground beef is "simmered for hours" with tomatoes, onion, garlic, peppers, pimentos and peas. Picadillo is also used to fill another appetizer, Papas Rellenas (stuffed potatoes). Egg-shaped ovals of mashed potatoes are formed around the ground beef mixture and deep fried. But my absolute favorite way to eat the picadillo, once he's added small, browned cubes of potatoes, is with a couple of fried eggs on top, a side order of white rice and the heavenly plantain maduros (fried plantains) – a typical Cuban almeurzo (lunch) dish.

The snow-white, fibrous yucca is a wonder both ways he prepares it – barely boiled then deep fried as an appetizer; or as a side dish – boiled, cut in large chunks with craters of mojo (garlic sauce) floating on top.

Mojo is a sauce often used as a marinade, baste, or dip in the Cuban household. It is traditionally made with chopped garlic, lime and lard. Not exactly for the faint of heart (or diet), but Piquet says that he prepares two mojos – the standard one with lard, and an olive-oil-based mojo – and gives the customers a choice. It is offered as a dip for both the fried yucca and the mariquitas – plantain chips – huge, yellow ribbons of freshly fried plantains that Piquet cuts to order on a ham slicer.

El Cubano, with pork, ham and cheese, is the best known Cuban sandwich, but the sandwich that makes me salivate just to think about it, is the Pan Con Bistec steak sandwich. Piquet agrees, "It is my favorite sandwich. I make it with one of the little Palomilla steaks, shoestring potatoes, grilled onions and sliced tomatoes." It is served on a thin, toasted loaf of bread that he tells me is as close as he can get to Cuban bread. "It's made by the Royal Bakery by Cubans." It is a great sandwich; a classic case of different flavors and textures coming together to make something truly wonderful.

The first dish listed under "House Specialties" I probably wouldn't have ordered if the usually modest Piquet hadn't boasted that they served "the best chicken breast in all of Houston." This is not an exaggeration. It doesn't suffer from being either skinless or boneless. A whole eight ounce chicken breast is butterflied, slathered with mojo, then browned on the grill with onions. I'm not at all surprised to hear that it is the number one seller at Cafe Piquet. It comes with white rice, fried plantains and the beloved Frijoles Negros (black beans). Closer to a soup than a side dish, they are dense, richly flavored and black as a moonless night. Black beans accompany most orders, but are worth ordering on their own if you have a steak sandwich, for instance.

When the black beans are cooked with rice it is called Moros, short for Moros y Cristianos (Moors and Christians), a reference to the invasion of Spain by Moors in the 8th century. The dish is moist and full of flavor almost like a risotto.

The Pernil Asado (roasted pork), "always popular with Cubans," Piquet says, is cooked slowly for ten hours. But I liked the succulent, fat-edged nuggets of Masitas Fritas (fried pork chunks) even better. This is definitely a case where the natural sweetness of the caramelized fried plantains seems to suit the salty richness of the pork especially well.

Almost as popular as the picadillo is the Cuban classic, Ropa Vieja. The name "ropa vieja" or "old clothes" comes from the practice of first boiling the beef for broth then shredding the beef (using it "secondhand") to make a sort of beef hash. I don't remember tasting a better rendition.

The Camarones Enchilados Cuban (shrimp creole) "is an old family recipe," Piquet tells me. The shrimp are cooked in a tomato sauce that has been simmered for "about two hours like a spaghetti sauce" until the onions, garlic and peppers have become tender. The heat is provided by "lots of black pepper."

However, even better in the seafood genre is the Pargo Entero Frito (fried whole red snapper). "That's one of my favorites," Piquet agrees. It is available only when he is able to get fresh red snapper, "about 90% of the time," he says. "I never freeze it." He cleans the fish, seasons it with a little salt and garlic powder, fries it quickly in canola oil, and brushes a little mojo on top.

Dessert is a must. Cubans have a natural, almost patriotic reverence for sweets. Bread pudding is apparently as popular in Cuba as it has become recently (again) in the United States. Piquet says that it is his mother's recipe and it is divine, distinguished by a gooey layer of caramelized sugar on top. I preferred it by itself rather than topped with coconut cream listed as an option. The flan is excellent with just the faintest hint of lemon peel, and the rice pudding served in thick glass jars is soothing and delicious. Fans of Tres Leches, the Central American specialty, will enjoy the one served at Cafe Piquet.

This is real celebratory eating and goes well with a robust glass of (for instance) good Spanish red wine, but since Cafe Piquet has no liquor license, they are happy for customers to bring their own.

Cubans are known for their coffee which is served in cups smaller than espresso cups, called "tasitas." They believe that coffee should be, like the letters for the word "café," *caliente* (hot); *amargo* (bitter); *fuente* (strong); and *escaso* (scanty).

CARTER & COOLEY

375 West 19th Street
Houston, Texas 77008
713/864-3354

Type of Cuisine: Delicatessen
Bar: No
Dress: Casual
Entertainment: No
Payment: All Major Credit Cards
Sandwich Prices: $4.50-$5.75
Recommended Dishes:
BLT
Reuben
Liverwurst on Pumpernickel
Muffaletta
Thanksgiving Supreme Wrap
Baked Potato Soup
Desserts: Blueberry Pie
White Chocolate Cookies
Chocolate Chip Cookies
Hours: Monday-Friday, 9:00a.m.-3:30p.m.
Saturday, 9:00a.m.-5:00p.m..
(Closed Sunday)
Reservations: Not Accepted

Picture this. You're a kid. You're sitting at the kitchen table. Your mom has just made you a BLT and poured you a glass of cold milk. The bread is soft and white. The bacon is crisp, smokey, and there's lots of it. The "L" is curly, fresh Butterhead lettuce and the "T" is a thick slice of juicy beefsteak tomato. Are you dreaming?

No. You are lunching at Carter & Cooley in the Heights.

The old saying that the whole is greater than the sum of its parts could have been written about the simple act of making a sandwich. Neil Sackheim, who co-owns the charmingly nostalgic lunchtime deli with Randall Pace sees it this way, "If you start out with the very best quality raw ingredients, all it takes is putting them together in the right order, the right proportion, so that you get a taste that combines to make your palate agreeable. Our breads are all made daily to our specifications. Our meats are shipped in weekly from New York. We go to the Farmer's Market to select the best lettuce and tomatoes."

But, let's get back to the perfect BLT. With the kind of solemnity normally reserved for a disarmament conference, Sackheim says, "The problem is, most places you order a BLT, people don't take it seriously that you are ordering a BACON, lettuce and tomato sandwich. We put eight full slices of bacon on any of our BLT's or club sandwiches, so you're getting bacon as the main ingredient and not just a taste. Plus, it's extra thick, hickory smoked Texas bacon that we bake off first, so it's always crisp and greaseless."

The Reuben runs a close second to the BLT and is good enough to draw regular customers from as far away as Kingwood, Baytown and Spring. Rich ribbons of real New York corned beef, buttery sauerkraut, melted Swiss cheese, and toasted rye bread slathered with good, homemade Thousand Island dressing. It tastes like it was made by someone who grew up eating great Reuben sandwiches. It was.

"The idea of having (my own) delicatessen has been in my mind for many, many years." says Sackheim, "So, in late 1988, a situation came up where the Houston Heights was proposing a downtown revitalization district through what was called Main Street Project for a small urban city within a city. Since Randy (Pace) and I both lived in the Heights, we saw the need for a delicatessen."

"Randy and I designed the deli to reflect the historical virtues of the Heights using the original features – 17 foot high, original tin ceilings, the transoms above the doors, the lighting and the ceiling fans. All of this gave you a feeling that your were walking into an historical ambiance." They named their restaurant for Oscar Martin Carter and Daniel Denton Cooley who, "came from Nebraska in 1892 with the intention of establishing a totally planned community complete with an industrial district, business district, and most importantly, a residential district," explains Sackheim. This land was elevated some 23 feet above Houston, hence the name Houston Heights. They purchased the property in April 1892, and both Carter and Cooley were still living there when the Heights was annexed to Houston in 1918. Carter was called the "Founder of the Heights" and Cooley, grandfather of renowned heart surgeon Denton Cooley, was known as "Father of the Heights."

When they opened for business April 4, 1989, the 68th anniversary of the Simon Lewis Building, Sackheim tells me that their menu had "a few more ethnic specialties – things like blintzes, bagels and lox, and cabbage soup – dishes from my own background." Few of these "Jewish specialties" remain except a coarse, authentic-tasting chopped liver (best on pumpernickel with onion), and old-fashioned potato salad – both recipes be attributes to his maternal grandmother. Also great on pumpernickel (or rye) with mustard and onion, the Liverwurst is the real thing. "Oh yeah," Sackheim laughs, "We have one gentleman who comes in exclusively for the Liverwurst!"

I'm sure he has a lot more who come in for his fabulous

rendition of the New Orleans classic, the muffaletta. He just recently added the muffaletta to the menu and, "we're selling the hell out of it!" Under the heading of practice makes perfect, Sackheim says that it's taken them two years to strike just the right balance of meats, cheeses and the all-important olive salad – a piquant, vinaigrette-based mixture of garlic, olives, capers, onions and oregano. "Frankly, I think it's my favorite sandwich."

One of my least favorite recent food trends, the "wrap," makes an appearance as the Supreme at Carter & Cooley and although I ordinarily find the wrap concept a little like eating a rolled up newspaper, Sackheim seems to have gotten the essential mix of flavors and textures right. Of the five to choose from, my favorite is the Thanksgiving Supreme. Warm, crusty pieces of old-fashioned southern corn bread dressing, moist slices of turkey breast, chunky homemade cranberry sauce, lettuce and mayonnaise on a five-grain flour tortilla – a fragile, but delicious composition that must be held gingerly not to spill its content on the way to your mouth.

The salads were a bit of a disappointment, but I'm sure Carter & Cooley has as many fans for its soups (which rotate) as it does for its sandwiches. The three I sampled were spectacular. The black bean had the assertive, lingering taste of cumin and a fine, smooth texture. The chicken and dumpling (irregularly available) has soft, doughy dumplings in a dense, chicken flavored broth with orange flecks of diced carrots and shreds of not only breast meat, but dark meat, too, for extra flavor. But the best, and best known of all, is the Baked Potato Soup. A silky, cream-based potatoey soup – a sort of chunky vichyssoise with all the trimmings – crumbled bacon, chopped scallions and shards of freshly grated Cheddar cheese. It is homey, deeply satisfying, and conjures images of cool nights in front of a warm fire.

Saving the best for last. Do not leave without trying at least a bite of one of the little individual pies. The blueberry was our favorite. The buttery sweet crust was stained dark purple form its rich contents bubbling through in the oven. The cinnamon apple was almost as good as the blueberry, followed by a bright red cherry pie. All begged to be warmed, then topped with a scoop of vanilla ice cream. You might want to consider leaving with a sackful of soft, freshly baked homemade cookies – white chocolate, macadamia nut, peanut butter, chocolate chip or oatmeal raisin. My favorites were the white and regular chocolate chip. Back to that kitchen table and tall glass of cold milk.

CAVATORE

2120 Ella Boulevard
Houston, Texas 77008
713/869-6622

Type of Cuisine: Italian
Bar: Full
Dress: Nice Casual
Entertainment: Piano Sunday-Thursday 7:00p.m.-10:00p.m.
Friday-Saturday 7:00p.m.-11:00p.m.
Payment: All Major Credit Cards
Entrée Range: $9.50-$19.95
Recommended Dishes:
Appetizers: Tortellini in Panna
Calamari Fritti
Insalata dei Cesari (Caesar Salad)
Entrées: Costoletta di Vitello (Veal Chop)
Pollo Valdostano (Chicken Breast)
Penne alla Mafia (Penne with Sausage and Peppers)
Hours: Lunch: Monday-Friday, 11:00a.m.-2:30p.m.
Dinner: Sunday-Thursday, 5:30p.m.-10:00p.m.
Friday-Saturday, 5:30p.m.-11:00p.m.
Reservations: Accepted

I recommend that anyone who took a New Year's vow of dietary abstinence avert their eyes now, because, although it is possible to dine fairly abstemiously on grilled chicken with marinated vegetables, and what may well be the best Caesar salad in town, where Cavatore Italian Restaurant really excels is the sturdy, cream-enriched sauces of North Central Italy.

Known as Emilia-Romana, this region is distinguished by its farm lands... and what this style of cooking lacks in subtlety, it makes up for in real, soul-satisfying substance.

When Sonny Lahham and Giancarlo Cavatore opened Cavatore in 1984, Giancarlo encouraged his mother, Olga, to come from Italy "to teach our first chef her recipes from sauces to sausage-making. 85% of the recipes we still serve are Mrs. Cavatore's." Lahham continues that "she's 86 years old and lives in Milan now, but she was from Bologna originally"(a city famous for its fabulous food and pork products).

In fact, what we know as bologna, the much maligned sandwich meat, began as mortadella in Bologna and is featured on the menu cubed with mozzarella cheese and tossed with a simple oil and vinegar dressing in Insalata Cavatore.

It is the first of three excellent salads listed on the menu. The Insalata di Spinaci is a terrific traditional spinach-egg-mushroom salad with a good vinaigrette, but the Insalata dei Cesari, Caesar salad, (for two people) is the fine work of Cavatore's chef of ten years, Greg Torres, a native of Monterrey,

Mexico. Suitably tart with lemon juice and not creamy as we have come to know it elsewhere, Torres points out that his Caesar salad seems authentic because it is so similar to the recipe that Italian brothers Alex and Caesar Cardini created for their restaurant in Tijuana, Mexico, in the late 1920's with a minor omission for health security's sake: the raw egg yolk.

The Tortellini in Panna is definitely not for the faint-of-diet, but worth the drive alone. Pasta rings are filled with veal and topped with a heavenly mixture of cream, butter and Parmesan cheese. This is a dish with origins deep in the heart of Emilia-Romano. Only in Italy could a simple doughnut-shaped, meat-filled pasta tortellino, in the singular inspire not one, but two different stories. Was it created by the besotted cook of the Cardinal of Bologna in memory of the navel of the beautiful daughter of a country innkeeper on their journey to Rome as some Emilians claim? Or is it actually the navel of Venus immortalized by the cook at a trattoria in Castelfranco back in the days when they believed Greek gods roamed the earth?

My second favorite pasta is the whimsically named Penne alla Mafia apparently for its earthy, Sicilian-inspired qualities. The sauce is a forcefully-concentrated marinera rich with garlic and sweet peppers. But the highlight is Mrs. Cavatore's own recipe for homemade Italian sausage – spicy without being hot and studded with fennel.

Incredibly, Lahham says that among the other choices of pasta, the Linguini con Vongote (with clams) is one of the most popular, "especially the one with white clam sauce." Lahham admits that the clams are not fresh, but people love it, especially the intensely-flavored sauce of fish broth, white wine, garlic, fresh basil and crushed red peppers.

Listed under Pasta Fresca are classic homestyle renditions of the kind of standards you'd expect to find at Cavatore. The two standouts are Fettucine Carbonara with a creamy liaison of eggs, cream, butter, pieces of prosciutto ham and Parmesan cheese; and the equally-satisfying Lasagna al Forno, classically made, baked in sheets, then cut into individual portions which are topped with cheese, marinera sauce and reheated in an oven until it is brown and crisp on the sides.

Among the soups, I was happy to see the delicate, old-fashioned Stracciatella. Equally popular in Rome and Bologna, their version of this chicken broth-based soup has fresh spinach and is laced with whole egg – broken, beaten and stirred into the soup while almost boiling.

There are six different veal dishes to choose from and, while I liked the Vitello Piccata very much, I find it hard to pass up a good veal chop when I see one. A relative newcomer on the menu (and the only veal recipe not courtesy of Mrs. Cavatore) – the Costoletta di Vitello Capri, is not a dainty little thing either in portion or presentation. A whopping ten ounces of tender veal chop is quickly grilled, covered with a mixture of cheeses, then flamed with brandy. Call the food police now and arrest me – I love this dish.

Lahham says that those looking to satisfy their craving for a large piece of meat often opt instead for the Filetto de Mamzo al Brandy – a filet sautéed in butter, enriched further by a "touch of cream" and then flambéed with brandy.

We have Lahham's wife, Giuliana, who is from Genoa, to thank for the best of the chicken dishes, Pollo Valdestano. A chicken breast is lightly breaded, sautéed in butter, and placed over a bed of fresh asparagus covered with marinera sauce and melted mozzarella cheese. The Pollo Cacciatore (chicken "hunter's style"), a dish my grandfather loved, is prepared according to the well-founded custom with a robust marinera sauce full of sweet peppers and onions. Lahham says the Pollo al Rosmarino – rosemary chicken sautéed with garlic and mushrooms – is the most popular of all.

All of the desserts I sampled are outstanding and made by Torres himself. His favorite appears to be the Tiramisu which he says "is made with love" (and only made on weekends). "It goes pretty fast. Sometimes we sell out on Friday night." Of the other fourteen or so regularly available choices, it's a toss-up between the White Chocolate Mousse which I would ordinarily not recommend over Dark Chocolate Mousse, but prefer in this case and a wonderful rendition of that old Sicilian specialty, Cannoli. Cylindrical pastries are piped full of a divine mixture of fresh whipped ricotta cheese, tiny chocolate chips, a little vanilla extract and chopped raisins and pecans. Although sometimes an acquired taste, Torres' cannoli are perfect.

Cavatore is directly across the street from Giancarlo Cavatore and Sonny Lahham's first successful venture together, the cozy French restaurant in a log cabin, La Tour D'Argent. As a nod to "Texas and the United States," Cavatore says they lovingly dismantled a hundred-year old barn in Bastrop, Texas, and reassembled it on the site that had been used as a parking lot for La Tour D'Argent.

The barn is just one of the rooms where it's possible to sit and it might be your first choice if you enjoy live entertainment in the form of a piano player (Monday through Thursday 7:00 p.m. 10:00 p.m., Friday and Saturday until 11:00 p.m.). There is also a series of slightly cozier, smaller rooms.

CHEZ GEORGES

11907-J Westheimer at Kirkwood
Houston, Texas 77077
281/497-1122

Type of Cuisine: French
Bar: Wine and Beer
Dress: Coat Required
Entertainment: Piano Tuesday 7:00p.m. – 10:30p.m.
Payment: American Express, MasterCard, Visa
Entrée Range: $7.95-$28.00
Recommended Dishes:
Appetizers: Salade de Magret de Canard Fume (Salad with Smoked Duck Breast)
Paté Maison
Chausson d'Escargots
Lobster Bisque (Lunch)
Entrées: Poisson de Jour en Parchemin (Fish of the day in parchment)
Baby Rack of Lamb
Bouillabaise (Lunch)
Salade Nicoise (Lunch)
Hours: Lunch: Tuesday-Friday, 11:00a.m-2:00p.m.
Dinner: Tuesday-Friday, 5:00p.m.-10:00p.m.
Saturday, 4:00p.m.-10:00p.m.
Sunday, 11:00a.m.-8:30p.m.
(Closed Monday)
Reservations: Accepted
Smoking: Not Permitted

In *France, The Beautiful Cookbook* writer, Alexandre Vialatte, is quoted as saying that the mountainous, volcanic region of central France known as the Auvergne, "produces government ministers, cheeses and volcanoes"; and I would like to add, in the case of Georges Guy, chef and owner of Chez Georges – one very talented chef.

Uncharacteristically nomadic for a French couple, Georges and Monique Guy have moved no fewer than eleven times in their twenty-seven years of marriage. Fortunately, two of the moves have been to Houston, the first in 1982 to join his brother and his family who were already living here and the last in 1987 to open the small, unpretentious Chez Georges on the corner of Kirkwood and Westheimer.

A veteran of just more than three decades as a chef, Georges Guy earned his first star in the prestigious Michelin Guide in 1981. Although he was born "by accident" he jokes, in an area well known for its hearty, rustic, rib-sticking style of cooking, he says his tastes in cooking (and living) lean heavily toward the warm, sunny, herb-rich region of Provence where his parents moved their family of eleven children when he was seven. After seven happy years in Aix-en Provence, the army relocated his father back to the Auvergne, but the die was cast and he knew he was destined to return. He eventually did return briefly with his own family just before his last and hopefully, final move to Houston seven years ago.

His love for the South of France is reflected not only in the Provencal-style decor of their restaurant, but particulary in his deft and generous use of fresh herbs.

Each meal I've eaten at Chez Georges has been like taking a little trip to France and not just because it's taken me practically that long to get there and back.

The lunch menu is quite different from the dinner offerings and features such old friends as French onion soup, bouillabaise (fisherman's soup), lobster bisque, salade nicoise and steak au poivre (pepper steak).

The Onion Soup, often referred to by the French as "gratinée" for the crust of cheese baked on top of the crouton in the last stage of cooking, is especially good – distinguished by the use of duck stock as opposed to the usual chicken or beef.

The Bouillabaise is a successful re-creation of a dish which originated in Marsailles, a fish stew which he makes by substituting Gulf snapper and shrimp for the red mullet, sea bass and langostines of the Mediterranean – something purists will tell you should not even be attempted. The densely-flavored fish broth is chock full of seafood and served with the traditional garnishes of a crouton, shredded French Gruyère cheese, and a small dish of rouille – a garlic, red pepper and saffron-based mayonnaise.

The Lobster Bisque is an accurate recollection of an old favorite and will be available on the Sunday brunch menu starting Easter Sunday. Both salads at lunch were wonderful and very satisfying. The first one listed is Salade du Berger, which is topped with thin slices of caramelized onion, bacon and goat cheese. The Salade Niçoise is a superior treatment of an old bistro-style classic. Both salads benefit from the house vinaigrette made creamy by the addition of an egg yolk.

The Steak au Poivre, a dish that was first prepared by chef Emile Lerch in 1920 at the Trianon Palace of Versailles, was tender, cooked to roseate perfection and topped with a piquant pepper cream sauce.

Any of these dishes are good enough to single-handedly rekindle the fashion for French food in this town – something I'd love to see happen!

The dinner menu runs the gamut from the elegant simplicity of an impeccably prepared fish of the day (red snapper, in our case), wrapped in parchment, to the elaboration of one of the chef's innovations, an appetizer of escargots sautéed with bone marrow in a red Burgundy wine sauce served in a puff pastry shell. This is where Georges Guy's virtuosity really shines.

The inspiration of two of the world's finest chefs, the remarkable Troisgros brothers, Pierre and the late Jean, with whom he worked some twenty-three years ago in the tiny town of Roanne (near Lyons) is evident in his especially masterful treatment of fish. This is truly where the French excel. I defy anyone to not be converted into a full-fledged fish lover by either the Grilled Snapper with a sauce of rosemary and the sly variation of red (as opposed to white) Burgundy wine or the Grilled Oregon Salmon served with fresh spinach and a julienne of tomatoes with basil.

The Auvergne is famous for its lamb, so it stands to reason that both the Grilled Lamb Chops at lunch and the roasted Baby Rack of Lamb are excellent, redolent of fresh thyme and right on the mark.

Another especially memorable dish was the appetizer salad of mixed greens garnished with finely sliced smoked duck breast and a warm, creamy disk of goat cheese enclosed in a light, crispy pastry shell, dressed this time with hazelnut oil and fresh rosemary.

The desserts are every bit as good as you would hope to find at a French restaurant; the stand-outs being a heavenly Chocolate Mousse Cake, more mousse than cake; a classic Bavarois – a light, fruit-flavored mousse supported by a thin layer of cake; and that old standard Profiteroles – vanilla ice cream in little puffs of pastry topped with melted chocolate and whipped cream.

The Guys have pretty strong feelings about how their food should be eaten and what should accompany it. For instance, there is a noticeable absence of salt and pepper on the table although they will provide it if you ask. (I do recommend tasting your food first to see if it's needed.) They also made a decision long ago to not offer liquor as they firmly believe that wine is the only true complement to their style of cooking and this opinion is taken further by the exclusive offering of French wines (with a preponderance of Bordeaux) on the wine list.

Both the wine list and the recently added wine bar are the particular domain of Monique Georges. She sees this an an opportunity for people who don't want to eat a full meal to stop in, have a glass or two of wine, "a small dish" of something, maybe some charcuteries (French sausages and paté) and a little cheese.

The last Wednesday of every month Chez Georges has

an evening with a pre-set menu highlighting dishes from a particular region of France. They call it "Le Tour de France" after the annual bicycle race and they say it's been very successful since they began in January. How wonderful to taste regional specialties that wouldn't ordinarily appear on a menu here!

Chez Georges seats only eighty people. It's especially fun to invite(at least) two other couples and reserve the very cozy private dining room. If you do, you might want to try the special six course tasting menu which is dictated by the season, and the whim and imagination of the chef.

The Guys are a success story in every way – a close family with three grown children and two grandchildren. They say, in spite of working hard, something people from this region are also known for (Monique, Georges and son Phillipe are there every day and night), they lead a "happy, relatively stress-free life here in Houston" which they attribute to the easy warmth and enthusiasm of their very loyal clientele. Although Monique Guy, who clearly has more affection for the Auvergne than Georges, says there is an expression that "Auvergnias have dirt on their shoes" meaning that those from the Auvergne may travel, but they always keep some of their home deep in their hearts.

When I marveled at their longevity personally and professionally, she explained it like this: "Georges is good. He is a good husband, a good father and a good chef." I especially agree with the last sentiment.

CHIMI CHURRI'S

5712 Bellaire Blvd.
Houston, Texas 77081
713/661-1325

Type of Cuisine: Argentinean/Uruguan
Bar: Wine and Beer
Dress: Casual
Entertainment: Friday, Saturday and Sunday nights
Payment: All Major Credit Cards
Entrée Range: $8.75-$15.95
Recommended Dishes:
Appetizers: Chorizo a la Parilla (Grilled South American Sausage)
Grilled Blood Sausage
Potato Salad
Entrées: Parillada "Completa" (Mixed Grill)
Churrasco (Ribeye)
Entrana (Skirt Steak)
Asado (Beef Flat Ribs)
Hours: Lunch: Monday-Thursday, 11:00a.m.-3:00p.m.
Dinner: Monday-Thursday 5:00p.m.-9:00p.m.
Friday-Saturday, 11:00a.m.-11:00p.m.
(Closed Sunday)
Reservations: Accepted

"I am going to tell you a story about chimi churri," begins Gustavo Saldivia, who with his father, Mariano, owns Chimi Churri's South American grill.

"About fifty or sixty years ago, in the country side of Uruguay, there was a land owner who before he went out to do his duties told his cook, 'make me a steak with chimi churri.' What he meant was, 'make me a steak with something or other, and the word he used was chimi churri. So, this cook made up a sauce with garlic, parsley, olive oil, vinegar, oregano and a touch of red pepper. And she made him a steak. He loved it so much that whenever he had big parties at the ranch, he offered it to their guests. It became very popular with every grill item in South America.

"Now chimi churri is on any table in South America. This is a must. It would not be absent. It's almost like ketchup here with French fries."

The Saldivia family came to Houston nearly twenty years ago from the city of Montevideo on the southernmost tip of Uruguay. In June of 1994, they opened Chimi Churri's with the intention of offering a menu that is exclusively Rio Platense – a style of cooking and eating unique to Uruguay and Argentina, "two very, very close countries divided by a river, Rio de la Plata, but the people are the same," the younger Saldivia with whom I spoke, explains. "There is nothing on this menu that you won't find there."

At the very heart of Rio Platense cuisine is the parrillada – a mixed grill that includes asado (beef flat ribs), South American chorizo (sausage) and an assortment of what are euphemistically known in this country as variety meats – sweet breads, tripe, and kidneys.

"The Parrillada is our specialty. I wanted to be authentic so I took a chance on putting the mixed grill on the menu, even though I know Americans would not eat kidneys, tripe or sweetbreads."

In the name of research, I ordered the less heroically portioned appetizer version which included everything but the flat ribs (the Picada). What I found was that the Chorizo, which can and should be ordered on it's own to sample, was earthy and divine with a flavor that falls somewhere between sweet and hot Italian sausage. The Sweetbreads were sliced quite thin, had an appetizingly crisp exterior and tasted distinctly of the grill. The kidneys and tripe were about a 10½ on the "gak!" meter.

Saldivia laughs and says that many American customers like the mild flavor and crunch texture of the sweetbreads and sometimes order them alone as an entrée or grilled and eaten on a sandwich, but that "you usually have to be born to it to like the stronger tasting kidneys and tripe."

They have both ham and cheese and the more classic beef-filled Empañadas, but I can't think of a better way to start a meal at Chimi Churri's than with the Chorizo a la Parilla. Garlicky and juicy, the grilled sausage is served with warm, freshly baked, buttered slices of French bread and a slightly chunky, superior version of the already well known chimi churri sauce. Saldivia agrees, "My favorite appetizer is the chorizo. I like to eat sausage and red wine before I start...and French bread."

He's right. Almost everything on the menu cries out to be washed down with good, hearty Spanish or Chilean red wine. This earthy, seductive food marries perfectly with the bold Spanish Vino Cubrero, Montecillo. It is less expensive and has less bite than the better known Rioja, Marques de Caceres. Or why not try one of seven choices of Chilean Cabernet Sauvignons?

The third appetizer listed, Provoleta, is provolone cheese melted over slices of tomato that have been doused with chimi churri sauce. It goes well with the grilled sausage, but I liked the idea that in Uruguay the melted cheese alone is eaten with a grilled steak.

When available, another appetizer, Matambre Con Rusa,

is worth ordering. Literally translated, "mata hambre" means to "kill hunger." Saldivia tells me that "the gauchos used to take that in their packs when they went out in the country on their horses. When they were hungry, they would just cut a piece of matambre and put it on a slice of bread." This unusual cut of beef between the ribs and the skin is stuffed with spinach, carrots and hard boiled eggs. It is then rolled, grilled and served cold with "Russian potato salad." The small pieces of beef are so difficult to get that Saldivia says he plans to offer Matambre exclusively on weekends.

The Russian Potato Salad deserves special comment. It is the sort of potato salad that you would find at a charcuterie or delicatessen in Paris. Homemade mayonnaise is used to bind uniformly diced cubes of potatoes, carrots and sweet peas. In South America, it is the classical accompaniment of Milanesa a thin sliced, breaded beef or chicken cutlet. We found that it complemented perfectly the intense richness of the off-the-menu, irregularly available, Grilled Blood Sausage.

Saldivia actually brings the blood sausage himself on the plane when he travels to Miami where he says it's easier to get because there are more Argentineans living there. "I always want to have it for the people who know it and love it." Count me in.

The house specialty, the parrilladas are available in varying combinations of meats. One with a grilled chicken breast, the fabulous sausage and the asado or beef flat ribs that I adored; or the "Completa" with flat ribs, sausage, sweetbreads, kidneys and tripe. Saldivia says that they are happy to substitute other meats in place of the innards with an adjustment to the price.

On two occasions we were surrounded by groups of six or more enjoying the parrilladas piled high on portable grills in the center of the tables, as much for the pleasure of the conviviality of it, Saldivia claims, as for the contents of the meal itself.

But for me this is a steak house and I plan to return often for both the Churrasco (rib eye) and for Saldivia's personal favorite, the Entrana (skirt steak). Both steaks were unbelievably tender, grilled to roseate perfection, and arrived with the distant remnants of having been basted with chimi churri sauce before being placed on the grill. Unlike fajitas, Saldivia explains, "The Entrana is the outside skirt, so it doesn't have the veins and nerves that the fajita does. So, it is very tender meat. We are very proud of our Entrana."

I also highly recommend the Asado (beef flat ribs). They are meaty, butterflied, also basted with sauce, and grilled. Mariano Saldivia believes that a lot of the extraordinary flavor comes from the meat being grilled while still attached to the bone. (I happen to believe this is true about everything including chicken.)

Another winner, the Carre dé Cerdo, is an exceptionally tender roasted loin of pork napped with a voluptuous, mushroom-strewn cream sauce.

All entrées arrive on a plate wreathed with seasoned, grilled slices of zucchini, squash, carrots, and golden, well-crisped wedges of skinless red potatoes – "The #1 side order in South America," Saldivia says. Even the Milanesa, offered six different ways, is served with the roasted potatoes instead of the Russian potato salad as it would be in South America, because "customers preferred it," he says. The Milanesa I sampled was the "al Plato" or "breaded beef cutlet," and it was pretty much exactly what you would want a chicken fried steak to be – tender – with a crisp, well-seasoned batter.

When I asked about the three pasta dishes featured on the menu, Saldivia explained that "Uruguay and Argentina are very much Italian countries. Every menu you see in every restaurant, you are going to find 15 or 20 different pastas. Pasta in South America is as popular as hamburgers are here."

The Cannelones had a wonderful homemade quality. Stuffed with puréed spinach, ricotta and Parmesan cheese, it arrives bubbling from the oven in individual metal gratin dishes, covered in a well-seasoned tomato sauce and melted mozzarella cheese.

For dessert, the Flan is excellent and is enhanced with a distinctive dollop of a heavenly mixture called dulce de leche – sweetened condensed milk with sugar – a real South American touch. Also unique to Chimi Churri's is a dessert called "Martin Fierro" – two pieces each of mozzarella cheese and candied, puréed guava, meant to be eaten with the good, crusty bread while you finish your wine. It is named for a famous Argentinean gaucho, Martin Fierro, although Saldivia tells me that Argentineans insist on calling it "postre de vigilante" because it is what soldiers or "vigilantes" were once fed for dessert in the barracks in Argentina.

Chimi Churri's seats only fifty-four people in the main dining room and twenty-four in a smaller side room that he calls the wine cellar. The cozy little restaurant is abuzz with entertainment on weekends. Friday nights, there is traditional folk music from the Andes. Saturday nights there is a duo playing and singing what he describes as "romantic ballads and tango music."

THE CLADDAGH IRISH PUB AND GRILL

5757 Westheimer #105
Houston, Texas 77057
713/789-4858

Type of Cuisine: Irish
Bar: Full
Dress: Casual
Entertainment: Live Music Saturday Nights
Payment: All Major Credit Cards
Entrée Range: $5.95-$11.95
Recommended Dishes:
Appetizers: Jumbo Sausage Rolls
Potato Cake
Entrées: Full Irish All Day Breakfast
Bangers and Mash
Cottage Pie
Hours: Monday-Sunday, 10:30a.m.-2:00a.m.
Kitchen Open, 11:00a.m.-10:00p.m.
Reservations: Not Accepted

In *The Book of Household Management,* 19th Century English culinary authority Mrs. Isabella Beeton wrote, "To begin the day well is a grand thing, and a good breakfast at a reasonable hour is an excellent foundation for a day's work … or even pleasure."

The Full Irish All Day Breakfast at The Claddagh (pronounced claw' dah) Irish Pub and Grill is just this sort of breakfast. It is a masterful piece of work that general manager and County Wicklow native Tim O'Gara says, "From ten in the morning until ten at night outsells all the other entrées put together." O'Gara is as proud of the quality of the various components of the breakfast as he is of the authenticity. "Anyone coming off the plane from Ireland – it's the exact same breakfast that they would have had at home the day before – there's not a difference."

In Ireland it is considered the most important meal of the day. One of the few differences that I can see is that there this heaping plateful would be preceded by a glass of fresh juice and a steaming bowl of porridge.

A meal of this scope and magnitude always seems like a better idea to me late at night than it does early in the morning. O'Gara explains that, "Traditionally in Ireland, the breakfast wasn't served until about eleven o'clock in the morning anyway. In rural life, everyone would have to be our on the land before seven, and they'd have gone out with an empty stomach. They'd come in and the woman of the house would serve up everything that was in the fridge. She'd fry it on an agate cooker where you'd have to put the coal logs in one side. That's where the Irish breakfast came from, which was bacon, sausage, eggs, pudding, tomato or mushroom ... whatever was in the fridge ... and served them out some homemade bread, which would be soda bread. That's how the tradition started out in Ireland and became so popular. Because people would be so hungry coming off the land at that hour."

Diners are given the option of Fried Potatoes or Potato Scones with their breakfast. There is no contest. Not only because, as O'Gara says, "You're not likely to eat potato scones anywhere else in town," but because the welcome crisp wedges are so good and suit the rest of the breakfast so well. Cold, seasoned mashed potatoes are mixed with an equal measure of flour, rolled out and baked in a twelve inch pizza tin. It emerges from the oven colored brown, and transformed into a potato scone. As O'Gara points out, each distinctive ingredient of the breakfast exists as a testimony to the thriftiness of the rural Irish household.

Grilled medallions of black and white pudding are a hold-over from Irish rural life when a pig was slaughtered and absolutely nothing went to waste. I happen to love both of them and the less said about their composition the better, except that they are delicious – a must to sample – and are being imported directly from Ireland along with the Irish bacon and sausage.

A fat-edged rasher or slice of Irish back bacon graces the plate. It is closer to a grilled slice of ham or Canadian bacon than standard American, or what the Irish call "streaky" bacon. Given a choice between the Irish or English sausage or "bangers," I lean toward the four-inch, finely-ground Irish imports. Add a couple of eggs (best ordered over easy or sunny side up) and – as O'Gara says, "As much soda bread as they like – white or brown – whatever's made in the kitchen." Irish Soda Bread is a quickly-made bread leavened with baking soda. It is made with buttermilk and white flour or, in the case of brown soda bread, whole wheat flour.

The plate is rounded out nicely by a half of a grilled tomato although in Ireland a few grilled mushrooms would also accompany the breakfast. O'Gara says he actually prefers the mushrooms to the tomatoes, and that the kitchen usually has them if the customer prefers.

Owner Michael Quigley, who grew up in Cleveland, Ohio, but has family and deep roots in County Mayo, says that when he opened Claddagh in January 1997, his intention was "to come up with a traditional Irish pub and restaurant ... someplace where everyone would feel comfortable." He says the bar was named for the Claddagh ring, "a promise ring (in

County Galway) that signifies friendship and warmth – the qualities that go well with the atmosphere of the pub."

Quigley says that "the menu is a selection of the best (Irish/English) recipes that Tim (O'Gara) and I were familiar with, that we thought would go over well with the American palate." In fact, many of the recipes originated with O'Gara's mother or aunt.

Hot or cold, I never met a Scotch Egg I liked. This is classic pub fare – a hard boiled egg covered in an almost imperceptible veil of sausage, dipped in beaten egg, rolled in bread crumbs and baked in the oven. It is served cut in quarters with pickled onions and a tart, nearly black English relish called Branston pickle.

On the other hand, the Jumbo Sausage Rolls are something to write home about. The hefty, pale English pork sausages are being made locally and supplied by an enterprising young businessman from South Africa who craved English pork products and couldn't find any in Houston to suit his taste. O'Gara says, "It's a much better quality than the English bangers we were getting because he imports the spices, but uses local pork. He minces it himself – so there's no need for preservatives or for it to be frozen or anything." These fresh, lovely, mild sausages are cooked and then encased in buttery, unexpectedly light puff pastry.

The sausage rolls are served with a jar of bright yellow, sinus-clearing English Coleman's mustard. It is a sharp, freshly-made mustard – particularly if you buy it in England – that I find highly addictive. It goes so well with pork of any kind and bears so little resemblance to the Coleman's mustard found in supermarkets here, that I've actually had friends bring it back from England for me. O'Gara says that they get it from the same company that's importing the bacon, sausage and Branston pickle. "A brother of mine in Ireland says, 'If God intended us to be vegetarians, he wouldn't have invented Coleman's mustard.'"

Listed unfairly as an appetizer, the Potato Cake is ample enough to make an appealing, but devastating assault on anyone's appetite. O'Gara says that the recipe is courtesy of a friend in Dublin. "They'd have boiled bacon and cabbage for dinner two or three times a week when he was growing up and the next day for lunch his mother would make potato cakes, which was left over mashed potatoes, bacon and cabbage all made into a large cake or pie and fried up in a skillet."

On the short list of entrées, my second favorite after the breakfast is Bangers and Mash which O'Gara says, "American customers think sounds like a car crash." It is sturdy, nicely-seasoned mashed potatoes and a choice of English or Irish sausages (bangers) cooked on the grill. Try some of each.

"The Cottage Pie and the Irish Lamb Stew recipes came from my mother," O'Gara says, so naturally they are his favorites. They are both good, hearty dishes. I think the Cottage Pie may be my preference. It is sautéed ground beef with diced carrots and peas, "whatever's in the kitchen," O'Gara says, covered with mashed potatoes and baked in a huge oval ramekin until a crust forms on top.

Naturally, the drink of choice appears to be the Irish beer, Guiness, on tap. "Oh yeah. We sell as much Guiness as the rest of the beers put together. A lot of our customers say that we have the best pint of Guiness in town," O'Gara adds.

The Claddagh is wedged into the corner of a strip center between a women's bathing suit shop and a hairdresser so don't go looking for a charming, thatched roof cottage. The authenticity (and charm) comes from within.

When asked what distinguishes an English pub from an Irish one, O'Gara says, "You'll rarely get any (live) music in an English pub, where an Irish pub will do traditional Irish music on a regular basis. At Claddagh, I hire the best bands available on Saturday nights, and in September we have a 'Half Way to St. Patrick's Day Party.' I hire Rover's Return, the best Irish music in Texas, and the Houston Highland Pipers, and have Irish dancers as well."

CLARY'S RESTAURANT

8509 Teichman Road
Galveston, Texas 77551
409/740-0771

Type of Cuisine: Seafood
Bar: Full
Dress: Nice Casual
Entertainment: Classical guitar Friday and Saturday nights
Payment: All Major Credit Cards
Entrée Range: $13.75-$21.50
Recommended Dishes:
Appetizers: Boiled Shrimp
Grilled Oysters
Hors d'oeuvre Plate (for two)
Gumbo
Entrées: Special Batter Lump Crabmeat
Grilled Fish with Court Bleu Sauce
Seasoned Baked Crab
Flame Broiled Shrimp
Hours: Lunch: Tuesday-Friday, 11:30a.m.-2:30p.m.
Dinner: Tuesday-Friday, 5:00p.m.-10:00p.m.
Saturday, 5:00p.m-10:00p.m.
Sunday, Noon-9:00p.m.
(Closed Monday)
Reservations: Accepted

Every now and then I eat a dish that sticks in my memory bank like glue. I dream of it and wake myself up imagining how it would be in other incarnations...could I make a sandwich of the dish? How would it be on top of poached eggs slathered with hollandaise as an addition to Eggs Benedict? Clary's grilled oysters is that sort of fixation.

An oyster dish so rich, so delicious, so unique, that it would give my beloved Oysters Foch at Antoine's in New Orleans a run for their money. I defy anyone who even thinks they don't like oysters not to be converted by these little individual pancakes. Fresh oysters are removed from their shells, coated with seasoned flour, flattened and turned with a spatula as they crisp in butter on a flat grill.

As is often the case with truly memorable dishes, Clary Milburn, owner of Clary's, says the dish was created by accident for a group for lunch before his restaurant had really even opened for business. "We made up a flour that was special for the oysters and realized that we didn't have oil to deep fry them in, so we just stuck them on the grill. When they brown, we flip them over like pancakes." They are heaven on their own with a little of the house red or tartar sauce or, dangerously close to gilding the lily, doused with the darkly delicious

Court Bleu sauce. Named for both a bayou and a fishing worm near where Milburn grew up in Opelousas, Louisiana, the sauce is "something I came up with that starts almost like a gumbo roux, but I add granulated garlic to the butter and get it real hot before I add my flour, then my seasoned water." The sauce was created to be served over a piece of grilled fish or snapper and it was fabulous like that, but spectacular as an embellishment to the already wonderful grilled oysters. "I made it to put on the fish, but I guess you could eat it with anything."

A close contender for second place in my affections on the menu is the "Special Butter Lump Crab Meat." Here is the absolute simplicity of huge, flawless nuggets of sweet lump crab meat mixed with butter, chopped scallions, a little bacon, shredded Cheddar cheese and broiled in individual ramekins until the cheese melts and seeps down between the pieces of crab meat. Milburn's soft spoken, modest response to my rave is that "it is another one of those recipes we kind of played around with. We started with just crab meat and butter, but when people started asking me for crab meat au gratin, it was just my way of combining the two. Being from Louisiana, it's important to me that food has a flavor – a unique flavor."

Although Milburn says he's expanded since the early days, the restaurant appears to have changed little. The setting is tranquil, perched on a bulkheaded inlet off Offats Bayou. Shrimp boats glide by the windows on their way to and from a day's shrimping in the Gulf. Clary's is blissfully old fashioned and civilized. My favorite time to visit is the weekend when the lights are dimmed a bit and the air is full of soft, classical guitar (from 6:00 p.m. until closing on Friday and Saturday nights) thanks to the talented Bryan Kile who has been performing at Clary's for three years. Milburn says, "I have learned that people who come to this particular restaurant come to dine, to spend the evening."

Indeed, from the time the diner arrives, he is rewarded with a dish of complimentary hot Boiled Shrimp. Careful, they are addictive. One fellow diner commented that he'd be happy with a heaping plate of them and a little drawn butter for dipping. Milburn says he believes the shrimp, listed on the menu as an appetizer, are better eaten in small doses than made a meal of.

My advice is to start with the Hors d'oeuvre Plate (for two), that way you get to sample the grilled oysters, fried fish fingers, fried crab claws and an extra helping of hot boiled shrimp served on a platter garnished with a few pickled okra, carrot sticks and dill pickles. The Fish Fingers are succulent, greaseless chunks of filet of red snapper or trout dipped in a milk and egg batter, then cracker meal and deep fried to flawless perfection.

A cup of Gumbo is a must, but who then would want to choose between the special butter lump crab meat, the seasoned baked crab or the grilled fish with the divine Court Bleu sauce? Fortunately, several of the best dishes can be found grouped together on various combination platters always a great idea, as long as each individual component is accorded the respect it merits and the portions are well-balanced and not overwhelming.

For instance, the seasoned baked crab claw meat mixed with a finely minced mixture of sautéed and well-seasoned green onions, white onions, garlic, green peppers and a little Worcestershire sauce is molded into the body of a crab and baked in a hot oven until crusty on top. It is coupled with one of Milburn's favorites, the Flame Broiled Shrimp – raw shrimp peeled, dry-seasoned and left to marinate for hours in their own juices and then cooked on the grill rather than "broiled." The "seafood platter" is rounded out with a piece of impeccably grilled fish, a few broiled scallops and grilled oysters.

Another option is the "Saralyn B. Platter," named for a regular customer who also had difficulty making up her mind between the butter lump crab meat, the baked shrimp and the grilled oysters – "we surprised her and served all three at once."

Even the house salad dressing combines two favorites: a puckery Italian dressing faintly tinged brown by the addition of a little Worcestershire Sauce, topped with a heaping spoonful of creamy bleu cheese dressing. The Lyonnaise Potatoes are mixed with onion and browned on the grill and would be my choice over the rice as a side dish.

The kitchen duties are in the capable hands of Milburn's sister, Alice Perry, his son, Dexter and chef, Michael Hypolite, whom he says has been with him on and off for sixteen years. Another son, Dwayne works as both dining room manager and bartender. Most of the wait staff have worked at Clary's for ages, and it shows. The service is perfect.

Save room for dessert. The old-fashioned Bread Pudding has chunks of apple in it and is served warm with vanilla sauce. The Chocolate Sour Cream Cake was terrific, and the Pecan Pie was one of the best I've ever eaten.

It's not a requirement, but Milburn, who describes Clary's as a "nice, casual restaurant" says, "Coats are suggested." Reservations are also a good idea if you're driving from Houston, and if you have your heart set on the special butter lump crab meat, it is seasonal, so you might ask if it is available, although Milburn says, "Of course, depending on the weather, we're able to get it most weekends. We shop for quality and if it's not excellent, we won't have it."

CLAUDIO'S PIANO BAR RESTAURANT

700 Kipp
Kemah, Texas 77585
281/334-4427

Type of Cuisine: Italian/Seafood/Steaks
Bar: Full
Dress: Nice Casual
Entertainment: Piano Bar Tuesday-Saturday 7:00p.m.-2:00a.m.
Payment: All Major Credit Cards
Entrée Range: $11.95-$25.95
Recommended Dishes:
Appetizers: Clams on the Half Shell
Stuffed Mushrooms
Pastas: Ziti al Salmone (Ziti with Salmon)
Capellini al Granchio (Angel Hair Pasta with Crabmeat)
Entrées: Broiled Baby Flounder
Stuffed Lobster Tails
Baby Lamb Chops (occasional special)
Hours: Happy Hour: Tuesday-Friday, 4:00p.m.-7:00p.m.
Dinner: Tuesday-Thursday, 5:00p.m.-11:00p.m.
Friday-Saturday, 5:00p.m.-12:00a.m.
Sunday, 4:00p.m.-10:00p.m.
Reservations: A must

Sometime in the Fourth Century A.D., Saint Ambrose, the Bishop of Milan, advised his colleague, Saint Augustine, "When in Rome, live as the Romans do; when elsewhere, live as they live elsewhere," and it's still great advice, especially if the Roman in question is the multi-talented tenor Claudio Sereni, padrone of Claudio's Piano Bar Restaurant in Kemah.

With equal emphasis on the "piano bar" and "restaurant" part of the name, this lover of music and food has created an environment where both elements shine and a rousing good time is had by all. If the food wasn't so great, the music alone would be worth an evening's entertainment, but the kitchen keeps tempo, measure for measure with the high standards set by Sereni, with his wife, Crista, at the piano bar.

His partner in this endeavor is John Bell, a New Yorker, with whom he had worked at Bertolotti's and Villa Capri. "John and I were great friends and for years we'd sit at his house or mine and daydream 'if we had a restaurant, what would we do?' He'd do his side of the menu, things like broiled fish and steak, and I'd do my Italian side." Indeed, the menu reflects the respective passions and talents of each owner. Sereni says it can almost be divided right down the middle.

After an extensive renovation they opened on a trial basis without any advertising. "The restaurant seats eighty-two people and that night we served eighty dinners." They have played to a packed house ever since. It's easy to understand why.

There is something for everyone on this menu, from the elegant simplicity of a perfectly-broiled whole Baby Flounder to the tender, melt-in-your-mouth, fall-off-the-bone Baby Back Ribs marinated in pineapple-sweetened barbecue sauce and roasted until crisp around the edge. Seafood is highlighted, and fresh clams, a rarity in this area, are one of the stars of the show. Sereni says, "We sell so many Clams on the Half Shell , it's unbelievable. Once a week they come from Maine alive in salt water. We change the water every day, throwing out any that have died."

Of the pastas, Sereni says his biggest seller is the Capellini al Granchio – angel hair pasta in a light Alfredo sauce with crab meat – but it could not top my favorite, Ziti al Salmone. The ziti, large tubular pasta, are the perfect vessel for the ambrosial "pink sauce" – a dense tomato sauce thinned with whipping cream and enlivened imperceptibly with Russian vodka. A thin slice of smoked salmon is perched on top. Also wonderful was the Linguini al Frutti di Mare. A heaping mound of sea creatures – clams, mussels, shrimp and calamari – sautéed with linguini in Sereni's mother's own marinera sauce. The very lifeblood in this type of Italian cooking, it is the robust, powerfully concentrated sauce that he says he grew up eating. It is rich with red wine, onions, garlic, fragrant with fresh basil and simmered for hours.

Sereni claims that "people go crazy for the Veal Saltimbocca." It is prepared Roman-style, flat instead of rolled. Thinly sliced veal scaloppine and imported Italian proscuitto are sautéed in sage-scented butter and olive oil and placed on a bed of spinach barely cooked with a little garlic and olive oil. Claudio's rendition does "jump into the mouth" as the name implies.

One of John Bell's greatest talents is his ability to cook meat, according to Sereni. Although I didn't try the steaks which he says are the best he's ever eaten, "even better than my mother's," if the Lamb Chops I sampled one night are any indication, he may just be right. An occasional special, I'd be happy if they remained a constant. They were delicate little chops cut fresh from the rack, marinated overnight in olive oil, garlic, lemon and rosemary, cooked quickly on the grill and finished off with a little rosemary sauce on top. I was surprised to see that they were served with the traditional British accompaniment, fresh mint sauce, on the side. When I asked Sereni about it, he said headwaiter, Englishman John Blythe, "grows his own mint at his house and once a week he brings it in and makes the real sauce." On this particular night, the lamb chops were offered with Stuffed Lobster Tail, and although I would ordinarily hesitate to order these two together or anything that I know has to be frozen, like lobster tails, it was spectacular. The lobster tail itself was sweet and succulent showing no sign of its tenure in the freezer, and the stuffing I would probably eat if it was baked in an old shoe. It is that gutsy, vibrantly-seasoned, New York-Italian style stuffing with finely minced clams, shrimp, scallops, bound lightly with bread crumbs and flavored with lots of garlic and oregano. Clearly John Bell's influence, the stuffing is worth trying either mounded on a mushroom and browned as an appetizer, wedged into a filet of fresh flounder or snapper and baked, or of course, an order of the lobster tails on their own.

The desserts are the domain of South American chef, Marleny Marquez who shares kitchen duties with Bell and Werner Ortiz, and they are right on the mark. Tiramisu, a relative newcomer in the Italian dessert family created only thirty years ago by a chef in Veneto, shares billing with an outstanding Italian Flan and the ancient Italian confection, the Bomba. Sereni says, "It is the dessert my mother used to make. You can have it nowhere else!" Sponge cake is doused with kahlúa, espresso, cappuccino, layered with cream and mascarpone cheese, and flecked with chopped Italian candied fruit. It is Claudio's most popular dessert.

The late night menu offered from 11:00 p.m. to 1:00 a.m. Thursday through Saturday features items chosen by the collaborative effort of his waiters and kitchen staff, and is a good example of Sereni's management style. The service is excellent and so versatile. Sereni agrees, "That's the most important thing. I have the best waiters and employees I've ever worked with. They had all worked for me before and asked for a job when they knew I was opening a restaurant. There's Fabio Gasponi from Rome who can sing Roman country music with me. John Blythe, my head waiter, probably the most experienced waiter in this town, used to sing in a club in England."

There is an atmosphere of casual sophistication about Claudio's. Although the décor is elegantly spare with its white walls, deco wall sconces and oak floors and bar, Claudio's has all the warm, familiar conviviality of an English pub. The clientele is elbow to elbow at the very animated bar, dressed in everything from Hawaiian shirts and shorts to slinky black cocktail dresses.

A word of warning, reservations are a necessity on any night and weekends are sometimes booked days in advance. The most coveted tables near the music in the bar area are often occupied all evening by diners who come early and stay late. Who can blame them? The other larger, less popular room is nonsmoking and quieter – the diner has the advantage of being able to hear dinner partners when they speak.

When I asked Sereni the secret to his success, he said, "I love my clientele. Most of them I've known for years. They come here and spend six or seven hours, eat dinner, dance they don't have to go anywhere else. They have everything in one place. I believe that is the reason they have a good time."

COCO'S

5959 Richmond Avenue
Houston, Texas 77057
713/266-1188

Type of Cuisine: Japanese
Bar: Wine, Beer and Sake
Dress: Casual
Entertainment: No
Payment: All Major Credit Cards
Entrée Range: $5.25-$14.50
Recommended Dishes:
- All Sushi
- Quail Egg Yakitori
- "Aspara Bacon" (Asparagus, Bacon Yakitori)
- Chicken Yakitori
- Tsukune (Ground Chicken Ball Yakitori)
- Ika Geso (Squid Yakitori)
- Eggplant Yakitori
- Miso Soup

Hours: Monday-Saturday, 11:30a.m.-10:30p.m.
(Closed Sunday)
Reservations: Recommended for larger parties

According to a Japanese proverb, "If you have the pleasant experience of eating something you have not tasted before, your life will be lengthened by seventy-five days." If Mami Takagi had it her way, we "foreigners" as she calls her non-Japanese clientele, would outlive Methuselah.

On Halloween, 1995, Mami (pronounced "mommy") opened Coco's, fulfilling her ten year dream of introducing Tokyo-style yakitori to Houston. A sort of ultra-healthy fast-food, Mami says that yakitori, sold by street vendors and in specialty restaurants, can be found on practically every street corner in her native city of Tokyo. Most Americans who frequent Japanese restaurants will recognize the term "yakitori," always listed as an appetizer, as small cubes of chicken (sometimes white, but usually the more succulent dark meat) threaded onto small bamboo skewers with alternating pieces of naganegi onion or scallion, basted with a sweetened soy-based sauce and grilled over hot coals.

This style of cooking in Japan is known as "yakimono" – "yaki" means "to sear with heat" – and at yakitori restaurants in Tokyo, all manner of things are skewered and grilled in one of the oldest methods of Japanese cookery.

Concerned that a restaurant serving yakitori exclusively would be too strange and specialized to lure Houstonians, Mami, who moved here from Tokyo in 1976 with her two small children, encouraged son Ken, now twenty-five, to learn the ancient art of preparing sushi and sashimi.

Ken apprenticed in two Houston restaurants – first Japon, and then Miyako. He learned his lessons well. This very Western young man prepares some of the most exquisite sushi in town. Mami says that Ken has coaxed the young, attractive crowd that fills the place to eat sushi Friday and Saturday nights into trying the various goodies cooked in the style of yakitori by offering to buy the two a la carte "sticks" if they don't like them. "He hasn't paid for one (order) yet!"

I can't imagine even the most unadventurous diner not being completely won over by either the Quail Eggs – hard-boiled, carefully impaled on bamboo sticks, dusted with sea salt, and gently grilled (two eggs per stick, two sticks per order); or Ken's invention – "Aspara Bacon" – medium-thin pieces of barely blanched asparagus wrapped in pieces of smokey bacon, grilled to perfection, and enhanced at the table by a little squeeze of lemon.

The first dish listed on the "yakitori kushiyaki à la carte menu" is Yakitori, the best-known of foods cooked in this manner – pieces of scallion and tender morsels of chicken glazed with a mixture of sake, rice wine, dark and light soy sauce, mirin (sweet cooking wine) and a little sugar. The Ebi (shrimp) receives the same glorious treatment as the chicken yakitori. Both are excellent.

The Tsukune (ground chicken balls) were an unexpected delight – finely-ground chicken seasoned with ginger and onion, formed into balls, brushed with glaze and browned.

I was not mad about the nearly naked Chicken Wings (Mami says that the Japanese adore them!), but the Chicken Gizzards were interesting – cut in thin strips, threaded onto the skewers, and seasoned simply with a little sea salt.

For those fans of squid , the Ika Geso (not identified on the menu as squid) is elegant in its simplicity – sliced into ribbons, flavored with salt and grilled. It tastes a lot like the ocean from which it came.

Of the choices of vegetables cooked this way – the Japanese mushrooms, green onions, or green pepper – my favorite was the Japanese Eggplant, a sort of Asian popsicle – slender chunks of eggplant, basted this time with sweet soy bean paste, placed on sticks large enough to support the weight of the eggplant and grilled long enough for the sauce to caramelize with the natural sugar in the eggplant.

This style of cooking seems almost abstemiously plain – with a lightness that borders on spa cooking, but the flavors of all the impeccably fresh ingredients are vibrant and incredibly satisfying.

Mami tells me that the name "Coco" has no particular significance – she just liked the sound of it. The restaurant seats only fifty people at both sushi and yakitori bars and at the few tables in the back. It is a little gem of a place with minimal decoration and a relaxed, cozy neighborhood atmosphere – just what she had in mind. "It's just a bar – nothing traditional, everything is contemporary – a place to have fun and talk to people." Although, it is interesting to note, Mami observes the traditional Japanese ritual of bowing to greet and bid farewell to entering and departing customers. The appropriate response is either to bow in return or to simply say " hello" or "good-bye."

Coco's was originally geared to a Western clientele. Mami assumed that all Japanese diners would be as critical of her food as she says she is of others', but the restaurant is invariably at least half full of Japanese businessmen, "so I must be doing something right."

While I study the menu and decide what to order, I always ask for a bowl of Edamame (soy beans) – boiled, salted and meant to be popped out of their shells directly into your mouth. (I prefer to eat them warm. They don't usually serve them that way, but are happy to heat them a little for you.)

As all of the yakitori choices are served à la carte, ranging from one to three little skewers per order, it is possible to try everything I've recommended. Yakitori etiquette requires the eater to remove the food from the bamboo skewers directly onto the plate with either chopsticks (or a fork) and eat them with either choice of utensil, but never directly off the sticks. Empty skewers are placed in attractive white porcelain footed cups placed on the table for this purpose.

As it's possible to find lighter, crisper tempura (battered and deep fried vegetables and shrimp) elsewhere, if you're still hungry (and game) after sampling the yakitori and whatever sushi you've ordered, you might venture into the fascinating world of Japanese noodles. There are eight dishes listed in this category – really sixteen, when you consider that you have either udon (soft, thick, large white noodles made of flour) or soba ("buckwheat", or "buckwheat noodles") to choose from.

Udon noodles are usually eaten swimming in a rich broth of dashi, sake, sugar and soy sauce topped with tempura shrimp and sometimes onions and mushrooms. Dashi is a stock made from katsu bushi (dried bonito flakes – something that Coco's manager Seiko Corbett says is the very heart of Japanese cooking) and kombu (dark green dried kelp or sea tangle).

Soba noodles are often served cold as in the case of "zaru soba" named for the basket on which it is served, topped with crisp strips of nori (seaweed) and dipped in a broth of dashi, dark soy sauce and mirin.

There's also a short list of Donburis – another Japanese speciality whose name actually describes the bowl in which it's served. The "big bowl" or "donburi" contains short-grain white rice topped with everything from yakatori (chicken), shrimp tempura, to my personal favorite, unagi (fresh water eel) and laced with cooked beaten eggs.

Unagi is imported, already grilled, from Japan where it is believed that if you eat unagi on the Day of the Cow, during the summer solstice, you will live healthy all year. I never miss ordering it as sushi where it is lightly grilled again, glazed with tare (a sweet, smokey sauce that takes two days to make) and formed onto rice. The sauce is so divine that this type of "nigiri" or "hand-pressed" sushi is not meant to be dipped in soy sauce before eating.

The Miso Soup is especially good here. A staple of the Japanese diet, it is dashi flavored at the last moment of the cooking process with miso (the mildest, sweetest of the three varieties available of fermented soy bean paste) and served with jewel-like flecks of tofu and pieces of green onion. It is easily digested, rich in vitamin B and protein, and is served in the traditional little covered lacquer bowls. Miso soup is meant to be sipped directly from the bowl throughout the meal. It's so soothing and health-giving – it's easy to understand why the Japanese start their day with a bowl of it.

Dessert is ice cream made from ocha (green tea – considered essential to life in Japan) topped with azuki (a purée of red beans and sugar) served in wonderful little sundae glasses. This may be an acquired taste, but worth trying as a novelty and is definitely in keeping with the spirit of that Japanese proverb.

As they say in Japan, "Itadakimasu!"...Bon appétit.

COLLINA'S ITALIAN CAFE

12311 Kingsride
Houston, Texas 77024
713/365-9497

3933 Richmond Avenue
Houston, Texas 77027
713/621-8844

2400 Times Boulevard
Houston, Texas 77005
713/526-4499

Type of Cuisine: Italian
Bar: Wine and Beer
Dress: Casual
Entertainment: No
Payment: All Major Credit Cards
Entrée Range: $6.95-$11.95
Recommended Dishes:
 Appetizers: Stuffed Artichoke
 Salads: Mista Terra
  House Salad
 Entrées: Italian Muffaletta
  Pizza
  Lasagna
 Desserts: Butterscotch Squares
  Lemon Squares
  Chocolate Decadence
Kingside and Times Hours: Monday-Friday, 11:00a.m.-2:30p.m.,
 5:00p.m.-10:00p.m.
 Saturday, 11:00a.m.-10:00p.m.
 (Closed Sunday)
Richmond Hours: Monday-Thursday, 11:00a.m.-10:00p.m.
 Friday-Saturday, 11:00a.m.-11:00p.m.
 (Closed Sunday)
Reservations: Accepted

This is an ode to pizza – not the graceless, leaden variety with crust like cardboard and cheese like library paste – but the good stuff – the stuff that inspired music..."When the moon hits the sky like a big pizza pie...that's amoré!"

To make pizza like this, it *has* to be amoré! It's too hard to make great pizza without it. The crust alone, always the star attraction, requires infinite finesse and patience to produce just the right texture moist and chewy, but still crisp with plenty of flavor.

Paul Hill, chef and owner with his talented wife, Lisa, of Collina's Italian Cafe produces this kind of pizza. His ancestors, the Collinas, who changed their name to Hill when they came to America in the mid-1800's, would be proud. A Florida native, Paul began his apprenticeship in the food business by working for Vincent Mandola at Vincent's and Nino's for seven years. "Vincent always said that to succeed in the restaurant business it is important to do at least one thing really well." I'm happy to say they do more than one thing really well. In fact, they do several things spectacularly.

Paul claims that pizza sales account for only 50% of their business, but he admits it's what he's most proud of. He says the crust took him months to perfect, and it is that rare kind that you find yourself finishing long after the toppings are gone. There are eight choices of pizza to choose from in sizes varying from the eight inch gourmet pizette to a whopping twenty incher, and eighteen luminously fresh, ancillary ingredients to allow diners to create their own.

I usually like to load them up, ordering the one with everything; but this is pizza transformed from the prosaic to the poetic, so in this case, the simpler the better. Just the addition of cheese (a mixture of top-quality mozzarella, provolone and Romano) and pepperoni gave the crust a chance to shine.

The Italian Muffaletta runs a very close second to the pizza. Closer to a panini than an actual muffaletta, the Italian sandwich created in New Orleans in the early Twentieth Century, Collina's muffaletta is constructed inside warm, heavenly wedges of focaccia, the rustic Italian flatbread. Taken from the Latin word "focus" for hearth, the flat round loaf is creased with deep indentations infused with fruity olive oil, rosemary, and Romano cheese, then baked in an oven instead of under the ashes in a hearth as it was originally in Italy. The focaccia, Paul believes, is their second best accomplishment and serves as a perfect foil to the thinly sliced turkey breast, mortadella, capicolla (highly seasoned, peppery imported Italian ham), provolone cheese, romaine lettuce and the traditional muffaletta green and black olive vinaigrette dressing. The contrasting flavors and textures of this sandwich, served warm, were good enough to inspire a fist fight to finish it at our table. A whole focaccia is twelve inches in diameter and it is possible to order an Italian muffaleta that size for as many as six people ($25.50) a perfect idea for a lunch meeting! They also make a vegetable muffaleta and are happy to make any portion of the twelve inch size vegetarian. For a warm, crusty sandwich it travels surprisingly well.

In fact, it all travels well, which was part of Lisa and Paul's plan of "good food, at a fair price and even have it delivered." Sixty percent of their business at the three-year-old Richmond location is delivery and a much smaller percentage at the larger location in the Village. According to the Great Food

Almanac, Americans eat an astonishing ninety acres of pizza per day, and I'd be willing to guess a huge percentage of it is consumed in the comfort of their homes. There are many conflicting stories about this, but if we are to believe the "Dictionary of American Food and Drink," America's first pizzeria dates back to 1905 in New York's Little Italy.

Particularly wonderful are Collina's Stuffed Artichokes. Stuffed with a savory mixture of fresh bread crumbs, oregano, rosemary, garlic, butter, Romano and Parmesan cheeses, then baked – they are messy to eat and without competition!

While the Caesar Salad was good (with or without chicken), the three other salads the Mista Terra with Roma tomatoes, pepperoncini (little Italian peppers), red onion, roasted bell peppers, eggplant, feta cheese and black olives; the Pomodoro Basilico with tomatoes, basil, artichoke heads, red onions and black olives; and the House Salad all benefit from a vinaigrette good enough to drink. The spunky house vinaigrette sparked by the addition of onion purée, is a legacy of native Houstonian Lisa's parents, food lovers, great cooks and authors of "The $12 Gourmet," Boyd and Beverly Fadrique.

Of the ten choices of pasta available, my two favorites were a homey, heartwarming Lasagna and the large, round Ravioli filled with a mixture of Romano, ricotta, Parmesan and mozzarella cheese, and bathed in a tomato sauce thinned with cream.

The desserts are Lisa's exclusive domain and while it would be easy to miss the small print on the menu to "ask about our daily homemade desserts" – don't. The best, in order of preference, are the fabulous, unconscionably rich Butterscotch Squares, Lemon Squares, Chocolate Decadence Cake and the Chocolate-Pecan-Caramel Cheesecake (all available on an irregular basis).

There is a dizzying array of off-the-menu options available at sometimes less than 24 hours notice and a thriving catering business run by Lisa's younger sister, Devera Allday. All three locations are closed on Sundays, but can be leased for private parties.

The restaurant on Richmond seats only thirty-three people indoors and always seems to be packed, so if I'm not having these goodies delivered, I'd opt to eat at the still lively, but more comfortable Village location. It's twice as big and has the added civilized advantage of offering either beer or wine with your meal.

CORTES RESTAURANT

404 Shepherd (at Feagan)
Houston, Texas 77007
713/880-4295

Type of Cuisine: Tex-Mex
Bar: Wine and Beer
Dress: Casual
Entertainment: No
Payment: All Major Credit Cards
Entrée Range: $5.50-$10.95
Recommended Dishes:
Breakfast: Migas
Entrées: Liver and Onions
Chicken Fried Steak
Snapper with Caper Sauce (or sweetbreads)
Chicken Mole
Fajitas
Pechuga de Pollo
Spinach Enchiladas
Tamales
Torta (Milanesa)
Dessert: Flan
Tres Leches
Hours: Tuesday-Saturday, 7:30a.m-9:00p.m.
Sunday-Monday, 7:30a.m.-2:00p.m.
Reservations: Not Accepted

Go ahead. Throw a dart at this menu. Whatever it hits, I guarantee will produce groans of delight and words like . . . "Oh, my God. This is the best ________ I've ever tasted!" This has been my experience at Cortes Restaurant.

If you recognize the name, it's because the Cortes family has been in the food business in Houston for at least twenty-five years. Patrick Cortes who owns the restaurant with his mother, Esperanza ("everybody calls her 'Hope'") Rodriguez and his older brother, Luis, explains, "My father, who is from Chile originally, is a master chef. He was the head chef at Harrigan's on Kirby where Jalapeños is now and then Brennan's where he was (in 1980) when my mother opened Cortes Deli on West Alabama. In 1982, we doubled the size of Cortes Deli and my dad quit Brennan's and came to work with my mom because the business had grown to where it would support the whole family."

They owned a second, much larger restaurant for about a year ('96-'97) before deciding that smaller was better. ("Too much overhead and too much work," Cortes says.) If their lease hadn't expired in December '97, they might still be on West Alabama. But, three weeks before they would have been forced to close, they heard through a friend about the recently-vacated Feagan Street Restaurant on the corner of Feagan and Shepherd. "We went to take a look at it and it was perfect – same color combination of our other restaurant, same number of tables . . . the tablecloths even fit! My mother says she prayed for a miracle from God and she got it!" They closed on Christmas Eve and re-opened as Cortes Restaurant two weeks later in a cozy, pub-like atmosphere.

Cortes Deli was neither "deli" nor full-fledged restaurant. Cortes was – and probably still is – best known by its loyal followers as a place to eat breakfast (all day). And although their Migas (made with lean, homemade chorizo) are divine, breakfast barely scratches the surface of what they do well.

What's your pleasure? Liver as thin as a quarter, brown and crackling-crisp, covered in butter, caramelized slivers of onions (Higado Encebollado)? A huge filet of scarlet snapper, dusted with seasoned flour, browned in a pan, treated to a superbly peppery pungent caper sauce? (He did this same sauce on sweetbreads for me and it was spectacular.) Or maybe you're in the mood for what one fellow diner decreed "the best chicken fried steak in town," with old-fashioned cream gravy and rosemary-flavored mashed potatoes? And I haven't even gotten to the Mexican food yet!

Cooking duties are equally divided between Cortes and his mother, and all I know is that you have to love something a lot to do it this well. Cortes describes the fare like this, "We're a little Tex-Mex, a little authentic Mexican, but always with a continental flair."

For instance, the spinach for the Spinach Enchiladas is seasoned the way it would be in France – with a couple of grinds of fresh nutmeg – and the cream sauce is a classic béchamel which speaks with a Spanish accent when studded with finely-diced jalapeños and cilantro. Heaven.

"A lot of the recipes for the Mexican and Tex-Mex dishes originated with my mother's family. She grew up in McAllen down in the valley." But they both credit Cortes' father, Luis Cortes, who now lives in Chile, with expanding their culinary horizons and teaching them techniques they might not have learned otherwise. When complimented on what a fine cook (and saucier) she is, Rodriguez says, "I learned so much from my ex-husband."

If it's Tex-Mex or Mexican food you're after, prepare for the definitive rendition of everything from a sublimely earthy and intense Chicken Mole scattered with toasted sesame seeds to succulent, perfectly-seasoned, chargrilled Pechuga de Pollo and Fajitas. (Cortes says that his brother, Luis, prefers to work the front of the restaurant, but is responsible for concocting the superb marinades for both the fajitas and the splendid pechugas de pollo.)

Even the chips are memorable – thin enough to see through and served with the HOT! HOT! HOT! bright green house salsa. Their salsa, which seems to consist mostly of puréed jalapeños, is shipped to die-hard devotées all over the world. An interesting, brick-red secondary sauce is also placed on the table – the hot, slightly-bitter culprit this time is a roasted chile de arbol.

Cortes says the secret to guacamole this good is to make it constantly in "very small batches," but I dug further and discovered his mother's secret. Flawless avocados are mashed with "a pinch of salt and a squirt of heavy cream." (Who knew?)

Tamales, like everything else, are made from scratch. They come in three flavors – shredded roasted pork (my favorite), chicken, or chicken tarted up with finely-minced jalapeños. (Those with a strong food memory may recall these as the tamales sold at the venerable old Jamail Brothers Market.)

The Mexican sandwich, Torta, is constructed on fresh, crusty baguette-like "torta bread" with layers of iceberg lettuce, tomato and avocado slices, a slathering of sour cream, a thin veneer of smoky, pork-flavored refried beans and a choice of pork, chicken, fajitas or the most traditional filling – Milanesa. Cortes says, "We barely sold any at Cortes Deli, but here the Torta (Milanesa) is so popular, we can hardly keep the bread in stock. Another winner in the red meat genre, the Milanesa is wonderful – a piece of sirloin steak pounded into submission, cloaked in ground cascabel chile-flavored bread crumbs and deep fried.

The woodsy cascabel chile is also a major flavoring agent of homemade, spectacularly lean Chorizo. "The chorizo is a very old recipe – my mother's mother – and it's unique because we add no fat at all … only the leanest parts of pork, but seasoned intensely with salt, garlic, chile powder, paprika and, of course, chiles. It's pretty strong on it's own, but people come and buy it by the pound ($3.50)."

Lines form on Saturdays and Sundays for their famous Migas, "the single most popular dish on the menu – breakfast, lunch, or dinner," Cortes says. "Migas" means "crumbs" which doesn't nearly do justice to the eggs scrambled with chorizo, garlic, chopped onions, tomatoes and jalapeños, and the nearly-transparent tortilla chips. As a final howdy-do, they melt cheddar cheese over the top. "Oh, I love our migas," Cortes boasts. "I recommend them any time of day, and if they don't like 'em, I'll pay for 'em!"

Sunday regulars at Cortes Restaurant also know the Cortes

family tradition of serving a classic Spanish Paella for lunch. (They close at 2:00 p.m.) "We've been doing this for eighteen years. We only make so much, so people always know to call ahead and reserve some if that's what they want." The paella is cooked in the time-honored fashion with sunny, saffron-yellow rice dotted with pimientos. It is rich with seafood, sausage and whole chunks of chicken and pork.

For dessert, the Flan is eggy and dense with a pleasant aftertaste of cinnamon and the (also homemade) Trés Leches is a memory that lingers.

There is an assortment of California wines and domestic and imported beers to choose from. (You might skip the frozen margaritas. They are made from agave wine rather than tequila.)

Happily, the seating at Cortes Restaurant has just been doubled (from 40 to 80) by building a patio out front.

COSMOS CAFÉ

69 Heights Blvd.
Houston, Texas 77007
713/802-2144

Type of Cuisine: American/Eclectic
Bar: Full
Dress: Casual
Entertainment: Live Music Friday-Saturday 9:30p.m.-2:00a.m.
Big Band Music Last Sunday of the month 6:30p.m.-2:00a.m.
Payment: All Major Credit Cards
Entrée Range: $4.75-$13.95
Recommended Dishes:
Appetizers: Tuscan White Bean Ragout
Quesadillas
Goat Cheese and Pesto Terrine
Entrées: Cosmos Salad
Green Chili
Reuben Sandwich
Meatball Sandwich
Dessert: Mocha Toffee Seduction
White and Dark Chocolate Cake
Hours: Monday-Thursday, 11:30a.m-12:00a.m.
(Kitchen closes at 10:00p.m.)
Friday, 11:30a.m.-2:00a.m. (Kitchen closes 12:00a.m.)
Saturday, Noon-2:00a.m. (Kitchen closes 12:00a.m.)
Sunday, Brunch 11:30-3:00p.m., Full Menu 11:30a.m.-10:00p.m.
Reservations: Accepted

It's not Cosmo Topper, or even Cosmo Kramer. It is The Cosmos ... the galaxy, the universe ... you know, the great beyond. But while Cosmos Café has a decidedly David Lynch – Twin Peaks kind of atmosphere, it's the cooking that's strictly out-of-this-world.

The menu is regionally eclectic with strong breezes from the general direction of the Mediterranean (and the Southwest). There is something for everyone here. Flawless renditions of everything from a Tuscan White Bean Ragout that could easily come out of a farmhouse kitchen in northern Italy, to an impeccable reading of a classic Reuben sandwich oozing with Russian dressing.

Deanna Rund, who owns Cosmos Café with husband, Jean Silvey, is a gifted, largely self-taught cook with great food instincts, high standards and a total commitment to using the best, freshest ingredients ... not that she's a novice in the business.

Rund and Silvey have been together twenty-five years. "Since high school in Denver," Silvey says, and their first restaurant together was called the Buffalo Bar "in Idaho Springs about an hour west of Denver, in the mountains. This was about 1978 – '82." Rund tells me that the only holdover from those days – apart from the burgers – is her Green Chili. "I got a blue ribbon for that one time. That pleased me to no end!"

Not a soup for sissies, it is a slightly-searing, powerfully-concentrated chicken broth colored green from a heavy dose of cilantro, roasted poblano peppers, and lots of fresh, chopped jalapeños, with bite-size morsels of pork. "Green chili is really popular in Colorado and New Mexico. It's such a regional thing that when we opened (July 1996) I started to not even put it on the menu. You don't see it much in Texas. But, I'm glad I did. It's the dish I'm proudest of and probably most attached to." A bowl is a massive, sinus-clearing undertaking, but a cup would be a fine way to start a meal on a cool day.

I can't think of a better way to follow it than with one of their neatly-composed, perfectly dressed salads. You have to love salad to make a vinaigrette this good. (She does.)

I'm a sucker for a Spinach Salad and I haven't come across one lately that holds a candle to Cosmos'. Dark green leaves of cello spinach are tossed with toasted pecans, strips of sautéed mushrooms and fragile ribbons of shaved Parmesan cheese. It has a rich, mustardy vinaigrette with a lingering jolt of fresh, minced garlic. "It is our most popular salad," Rund says. "I think there are people who are actually addicted to it."

The Cosmos Salad runs a very close second in my affections. The electrifying house vinaigrette benefits from a good spike of balsamic and finely chopped shallots. The salad itself is a basic mix of seasonal greens – oak, frisée and radicchio on my visit – tossed with pan-crisped pieces of leeks, whole, nutty roasted garlic cloves, sweet Bermuda onions and wedges of Roma tomatoes.

There is a perfect rendering of a Greek Salad with all the usual suspects – briny feta cheese, pungent Calamata olives and a fine oregano-strewn vinaigrette. The Thai Beef Salad will remind Thai food fans of the smokey, marinated, then grilled flank steak dish called "Tiger Cry."

Among the appetizers, the Goat Cheese and Pesto Terrine is another dish Rund says she's been making for a long time. Little individual terrines are layered with goat cheese, a classic basil pesto, puréed sun dried tomatoes and studded with whole roasted garlic cloves – a more recent addition. It is served with a generous mound of mixed salad greens with the house vinaigrette and freshly-made crostini or croutons.

The earthy, deeply-satisfying Tuscan White Bean Ragout is meant to be spooned on to crusty slices of rustic Italian bread scored from the grill (a nice touch). Rund says, "Yeah. It's a real peasanty dish; a soup really, with vegetables – celery, carrots, onions, garlic and white beans. I cook it down with herbs and finish it off with fresh chopped spinach. The bread is pretty authentic Italian bread. Like all my other breads it comes from Dutch Regal which is the bakery for Whole Foods."

Someone must have passed a law lately that all menus of a certain type in the Greater Houston Area must include Quesadillas because almost all do, but not like Cosmos'. Rund's sly variation on an all-too-familiar theme is to combine fresh corn, julienned strips of zucchini, red bell pepper and onions with two kinds of cheese – Cheddar and Monterey Jack – (chicken is optional) and serve it with a puckery, palate-awakening salsa verde – a tomatillo sauce with diced avocado and onions – for dipping. Rund says the recipe for the quesadilla is an adaptation of her mother's, but that the salsa verde just seemed like a good idea to her (me, too).

Rund tells me that they serve more burgers than anything else and I'm not at all surprised. They are especially good – charbroiled, freshly-pressed patties of lean grade beef – "never frozen" she would like for me to point out – served on soft, toasted sesame seed buns (also from Dutch Regal). My favorite is the Half Moon Burger with two thick slices of sweet, smokey bacon, slathered with a sassy chipotle pepper (smoked jalapeño) sauce, all topped with Cheddar cheese.

However, if it's meat you're after, the Meatball Sandwich is good enough to win a blind taste test of Italian Americans in New Haven, Connecticut. Four golf ball-sized meatballs composed of well-seasoned pork and beef are lightened and made unbelievably moist from the addition of grated zucchini – "my secret," Rund says. They are covered with a heavenly homemade marinera sauce loaded onto a toasted hoagie roll, and have provolone cheese melted over the whole messy, but wonderful, thing.

Diners who order a Stellar Sandwich are given a choice of either homemade potato chips or a portion of one of the best potato salads in town. Although it is almost a crime (in my book) to pass up a homemade potato chip, the spectacular Reuben sandwich should be accompanied by potato salad. "We are proud of our potato salad," Rund says. "It's so good, some people have it by itself for lunch. Mary Ann (Elliot, who shares kitchen duties) won't let anybody else make it because she likes to lick the bowl." Firm wedges of new potatoes with their skin still on are mixed with hard boiled eggs, onions, celery, two types of pickles – sweet and dill – a little mustard "and really, really good mayonnaise." Rund continues, "It's my mother's recipe. She was always the best potato salad maker."

Among the entrées – listed as "Specialties" – the Grilled Pork Chops with Rosemary is the kind of dish that regularly tempts me. Lean, center cut pork chops are marinated in olive oil, garlic and fresh rosemary and cooked quickly on the grill. They are so homey and deliberately simple that Rund tells me, "I have customers who say, 'well, you need to have apple sauce with this.'" The plate is laden with a dense square of unimprovable cheesy potato and turnip gratin.

At least one piece of the aptly-named ambrosial Mocha Toffee Seduction should be ordered for the table. If "the table" can handle two, a close second choice is the White and Dark Chocolate Cake. It is almost like candy. Dense layers of white chocolate mousse alternate with dark chocolate mousse and is finished with a flourish of rich, chocolatey fudge topping.

Since Cosmos Café is about half a block from both Rockefellers and The Fabulous Satellite Lounge, from now on it is my first choice for an early or late dinner either before or after catching a show. If your visit falls on Saturday night, Cosmos Café has live music from about 9:30 or 10:00p.m. until closing at 2:00a.m.

CRAPITTO'S

2400 Mid Lane
Houston, Texas 77027
713/961-1161

Type of Cuisine: Italian
Bar: Full
Dress: Casual
Entertainment: No
Payment: All Major Credit Cards
Entrée Range: $7.95-$19.95
Recommended Dishes:
Appetizers: Portobello alla Griglia
Escargots
Sausage and Peppers
Insalata di Famiglia
Entrées: Grilled Veal Chop
Vitello Crapitto
Pasta Julio
Capellini di Mare
Mary Nell's Favorite
Dessert: Cheesecake
Spumoni
Hours: Monday-Friday, 11:00a.m.-11:00p.m.
Saturday, 5:30p.m.-12:00a.m.
(Closed Sunday)
Reservations: Accepted

Crapitto's doesn't feel like a new restaurant because, until very recently, it was Romero's – a twenty-year-old Italian neighborhood stand-by. Some of these customers were regulars of Romero's, but all are fans of the affable new owner, John Crapitto.

About a quarter of the old menu and almost all of Romero's staff remains. Two members of the team have worked in the building for seventeen years – chef Julio Minuta and manger Fazal Rehman (called "Raymond"). Crapitto has transformed this charming seventy-five year old farmhouse into a very nice place to be.

The menu now consists of some oldies-but-goodies, popular new favorites, and a handful of dishes inspires by and often named for various members of Crapitto's large, food-loving family. In fact Shrimp Nellie is named for his beloved grandmother Nellie Crapitto, at whose house the entire Crapitto clan (and extended members) gathered every Sunday. "My grandfather, Louis Crapitto, was born in Italy. He was a doctor, a G.P., and very busy so my grandmother did all the cooking. She cooked every night, but Sunday's were the big day. You know … the big meal. Sometimes as many as twenty people would be in and out of the house all day long."

Shrimp Nellie is wonderful – whole shrimp dipped in beaten eggs, sautéed until golden brown, then coated with a garlicky Alfredo sauce. But, my favorite contribution of Nellie's to the menu is the enticingly old fashioned Insalata di Famiglia.

A fine choice as an appetizer or an entrée at lunch, it is a bed of red tip lettuce with a generous mound of chopped, superbly dressed tomatoes, black olives, onions and celery. Crapitto says the fabulous Balsamic vinaigrette is his Uncle Louis' adaptation of his grandmother's salad dressing.

The vinaigrette really has a chance to shine when slathered over a huge, meaty, perfectly-grilled portobello mushroom. The Portobello all Griglia is a work of art – easily six inches in diameter, smoky and crisp from the grill.

My second favorite appetizer is a classic – Escargots. "I eat 'em like popcorn," Crapitto says. Chewy snails imported from France are prepared in the time-honored way, a la Bourguignonne, but tucked into six little indentations in a snail dish rather than back into their shells. (Who wants to fight with those shells to get to the really good stuff – the puddle of garlic and parsley flavored butter?)

An even heartier option as an appetizer is an off-the-menu Sicilian standard – Sausage and Peppers. The sausage is superb, fennel-flavored and juicy, and the red and yellow sweet peppers are caramelized appealingly in a frying pan with slivers of onions. The sausage and peppers are doused with a little of the hearty house marinera sauce and wedged onto a crusty, eight-inch baguette on Crapitto's new lunch menu. This is the Italian Sausage Sandwich. Not dietetic, but divine.

Two other sandwiches on the lunch menu that fall into that robust category are the Meatball Sandwich and the Monte Cristo. Massive, moist meatballs the size of a child's fist, are composed of an ideal ratio of Italian sausage to lean ground beef (40-60%). Three meatballs fit on a baguette. (Regulars know to order the – also off-the-menu – Meatballs and Spaghetti for dinner.)

I've never quite figured out what the Count of Monte Cristo did to deserve having this sandwich named after him, but I'm grateful. It is (let's face it) French toast with carefully constructed layers of ham, sliced turkey and, at Crapitto's, three different types of cheese – provolone, Cheddar and American. It is dipped in egg batter, cooked in butter on a flat grill and served dusted with powdered sugar.

There are lighter alternatives for lunch. Most memorable from the main menu is, of course, the Insalata di Famiglia, but also, the Insalata Pesce made a light but satisfying lunch on one recent visit. Warm, well-seasoned grilled shrimp and scallops (three of each) were perched on top of a tossed salad of arugula, radicchio and crumbled goat cheese. Very nice.

The House Salad is a neat composition of Romaine lettuce, wedges of tomatoes, sliced domestic mushrooms and croutons made from the fresh sourdough bread that is served at Crapitto's. But, the best thing about the house salad is the Italian Roquefort dressing – a tart vinaigrette with crumbled Wisconsin Bleu cheese, rather than Roquefort.

My favorite pastas – in descending order – are Pasta Julio, Capellini di Mare and Mary Nell's Favorite. A holdover from Romero's menu, the Pasta Julio is the brainchild of Chef Julio Minuta. Shrimp are sautéed, then chopped and blended with garlic-seasoned spinach and ricotta cheese. Huge sheets of pasta are then folded over this mixture to make "one big tortellini," as Crapitto says. They are cooked, warmed in garlic-flecked olive oil, and arrive with four grilled shrimp balanced on top.

Lump crabmeat marries well with grilled shrimp, a creamy Alfredo sauce and angel hair pasta for the rich, but heavenly Capellini di Mare.

"Mary Nell's Favorite is a combination of some of my Aunt Mary Nell's favorite things – bowtie pasta tossed with basil, fresh tomatoes and garlic. She's the Queen of Garlic!"

I loved the Snapper Dr. Louis, named for Crapitto's grandfather "because he loved crabmeat," he says. A filet of red snapper is "menuired," as it says on the menu. (I don't think I've ever seen the French term for dusting a piece of (usually) fish with seasoned flour and cooking it in butter, meuniére, used as a verb before, but I like it.) The crisp, buttery filet is covered in a white wine-flavored sauté of red, yellow and green pepper, sliced mushrooms and whole lumps of sweet crabmeat.

There were two veal dishes of note. The Vitello Crapitto is a thin scallopine of veal – crusty with an outer coating of fresh bread crumbs and Parmesan cheese, topped with a salty pink slice of proscuitto ham, a layer of gooey melted mozzarella cheese, artichoke hearts and finally, a little Alfredo sauce.

Still, there's nothing simpler or better than an impeccably-grilled Veal Chop basted with rosemary, basil and thyme-flavored oil. It is a ten-ounce chop that came with crisp wedges of Parmesan and parsley-cloaked oven-baked potatoes.

The two best desserts are a citrusy homemade Cheesecake and a classic tri-colored Spumoni made for Crapitto's by Oscar's Creamery.

Italy and California are equally represented on the well-priced, well-thought-out wine list.

The pretty patio is a popular place to linger on temperate days and balmy evenings. As they say in Italy, "Dolce fa niente!" How sweet to do nothing!

CRAZY CAJUN FOOD FACTORY

2825 NASA Road 1
Seabrook, Texas 77586
281/326-6055

Type of Cuisine: Cajun/Seafood
Bar: Wine and Beer
Dress: Casual
Entertainment: No
Payment: All Major Credit Cards
Entrée Range: $5.95-$22.95
Recommended Dishes:
Appetizers: BBQ Shrimp Terrell
Angels on Horseback
"Spicy Thang" Appetizer Combination
Boudin Ball
Stuffed Jalapenos
Andouille Sausage
Entrées: Stuffed Rib Eye
Panéed Shrimp
Boiled Crawfish
Jambalaya
Hours: Monday-Thursday, 11:00a.m.-10:00p.m.
Friday-Saturday, 11:00a.m.-11:00p.m.
Sunday, 11:30a.m.-10:00p.m.
Reservations: Recommended for larger parties

John La Farge, an American artist who was born in the early 19th Century believed that "the full use of taste is an act of genius." I don't know if it's an act of genius, but it is at least the act of someone who is very, very smart about combining ingredients and seemingly disparate elements and coming up with highly individual dishes of piercing, eye-popping flavor. While it has long been my opinion that a talent like this is God-given and not taught, Sonny Payne, owner of the Crazy Cajun says he learned much of what he knows from Cajun men in Northeast and then South Louisiana, who did almost all the cooking for company. "Different families would come together every weekend. We used to catch crawfish every Saturday and boil them when it was crawfish season and we'd be barbecuing on the lake on Sunday. It was just the way of life for us. Your eatin' and your lovin' to a Cajun are the most special things in the world."

He's still boiling crawfish and barbecuing by the lake, but fortunately for us, it's Clear Lake.

"When I first opened the Crazy Cajun on October 28th, 1982, I didn't even have a stove. I had to bring a Coleman cook stove. I used Igloo coolers for refrigerators. I had two deep fryers and I borrowed a little electric barbecue pit from my neighbor to barbecue my steaks and shrimp on – but being a dreamer...I thought I was going to take over the world." He nearly has. That original forty-seat restaurant now seats two hundred and he's opened a steakhouse on I-45 and NASA Road 1.

At the original Crazy Cajun that simple, hand-written menu offering barbecued shrimp, boudin, andouille sausage, étouffée and steak has become a mind-boggling proposition of over sixty dishes prepared and offered in seemingly infinite varieties and combinations.

Let's navigate this vast, worthwhile territory. Many of the dishes that he prepared so primitively in the beginning have evolved into near-masterpieces. Starting with appetizers, "the Barbecue Shrimp is something I started doing fifteen, twenty years ago." He wraps a shrimp with a piece of bacon, secures it with a toothpick, glazes it with his barbecue sauce which he says has more than 130 ingredients and cooks it on a pit over four different kinds of wood – oak, hickory, pecan and mesquite. I know that sounds good, but what's even better is the BBQ Shrimp Terrell. Here he splits the shrimp, stuffs it with a small piece of jalapeño pepper and cheddar cheese, wraps it with bacon, bastes it with sauce and barbecues it again, to a deep mouth-watering bronze. Under the heading of gilding the lily, he has further enhanced this already spectacular dish by adding an oyster just under the bacon of the BBQ Shrimp Terrell. He calls this Angels on Horseback and says it is available at all locations.

The Alligator is worth trying as a novelty item. It is actually the tenderized tail of the alligator. Offered sautéed, but better fried, it is one of those things like frog's legs or rabbit that your parents got you to try by telling you it tastes "just like chicken." (It does, only chewier). A little goes a long way. So I recommend ordering it as part of one of the combination appetizer plates called "Spicy Thang." That way you get to try fried crawfish, his stuffed jalapeño and the Boudin Ball – one of the most inspired pairing of ingredients since peanut butter met jelly. The boudin ball is homemade boudin (long on pork meat and short on pork liver) mounded around a piece of cheddar cheese, battered and fried. Ordered on its own, the boudin ball is the size of a softball and is a little overwhelming, but the "boudin ball puppies" are more manageable, the size of golf balls, finger food really, crisp on the outside with the welcome surprise of melted cheese and creamy boudin when you bite into it. Payne also makes them with seafood boudin – boudin mixed with seafood étouffée and pieces of lean, slightly searing homemade andouille sausage. His stuffed jalapeños distinguish themselves by being halved, surrounded by a choice of meat or seafood boudin, battered, deep fried and served with spicy buttermilk dressing. Payne has been making his own sausage for more than ten years now and claims he's "makin' it the best way I know how – like I'm makin' it for God himself."

Known primarily as a seafood restaurant, Payne boasts, "I really take pride in my steaks and my barbecue. That's my first true love – the barbecue pit. I tell people 'if mine isn't one of the best in the world, one of the best they've ever had, from anyone's backyard or café *anywhere* – we have to buy it back.' I'd rather they get something else."

I thought this was a pretty bold statement until I tried the off-the-menu, but regularly available Stuffed Rib-eye. The dish is a wonderment; the one pound rib-eye – excellent, tender and juicy on its own – is split, stuffed with seafood boudin, dusted with Payne's special, eighteen-ingredient dry seasoning mixture, and cooked to roseate perfection on the pit. A pan is placed underneath the steak to catch the boudin and stuff it back in as the steak cooks.

Of the dizzying array of seafood choices, the winner hands-down is *anything* panéed. Shrimp, oysters, fish or all three in a "combeaux" are coated with a "special" sauce, lightly battered, then pan-fried in butter or "panéed" until golden-crusted. An all-out splurge, this dish is outrageously rich, but absolutely wonderful.

The Boiled Crawfish are exceptional – assertively-seasoned without being painful and large enough to qualify as small lobsters. "We have them all year. We're bringing them in from a farm that's a little north of us and it's cold water, so it's just the beginning of the season now. They're big ones with claws like lobsters." If you are going exclusively to eat these lovely little monsters you might call first to make sure they have them. Payne admits, "I might be out one or two days a week if there's been a run on them, since we only bring in a certain quantity."

Payne claims he invented Battered French Fries and they are good, but so are the Smothered Taters – skin-on French fry cut potatoes seasoned and smothered in a covered pan with onions and garlic. The real stand-out though are the Hush Puppies. Now, I've never much seen the point of hush puppies, but these are remarkable – well-crisped on the outside, moist and tender on the inside with chewy whole kernels of corn. When I asked about them, Payne said, "It's my Mama's recipe that makes 'em so special. I tell everybody 'she's with the Good Lord now, but she showed me how to do it before she went on.' I can tell you, a lot of people make hush puppies – just not many people make 'em good."

While the roux-based étouffée alone seemed a bit heavy-going to me, the Jambalaya is full of andouille sausage, cochon de lait (roast pork) and deep fried turkey (both available as lunch specials with Payne's latest favorite side dish – Pecan Praline Sweet Potatoes).

Payne prides himself on the extreme diversity of the menu and says he offers so many combinations and tasting dinners because he "doesn't like making a meal out of just one thing."

It is possible to try almost everything on the menu (for $35.00 per person) by ordering the Dolly Parton a la carte Feast where they cook and serve one dish at a time. "You can eat like a millionaire but you don't have to be one. It's twenty-five to thirty courses – a bite of this, a bite of that. Everybody at the table has to order it. It's a progressive dinner that takes between two to three hours depending on how much fun you're having." (I might think twice before I parked my pants on those hard picnic benches for two to three hours at the NASA Road 1 location. He says the Crazy Cajun on Westheimer has comfortable booths.) For shrimp fans, another regularly available special is the Bubba Gump Dinner – thirteen shrimp, cooked thirteen different ways on one plate with two kinds of potatoes.

DANIEL WONG'S KITCHEN

4566 Bissonnet
Bellaire, Texas 77401
713/663-6665

Type of Cuisine: Chinese/Whole Hams
Bar: Wine and Beer
Dress: Casual
Entertainment: No
Payment: All Major Credit Cards
Entrée Range: $6.95-$9.50
Recommended Dishes:
Appetizers: Road Kill Pork (Barbecued Pork)
Entrées: Ham
Garlic Lovers Pork
South of the Border Turkey
Salt and Pepper Shrimp
Fiesta Spicy Shrimp
Sautéed Red Snapper
Sliced Ham with Hunan Sauce
"Good Morning to You" (Stir Fry Chicken and Okra)
Hunan Fried Rice
Hours: Monday-Friday, 11:00a.m.-9:30p.m.
Saturday-Sunday, 12:00p.m.-9:30p.m.
Reservations: Accepted for larger parties

Daniel Wong is that rarist of all human creatures – a complete original. Not content to merely offer Houston his ever-evolving, utterly distinctive style of Chinese cooking, he wants to make your Thanksgiving dinner, too. After having sampled his moist, precisely cooked, perfectly seasoned turkey, natural gravy, classic cornbread dressing and the best yams (candied with slices of lemon and orange) I've ever tasted – I'd let him.

The only form of tradition Wong feels compelled to uphold is the tradition of serving consistently excellent food that began thirty-six years ago at Ming Palace on West Gray.

A native of Canton, a region of China known for producing excellent chefs, Wong says he began his cooking career working part-time at a Chinese restaurant in Honolulu in 1949. His first encounter with Thanksgiving turkey and cooking American food was when he was "asked to cook in the Army during the Korean War. I was the mess sergeant when I was stationed in Los Angeles, from 1956-1957, after I had returned from a sixteen month tour of duty in Korea." Wong stayed on in Los Angeles after he was released from the Army and in 1958 went to Hong Kong to visit his parents. There he met his wife whose father, Kwongsee Chow, co-owned one of Houston's first Chinese restaurants, Ming Palace. He came to Houston in 1958 and on June 6, 1960, "joined the team in the kitchen at Ming Palace" where he became known for serving Chinese banquets and introducing Houston to authentic Chinese dishes.

"In those days, there weren't so many restaurants with a real Chinese menu. They had American things like chop suey and chow mein. I served more exotic dishes like bird's nest soup and duck – a lot of new things they hadn't heard about. I created a complete Chinese menu. On Sunday nights, I served as many as six hundred people in the Chinese community a nine course dinner – a Chinese banquet." Thirty-six years later, at Daniel Wong's Kitchen life is simpler, but with a little notice, he is still happy to regale a party with a nine course blow-out.

In 1977, he bought Ten Fathoms Restaurant downtown on Milam and Polk and ran both restaurants until 1980 when Ming Palace closed "so the location could be leased to someone else." He opened Daniel Wong's Restaurant at 3130 Richmond on June 15, 1984, where he continued adapting his recipes to the times. "I like change. I change all the time – everything must be up to date. I never wanted to just serve the same old recipes my grandfather used to make." He closed Daniel Wong's in June, 1991, to take a break. He used the first month to record his highly individual recipes in a yet-to-be published cookbook and the rest of the five years he traveled, first to the West Coast then to the East.

By May of 1996, he was ready to open Daniel Wong's Kitchen – a casual, clean-cut setting with a menu geared "towards the 20th century – everything must be healthy – all food must be fresh. I only cook what I can get fresh at the market. Now, I just cook what I like."

Fortunately for us, the repertory of what he likes is vast and wonderfully varied. Before I even address his new menu, I must talk ham.

In a culture where the pig is so celebrated that in Chinese script, the character for home is an ideogram of a roof over a pig, and there is heated rivalry between provinces as to who produces the finest ham in China, it shouldn't be altogether surprising that the finest ham I've ever tasted is produced – boiled and baked to sweet, tawny succulence – by Daniel Wong. If you like ham or even think you like ham or know someone who likes ham, you will want to pick up a phone now and order a ham from Wong.

"I know what ham tastes like and it's salty. So, I tried to think of a way to get the salt out before you sugar cure it." Using a method he began developing back in his days in the service, he first boils the ham for an hour in water with lemon and the same seasonings that will be used to bake it – cinnamon, allspice, clove and bay leaf. He lets the ham rest, then he rubs it with brown sugar, the seasoning mixture, then surrounds the ham in the pan with a cup or so of that ancient Chinese ingredient – 7-Up! Wong plans to offer it at the restaurant as an off-the-menu special so customers can taste this melt-in-your-mouth treat.

But don't let it keep you from ordering my favorite appetizer, the whimsically titled Road Kill Pork. "In China when I was real young, someone told me that when you pick something up from the road – if you don't kill it yourself, you have to season it heavily with garlic and ginger." Wong assures me his number-one selling dish, virtually inhaled at our table, is store-bought and was created exclusively for this new menu. When the garlic-laden, rich brown sauce and sliced barbecue pork are combined with snow peas and carrots further down the menu, it becomes Garlic Lovers Pork.

Another departure from convention is the South of the Border Turkey – a dish using Southern Chinese methods with South/Southwestern sensibilities. Wong admits, "Most Chinese restaurants use chicken, but I like to create something different. Turkey is a good meat but tends to be a little dry, so if you marinate it and cook it right, it can have a good flavor." In fact, he marinates the thin slices of turkey in a combination of egg white and cornstarch and cooks it quickly in a wok with lots of garlic, cilantro, sweet basil and especially black pepper.

I have two favorite shrimp dishes. The first is the Salt and Pepper Shrimp. Equal parts salt, pepper and sugar, the plump, pepper-flecked shrimp are sautéed with carrots, zucchini squash and sliced red onion "for color and because they're sweet." My second favorite is the Fiesta Spicy Shrimp. Oyster sauce, soy sauce and wine are joined with gentle, seductive breezes from the Southwest – cilantro and a little sliced jalapeño to create a vibrant, precisely balanced sauce.

One of the few recipes carried over from Daniel Wong's, the Sautéed Red Snapper is barely recognizable slices of red snapper sliced with the grain, combined quickly with black beans, garlic and whole slices of fresh ginger as a bracing counterpoint to the otherwise rich ingredients.

The Sliced Lamb with Hunan Sauce is one of the many instances of Wong's use of asparagus on the menu. These two springtime favorites are wisely paired in a dish that Wong says dates back to a time when asparagus was incredibly expensive and hard to get in Houston. "I created this recipe at Ming Palace, so I've been using asparagus a long time. It's even more popular now than it was then. I try to buy the thin asparagus – the skinnier it is, the better the flavor." One diner who normally doesn't eat lamb commented how unlamb-like it tasted, and Wong says it's because he's "careful to trim the meat of all animal fat, so it doesn't taste gamey."

That much-maligned vegetable, okra, makes an unexpected, but welcome appearance at Daniel Wong's Kitchen. Not only does he serve quite a respectable Seafood Gumbo, but it is featured in two dishes called "Good Morning To You" because they "are good enough to eat for breakfast." Sweet, crisp, emerald green slices of okra are combined with chicken in one dish and a sauté of assorted fresh vegetables in the other. Wong admits that "most people think they don't like okra because most people don't know how to cook it. It doesn't have to be cooked to death."

The Hunan Fried Rice has great depth of flavor – a deep, rich brown from the addition of oyster sauce and full of scrambled egg, pork, chicken and beef with a lingering tingle of hot chili oil. It just barely wins in my affections over the welcome nutty flavor of Wong's inventive Fruit and Nut Fried Rice. Toasted sesame seeds, peanuts and almonds are wok-fried with a generous studding of diced dried pineapple, papaya, coconut and raisins. ("I make two kinds – salty and spicy. ") Lighter and fresher-tasting than most fried rice dishes – it is the perfect foil to any of the more complex entrée dishes I've recommended.

A warm home-baked almond cookie is a nice way to finish this meal.

As low key as Daniel Wong is, make no mistake about it – this is heady, virtuoso cooking that displays infinite application of both imagination and experience.

Wong has an uncommon generosity and love for what he does and is anxious to share. He's already given cooking demonstrations on all the local television stations and looks forward to giving classes. "I'd like to pass on what I know – to teach people to cook well and simply." He sees himself as a perpetual student. That may be one of the reasons he's so good. "I like the restaurant to be busy. The more I do – the better I get."

DENIS' SEAFOOD RESTAURANT

12109 Westheimer
Houston, Texas 77077
281/497-1110

Type of Cuisine: Cajun/Seafood
Bar: Full
Dress: Casual
Entertainment: No
Payment: All Major Credit Cards
Entrée Range: $8.95-$21.95
Recommended Dishes:
Appetizers: Oysters Rockefeller
Steamed Oysters
Fried Crab Balls
Shrimp and Oysters en Brochette
Entrées: Fried Catfish
Seafood Enchiladas
Rib Eye
Hours: Sunday-Thursday, 11:00a.m.-10:00p.m.
Friday-Saturday, 11:00a.m.-11:00p.m.
Reservations: Accepted

In *Consider the Oyster,* America's "epicure laureate," M. F. K. Fisher wrote in 1941, "There are too many legends, really, about oysters Rockefeller for anyone to dare say what he thinks is the true one. It is equally foolish to say what is the true recipe since every gourmet who has ever dined in that nostalgically agreeable room of Antoine's on St. Louis (in New Orleans) figures, after the third or fourth sampling if not the first, that he has at last discovered the secret."

I don't know if Denis Wilson, chef/proprietor of Denis' Seafood, has discovered *the* secret, but he's discovered **a** secret and he's not telling. They're certainly the finest rendition of oysters Rockefeller I've eaten this side of the Mississippi.

I do know that he takes his freshly shucked raw oysters, cold, briny and perfect in their raw state, and covers them with a rich green blanket – a mixture of what he'll only say includes butter, garlic and puréed spinach and crisped briefly in a 500° oven. That's just the beginning of what he does well. After the oysters in raw and Rockefeller states, my third favorite treatment of the beloved bivalve is the unusual steamed oyster – napped with finely chopped garlic and butter and steamed in a convection/steamer until the butter runs off and all that's left is a heavenly residue of garlic. Denis says these are improved even more by adding a squeeze of lemon and a couple dashes of Tabasco® at the table.

Another appetizer we love is the Fried Crab Balls – surprisingly light, crunchy pillows of mostly crab meat rolled in flour, then bread crumbs, and fried quickly in cottonseed oil – the only oil he ever uses. In fact, all of the fried dishes are as you visualize them in your fondest dreams – crisp, light, moist and (most importantly) greaseless. This is another culinary secret he brings from his home state Louisiana, one that they share with the French and maybe the Chinese – that food seasoned, lightly coated with some substance (a mixture of both corn flour and corn meal in his case), and fried quickly in good oil at the right temperature, seals in the flavor and produces something much nearer a dream than the nightmarish, heavy, grease-sodden mess that gave fried food a bad name to begin with.

The Fried Catfish was especially good – luminously fresh, "wild, not pond-raised" like Wilson says he "grew up eating," blissfully free of that muddy taste that catfish so commonly has.

One of the things that distinguishes Denis' Seafood from other restaurants is the variety of fresh fish available daily, mostly caught (with the obvious exception of tuna or salmon) by Wilson's own fisherman in local waters. Buttery-fleshed Angel Fish, rarely seen outside an aquarium, was a highlight of one meal. Any of the fish, in fact anything on the menu, is available prepared virtually any way the diner can dream up. Wilson says his objective from the beginning was to serve the freshest fish in town, and that preparing exactly what the customer wants to eat, exactly how he wants to eat it "is a gift." He's right. It is a "gift" to us and great testimony to his (and all of the kitchen crew's) innate skill and versatility as a chef.

He comes by it naturally. Wilson grew up in Lafayette, Louisiana, and was raised by two talented amateur cooks. He says his mother was a great short order cook. Her deviled egg recipe is used daily to top the Shrimp Slaw, a creamy coleslaw sweetened with honey and generously studded with little shrimp and garnished with larger shrimp.

His father, on the other hand, cooked for a day and a half at a time and passed on his recipe for the labor-intensive, time-consuming dishes that are often considered the very hallmark of a good cook in Louisiana – dishes like Crawfish Bisque, intensely flavored with the fat of the crawfish; Crawfish Court Bouillon (pronounced "coó-buyon") – a thicker tomato based background to the delicious little crustaceans; and my personal favorite, the Crawfish Stew – outrageously lush, chock-full of chopped onions, green peppers, scallions and served over white rice. He learned his lessons well.

His two daughters, Heather and Shannon work at Denis' as floor managers. Heather waited on our table one night and clearly knows the family business; and Shannon, on a different night working as bartender, whipped up the house martini for us. (It's called a Sledge Hammer for obvious reasons and is made by first rinsing the glass with Courvoisier, burning the cognac off with a match, flaming an orange peel and rubbing the rim of the glass with it, and straining a shaker full of ice and Stolichnaya Krystal into the glass garnished with an olive.)

In November 1988, he opened Denis' Seafood, a free-standing black tile and stucco building in front of the dollar cinema on Westheimer between Kirkwood and Dairy Ashford. You can't miss it. It looks more like a huge aquarium with giant crab, angel fish, redfish and swordfish swimming by painted on the stucco walls and etched into the windows by local artist, Joe Jones.

The interior is especially handsome – reminiscent of New Orleans with black and white tile floors, ceiling fans, stained oak walls and red leather booths softly individually lighted by small brass fixtures with little black shades.

Denis' Seafood may be as famous in some circles for their off-the-menu specialities as those on the menu. Two of the best are both the Shrimp and Oyster en Brochette – impeccable specimens simply wrapped in good smoky bacon, broiled until crisp and served with both red and Louisiana-style remoulade sauce. Another outstanding dish that's just gone on the menu is the Seafood Enchiladas, the chef's own invention – thin white tortillas filled with étouffée and topped with the aforementioned court bouillon (that interestingly ends up tasting a bit like mole in this guise) and a generous melting of Wisconsin cheddar cheese. The enchiladas are served in Tex-Mex fashion but with a side order of Creole Rice this time. All of the rice and potato dishes are given special attention and it shows.

Of the non-seafood dishes, the fourteen ounce Iowa corn-fed Rib-Eye was an unqualified success – pan-broiled in butter and served surrounded by a sauce made from pan drippings and vermouth, thickened with a little roux.

My two favorite desserts were the White Chocolate Pound Cake topped with fresh whipping cream and drizzled with puréed strawberries, and the hard to beat Chocolate Pecan Sundae – elaborately constructed layers of vanilla ice cream, warm chocolate pecan pie and whipping cream served in an old-fashioned sundae dish with a long spoon.

DIXIE'S ROADHOUSE

8135 Katy Freeway
Houston, Texas 77024
713/681-4200

Type of Cuisine: American/Eclectic
Bar: Full
Dress: Casual
Entertainment: No
Payment: All Major Credit Cards
EntrÈe Range: $5.95-$22.95
Recommended Dishes:
Appetizers: "Tabasco®" Pepper Angus Filet
Crispy Select Oysters
Shrimp Quesadillas
Seafood Gumbo
Entrées: Chicken Fried Steak
Spicy Thin Catfish
Smoked Prime Rib
Hours: Sunday-Thursday, 11:00a.m.-10:00p.m.
Friday-Saturday, 11:00a.m.-2:00a.m.
Reservations: Accepted for Larger Parties

Dixie's Roadhouse is a neon red painted lady with a reputation for fun. As evidence, when I called directory assistance for the number of the then three-month-old restaurant, the operator corrected me. "It's Dixie's RED HOT Roadhouse!" I asked if that's how it's listed and she said, "No, I just ate there." When I asked how it was, she said, "Oh, absolutely delicious and lots of fun!" I pressed her to find out what was so good (and so much fun), she demurred, "I'm not really allowed to say. But I'll bet you'll enjoy it!"

This was music to the ears of owners James Hillyer and Bob Wilson. Both veterans in the restaurant business, they have owned six or seven restaurants between them. Hillyer says, "This is our business and we like to have fun with it. Bob and I set out to create a new concept based on our belief that it's not enough just to feed people, customers must be entertained, too; not so much a dining experience as a fun experience. We wanted to create the ultimate roadhouse with the kind of regional food we all grew up eating – only better, fresher and not just seasoned with salt and pepper anymore."

Indeed, "Red Hot" is a reference to the partners' mutual affection for hot sauces of any origin, and assertively-seasoned food. Hillyer adds, "Spices are really big now. I mean, there are hot sauce conventions, magazines and web sites. Habanera futures – that's what they say buy!"

Drinks are elevated a notch or two by using freshly

squeezed juices. Entrées are preceded by a basket of exquisitely moist, hot, out-of-the-oven miniature jalapeño corn muffins – a recipe so dear to Hillyer's heart that he jokingly says he won't even share it with his eighty-year-old mother. A great impression is made instantly.

Starting with the appetizers, the most distinctive dish and the one I will return for again and again, is the "Tabasco" Pepper Angus Filet. A tender piece of "certified angus filet" is marinated for twenty-four hours in Tabasco® Sauce and then literally "smoked" in a hot wok. It's sliced and served with an (almost) unnecessary, and absolutely incendiary, homemade Habanera sauce that makes an appearance in several guises on the menu.

The habanera peppers, tomatoes and other ingredients of the sauce are charred on the grill so it has a wonderful, smoky flavor. It is my choice to accompany another appetizer – the incredibly light, very nearly perfect, Crispy Select Oysters.

If you crave something hot and cheesy – as I often do – the Queso served with warm, freshly-made chips, salsa and guacamole or the Quesadillas are hard to beat. They benefit from being made with the soft, white slightly-salty Mexican cheese called Chihuahua.

The Seafood Gumbo has a heady, pitch-black, darkly delicious roux with shrimp, crawfish and oysters – a fabulous recipe courtesy of Hillyer's mom, he says.

I was a little surprised to see Beefsteak Tomato and Onion with Fresh Bleu Cheese escape from a steakhouse menu. Wilson explained they both just love the salad. "I mean, we almost put smoked salmon on the menu," but fortunately, cooler heads prevailed. "We finally said, 'Look, this is madness. We need some reality here!'" They were determined to serve the dishes "we both really like to eat," he says.

The Tacos and Burritos are a good example. Hillyer was the original owner of the restaurant Cabo, and has since sold it. He has some experience with and a real affinity for soft tacos. Although he prefers either the chicken – seasoned and cooked "Cuban style," he says – or beef. The tacos are a little awkward to eat, but they seem to have gotten that essential balance of flavors and textures right with just enough lettuce and a sassy little serrano pepper and yoghurt-based salsa.

If you can find two (or ten) people who like their burger cooked and dressed the same way, the ten-inch Giant "Mack" Burger is a marvel to behold. It is as big as a Mack truck or at least a standard size Frisbee, is cooked-to-order on a charcoal grill and arrives fully loaded. "All the way," Hillyer says. "We prepare it for you . We don't serve it open face. I just don't like open face hamburgers that you have to 'make' yourself. We do cut it in quarters for you." I recommend it with a pound or two of bacon and jalapeño Jack cheese on top.

Also in the beef genre, it's a tough call between one of the city's best Chicken Fried Steaks and Smoked Rib-eye. Listed as a Roadhouse Platter, the chicken fried steak is blessed with two fine entities – perfectly seasoned batter and a tender veal cutlet pounded thin to considerable acreage. Hillyer says, "I'll give that to my mother. That's how I grew up eating it. She always used veal (instead of beef)." It is topped with rich, peppercorn-flecked cream gravy and served with a side order of the nearly ubiquitous, but well above average, Garlic Mashed Potatoes.

The often pedestrian Prime Rib absolutely sings with the flavor of smoke. "We smoke them for about six hours and the flavor really gets in there." Hillyer says that they run out every night. It comes with a horseradish cream sauce and a sultry, smoke-flavored natural "jus."

The Spicy Thin Sliced Catfish is a novel presentation and a winner among the Fresh Gulf Seafood. Catfish filets are sliced thin horizontally – an idea Hillyer got from a little restaurant on the bayou outside New Orleans. Like the Crispy Select Oysters, the pieces of catfish are cloaked in a light, aggressively-seasoned batter, the secret of which is corn flour and not corn meal, as Hillyer says. The catfish itself has that clean, almost sweet flavor, a tell-tale sign of being farm-raised. It comes with French Fries and freshly-cut and battered Onion Rings (both excellent), but I wouldn't miss asking for a side of cool, crunchy coarse grain mustard-flavored Cole Slaw.

I'm always pleased to see particular care taken with side dishes and there's a lot to recommend at Dixie's. A nice, homey touch is a Jumbo Sweet Potato baked and served with cinnamon sugar. Corn on the Cob is roasted and dramatically presented with its husks stripped back. A good case could be made for an order of sweet, caramelized Wok-Seared Onions. The Wok-Steamed Asparagus – another steakhouse favorite – were fat as a billiard cue, slathered with butter, and cooked to al dente perfection.

The desserts need a little work. Of the three pies available, the Pecan Pie tasted the most homemade. (As I correctly assessed, neither of these guys is a dessert eater.)

All in all, directory assistance was right. I did enjoy it. As the neon sign over the kitchen says (sort of tongue in cheek!), it is "The Finest in Roadhouse Cuisine."

DON PEPE

4010 Highway 6
Houston, Texas 77082
281/531-7673

Type of Cuisine: Chilean
Bar: Wine and Beer
Dress: Casual
Entertainment: No
Payment: All Major Credit Cards (except Diners)
Entrée Range: $3.95-$12.95
Recommended Dishes:
Appetizers: Empanadas (Queso or Beef)
Entrées: Chancho al Jugo (Pork Loin)
Congrio (Conger Eel)
Pollo Montina (Chicken in Pastry)
Charquican (Puréed Squash with Vegetables and Beef)
Dessert: Brazo de Reina
Hours: Tuesday-Thursday, 11:30a.m.-9:00p.m.
Friday-Saturday, 11:30a.m.-11:00p.m.
Sunday, 12:00p.m.-9:00p.m.
(Closed Monday)
Reservations: Not Accepted

The handwritten sign on the door says, "This is not a Mexican restaurant!" This isn't so much a warning as a declaration that inside this cozy, family-run hideaway you won't find nachos, enchiladas or fajitas. What you will find is a short list that represents all major points of interest on the Chilean culinary landscape. Dishes like Pastel de Choclo, Charquican and Chancho al Jugo – all new (and welcome) additions to my food vocabulary.

Santiago native, Rick Fonseca, is proud of his culinary heritage. He opened Don Pepe in September, 1993, with the help of his parents – his mother, Nora who cooks, and father, Jose who manages. "Our intention was to introduce Houston to Chilean food." Indeed, the menu boasts that Don Pepe Chilean Restaurant is "The only one in Texas."

It's common knowledge now how highly regarded Chilean wine is. What I'm just now learning is how remarkable and completely distinctive the food is that goes with it. Fonseca feels that this is particularly true of South America's favorite snack food – the Empanada. There are four types to choose from as an appetizer – three fried and one baked. "I always recommend that people try the Pino Horno, the baked meat-filled pie, because that's the one most Chileans eat...with a bottle of red wine. That's how you eat the empanada." The classic Chilean meat empanada is filled with a moist, superbly-seasoned mixture of finely ground beef, two kinds of raisins, olives, hard-cooked eggs and onions.

The same filling fares equally well in the fried rendition – Pino Frita. But best of all is the Queso (cheese-filled) empanada. Fonseca says that his mother uses Monterey Jack "because the cheese should run out and hang when the empanada is cut, and it comes the closest to the cheese that would be used in Chile for this purpose." A sultry Santa Rita 120 Cabernet Sauvignon went especially well with the empanadas and in fact with all the dishes we sampled during this meal.

Before you've even ordered, wedges of warm, freshly-baked Pan de Masado arrive. It is interesting. "Typical Chilean bread," Fonseca says – flat, round, dense, almost biscuit-like with a slightly sweet flavor.

Although they are happy to supply butter, it's meant to be eaten with the vibrant, fresh-tasting, homemade salsa. It is bright green, tart with vinegar, composed of finely-chopped cilantro, garlic, onions, and has the lingering tingle of finely minced jalapeno peppers. The Fonsecas call it "Peure" and it has become so popular they sell it by the jar ($2.95 for 12 ounces). "Once customers taste it, they almost always want to buy it! I've seen them put it on everything – even Pastel de Choclo, which I don't recommend."

Me neither. This would disturb the delicate balance of Chile's most unusual and oldest specialty. Fonseca says, "It's our main dish and has existed as long as Chile has," which could conceivably date as far back as the Aruscanian Indians who inhabited Chile until colonization of the Spaniards in 1541.

It is a rustic dish that is constructed by placing a baked chicken drumstick in the bottom of terra cotta casserole. Next comes a layer of well-seasoned ground beef and onions that is probably the same filling that's used to make the meat empanadas. Then the chicken and beef are covered in sweet, white corn that has been ground, then stirred for hours with sugar. The casserole is baked until an appealing crust forms on the top. "I always encourage newcomers to try pastel de choclo and 99% of the time they love it. I'm very proud of it because Chilean customers tell me that my mother's secret recipe is better than they remember eating in Chile." (One word of warning – if you're from the school of thought that entrees should always be savory and not sweet, Pastel de Choclo may not be for you!)

Another specialty of the house is Congrio. Advertised cryptically as "Chilean fish," it is actually the scaleless, saltwater conger eel – a distant relative to the common eel and a delicious gift to Chile from the bordering Pacific Ocean. This "monster fish" that often grows as large as ten feet, is more beauty than beast as it appears before you at Don Pepe. Huge fileted chunks of the firm, white-fleshed fish have been seasoned simply with lemon and garlic, dusted with flour and fried very quickly in a Chinese wok. The flavor is mild, almost sweet and quite distinctive. It is complemented perfectly by the bright, fresh flavors of what Fonseca calls Chilean salad – chopped tomatoes and onions dressed with a light vinaigrette. (When I commented that the onions seemed unusually sweet, Fonseca told me that the secret is that they soak them overnight in saltwater "to remove the bitterness.")

Almost all Latin countries have their own highly individual version of paella. At Don Pepe it is called Arroz a la Valenciana in honor of the city on the eastern coast of Spain where paella originated two centuries ago. Colored a sunny, persimmon-yellow with saffron, it is moist and packed with seafood – clams, mussels and crawfish tails, and small nuggets of chicken, pork and sausage.

Since Chile is framed to the west by the Pacific Ocean and to the east by Argentina and Bolivia, it is not surprising that beef and seafood get equal billing.

I love the hearty simplicity of the first two dishes listed under Platos de Carnes. The first is Bistec a lo Pobre. This "poor man's steak" is a choice of well-seasoned, marinated beef shoulder or rib-eye pan fried with sliced onions and topped with two fried eggs and French fries. The second is Chilenazo – Chilean slang for "something really big ... bigger than Chile!" Fonseca says. This time your choice of steak is accompanied by saffron-scented rice, two fried eggs and Chilean Style Beans – kidney beans that have been cooked with fettucine broken into small pieces. Fonseca tells me that he doesn't know how that got started. "My father says they've been eating beans like that in Chile since he was a kid."

Most interesting of all the meat dishes is Charquican. The menu's description, "mashed squash and potatoes with mixed vegetables," doesn't begin to do it justice. It is a mound of puréed yellow squash with peas, corn, lima beans, green beans and tiny cubes of potatoes that have been added to sautéed, small, bite-sized nuggets of beef and onions. It tastes of garlic and cumin and comes with or without steak. "Many people eat it without (the extra meat)," Fonseca says.

A chicken dish I enjoyed even more than Pastel de Choclo is called Pollo Montina. It can only be described as rustically sophisticated. An earthy sauté of what we might think of as smothered chicken (with bones still attached), sweet peas, onions and carrots finds its way into a delightful piece of pastry fashioned into a basket with a flower-shaped handle on top. The rich brown gravy soaks through the dough and makes it a pleasure to eat when you've finished its contents.

Saving the best for last, I would have to strain to think of a finer treatment of a pork loin than Don Pepe's Chancho al Jugo. A whole tenderloin of pork is covered in onions, carrots, garlic and green peppers surrounded by white wine and baked to juicy, eye-popping perfection. It is offered with rice or French fries, but I don't think you could do much better than the house mashed potatoes to absorb the heady, red-tinted sauce.

Nora Fonseca's talent does not stop there. A gooey confection called Brazo de Reina comes close to replacing the milk-soaked Central American cake, trés leches, in my affections. Moist yellow cake is iced with cooked, caramel-flavored sweetened condensed milk, then covered in chopped walnuts. "Brazo de Reina" means "arm of the queen," presumably because of its shape, and can be purchased whole – with a little notice – for you next dinner party.

DUCHO'S STEAK HOUSE

633 Heidrich
Houston, Texas 77018
713/692-9074

Type of Cuisine: Steaks/Barbecue
Bar: Wine and Beer
Dress: Casual
Entertainment: No
Payment: All Major Credit Cards
Entrée Range: $7.95-$14.95
Barbecue Prices: $3.95-$6.25
Recommended Dishes:
Appetizers: "Wings of Fire" (Buffalo Wings)
Entrées: Fried Catfish
Burgers
Chicken Fried Steak
Pork Chops
Barbecue: Turkey Breast
Ham
Sausage
Potato Salad
Coleslaw
Hours: Lunch: Tuesday-Friday, 11:00a.m.-2:00p.m.
Dinner: Tuesday-Friday, 5:00p.m.-10:00p.m.
Saturday, 4:00p.m.-10:00p.m.
Sunday, 11:00a.m.-8:30p.m.
(Closed Monday)
Reservations: Accepted

The nearly thirty-year old neon sign with the flashing red arrow reads "Ducho's Steak House…Cocktails." That barely scratches the surface of what this Garden Oaks institution does well. As far as I'm concerned, Joanne and Calvin Ducho hold the bragging rights to some of the best Texas/Southern home style cooking this side of the Mason-Dixon line.

The appetizer to go for is called "Wings of Fire" which sounds like a lot more like a series on the Discovery Channel than what it is – the best Buffalo wings I've ever tasted. They are dry-seasoned, deep fried, then liberally doused with Louisiana Hot Sauce. Ask for the chunky, garlic-flecked, homemade blue cheese dressing instead of the ranch that normally accompanies them and don't plan on sharing them with more than one person. They're too good!

There's so much to recommend next, I hardly know where to start. I'm a fairly recent convert to Catfish and I've never enjoyed it more than at Ducho's. The clean-tasting, white-fleshed filets are Alabama farm-raised from a company called "Delta Pride." They are lovingly prepared in the time-honored fashion – bathed in seasoned milk, lightly encrusted with fine cornmeal and impeccably deep fried so they are crisp and golden on the outside and moist on the inside – and served with the traditional hush puppies, freshly-cut French fries, and a trip to the salad bar. The distinctive vinaigrette-based cole-slaw goes especially well with the catfish. Already an incredible bargain at $7.95 an order – regulars clamor for Ducho's all-you-can-eat catfish special on Fridays, Saturdays and Sundays for the same price.

The flame-broiled half-pound Burger is one from your fondest dreams. Ducho rightly says, "I'll put them up against anybody's in the city. The big difference is that I grind my own hamburger meat which almost no one else does."

First in the affections of many Texans, the Chicken Fried Steak is fabulous – heroically portioned, unbelievable tender, lightly-breaded and takes well to the silky, black pepper-studded cream gravy. I enjoyed it almost as much as the Southern Fried Chicken – available three pieces to an order – all-white, all-dark or a mixture of the two. Even the breast meat is moist and juicy under a thin, well-seasoned batter.

The eight ounce loin cut Pork Chops are succulent, full of flavor and appealingly-scored from the grill. They are served with long grain and wild rice, and an order of irresistible garlic toast – thickly sliced white bread slathered with melted butter and chopped garlic, and toasted on a hot griddle.

Ducho's Steak House was opened in 1965 by Calvin Ducho's brother, Edgar. Ducho says his brother opened the steak house, a stone's throw from his existing barbecue business on North Shepherd, The Hitching Rail, mostly because "there weren't any steak houses out here." He bought his brother out in 1984, and Edgar and his wife have since retired to the Ducho's hometown of Moulton, Texas.

There are twelve different, moderately-priced cuts of steaks to choose from. He says that "the 30 ounce sirloin for two people is our main steak and I have it on special every weekend for $20.95." He seasons his steaks with salt, pepper and garlic, "mops 'em with butter," and charbroils them on a grill. When I ask if that's what makes them so good, he says, "We just cook 'em right."

EL MESON

2425 University Blvd.
Houston, Texas 77005
713/522-9306

Type of Cuisine: Cuban/Mexican
Bar: Wine and Beer
Dress: Casual
Entertainment: No
Payment: American Express, MasterCard, Visa
Entrée Range: $8.95-$11.95
Recommended Dishes:
Appetizers: Nachos Cubanos
Nachos al Meson
Tapas: Gambas al Ajillo en Cazuela
Chorizo Riojano al Jerez
Entrées: Solomillo
Ropa Vieja
Picadillo
Enchiladas del Mar
Carne Asada a la Tampiquena
Pollo en Molé
Hours: Monday-Thursday, and Saturday, 11:00a.m.-9:45p.m.
Friday, 11:00a.m.-10:45p.m.
Sunday, 12:00p.m.-9:45p.m.
Reservations: Accepted

"I think we are known now as a Cuban restaurant," explains Peter Garcia, Jr. as he proudly maps the sixteen year evolution of El Meson.

"At first, we called ourselves a Spanish/Mexican restaurant. Then, we called it a Cuban/Mexican restaurant. Now, we just say that it is a Cuban restaurant."

Indeed, there it is in bold print on the cover of the new menu, "El Meson in the village ... Cuban Restaurant."

Any confusion could be forgiven since the menu has a distinctly dual personality. It is divided (exactly) equally into categories of Cuban specialties, classic Mexican dishes, with the odd Spanish influence.

Native Houstonians may remember this site as the original location of El Patio (built in 1957). The Garcia family moved to Houston in the spring of 1981 from New York where they owned and operated a successful Cuban restaurant. They bought El Patio and as Garcia tells it, "We did the closing at 3:00 p.m., and at midnight it was ours lock, stock and barrel. The next day we opened for business without skipping a beat, and no one had a clue about guacamole or enchiladas."

They changed the name to El Meson ("the inn") and within a week began introducing some Cuban dishes to the clientele.

"The Picadillo was right at the top. That was easy. And, of course, Arroz con Pollo and Ropa Vieja. The Chuletas, that's pork chops, were out there right away. And the Palomillo."

Still, El Patio had its fans. Many of the Mexican dishes are hold-overs from those days – refined versions of the original recipes. "I have customers who have been coming in for thirty years eating the same thing. One regular, Dr. Red Duke, has been coming (to the restaurant) much longer than we've been here. He always orders the same dish. He says, 'Now, Peter, don't go messin' with my Compuestas!' All the combination dinners are left over from the old days. I don't dare change them. I'm superstitious!"

The great news about El Meson is that every dish, whatever its origin, is prepared with equal measures of love and respect. There are no cursory efforts here.

Let's start at the top – one of the areas where the two cuisines happily overlap – like the Nachos Cubanos.

Nachos are transformed into a tropical delight when crisp blue corn tortillas bear up under the substantial weight of Cuban black beans, a chunk of sweet plantain and melted Monterey Jack cheese. Sliced medium-hot jalapeños are piled neatly in the center to garnish at will. They are an asset. The equally good Nachos al Meson require no further embellishment as the wonderful, assertively-seasoned Cuban beef hash – Picadillo – is substituted for the usual fajita meat. Try a half dozen of each.

Tapas – the Spanish bite-size bar food – are given their due on the new menu as a sort of gastronomic tip of the hat to the Spanish culinary roots of Pedro Garcia, Sr., Peter's late father. Tapas Variadas is a sampling of imported Spanish cheeses such as the semi-hard, salty Manchego from the plains of La Mancha, and the divine Spanish blue cheese, Queso Cabrales – "when available" as it says on the menu – and two different types of garlicky, paprika-flavored chorizo, or sausage, and smoked dry-cured pork tenderloin – Lomo Embuchado.

The Spanish affinity for garlic is exemplified in the tapas classic Gambas al Ajillo en Cazuela. Shrimp bob in fragrant Spanish olive oil and garlic ("al ajillo") in traditional individual glazed pottery ramekins. (It is customary – in fact, encouraged – to use pieces of good crusty bread to soak up any remaining garlic and oil from the cazuela.)

The heartier of the two imported chorizos – the Chorizo Riojano (from "Rioja") – is sliced, sautéed with onions until the skin crisps and finished off with a welcome dose of fine Spanish sherry in the tapas dish – Chorizo Riojano al Jerez.

Tortilla Espanola – the potato and onion filled omelet

enjoyed in Spanish homes from breakfast through cocktail hour – rounds out the short list of tapas.

The Spanish national dish – Paella – as beloved by Cubans as it is by Spaniards, is featured under Mariscos ("seafood") on the menu. It is prepared with either seafood "Marinera" – or, my preference, "del Meson" – with added chicken (plus, pork and chorizo if you ask for it). The most notable difference is El Meson's use of long grain, instead of Valencia or short grain rice. It needs little other than a squeeze of lemon and a pinch of salt to be perfect. (Fans of paella should phone ahead, as it requires a minimum of an hour to prepare paella properly.)

Another favorite seafood dish – Camarones Enchilados – is, I'm sure, a source of great confusion. This Cuban specialty is shrimp sautéed "enchilados," literally "in sauce." The sauce, called Salsa Espanola on the menu, is a robust garlic and sherry-flavored reduction of tomatoes and vegetables.

There's so much to recommend among the Cuban entrées, I can only start with my very favorites. The Solomillo and Pollo al Ajillo battle it out for first place. Solomillo, the name for tenderloin of pork, is – as Garcia correctly claims – "to die for." The impossibly-tender piece of pork is marinated overnight in a classic Cuban mojo, a sauce of olive oil, garlic and naranja agria (sour orange), then quickly charbroiled. Like both the Masitas (pieces of pork tenderloin) and the Chuletas (pork chops), the Solomillo is complemented by pieces of yucca (the white root vegetable), boiled and dressed with a little mojo.

The Pollo al Ajillo easily earns its reputation as El Meson's most popular dish. A skinless chicken breast is marinated, scored quickly on the charbroiler, then finished in a skillet with an earthy mixture of onions, garlic and olive oil.

The previously-mentioned Cuban beef hash, Picadillo a la Criolla, is perfectly seasoned and improved only by the addition of a couple of fried eggs – a Cuban practice that Garcia says is known in Cuban diner parlance as "Adam and Eve in El Paraiso" (in paradise).

Tasajo – shredded salt-dried beef – gives El Meson's tomatoey Ropa Viejo extra depth and harmony. Garcia tells me that there was a time when Ropa Viejo – which literally translates to "old clothes" – was made exclusively with tasajo instead of the beef brisket, boiled and shredded, that is commonly used now.

Bistec Encebollado is thin, bone-in rib-eye steak of considerable acreage, again marinated, char broiled and blanketed with onions ("encebollado").

But, if it's steak you're after, my absolute favorite thing among the Mexican entrées – the Carne Asada a la Tampiquena

– is definitely the way to go. An absolutely flawless "flame-cooked" ("asada") skirt steak is central to this combination plate that includes a cheese enchilada and a flauta de pollo. One of the few combination plates that's actually eaten in Mexico, Carne Asada a la Tampiquena has been served at this location since El Patio opened in 1957.

An exquisite brownish red mole poblano is updated when paired with plump, skinless chicken breasts. Another nod to the nineties – Enchiladas de Vegetales – enchiladas filled with vegetables sautéed in a garlicky tomato sauce – are good enough to convert even the heartiest carnivore. But, the best of the enchilada adaptions is the one filled with the garlic-studded shrimp (Gambas al Ajillo) and covered with cheese. Mexican entrées are all accompanied by yellow rice and excellent refried beans.

All dishes listed as Mariscos or Cuban Entrées come with a cup of soulful, deeply satisfying Cuban black beans that taste faintly of dry sherry, slightly-sticky white rice, and glorious chunks of ambrosial fried sweet plantains. The sweet/salty contrast of flavors is one of the elements that makes Cuban dining so distinctive.

Spain and Chile are well-represented on the wine list. I especially liked the Spanish rosé by Marqués de Caceres Rioja with the paella. The margaritas are strong, made from real lime juice, and there are more than 54 beers, ales and lagers to choose from.

Either Tres Leches or a wonderful, eggy Flan are a fine way to end the meal. Plus, of course, a tasita of good strong Cuban coffee.

El Meson feels like a cozy, neighborhood restaurant. Clearly the Garcias love what they do and believe as did Epicurus, the Greek philosopher who's quoted on their menu … "So we must exercise ourselves in the things which bring happiness, since, if that be present, we have everything."

EL PARAISO

2320 Crocker (at Fairview)
Houston, Texas 77006
713/524-0309

Type of Cuisine: Mexican
Bar: Beer and Margaritas
Dress: Casual
Entertainment: No
Payment: All Major Credit Cards
Entrée Range: $4.50-$8.00
Recommended Dishes:
Best Salsa
Breakfast: Machacado con Huevo (Eggs with Dried Beef)
Migas
Appetizers: Nachos con Chorizo
Queso Flameado
Entrées: Tamales
Entomatadas
Sopes
Milanesa
Hours: Sunday-Thursday, 7:00a.m.-10:00p.m.
Friday-Saturday, 7:00a.m.-11:00p.m.
Reservations: Not Accepted

What are your criteria for a great Mexican restaurant? We all have them. The chips? Are they warm? Fresh? Thin enough? The margaritas? Are they strong? Tart? Or, God forbid, made from a mix? Or maybe the flour tortillas? Are they buttery soft? Do they taste freshly made?

The litmus test for me is always the same – the salsa. Block by block in this town, there are more variations of America's favorite condiment than Elvis could shake a hip at.

The same list of suspects is lined up in almost every kitchen – tomatoes, onions, jalapeño peppers and cilantro – but used so differently that each restaurant inevitably produces a differnt result. There is salsa cruda or fresca where the ingredients are raw or nearly-raw and served cold. Or, the cooked salsas that are tomato-based, often served warm, and seem closer to a classic ranchero sauce. Or, of course, there's green salsa made from the little husk-covered tomatillos (green tomatoes).

My vote for the best salsa in town goes to El Paraiso. Owner, Roberto Torres, admits that "it is the secret to our restaurant." This is not a salsa for sissies. It is hot, but not so hot that it makes your eyes bug out...just hot enough to think twice before you'd invite the uninitiated (a non-Texan) to eat there. Torres' wife, Beatriz, says that those who visit the restaurant from out of town often stop back by to take a quart or two home with them. The hot culprit, along with the standard fresh jalapeños, is the devil's own chiles de árbol – incendiary little suckers similar to the cayenne pepper. The Torres' will share little else with me, except that like almost all of the recipes at El Paraiso, the salsa is a legacy of the original owner, Beatriz's mother, Helena Leal.

Señora Leal opened El Paraiso in 1978 in a little wooden house on stilts. The neighborhood according to the Torres', was almost exclusively Mexican at the time. The restaurant seated only forty people in those days, and the style of cooking, Roberto says, was Southern Mexican. Beatriz says, "The recipes are quite typical of my mother's native Guanajuato." The Torres' bought the business from Señora Leal in 1981, but she taught Lupe Montano, the cook, how to prepare these classic dishes before she left, so her tradition has continued. One huge difference is that the clientele is now "probably only 25% Hispanic/75% neighborhood people"... although she acknowledges that "the neighborhood has changed since then."

Fortunately, the menu has not – at least, not so you'd notice. My second criterion for greatness is authenticity, and like the salsa, many of the dishes at El Paraiso have the earthy, satisfying quality of Mexican homecooking. Beatriz attributes this to her mother's recipes, and the practice in her mother's day of making "all the platos from scratch when they're ordered, not before. You'd be surprised at how unusual that is."

El Paraiso opens at seven every morning and Beatriz proudly boasts that, "We're kind of famous for our breakfast." On weekends, regulars clamor for such favorite almuerzo (brunch) dishes as Huevos Rancheros, Roberto's favorite, maybe because the ranchero sauce is so good, Huervos Con Papas (egg scrambled with potatoes) or, what many consider to be Houston's best Migas. Taken from the Spanish word for crumbs, migas are eggs scrambled with crumbled tortilla chips and diced, sautéed peppers, onions and tomatoes.

I was pleased to see the unusual Machacado Con Huervo a La Mexicana on the menu – eggs scrambled with machaca (seasoned and airdried beef). Although Beatriz admits she's not a fan of the dish, she says many customers drive great distances to eat it. Happily, breakfast is served all day until closing at night with a minimal ($.75) charge after 11:30 a.m.

On my first visit to El Paraiso, the restaurant won my heart by regularly serving another traditional almuerzo dish, Menudo. Known in Mexico as the "Breakfast of Champions," this beef tripe and hominy soup (if you can find it at all) is normally only served on weekends not only because it is so time-consuming to make, but most especially because it is famous for its restorative powers after a night out on the town.

Still, those powers can be no greater than their Caldo de Pollo – a chicken soup to cure what ails you. A meal in itself, the ample bowl is laden with hearty chunks of potatoes, onions, carrots, cabbage and cilantro in a spectacularly rich chicken broth. A quarter of a chicken has been removed from the soup, and rests on the plate next to the bowl, for the eater to shred into the soup. Beatriz says the Caldo de Res (beef soup) is almost as popular as the chicken.

The margaritas are served in glasses big enough to swim in and you just might want to. They are delicious – puckery and potent. Among the appetizers, they go especially well with the Nachos Con Chorizo (nachos with scarlet-colored, molten-hot Mexican sausage) that is also featured in their Queso Flameado – a shallow dish of melted or literally "flamed" white asadero cheese. The Chile Con Queso stands out because it is not the melted processed cheese dressed up with a little chopped pepper that has become our expectation.. It's the real thing.

So are the Tamales. They are exceptionally large, filled with minced pork, and arrive already shucked, three to an order. It's easy to imagine, as legend has it, that tamales this wonderful were offered as gifts to the gods during the twelfth month of the eighteen-month long Aztec year.

For those who crave variety, there are three Mexican Plates of varying composition from which to choose; enchiladas, tacos, chalupas, burritos, etc. Roberto says the Mexican plates do well, but by sticking with these standards you might miss what they do best.

There are several other regional Mexican dishes that are a happy diversion from the usual TexMex dining experience. One is Entomatadas – simple enchiladas where the tortillas have been folded into quarters then cooked in a sort of ranchero sauce.

The citrusy green tomatillo sauce on the Enchiladas Verde make them a fine choice, but if your tastes lean (as mine do) to something more exotic, you might try instead the enchiladas under a rich, brown blanket of Señora Leal's classic Mole – another Southern Mexican specialty – originally created in 1650 by a Dominican nun in Puebla for a special dinner for the viceroy of New Spain.

The Steak a La Mexicana is not chopped steak as advertised, but minicubes of beef in an intense, rust-red tomato sauce full of onions and peppers – a nice departure from the usual fajitas.

A favorite Central Mexican snack food that I just recently discovered is Sopes. Similar to both chalupas and gorditas, sopes are puffy "little boats" of corn masa with their rims pinched up to contain various fillings – minced beef, shredded chicken, or diced avocado, all garnished with shredded lettuce, tomatoes and crumbled cajete (fresh white cheese).

Another recent revelation for me has been Milanesa – the Mexican version of the Italian dish, veal Milanese. Although beef is often used in Mexico to make Milanesa, this is not the case at El Paraiso. A veal cutlet is pounded paper-thin, lightly coated with a well-seasoned batter and fried parchment-crisp. Even better, ask for a fried egg on it and turn it into a sort of Mexican veal Holstein. It is served with the better-than-average rice and beans and the house papas fritas – huge wedges of fried potatoes.

The Torres' have renovated recently, so El Paraiso can now be "paradise" to up to ninety people at a time. Fortunately, none of the cozy, neighborhood feel has been lost. Beatriz says they draw quite a crowd from the downtown area at lunch time, but are happy to hold a table if you call ahead. They also take orders over the phone so your food is ready and waiting when you arrive. "Some people are in a hurry, you know."

EL PUEBLITO PLACE

1423 Richmond Avenue
Houston, Texas 77006
713/520-6635

Type of Cuisine: Guatemalan/Mexican
Bar: Wine and Beer
Dress: Casual
Entertainment: No
Payment: American Express, MasterCard, Visa
Entrée Range: $2.99-$6.95
Recommended Dishes:
Quesadillas: Las Locas, Vegetariana
El Costeño Plate (Beef)
Pollo Maya
Tacos Marinos (Fish Tacos)
Snapper Tilapia (Special)
Caribbean Snapper
Fried Plantains
Dessert: Flan
Hours: Breakfast: Monday-Sunday, 7:00a.m.-11:00a.m.
Lunch and Dinner: Sunday-Wednesday, 11:00a.m.-9:00p.m.
Thursday-Saturday, 11:00a.m.-11:00p.m.
Reservations: Accepted

Warm, sultry breezes blow from the general direction of Central America. It isn't just the Gipsy Kings playing in the background, but the merrily-syncopated sounds of cumbia – an upbeat conga-like dance music. El Pueblito Place looks like another brand-new Mexican restaurant, but it's not. The short menu successfully navigates the border between owners, husband and wife, Eduardo and Monica Lopez's native countries, Guatemala and Mexico. There is his side of the menu and her side of the menu, but always with the objective to keep dishes as light and healthful as possible.

"Make it colorful. Make it delicious. Make it fresh," says the young, fit-looking Eduardo Lopez. "That is our goal. So you can eat and not feel guilty about it. We don't want to spend too many hours in the gym!"

Tropical fruits and chiles – dried and fresh – are skillfully combined from the beginning as chips are placed on the table with not one, but two salsas – a smoky tomato-based salsa that Lopez refers to as a Chirmol and the house signature salsa made with crushed pineapple.

A good impression is made instantly by this sunny-yellow salsa with the snap of serrano peppers, garlic, lime and just the right amount of cilantro. It contrasts nicely with the chirmol, a recipe that takes Lopez back to childhood in Guatemala City.

"I can remember when I was about seven, watching my

mother and grandmother placing tomatoes, serranos and onions on the hot charcoals." When the skins would brown and their natural sugars caramelize, he says they would remove them from the fire and crush them coarsely with a rock. How did they eat the chirmol in Guatemala? "With freshly made tortillas," he says.

Fresh flour tortillas are made twice a day at El Pueblito. This is rare these days and it makes a huge difference.

He says his mother, who lives here now and supervises the kitchen, had a little tortilla factory in Guatemala City, but that is was his wife, Monica, who insisted they make tortillas from scratch so that their food would be "fresher, more authentic and more like homemade food."

Indeed, all seven dishes on Monica's side of the menu from the Texas Burrito to the Las Locas Quesadillas feature the divinely-thin crisp tortillas.

Quesadillas are fashioned with a choice of four fillings and they are superb. My favorite is Las Locas ("the crazy ones") with a perfect mix of grilled chicken, beef fajitas, Monterrey Jack and Cheddar cheese. The Quesadilla Vegetariana – with sautéed mushrooms, spinach, Cheddar cheese and Queso Fresco Mexicano – runs a very close second. The crawfish-filled Bayou Quesadillas, on the other hand, is the only dish on either side of the menu that I cannot recommend. They were oddly-seasoned and made with crawfish that doesn't live up to the same high standards of freshness as the other seafood at El Pueblito.

The Tacos Marinos ("fish tacos"), created with the whole sweet chunks of grilled red snapper are a fine example. They are excellent and take especially well to a spoonful of the sweet/tart pineapple salsa. The two tacos marinos come with a cup of good, garlicky black beans simmered slowly, "like my grandmother used to make us for practically every meal when I was growing up. I use all the seasonings she used – garlic, onions, cilantro, but no pork!" Lopez continues that "in the beginning I wanted to serve black beans with all the plates." I'm glad, however, that Monica prevailed because the Mexican-style charro beans that accompany most of the quesadillas and about half of the other dishes are spectacular. It is the inspired pairing of a little pineapple salsa with the other usual ingredients – oregano, onions and garlic – that transforms these pinto beans from the mundane to the sublime.

On the flip side of the menu, food friends have raved about the filleted Red Snapper prepared a couple of different ways and it's good, but it's the Carne Asada that I consider to be El Pueblito's finest accomplishment.

"They are similar to what you call 'fajitas' here," Lopez says, "but I'm using the tender, inside skirt of the cow." Plus –

and this is the important part – he is marinating the beef overnight in a purée of, among other things, poblano peppers, garlic and papaya, which serves as both a natural tenderizer and flavoring agent. They are grilled quickly so they are crusty on the outside and juicy on the inside. My choice is the El Costeño Plate where the carne asada is sliced and presented simply with flawless guacamole, and Rice "Colorado" – a nicely-seasoned rice with onions, carrots and peas – charro beans, and a couple of homemade tortillas.

Like the carne asada, the Pollo Maya is a recipe that originated with Lopez's mother. Again, pains are taken to marinate the chicken breast, he says, a minimum of eight hours before it is cooked on the charbroiler. The result is an incredibly moist, well-seasoned chicken breast.

It's a toss-up between the two snappers on the menu – the Caribbean and the Santa Monica. In both cases, the snapper is filleted, marinated in pineapple salsa, then cooked covered on the flat grill. I lean toward the Caribbean because it is served with black beans and long sweet ribbons of plantains grilled in butter, but I liked the Santa Monica fashion – cooked with a little butter and lemon the way (Lopez says) his Santa Monica prefers it.

The Snapper Tilapa, an occasional weekend special, was best of all. The filet of snapper is tucked into a banana leaf with a little chirmol, a piece of white, soft Queso Mexicano and spinach, tied and steamed in a hot oven.

Another special – off-the-menu, but available by request – is what Lopez calls Mixed Appetizer. Chunks of carne asada, chicken breast, and marinated and grilled shrimp are threaded onto wooden skewers with pieces of onion, bell peppers and tomatoes, and spiked into a hollowed-out pineapple with a sterno can placed in the center to create a fire. It's a festive dish and a nice way to start the meal, particularly if you're having a little party.

There is one red or white California wine and a better selection of Mexican or domestic beers to choose from.

For dessert, Fried Plantains can be ordered a la carte. They come with sour cream, but Lopez says that in Guatemala they would sprinkle sugar on them if they were eating them as a "sweet." Or, a small dense square of Flan is a fitting finish to the meal. It is flavored with a little brandy and embellished further by a drizzling of cajeta – caramel-like sweetened, Mexican dark cream. I love that time taken to decorate the dessert plate with icing make from colored sugar. A nice touch.

EL REY

910 Shepherd Drive
Houston, Texas 77007
713/802-9145

Type of Cuisine: Cuban/Mexican
Bar: No
Dress: Casual
Entertainment: No
Payment: Cash Only
Entrée Range: $2.99-$5.00
Recommended Dishes:
- Chicken Tortilla Soup
- Hot Acapulco Sandwich
- Cuban Sandwich
- Grilled Fajita Steak
- Rotisserie Chicken
- Cuban Coffee

Hours: Breakfast: Monday-Thursday, 7:00a.m.-10:30a.m.
Friday-Saturday, 7:00a.m.-12:00p.m.
Full Menu: Monday-Thursday, 8:00a.m.-9:30p.m.
Friday-Saturday, 8:00a.m.-10:00p.m.
Reservations: Not Accepted

Central Mexico meets Havana on the southeast corner of Shepherd and Washington. This is drive-through heaven where a classic Cubana (Cuban sandwich) shares equal billing with the best Chicken Tortilla Soup this side of Tijuana.

Cuban expatriate, Manny Diaz, says that when he bought and gussied up this twenty-year-old Kentucky Fried Chicken site, he couldn't figure out which way to lean. "I couldn't decide to go on the Cuban side or the Mexican side. I like both (cuisines) and I've been pretty much involved in both cultures. So, I decided 'why not a little bit of each?'"

Diaz's Cuban grandmother's powerfully-concentrated caldo de pollo is transformed into a full-fledged work of art when combined with nearly-translucent ribbons of tortillas and clumps of fresh avocado, and three different kinds of cheese. Chockfull of shredded rotisserie chicken – another specialty – and tinted orange from tomatoes and ground cascabel and chipotle chiles, it is rich with garlic and has the citrusy aftertaste of lime. One suggestion. If you're ordering the Chicken Tortilla Soup to go, take twice as much as you think you need. You won't want to share.

Since opening nine months ago, Diaz says he's surprised that customers come (at lunch) from "as far away as the Galleria for a cup of soup or a Cuban sandwich." I'm not surprised.

All three sandwiches listed under House Specialties are

neatly constructed on long narrow loaves of what Diaz calls Cuban bread, baked especially for Cuban restaurants by a Cuban baker at Royal Bakery. The sandwiches are then pressed in a plancha – a sort of waffle iron used expressly for this purpose.

"I'm particularly proud of the Cuban sandwich," Diaz tells me. "It took me three months to get that right." Great pains have been taken to achieve authenticity. Until he could find just the right jamon en dulce (Cuban sweet ham), dill pickles and Swiss cheese (he uses Emmentaler), he was having his sister ship the genuine articles from Miami where she lives. Thin slices of tender pierna de puerco (roast pork) round out this quartet of ingredients. The roast pork is marinated overnight in naranja agria (sour orange), fresh garlic, black pepper and oregano, tied off and roasted for what seems like an eternity (eight hours).

The Cubana is a fine piece of work. But so is Diaz's invention – the Hot Acapulco Sandwich. Pan Cubano (Cuban bread) is slathered with a smoky paste of ground chipotle chiles, a thin layer of the (Mexican) frijoles a la charro, chunks of rotisserie chicken and Swiss cheese, all warmed (and flattened) in the plancha.

Another winner, the Steak Sandwich, is made with a thin bistec de palomilla – round steak cooked quickly with lots of sweet onion on the flat top grill. As good as it is alone, it is improved by requesting that a piece of Swiss cheese be added before its trip into the plancha.

There is a choice of eight Mexican style sandwiches or tortas. Unlike the Cuban sanwiches, the Mexican tortas distinguish themselves by being made on the doughy bobbin-shaped bolillos (rolls).

The best is the Torta de Milanesa de Res (grilled breaded steak). Round steak is pounded paper-thin, dusted with seasoned flour and grilled crisply brown. Iceberg lettuce, cool slices of tomato and avocado top the buttery, golden-crusted Milanesa.

The Chicken Fajitas are good, but the Beef Fajitas are fabulous. Sliced thin as a quarter so the edges curl appealingly when they are cooked on the grill, care is taken to marinate the beef in garlic, chiles and lime. The fajitas are covered with onions caramelized on the grill.

The smallish, crisp-skinned Rotisserie Chicken is in a category all its own. Available "entero" (whole) or "medio" (half), the chicken is marinated overnight and cooked slowly on a gas rotisserie "made for us in Mexico," says Diaz. If you order the rotisserie chicken as a plato (lunch plate), you get good Mexican charro beans and way-above-average Mexican rice. But why not go tropical with an order of fried green plantains (Plantanos Fritos), and the Diaz family Cuban black beans (Frijoles Negros) cooked for hours with sofrito – chopped and sautéed onions, garlic and peppers – in the time-honored fashion.

El Rey opens at 7:00 a.m. and features breakfast for several hours. There are Huevos Rancheros, and eggs with assorted pairings of chorizo (sausage), papas (potatoes), and my favorite – Huevos a la Mexicano (tomato, onions and peppers). Best of all, though, is the Menudo, "breakfast of champions" (available exclusively Fridays and Saturdays). Go early, especially if the weather is cool. The menudo's fine reputation has spread, and they sell out quickly.

Tiny, glorious tacitas – thimble-size cups – of fragrant, head-clearing Cuban coffee are consumed all day by customers perched on one of the twenty black vinyl bar stools or simply standing at the counter.

But whether you eat-in, call-in-and-pick-up, or drive-through, Diaz – who hopes this is the first of several El Rey's – is well on his way to giving fast food a good name.

EMPANADAS BY MARINI

6154-B Westheimer
Houston, Texas 77057
713/952-5111

Type of Cuisine: Argentinean
Bar: No
Dress: Casual
Entertainment: No
Payment: American Express, MasterCard, Visa
Prices: Empanadas $1.75 a piece, $2.75 doublesize
Recommended Dishes:
Empanadas: (#1) Beef "Gaucho Argentino" (with cheese)
(#4) Texas Bar-B-Q (with cheese)
(#5) Italian "Marcello"
(#7) Ham and Cheese
(#9) Viva Zapata
(#11) Fugazetta
(#12) The Vegetarian
(#13) The New Yorker
Sweet Empanadas: (#28) Carnival of the World
(#25) Guayaba (with mozzarella)
(#18) Bananas with Everything
(#19) Apple with Everything
Hours: Monday -Saturday, 11:00a.m.-10:00p.m.
(Closed Sunday)
Reservations: Not Accepted

Pelusa Marini likes to tell a story about the days in the early 70's when she and her husband Marcello first introduced Houstonians to the joys of the Argentinean empanada.

It seems that a customer wandered into their (then) Montrose-area empanaderia, took one look at the picture-perfect, golden brown, half-moon shaped pastries sealed with the distinctive Argentinean flourish – the braided gaucho rope tie – and assumed the empanadas must be made by machine. "He said, 'Do you have a special machine from Argentina?' And my husband said, 'Yes, we have a special machine!'" she laughs. "He called me out of the kitchen and said, 'Here is the machine!' That guy was from Channel 13. I showed him how I made the empanadas by hand and he put us on the 5:00 p.m. and 10:00 p.m. news! After that, we were packed and for 17 years people came from all over to eat our empanadas."

At one time the Marinis had five empanada houses, but when the kitchen of the location in Montrose caught fire in 1985, they "stopped making empanadas," Pelusa says. Fortunately for us, as of December, 1997, they are back in business with partners, fellow Argentineans and tango fanatics, Alicia and Juan Carlo Suarez.

Their mission this time was two-fold. In addition to serving the celebrated empanadas, they hoped to put Alfajores, the unique cake-like Argentinean cookie, on the map. "Oh, they are big business in Argentina, but until now, nobody has them here!" They are superb – buttery cookies filled with creamy caramel (Dulce de Leche) and covered with chocolate. The almond-flavored alfajores look like the white chocolate-covered Oreos that grocery stores sell at Christmas, but trust me, unless you're from Argentina, the flavor will be a revelation to you.

My two favorite types of alfajores – of the four, or sometimes more, available – are the white chocolate-covered almond, and the espresso-flavored coffee alfajores where both the delicate cookie batter and the thin milk chocolate coating benefit from the subtle but rich aftertaste of good espresso.

The putty-colored caramel-flavored dulce de leche is made in the time honored tradition. Whole milk, sugar and a vanilla bean are stirred for hours in a heavy pot on the stove. It is sold in plastic half-pint containers. "We use dulce de leche for everything in Argentina," Pelusa tells me. She adds that Argentinean customers buy it to use as a spread on toast with butter or sometimes cream cheese. (I tried this on a warm, very grainy whole wheat toast and it was divine.) I also liked it sandwiched between two crisp meringue kisses and as a filling for Delicias de Nuez – a chocolate-covered tart with a white chocolate zig-zag on top.

Marini's could easily become known for their pastries now, but as Pelusa says, "People just go crazy for empanadas!" This go-around, the empanadas are fashioned by three generations of Marinis – Pelusa, daughter Debbie, and her sixteen-year-old daughter Ellie. Originally there were one hundred varieties of empanadas to choose from. This time they have (I think wisely) limited themselves to twenty-eight. In the name of research (of course!), I've sampled every single one of them, plus a few off-the-menu combinations. This is how they rate.

Carnival of the World (#28) produced groans of delight all around. Twice as big as the standard size, it is one of the eleven Sweet Empanadas. Debbie Marini says it was inspired by a nut-covered caramel apple she once ate at a county fair in Iowa. Small, still-crisp squares of Granny Smith apples are warmed with dulce de leche, chopped nuts, raisins, a little cinnamon and extra large chocolate chips. The filling is spooned onto a rich round of dough, folded, elegantly sealed and deep-fried in vegetable oil until it bobs to the surface. The outsized specimen is then split open and piped full of freshly whipped cream flavored with dulce de leche with more dulce de leche drizzled on top – truly testimony to the theory that it is impossible to get too much of a good thing!

My second favorite is Guayaba with cream cheese (#25). Guayaba is Spanish for guava, and satiny, deep-red guava paste that tastes like a cross between pineapple and strawberries is paired even more successfully with mozzarella cheese. (This was Pelusa's suggestion and I loved it.)

In fact, I returned to try several of the Meat Empanadas with mozzarella added because Pelusa said she prefers them that way. I quite agree. Starting at the very top with the Beef Gaucho Argentina (#1), "My grandmother's recipe," Pelusa says. Beef is king in Argentina and this is the most traditional empanada. It is filled with ground beef, onions, olives and hard boiled eggs, seasoned with salt, red pepper flakes, oregano and cumin. The Gaucho Argentina was and remains their number one best seller. The tart, emerald-green Chimi-Churri sauce is meant to be spooned onto the meat or any of the empanadas. Or, taken home to use as a marinade for beef or chicken as they do in Argentina. The chopped parsley, garlic, vinegar and oil-based Chimi-Churri sauce is sold by the half-pint.

Another invention of Debbie's, the Texas Bar-B-Q (#4) was wonderful – a lot like a neatly-contained Sloppy Joe with a nice, tomatoey barbecue sauce. (Again, Pelusa was right, the Texas Bar-B-Q empanada was even better with cheese in it.)

Italian Marcello (#5) is an Italian sausage-and-tomato pizza-in-a-pastry, inspired this time by Marcello Marini's grandmother who, like roughly half of Argentina, is of Italian descent.

Of the four listed Cheese Empanadas, the Ham and Cheese (#7) was perfect – diced pieces of baked ham and mozzarella. Add Cheddar cheese and sliced jalapeños and you have Pancho Villa (#8). Viva Zapata (#9) is a sultry mixture of creamy, well-seasoned refried beans, Cheddar cheese, mozzarella, jalapeño slices with a little smoky chipotle pepper sauce. Very nice.

The Vegetarian Empanadas were a big surprise to me. In order of preference, the New Yorker (#13) with whole flowerettes of broccoli in a velvety-bechamel sauce was downright irresistible. The Vegetarian (#12), created on demand for a vegetarian customer twenty-five years ago, has a nice contrast of textures; the crunch of chopped (uncooked) tomatoes, onions and bell peppers, and gooey melted mozzarella cheese. (The Chimi-Churri sauce was particularly good on this one.)

Among the Sweet Empanadas, apart from the extraordinary Carnival of the World and the Guayaba with mozzarella, both the Bananas with Everything (#18) and the Apple with Everything (#19) are heavenly. The bananas and apples, respectively, are chopped and sautéed a little with cinnamon, sugar and walnuts, and marry happily with a little mozzarella cheese.

Sometime soon Empanadas by Marini may have a liquor license and will serve beer, wine and "our Sangria" as Debbie says. But in the meantime, there is a stunning assortment of fresh fruit juices to enjoy with you empanadas and pastries in a variety of combinations from Monkey Juice (with fresh coconut, pineapple and banana) to Paraiso Tropical (with puréed mango, guava and pineapple).

EMPRESS

5419A FM 1960 West
Houston, Texas 77069
281/583-8021

Type of Cuisine: Franco-Asian
Bar: Wine and Beer
Dress: Nice Casual
Entertainment: No
Payment: All Major Credit Cards
Entrée Range: $8.95-$22.50
Recommended Dishes:
White Glove Dinner
Appetizers: Grilled Foie Gras in Bordeau Apple Sauce
Avocados and Dungeness Crab
Entrées: Crispy Shrimp
Filet Mignon a la Empress
Grilled Jumbo Scallops
Grilled Mahi-Mahi
Baby Lamb Chops
Boneless Quail with Foie Gras
Desserts: Chocolate Soufflé
Triad of Creme Brûlée
Hours: Monday-Thursday, 11:00a.m.-2:30p.m., 5:00p.m.-10:00p.m.
Friday, 11:00a.m.-2:30p.m., 5:00p.m.-10:30p.m.
Saturday, 5:00p.m.-10:30p.m.
(Closed Sunday)
Reservations: Accepted

In the eighteenth century noted French gastronome, Jean-Anthelme Brillat-Savarin, wrote in *La Physiologie du Goût* (The Physiology of Taste) that "the discovery of a new dish does more for the happiness of man than the discovery of a star." This may explain why diners at the Empress seem to be having such a good time. On a nightly basis, owner and chef, Scott Chen, regularly creates one mini-masterpiece after another for his multi-course gourmet extravaganza that he calls the White Glove Dinner.

What began eleven years ago as a Chinese restaurant, Empress of China, in a new prospering suburb of Houston has evolved into a full-fledged gastronomic bungee jump. No longer fettered by any form of convention, Chen now fuses the best of various cultures to create his highly individual style of cuisine.

"Chinese cooking techniques are good, but the food is too fatty. So, I decided to open a Chinese restaurant and serve Oriental food with no fat, no grease and only use very light cooking oils when necessary."

In fact, he uses broth instead of oil to sauté most dishes.

None of his creations suffer by the absence of these less healthy ingredients. On the contrary, the flavors seem more immediate, more intense. So I see it as an added bonus that food this delicious happens also to be so low in calories and cholesterol that he's been recognized by both the American Heart Association and the American Cancer Society for his efforts.

His other idea for Empress of China was to expand his wine list as much as possible. "People didn't know as much about wine in those days. No one associates fine wine with Chinese food, but I thought 'why not?' I started doing wine tastings, actual seminars staged by vintners and their sales staff. I began developing menus – five or six courses of dishes I would create to pair with each wine. It was fun! Exciting! My regular customers, who were invited by mailing list, loved it!"

The wine list is so extensive now with such an extraordinary assortment of vintages and nationalities represented, that it weighs as much the unabridged version of *War and Peace.* It is not at all surprising that Empress has received the "Wine Spectator's" Award of Excellence for three years in a row. (It is important to note that Chen does not and has never served hard liquor in his restaurant.)

The White Glove Dinner evolved from those early tasting menus and Chen found that he loved to experiment, to be liberated from the confines of the menu. "The initial idea behind these new dishes was East meets West. Why not borrow the best from all cultures – France, China, Japan? I traveled a lot to New York and California, always eating at the finest restaurants, trying new dishes. When I go into a place I say 'what's this guy doing?' I come home, read some books and test it, test it, test it, in my kitchen. For instance, my Chocolate Soufflé which has no egg yolks or flour I must have tested a hundred times before I got it right."

When I tell him that the soufflé was flawless – light, with an intense, lingering flavor of chocolate – he says, "It's because I use the best chocolate I can buy." Which leads us to his current obsession. Quality has become his mantra in his quest internationally for the best possible ingredients. "Quality is most important. If you only order the best quality of things...it's easy to cook it."

Well, yes and no. In my experience, it takes some expertise to pansear even perfect foie gras to just the right degree of doneness – crisp on the outside, rosy and creamy on the inside. I'd drive to Wisconsin for his Grilled Foie Gras in Bordeau Apple Sauce, a regularly available appetizer. Chen agrees it's now one of his signature dishes and always includes foie gras in some incarnation in the White Glove Dinner. He says, "Some people are a little afraid of it, but those who know it, love it."

Those who don't know, should try it.

Chen's cooking style and emphasis had clearly changed, so a year ago he dropped "of China" and the name became simply "Empress." The current menu is divided into several distinct categories; White Glove Gourmet Dinner, Pacific Rim Cuisine and Oriental Favorites.

The Oriental Favorites still exist out of respect for his earliest customers. "I'd like to take some of these dishes off the menu but I have customers who have come here for ten years who would miss them."

Of the regularly available menu items, he cites two dishes listed under Pacific Rim as the restaurant's most popular entrées: Crispy Shrimp with Honey Coated Walnuts and Filet Mignon a la Empress.

The shrimp are remarkable – barely coated in an ethereal layer of egg white and quickly wok-fried, but the filet mignon is in a class by itself. Chen does not exaggerate when he claims that "you will not taste beef like this anywhere." (Again, he means the quality). He prepares the Filet a la Empress in a classic French steak au poivre studded with peppercorns, panseared and flambéed with cognac, but with no butter or cream to bind the sauce. He uses Chinese vintage oyster sauce and a light wine vinegar instead.

While it is possible to construct a perfectly delightful meal by choosing dishes off the menu, my suggestion would be to abandon all budgetary constraints, settle in, and let Chen work his magic. One surprise after another awaits the adventurous who are willing to put themselves in Chen's wildly innovative and extremely capable hands. The White Glove Dinner has become so successful, Chen claims that fifty percent of the meals served every night are these tasting menus. "Especially when people have a corporate account."

There are three options to choose from four ($48.00 per person), five ($58.00) or six (68.00) courses. Each dinner begins with two complimentary courses "from the chef and that doesn't include the dessert course. So, it's actually more like seven, eight and nine courses."

We ordered the White Glove Dinner with the maximum number of courses (in the name of research, of course) and found each course to be skillfully prepared and beautiful presented. One show stopper was the Avocado and Dungeness Crabmeat and jumbo prawns with tomato, sweet onion, jalapeño pepper and cilantro in honey horseradish. The avocado was sliced impossibly thin and folded over itself in delicate petals. When I asked how he does this, Chen says, "Practice! Practice! Practice!" and adds that he's prepared this dish on television on the Discovery Channel's Great Chefs series.

That was our first official course. It was preceded by two complimentary courses – a pastry, a sort of turnover filled with highly-seasoned minced beef placed on a light cream sauce; and a variation of the aforementioned Crispy Shrimp with Honey Coated Walnuts (this time in a delicate caviar sauce).

Warm, crusty freshly-baked dinner rolls distinguished by the addition of potato to the dough, arrives with a pot of sweet creamery butter Chen has lightened with a little honey and cream cheese. "I think regular butter is too heavy!"

Next comes silky medallions of crisped Foie Gras supported by a handful of stringent arugala and tomato dressed in a light vinaigrette. Then one perfect Ravioli filled with a mixture of minced veal, shrimp and chives garnished with pieces of poached lobster in a mushroom champagne sauce.

Our fifth (and favorite) course was the Grilled Jumbo Scallops with Basil with small seasonal vegetables and walnuts in light brown sauce. Again, when he says "grilled," technically he means panseared "quickly over very high temperature." The sauce is a reduction of beef consommé, red wine vinegar and soy sauce with a little black pepper.

The fish course, like everything, changes constantly. Ours was a delicious, deceptively simple, Grilled MahiMahi in Balsamic Vinaigrette with string beans, but the following week Chen said he had just received some fabulous yellowtail tuna from Japan.

The last course before dessert is always meat. We had a perfect Grilled Baby Lamb Chop propped against a risotto sweetened with finely diced Chinese wine-infused pork sausage, lop cheung. Another possible meat course might be Filet Mignon or something that sounds divine – Boneless Quail with Foie Gras.

I wish I could tell you we were full, but we were not. But the courses are small and it's a good thing too, because that Chocolate Souffle was just one of six desserts that comprised our last course, Assortment of Desserts. It shared the plate with a Fudge Brownie and Coffee Mousse with chocolate, strawberry and mango sauce, Chocolate Walnut Cheesecake in caramel sauce á la mode and a Triad of Créme Brulées: banana, chocolate and strawberry with fresh raspberries served á la mode. They were all exquisite, each better than the next.

Is it any wonder that this culinary wizard has been a guest chef for three consecutive years at the James Beard Foundation dinners? The Foundation's newsletter recently gushed with the following encomium, "His unique Franco-Asian cuisine left diners in awe. His striking presentations, startling flavor combinations and crosscultural wine pairings defied every . . . stereotype."

EPICURE BAKERY AND TEA ROOM

2005-C West Gray
Houston, Texas 77019
713/520-6174

Type of Cuisine: European-Style Café
Bar: Wine and Beer
Dress: Casual
Entertainment: No
Payment: All Major Credit Cards
Entrée Range: $5.50-$8.50
Recommended Dishes:
Entrées: Chicken Salad
Grilled Eggplant and Goat Cheese Sandwich
Tomato Basil Soup
Pasta with Tomato Basil Sauce
Italian Meatballs
Salzburger Beef Goulash
Pastries: Croquembouche
Gateau St. Honoré
Viennese Apple Strudel
Strawberry Napolean
Hours: Monday-Thursday, 8:00a.m.-8:00p.m.
Friday-Saturday, 8:00a.m.-11:00p.m.
Sunday, 10:00a.m.-8:00p.m.
Reservations: Not Accepted

If you long to fritter away the hours writing in your journal while nursing a cappuccino and nibbling on a piece of Viennese apple strudel or spend a leisurely afternoon catching up with an old friend over a salad and a glass of wine, I've got just the place for you – the Epicure Bakery and Tea Room.

A well-kept neighborhood secret on West Gray, just two doors East of River Oaks Theater, it is frequented by a particularly closed-mouth contingent of regulars. The Epicure is a comfortable, serene environment where classical music soothes the soul, tables are well-spaced, and customers are encouraged to linger. It's no accident that it feels exactly like a European café.

Iranian brothers Amir and Khan Esmailkhanloo opened the Epicure in May of 1990 as a "real Europe-style bakery – just pastries and coffee." Indeed, he says 90% of his customers are regulars, many of whom are European or South American, "real café people – they love that type of Viennese café atmosphere and they like the pastries. In Europe, they never rush – they sit, they enjoy their coffee."

Both brothers moved to Houston from Vienna where they had lived for fifteen years. They attended the Vienna Culinary School where they both became Konditor Miester or master baker. "In the beginning, it was just a bakery, then customers began asking, 'Why don't you have ice cream?'" So, naturally they began making their own and it is fabulous – light, fruity sorbets of mango and fresh raspberry share the bill with unconscionably rich vanilla, chocolate and a pistachio – good enough to convert even the most die hard anti-pistachio ice cream eaters.

Next came salads and soups. "Within six months, people began coming in asking what we had for lunch, so we thought, why not prepare a few simple things?" Khan says, "The Chicken Salad is the first salad we served here. It's one of my brother's recipes." It is sublime – shimmering slabs of tender, barely poached chicken breasts tossed with a creamy, but light liaison that Khan says is 80% homemade yoghurt and 20% mayonnaise, toasted slivered almonds, chopped scallions and seasoned with salt and a little white pepper. There is nothing simpler or better. Khan admits, "It is something I eat every day and I never get tired of it." There are ten salads to choose from now and they are all above reproach. From the good, garlicy Caesar made with three kinds of mustard offered plain or topped with grilled chicken breast (or grilled salmon as a special one day), to a heaping mound of freshly made tabouli served with a square of briny feta cheese, sliced onions and tomatoes.

Of the thirteen sandwiches listed, all served on freshly made whole wheat baguette, my favorite is the Grilled Eggplant and Goat Cheese – creamy goat cheese is spread luxuriously on one half of the whole wheat baguette and topped with sliced tomato, slender pieces of eggplant seasoned with virgin olive oil and garlic, then grilled, and fresh spinach leaves lightly dressed with a little balsamic vinegar and oil and warmed gently in the oven. All sandwiches are served with a fine Cole Slaw made simply of white and red cabbage, shredded carrots, vinegar, yoghurt, mayonnaise, salt and white pepper. Khan says it's a recipe from a Hungarian partner he once had.

In fact, any recipes that aren't Amir's, Khan has garnered from years of extensive travel through Europe. "Many of these recipes are very popular in Europe. I travel to Italy, Switzerland or Germany where I have many friends in the restaurant and hotel business, and when I try something new I like, I always ask for the recipe." This explains the internationally eclectic menu.

While the Tomato Basil Soup, fragrant with basil and thickened with almost-dissolved pieces of potatoes and onions warmed my soul one rainy day, the Pasta with Homemade Tomato Basil Sauce is one of the best and most satisfying pasta dishes I've eaten outside an Italian restaurant. A simple reduction of fresh tomatoes, basil and garlic is thickened with a little cream, ladled over penne, shell pasta "or any kind that holds the sauce well" and topped with freshly grated Parmesan cheese and chopped parsley for color. All entrées are served with creamery butter and a basket of freshly baked whole wheat focaccia bread.

The Epicure is not wed to dogmatic authenticity. For instance, the dish listed on the menu as Italian Meatballs is closer in appearance to what we might think of as Swedish meatballs than anything I've seen come out of an Italian kitchen, but I'd order them again in a second. Moist, finely minced grilled beef meatballs are aswim in a pool of mushroom-flecked light brown sauce. It is served over exotic, nut-like basmati rice with steamed broccoli.

Should you be peckish from the strain of following subtitles of the latest foreign film next door, some Scrambled Eggs with a little ham and cheese and a buttery croissant might be just the thing, or any one of the delicious, handsomely composed omelettes. Breakfast is served as long as the restaurant is open. All egg dishes share a platter with fresh seasonal fruit and a non-traditional preparation of the Swiss standard, Rösti Potatoes. Usually shredded and browned in a pan one side at a time like pancakes, Epicure's are left in big pieces, parboiled, peeled, then sautéed in a pan with butter and parsley until crisp.

Two other entrées not to be missed are the Salzburger Beef Goulash and the chicken curry. One of Khan's favorites, the goulash is an old recipe that a Hungarian family shared with him. It is a rich tomato-based stew seasoned intensely with garlic, onions, caraway, marjoram and, of course, a generous measure of sweet Hungarian paprika. He says the Chicken Curry is equally popular and the flavor of the yoghurt-laced homemade chicken broth-based sauce is wonderful.

Make no mistake though, as good as all these dishes are, their reason for existence is pastry. As Khan says, "It is, after all, our specialty." In *The Book of Household Management,* 19th Century English culinary authority Mrs. Isabella Beeton wrote, "If there be any poetry at all in meals, or the process of feeding, there is poetry in the dessert." She probably didn't have a Mississippi mud pie in mind when she said that, but something more akin to the elaborate French confection, Croquembouche – just one of the many classic desserts made to order at the Epicure. The croquembouche, which literally translated means "cracks in your mouth," is an impressive conical tower of little individual profiteroles or cream puffs cloaked in caramel, stacked on top of each other and finished off with a fine netting of spun sugar – a bargain at twenty dollars for a minimum of twenty-five pieces. Other classics are Gâteau St. Honoré, named for the patron saint of French pastry chefs, perfect Éclairs (both mocha and chocolate) and authentic Viennese Apple Strudel.

Often considered the national dessert of both Austria and Hungary, the strudel's roots go back much farther to the middle Eastern invention of phyllo dough brought West by the invading Turks in the 16th Century. Gossamer thin and crisp as parchment, Viennese pastry chefs boast that a good strudel dough should be "thin enough to read a newspaper through." (Epicure's is!)

Khan says the Strawberry Napoleon, alternating layers of puff pastry and créme patisiere studded with strawberries, is his most popular individual pastry, but I could write a sonnet or two about the dense, ambrosial Chocolate Mousse or what I think may just be the best Tiramisu in town.

Custom-made cakes for special occasions make up a large part of their business. One day I was in, they had just completed a wedding cake for three hundred people. It was spectacularly beautiful, with graduated tiers garnished with fresh lilies and orchids. I am certain it tasted every bit as good as it looked. According to the book I saw of past creations, one is limited only by one's imagination. Khan says everything is hand done, so at least a week's notice is necessary.

FUNG'S KITCHEN

7320 Southwest Freeway, Suite 115
Houston, Texas 77074
713/779-2288

Type of Cuisine: Chinese/Seafood/Game
Bar: Wine and Beer
Dress: Nice Casual
Entertainment: No
Payment: All Major Credit Cards
Entrée Range: $7.50-$28.50
Recommended Dishes:
Appetizers: Steamed Oysters on the Half Shell with Garlic Sauce
Shrimp Rolls Wrapped in Bacon
Crisp Duck Rolls
Pan Fried Dumplings
Entrées: All Seasonal Specials, i.e. Alaskan King Crab Steamed with Garlic and Ginger
Tsing Tao Lobster with Black Pepper Butter Sauce
Baked Soft Shell Crabs with Black Pepper Butter Sauce
Deep Fried Squid in Spicy Salt
Fried Crispy Stuffed Eggplant
Snow Pea Tips with Garlic
Shredded Pork Pan Fried Noodle
Baked Pineapple Fried Rice
Roast Quail
Sizzling Beef
Pork Ribs with Orange Sauce
Hours: Monday-Sunday, 10:30a.m.-10:00p.m.
Reservations: Accepted

"I cook Hong Kong style," Hoi Fung says plainly. This only begins to explain the intriguing variety of more than four hundred dishes offered at Fung's Kitchen, and the truly amazing inventiveness with which they are prepared.

Hoi Fung moved to Hong Kong in 1961 when he was six from the Canton region of China where, as he says, "there's a lot of famous cooking," and he quickly followed in the footsteps of his family. "My grandpa, my pa and all of my uncles were chefs. I began to learn to cook at my father's restaurant (in Hong Kong) in 1971."

There are many things that distinguish the "Hong Kong style" from other more traditional methods of Chinese cooking. In a practical sense, he says that a much larger wok (36 inches) is used and that foods are cooked quickly over very high temperatures. But more importantly, the chefs in Hong Kong tend to be young, classically trained, and – to hear Fung tell it – ride the crest of the ever-changing tastes and influences of their clientele.

"There's a lot of competition in Hong Kong. But the chefs are smart; they know the market. People in Hong Kong like seafood. They like something light – not too rich. Also they have some style." Apparently in Hong Kong a tremendous emphasis is placed on the presentation of the dish – something we're more accustomed to seeing at Thai restaurants.

"I can cut the carrot. I can make a bird. I can make an eagle. I can make a fish. Even for a very small party, I give them very nice decorations. Sometimes I go home and cut the carrots until midnight and I feel confident to prepare the party for the next day. People eat with their eyes as well as their stomachs, you know."

Fung says that many of the dishes on the menu are old family recipes. A good example is the deeply-satisfying Hong Kong style Wonton Noodle Soup available only at lunch. "It has been in the family for at least ninety years," he says.

Hang on to your gastronomic hats because much of the rest is pure invention. Fung says he loves to cook and often stays late after the restaurant is closed to experiment with new dishes in an effort to duplicate (or usually) improve upon dishes and sauces that he has sampled at French or Japanese restaurants on his travels. Not wed to dogmatic authenticity, he serves the Indian-inspired jasmine rice rather than the standard short or medium grain rice traditionally used in Chinese kitchens.

To prevent the task of ordering from being completely overwhelming, Fung has wisely divided the seemingly infinite assortment of choices into twenty-five neat categories. When asked why the elegant, leather-bound menu is so long, he says that he adds "new stuff" all the time to prevent regular customers he has had for the several years Fung's Kitchen has been open from getting bored.

As in Hong Kong, seafood is featured at Fung's Kitchen, and I can't think of a better way to whet the appetite than with the sublime steamed oysters on the half shell with garlic sauce. Perfect, plump oysters with translucent flecks of chopped ginger and garlic peek out from under a vivid green blanket of cilantro leaves and scallions. A masterful piece of work, they were good enough to convert al least one non-oyster eater at our table. (Like all other seafood dishes, they are available only when Fung is pleased with the raw product.)

Next an order of pan fried dumplings is a must; so delicate, the usual "pot stickers" seem oafish by comparison. (The Japanese influence is clear here.) The wrapper is handmade and rolled so thin that the filling is visible through it. Fung feels that the addition of garlic to the dipping sauce is one thing that makes them so special. Two other favorites that can be ordered individually or together are the Shrimp Rolls wrapped with bacon – well-seasoned, finely ground shrimp sheathed in almost transparent pieces of bacon – and the extraordinary Crispy Duck Rolls – small, bronzed cylinders of shredded duck wrapped in "Hong Kong style" egg roll skins rolled thin.

Fung prides himself on having "something that nobody else has," and in keeping with this notion the fish tank is teeming with some unfamiliar, fairly fierce-looking creatures. A good example is the geoduck clam which weighs about three pounds and has what looks like the last six inches of an elephant's trunk protruding from its shell. It's large enough – with the meat inside and outside the shell – for Fung to prepare it in two different styles.

A spectacular special not to miss is the spiky, prehistoric-looking Alaskan King Crab. The sweet, delicate meat bears no resemblance to the more familiar frozen variety and responds well to being steamed with a little ginger and garlic. The Alaskan King Crab season is extremely brief – so, if it has passed when you visit – look forward to ordering it next year.

Fresh codfish is another unique taste treat. Currently an off-the-menu special, the snow-white firm-fleshed fish arrives red-rimmed like Chinese barbecue pork and is served with a piquant, ruby-red mayonnaise-based sauce.

Lobster is done up in its best bib and tucker in Tsing Tao Lobster with Black Pepper butter sauce. Not so much a sauce as a thin veil of black pepper and finely shredded scallion flavored with a little butter, it is my absolute favorite of the thirteen various preparations of lobster.

Fung's distinctive black pepper butter sauce also takes well to the heavenly baked soft shell crabs. Squid fans should not miss the light, cornstarch cloaked Deep Fried Squid in Spicy Salt.

The two vegetables of note are the Fried Crispy Stuffed Eggplant listed under "Miscellaneous" and the absolutely exquisite sautéed Snow Pea Tips. The stuffed eggplant is almost like a fritter. A piece of eggplant is rolled around a mound of ground shrimp, deep fried, then garnished with bright red ringlets of red jalapeno peppers.

Snow pea tips are the greenery attached to the tops of snow peas and fare best when their slightly peppery, highly addictive fresh taste is coupled with a little chopped garlic. Fung says one of his favorite ways to eat the snow pea tips is to top a green tangled mass with fresh crab meat.

There are twenty-six possibilities listed under "Noodles, Fried Rice." One of my favorites is Shredded Pork Pan-Fried Noodle where a crisply fried bed of vermicelli noodles supports a sauté of tender shredded pork, scallion, mushrooms and bean sprouts.

The Baked Pineapple Fried Rice with Mixed Seafood makes a presentation as attractive as it is delicious. Jasmine rice is stir fried with all manner of sea creatures and diced vegetables, loaded into a pineapple that has been halved horizontally, then covered and baked for twenty minutes in the oven. The rice is moist, and is pineapple-scented rather than flavored, so it's not sweet. I also loved Fung's rendition of Sautéed Thin Rice noodle "Singapore Style" – a spicy, curry-flavored nest of noodles with shrimp, scallions and curly brown wrinkles of scrambled eggs.

Fung is at least as proud of his offering of exotic "Game Meat" as he is of his seafood. He says he thinks wild game is especially popular these days because it's considered much leaner and healthier than beef. I thought two of the best were the Ostrich Meat with Ginger Green Onion which has a flavor and texture that could easily be mistaken for beef, and the chewy but good Alligator Tenderloin with Spicy Salt.

A tamer and even better alternative to the game meat is the oven-roasted, mahogany-brown Roast Plump Georgia Quail served with spicy salt and a tiny saucer of Worcestershire Sauce.

Fung says that the Sizzling Beef is one of their best known dishes. Strips of beef arrive on a hot "sizzling" platter covered with caramelized onions. The dish looks a lot like beef fajitas but fills the room with the unmistakable fragrance of Chinese wine mixed with fresh cracked black pepper. Another standout is the Kung Pao Chicken – moist chunks of breast meat in a sweet, rich brown sauce.

But the absolute winner for me in the "Beef and Pork" category is the Pork Ribs with Orange Sauce. Succulent, bite-sized morsels of pork are still attached to pieces of ribs. They should be eaten with your fingers and are worth every bit of trouble.

Mango Pudding, another old family recipe, is a fine, soothing finish to what I can assure you is a remarkable dining experience.

Reservations are taken and honored. Beer and mostly California wine are served.

GOLDEN BO

8655 Southwest Freeway (at S. Gessner)
Houston, Texas 77074
713/988-1301

Type of Cuisine: Chinese/Dim Sum
Bar: Wine and Beer
Dress: Casual
Entertainment: No
Payment: All Major Credit Cards
Entrée Range: $5.75-$9.50
Recommended Dishes:
Dim Sum: Shrimp Bells
Shrimp with Bacon
Vegetable Dumplings
Siu My (Pork Dumplings)
Chicken Pie
Baby Clams
Flat Rice Noodles
Singapore Noodles
Szechuan-Style Green Beans
Chinese Broccoli
Pot Stickers
Har Goul (Steamed Shrimp Dumplings)
Sweet Coconut Tart
Hours: Dim Sum: Monday-Sunday, 9:00a.m.-3:00p.m.
Chinese Cuisine: Sunday-Thursday, 11:00a.m.-3:00a.m.
Friday-Saturday, 11:00a.m.-4:00a.m.
Reservations: Accepted

"A touch of the heart's delight" is the prettiest gastronomic interpretation I've seen of the ancient Cantonese practice of dim sum. When Golden Bo opened over twenty years ago the clientele was "almost exclusively Cantonese," owner Harvey Truong tells me, "Now, it's about fifty-fifty."

From the slippery to the sublime, Westerners have taken dim sum to heart and made a meal of what was originally intended to be snack food to accompany tea. Although it is available during the week, the weekend is the best time to sample the astonishing assortment of dim sum at Golden Bo.

Of the traditional dishes, the standard bearers for me are the panfried dumplings known as Pot Stickers (#55) on the dim sum menu; delicate Har Goul (#7) – steamed shrimp dumplings; sweet, doughy Char Siu Bao (#14) – steamed BBQ pork bun; Siu My, literally, "cook and sell dumplings" (#8) – steamed pork dumplings; Fresh Shrimp Cheun Fun (#1) – white sheets of soft rice noodles with whole shrimp folded inside; and Nor Mei Gai (#60) – chicken sweet rice lotus leaf. There are sixty-three dim sum dishes listed, all skillfully prepared, but what shares the cart with them is the seemingly infinite variety of new ideas.

Truong began as a waiter at Golden Bo some eighteen years ago and now owns it outright with his two brothers Jimmy and Charlie. After watching the evolution of Golden Bo, he explains that these days most of the glorious off-the-menu dishes are inspired by frequent conversations his chefs have with their counterparts in Hong Kong – the dim sum capital of the world. Golden Bo's repertoire is expanded even further by the addition of at least two favorite Vietnamese appetizers that I spotted – shrimp paste on sugar cane and the transparent soft spring rolls, a nod to Truong and his brothers' native Saigon.

Here are some other new-fangled favorites you are unlikely to see elsewhere. Shrimp Balls are baseball-sized minced shrimp impaled with feathery wisps of what Truong calls "chow mein noodles" are deep fried and absolutely delicious dipped in a mixture of the bright orange-red chili sauce, hot chili oil and soy sauce.

Equally good variations on the shrimp theme are: Shrimp Rolls – similar to spring rolls, the same subtly-seasoned minced shrimp is enclosed in delicate wonton wrappers; and Shrimp with Bacon – where it is molded into the shape of a two bitesize balls and deep fried.

The Vegetable Dumplings are actually a mixture of shrimp and vegetables colored a brilliant green through the clear wrapper by the distinctive addition of chives. These are available both steamed and pan fried. (Both excellent, but I preferred them steamed.)

The Chicken Pie was a revelation to me – Cantonese comfort food – round, flaky layers of buttery pastry filled with diced chicken, flecked with sesame seeds and baked golden brown. Two other "pies" are shaped into triangles and filled, one with barbecued pork and another with a savory minced curried beef. All three are worth sampling.

Tiny, kettle-shaped steamed Siu My in this instance are made with exotic shark fin meat mixed with shrimp instead of the traditional ground pork. They are wonderful and meant to be eaten with a few drops of hot chili oil.

Briny, sweet Baby Clams from Seattle still nestled in their shells are stir fried with pungent black beans and garlic. I was less crazy about the mussels prepared the same way.

Golden Bo is one of the few Asian restaurants in town that goes to the trouble to make their own noodles, and they are exceptional. The Flat Rice Noodles with beef and Singapore Noodles are available to order à la carte or passed as dim sum. Fans of the hearty Thai noodle dish called Pad Thai will love the smoky, densely-flavored Flat Rice Noodles with tender strips of beef, crisp bean sprouts and caramelized onions. It goes especially well with one of my all-time favorite vegetables, Chinese Broccoli – faintly bitter branches of broccoli with just a little green attached are steamed, stacked neatly, and drizzled with the powerfully-concentrated oyster sauce when you beckon them off the cart. Flawless Szechuan-style green beans are also passed.

The colorful, slightly-searing Singapore Noodles pack the kind of wallop they are meant to. Freshly made rice vermicelli is tinted bright yellow with curry and tumeric, and generously flecked with tiny shrimp and chopped vegetables.

Truong agrees that "there is a lot of labor in making your own noodles," but that, if you sell as many as they do, it's worthwhile. He says the noodles are popular all day long, but are featured late at night. Golden Bo is open until 3:00 a.m. Monday through Thursday and 4:00 a.m. Friday and Saturday. Troung says it's busy. "A lot of people know we're open late, especially restaurant people. They don't want to go to JoJo's or Denny's so they come to eat Chinese food. We serve mostly noodles and noodle soup. You don't need to have any more before you go to bed. We have a Hong Kong-style noodle bar."

There are several fine ways to finish a dim sum meal. My favorite has always been with an order of Coconut Pudding (#38) – a soothing jello made from coconut milk and cut in squares. Macaroon lovers will enjoy (#39) the Sweet Coconut Tart.

During the week, Golden Bo has a lunchtime buffet offering as many as forty mostly Cantonese specialties. A limited selection of dim sum is passed during the week, but any of the aforementioned can be ordered à la carte. In order to beat the rush on weekends, think about arriving before 12:30 p.m. or after 2:30 p.m.

For me, all that's needed to enjoy the extraordinary dim sum at Golden Bo's is a pot of chrysanthemum tea, a healthy appetite, and a sense of adventure.

GUS'

909 11th Avenue North
Texas City, Texas 77590
409/948-8112
409/948-8004

Type of Cuisine: Steaks/Barbecue
Bar: Full
Dress: Casual
Entertainment: No
Payment: All Major Credit Cards
Entrée Range: $5.95-$17.95
Recommended Dishes:
Appetizers: Colossal Onion
Steak Trimmings with Cheese
Chicken Wings
Entrées: Filet Mignon
Rib Eye Sandwich
Chicken Picata
Pork Chops
Chicken Wylie (Chicken and Pasta)
Potato Salad
Hours: Lunch: Monday-Friday, 11:00a.m.-2:00p.m.
Dinner: Monday-Thursday, 4:00p.m.-9:00p.m.
Friday, 4:00p.m.-10:00p.m.
Saturday, 11:00a.m.-10:00p.m.
(Closed Sunday)
Reservations: Accepted

In Mel Brooks' Western satire *Blazing Saddles,* one character asks another, "What is a dazzling urbanite like you doing in a rustic setting like this?" For those who don't know better, Texas City might sound like a town out of an old western and "rustic" is just the word Gus' owner Mike Tucker chooses to describe his restaurant.

Gus' really isn't a restaurant you'd come across by accident. After you take a left off Loop 197, the main thoroughfare through Texas City, and drive thirteen long blocks through a series of neighborhoods, even Tucker agrees that "you might easily mistake the bluish-gray building with white trim for an auto parts shop," but you'd be missing some good fun and great steaks served with snappy professionalism in a cozy, animated neighborhood setting.

In 1961, barbecue master Gus Guthier, of German descent from Rosenberg, Texas, opened Gus' at the insistence of his friends to sell his barbecue as part of a meat market in what was actually an ice house across the street from the present location.

His lean German style sausage, fabulous potato salad, brisket and ribs developed such a following that he moved to a larger building across the street, and in 1968 built the structure that is, at least from the exterior, what Gus' is today.

A native of Texas City, Mike Tucker came to work for Gus as a twenty-one year old in 1971. He worked as a manager and after about a year convinced his boss that Gus' should be serving steak as well as barbecue. "In the beginning, we used to have to beg 'em to eat steak. Everybody used to come in for barbecue." So in order to make his case, "I'd cut up these pieces of rib eye and filet mignon, season and cook them in a skillet the way my Mama has always cooked steak. I'd let them try the pieces and the next time they came in, they'd order steak. Now they order steak 70% of the time!" Full of ambition and ideas, Tucker had all sorts of plans for Gus' and on July 1st of 1980, he bought out Gus. Within twenty-four hours, ten friends armed with hammers and nails transformed Gus' four wide-open walls to two rooms with soft lighting (at night) and walls lined with cozy individual booths built "so people could have some privacy and do some business during the day if they wanted, but with spools at the top so I could see if anybody needed anything from the bar. All my friends who came and helped remodel brought the license plates that hang on the walls today. This is why we designed the menu to look like a Texas license plate, circa 1961."

Gus' still sells barbecue and the same two women who took over the task from Gus' wife have been making his famous Potato Salad for thirty years (the secret of which Tucker says, is boiling, peeling and seasoning the potatoes with pickle juice, among other things, while they're hot), but the real story is the steak.

"We cut all our steaks – our rib eye, our filet mignon and our strips. That way we can control the thickness. The Filet Mignon is nothing but center cut tenderloin," and I must say they are like butter. He says he has his mother to thank for how good they are. "My mother was an RN and my father was a locomotive engineer and she'd cook steak on weekends for my two brothers and my dad. She had a way with them. People would come from all over to eat steak at our house." He says his technique is pretty simple. "People think we do all this stuff to it. We just season it right before we put it on a flat grill." He says he sells the most of the filet mignon, "although the rib eye runs a close second since I put it on sale Mondays, Tuesdays and Saturdays a ten ounce rib eye with salad and baked potato for $10.95." After the filet mignon, my next favorite thing on the menu is the Rib Eye Sandwich. A succulent eight ounces of ribeye is paired with a freshly baked homemade roll or "steak bun made from scratch every morning. I send three hundred to five hundred a week out to the surrounding refineries."

He still cooks the trimmings of the filet and rib eye, but now sells these juicy, well-seasoned morsels as an appetizer on a platter with pieces of warm, buttery rolls and cubes of American cheese impaled with toothpicks. If you're not ordering steak as an entrée, it's a great way to try the specialty of the house. Otherwise, my choice as a hot starter is the Colossal Onion. Known to Chili's fans as the "Awesome Blossom," a large white onion is cut by a special machine (now you know), soaked briefly in ice water to remove some of its bite, battered, fried and served with a honey mustard sauce fired up with a little horseradish.

Tucker says his biggest seller after steak is chicken. "I go through forty to sixty cases of skinless, boneless chicken breasts a week. Served either blackened or dusted with a lemon pepper based dry seasoning mix, they are delicious, but the best chicken dish on the menu is the Chicken Picata – two chicken breasts dredged in flour, sautéed in clarified butter and topped with a mushroom-flecked, silky cream sauce made from white wine, lemon juice and whipping cream. A definite winner. I only wish the cream sauce had been warmer the night I sampled it. Also, listed under the "Specialties" are the exceptionally juicy, vibrantly-seasoned center cut grilled Pork Chops. The only dish I'd steer away from is the spaghetti and meatballs. If you're in the mood for pasta, a huge favorite at our table was the off-the-menu pasta dish, Chicken Wylie. Tucker named the dish after Betty Wylie, a favorite customer whom he called upon to try out new dishes. "She always gave me her honest opinion. The cooked spaghetti noodles are sautéed in virgin olive oil in a skillet with salt, pepper, garlic and parmesan cheese. You keep moving it, adding more parmesan cheese as you go until the cheese cooks into the noodles. Then, I grill the chicken breasts until they're almost done, remove the noodles from the pan, add a little white wine, lemon juice and the slices of grilled chicken breasts and a little parsley." Sound delicious? It is. We were grateful to our waitress, Jeanette, for recommending it.

Tucker refers to the atmosphere as "casual and laidback," but there is nothing casual or laidback about the service. He runs a tight ship! The uniformed waitresses in black skirts, white tux shirts and bow ties are attentive, well-informed and have definite opinions about everything on the menu. Sadly, such really great service is the exception rather than the rule these days and is such a pleasure when encountered. Tucker says he has very little turnover in that position, and that he has "a whole restaurant full of good people, thirty-eight employees. I have an excellent kitchen staff." His kitchen manager is Neil

Guthier, Gus' son. This may explain why the food comes out lightning fast. When I asked about it, he said right from the beginning he went after the petrochemical lunch business and felt that it was important to have the "food on the table and have customers out in thirty-five minutes." Whew! He clearly succeeded.

The restaurant is packed at noon, Monday through Friday. Locals gather on Friday nights and the atmosphere resembles a big party more like a neighborhood restaurant in New Orleans. He does a booming takeout business just next door to the restaurant.

The Chocolate Fudge Cake is a memory that lingers – warm, gooey squares of fudgey sheet cake. A perfect way to end the meal.

HARRY'S RESTAURANT

318 Tuam
Houston, Texas 77006
713/528-0198

Type of Cuisine: American/Homestyle
Bar: No
Dress: Casual
Entertainment: No
Payment: Cash Only
Entrée Range: $2.70-$5.95
Recommended Dishes:
Check for Daily Specials: Lamb Shanks
Chicken and Dumplings
Meat Loaf
Seasonal Vegetables
Breakfast: Pancakes
Pork Chops
French Toast
Hours: Monday-Friday, 6:00a.m.-4:00p.m.
Breakfast Monday-Friday, 6:00a.m.-10:45a.m.
Saturday Breakfast Only, 7:00a.m.-1:00p.m.
Reservations: Not Accepted

In the 1960 Jules Dassin classic "Never On Sunday," Illia tries in vain to explain the simple pleasures of life to Homer this way . . . "The sun shines on me. It makes me happy! I eat a good fish. It makes me happy!"

While the simple truth of these statements may have been lost on Homer, it is not on me or John Platsos, owner of Harry's Restaurant on the corner of Tuam and Bagby.

I'm reminded of these words because there, on the menu, under the listing of opening hours Monday through Saturday, are the words "Never on Sunday," an oblique, but telltale reference to the movie and the owner's native Greece.

It's practically the only one. This comfortable, thirty-eight year old restaurant serves basic American homestyle cooking in cafeteria style. Except for an occasional Greek accent, the flavor is predominantly Southern, using time-honored, twenty-five year old recipes for dishes like Squash Casserole and Chicken and Dumplings that I swear could have been stolen out of my family recipe file.

One thing that separates Harry's from other places that serve this style of food is John's slavish devotion to impeccably fresh, top quality meats and vegetables. All vegetables are selected at the Farmers' Market and the meats are the best money can buy – even when he knows he won't turn a profit on a particular dish.

It's easy to celebrate, like Illia, the simple perfection of nature's gifts like fresh Mustard Greens steamed with a little salt, full of flavor in their unadulterated state, or a juicy ten-ounce Pork Chop marinated briefly, then seasoned again and grilled with onions and green peppers (available Thursdays).

There is a short list of five daily specials (a few popular favorites are repeated), and there isn't one I wouldn't recommend. John feels that Harry's claim to fame is their Turkey and Dressing – "Thanksgiving every Monday and Thursday" as the sign says (and he has the crowds at Thursday lunch especially to prove it) but I don't think it's anywhere near what they do best! (The turkey and gravy are above reproach, but I like my dressing better. Doesn't everyone?)

Everything is prepared with impressive care – not only John's light, perfect touch with seasonal vegetables, but he clearly goes that extra mile with all of the daily specials. The Roast Beef is a perfect example – seasoned well and browned first on the stove to seal in the flavor and then roasted to fall-apart perfection with plenty of garlic, Worcestershire sauce, and red wine (fortunately available every day but Wednesdays and Fridays). You also couldn't go wrong by choosing the Chicken Fried Steak with cream gravy (Mondays and Thursdays) or the commendable Liver and Grilled Onions (Wednesdays), but the day I wouldn't miss is Tuesday.

Starting at the top of the list of Tuesday's offerings the Chicken and Dumplings are from your fondest dreams. Silky strips of dumplings and chunks of chicken are cooked down to a rich, creamy base – the very definition of "comfort food."

The usually pedestrian Meat Loaf bears a subtle, striking resemblance in flavor to a Greek dish called "soutzoukakia" or "rolo" when it's made into a loaf exactly as our meat loaf is. John admits that it is a Greek recipe and that it's not the only one on the menu. The Tuesday special currently known as Macaroni Casserole with meat sauce and cheese is about to become a full-fledged "pastitsio," the famous baked pasta classic that pre-dates Italian lasagna. It is layers of seasoned, cooked ground beef and long, thick Greek noodles that resemble uncut macaroni or ziti cooked in a tomato sauce, topped with a classic bechamel sauce and browned until crisp in the oven. My favorite dish any day of the week (but only available on Tuesday) is Lamb Shanks, an unmistakable tip of the hat to not only the Greek meat of choice lamb but also to the style of cooking it. For a lamb lover, the shanks are immensely satisfying – roasted simply with onions, garlic, salt and pepper, and enlivened by the addition of lemon juice, a uniquely Greek, nearly thousand year old practice.

Harry's opened as "Gene's" in 1948 and belonged to Eugene Pavlovich until he sold it in 1975 to Harry Michelis, Greek expatriate and brother of Nick Michelis, original owner of Cleburne Cafeteria. Harry sold Harry's to John Platsos several years ago when he was ready to retire and move back to Greece. Already in the cafeteria business, John had opened Heights Tower Cafeteria in 1984 and still manages to successfully run both businesses. John is from a small town called Larisa (midway between Athens and Thesaloniki) and began his career cooking gyros and shishkabobs as a young man in Athens, 150 meters from the Acropolis.

He moved here in 1968 and says that his toughest critics are his Greek customers "because they know good food." (Well, me too.)

The breakfast at Harry's is as popular as lunch and it's easy to understand why. The pan sausage, lean smoky ham, and bacon are all excellent, but again, I was particularly impressed with the hefty, handcut Pork Chops, instead of the skinny, dried up old hockey puck varieties that often pass for "breakfast chops" elsewhere. I thought the crisp, eggy French Toast was unimprovable and the pancakes or "hotcakes," a generous six inches in diameter, may just be the best in town. The coffee was great, but I do wish they served freshly squeezed orange juice.

Harry's doesn't take checks or credit cards. (Neither did Illia – only cash.)

HEIGHTS CAMPHOUSE BAR B Q

2820 White Oak
Houston, Texas 77007
713/861-2033

Type of Cuisine: Barbecue
Bar: Beer
Dress: Casual
Entertainment: No
Payment: All Major Credit Cards
Entrée Range: $2.95-$6.45
Recommended Dishes:
  Pork
  Ribs
  Chicken
  Camphouse Potatoes (au Gratin Potatoes)
  Potato Salad
  Coleslaw
  Pinto Beans
Hours: Monday-Saturday, 11:00a.m.-9:00p.m.
  (Closed Sunday)
Reservations: Not Accepted

Heights Camphouse Bar B Q is a recent entry and as far as I'm concerned another winner in the local barbecue sweepstakes.

"It's the little things that make the difference in a barbecue place," owner Wilfred Weiting says when I compliment him on just knowing that a little onion goes a long way, and slicing the onions for sandwiches razor thin. "I guess that's just what comes from being in the business as long as we have."

Weiting was so young when he opened his first restaurant that it had to be in his older brother's name, Henry. "This goes back to about 1960 when I was about fifteen or sixteen. It was called Hickory Bar B Q and was on Times Boulevard." Most of his methods and recipes have evolved from those days.

"When we started out my brother, my brother-in-law and my dad used to get together one weekend a month and make barbecue." His unusual coleslaw and creamy, mustard-based potato salad were the contribution of his mother and sister at these family gatherings. "It was mostly just trial and error in those days. They'd come up with things and we'd decide the pros and cons of all the dishes what worked and what didn't."

In thirty-seven years Weiting has opened and sold a series of successful barbecue restaurants – The Hickory Pit, The Hitching Rail and most recently, Amy's at Westpark and Gessner, named after his daughter. Between The Hitching Rail and

Amy's in 1989, he says he "needed a little break" so he moved back to his hometown of Moulton, Texas, "halfway between here and San Antonio" and opened Amy's Mexican Restaurant. Which explains why the Mexican relish of chopped tomatoes, onions, cilantro and fresh jalapeño – pico de gallo – is displayed with the other more predictable garnishes dill pickles, sliced jalapeños and sweet relish. "I just love pico de gallo and thought it would be great on barbecue. People seem to like it. We go through a gallon, gallon and a half a day."

He says the most common recipient of his pico de gallo is a hearty bowl of the house Pinto Beans. They are closer to a bowl of chili than a mere side dish to barbecue. I'm not at all surprised to hear that many customers come exclusively for a "double bowl of beans topped with pico de gallo." He also offers the more traditional molasses-based Barbecued Beans "that go back to the days of the coleslaw when we first started out," but I'd go with the pinto beans – thick, hot with chili powder and rich with garlic.

Almost as popular as the pinto beans are the au gratin or Camphouse Potatoes. "I make them like an old-fashioned macaroni and cheese, but I use diced potatoes instead of macaroni. Almost everybody who comes through the line will get them."

They do go well with the barbecue, but I'm not sure I'd want to miss his Potato Salad. It is tart with yellow mustard and whipped smooth with the welcome crunch of chopped pickles, celery and onions.

Weiting admits that "people are pretty particular about their sides" and that they either love or hate his Coleslaw. "It's the recipe I started with – just diced cabbage and shredded carrots tossed with white vinegar, sugar and a little water." It has a clean, bright, almost Oriental flavor to it.

He's right. What qualifies as good coleslaw is as highly disputed by most Texans as the family chili or barbecue sauce recipe.

His barbecue sauce happens to be just my cup of tea. Colored deep burgundy from the addition of Worcestershire sauce and molasses it strikes the ideal balance between hot and sweet. "The difference is probably the lemon juice. I've been working on my sauce for thirty years. It's a sauce you could eat a couple of times a week without getting bored with it."

Which brings me to the barbecue itself. As far back as 1880, journalists Alexander Sweet and John Knox wrote in *On A Mexican Mustang Through Texas,* "It is claimed that this primitive method of preparation is the perfection of cookery, and that no meat tastes so sweet as that which is barbecued."

Weiting attributes achieving "the perfection of cookery" to two things – experience and excellent equipment.

"I've upgraded equipment every time I've opened a new place. I've cooked on about every pit there is." He invested in an Old Hickory Pit when he opened Heights Camphouse Bar-B-Q in June and says, "It's about the finest there is on the market, almost foolproof."

"We use all good green hickory. The secret to great brisket is just knowing when it's ready – the right moment to pull it off the pit." He smokes the brisket eleven to twelve hours overnight and it shares the pit with my favorite – juicy Barbecued Pork.

"Most barbecue places don't sell pork, but I've been doing it from the beginning at Hickory Bar B Q." Sliced, with some onions, pickles or relish, it makes an even better sandwich than the brisket does. Weiting agrees, "If someone tries the pork, they usually stay with it.

"A little trick I learned over the years is that I freeze the pork shoulder as it comes in and put it on the pit still frozen with the brisket for two reasons: first, it keeps it moist and second, it then cooks exactly the same amount of time as the brisket. We load the pit around 7:30 (at night) and it'll be ready about 8:30 in the morning."

Weiting says that the Chicken runs a close second to the brisket in popularity. "This is the first place I've owned where the chicken outsells the ribs. Maybe people's eating habits are changing." (Or maybe because it's so good.) He dry seasons the chicken with a mixture of salt, pepper, chili, onion and garlic powders at night, refrigerates it so it absorbs the flavors and puts it on the grill in the morning with the ribs when he removes the pork and brisket.

The chicken is fabulous but so are the Ribs and Sausage. Weiting claims that "everybody thinks ribs are their specialty." They are sweet, meaty pork ribs cooked until the tender meat just falls off the bone.

The sausage is a type of Polish sausage Slovacek made in Snook, Texas, that he's used since 1984. "We steam it first to soften the casing, then smoke it quickly on the pit. We slice it thin because it stays on a sandwich better. It's great on a Po Boy. One of our most popular po boys is a combination of beef and sausage.

"We have our po boy buns baked fresh every morning for us at White Oak Bakery right next door."

There's that attention to detail again.

There is Carrot Cake and an assortment of pies to choose from for dessert – Coconut Meringue, Pecan and, through the holidays, Pumpkin and Chocolate Meringue.

HINZE'S BAR-B-QUE

3940 Highway 59 Loop
Wharton, Texas 77488
409/532-2710

2101 Highway 36 South
Sealy, Texas 77474
409/885-7808

Type of Cuisine: Barbecue
Bar: Beer Only
Dress: Casual
Entertainment: No
Payment: All Major Credit Cards
Plate: Wharton $6.25, Sealy $5.95
Recommended Dishes:
- BBQ
- Brisket
- Ribs
- Pork
- Chicken

Hours: **Wharton:** Monday-Thursday, 10:00a.m.-9:00p.m.
Friday-Saturday, 10:00a.m.-10:00p.m.
Sunday, 9:30a.m.-9:30p.m.
Sealy: Monday-Friday, 10:30a.m.-9:00p.m.
Saturday, 9:30a.m.-9:30p.m.
Sunday, 7:30a.m.-9:00p.m.
Reservations: Not Accepted

Rosemary Hinze tells a story about the mouth-watering appeal of the Brisket at Hinze's Bar-B-Que in Wharton, Texas, that goes back more than twenty years. "I'll never forget. When we first opened, we had windows in the little building there. People would come in and order a pound of meat. They'd stand three or four feet from me where I was carving the brisket, you know, on the counter. Well, I'd start on this roast, and they'd see the juice running out and they'd say, 'Oh, gosh! Let me have another pound of that!'"

And that's just the brisket! I am a recent convert to the joys of succulent, buttery-tender brisket with the sweet, smoky flavor of pecans and the telltale scarlet ring around the rim. "The ring of smoke is what the judge looks for – if he knows what he's doing at a barbecue cook-off," adds W. C. Hinze, Rosemary's husband and head of the Hinze (pronounced "hints") barbecue dynasty.

Son Carl, who owns Hinze's Bar-B-Que in Sealy with his wife Debbie, tells it like this, "My dad's the one who taught us that you got to be patient ... That's the number one thing when you're cooking barbecue. He was the type that never got in a hurry for anything. He'd say, 'Just make sure it's right.'"

And they do. Whether you're in Wharton or Sealy, soup to nuts, start to finish, you're unlikely to have a better all-round barbecue experience anywhere.

Let's begin with the freshly baked Sourdough Bread that according to Rosemary, almost causes a stampede when it comes out of the oven late morning. Then there is their homey, heart-warming sauté of Bacon and Onion Potatoes that Rosemary points out outsells the vast array of other sides and salads "probably because it just goes so good with the barbecue and because you can't really get them anywhere else." A snappy, Black-Eyed Pea Salad gives the soulful, slow-cooked pinto beans and classic barbecued baked beans a run for their money.

The sprightly vinaigrette-based Coleslaw is a bracing counterpoint to the richness of the barbecue. Carl, who uses most of his mother's original recipes for his side dishes and vegetables because, "You know, if it ain't broke ..." agrees that "people really like our coleslaw. It's something different. My mother got that from my grandmother, and that's just the way we've been doing it."

One big adjustment Rosemary recently made is a subtle but, she believes, vast improvement on the old family potato salad recipe. "I never used to like our potato salad ... isn't that terrible? So lately, just in the last six months, we've been adding a dash of fresh onion to it and I think that brings the flavor out. Now I think it's delicious." Carl says that although his mother "thinks it's great and that she's selling even more potato salad now that it has onion in it ... we're going to keep it like it is."

Where Carl does break rank with his mother is in the preparation of the family barbecue sauce. Both sauces are thick enough to stand a spoon in, but Rosemary feels that the secret to hers is the oil from the skin of the whole chunks of lemons that she uses. Carl prefers his sauce a little sweeter. "I put about half as much lemon juice and at least one container of orange juice in it, too, to kind of take the tanginess out of it." It is fabulous – a heavenly deep-flavored sauce that strikes an ideal balance between heat and sweet.

If the original Hinze's in Wharton was good enough to be listed among *Texas Monthly's* "50 best barbecue joints in Texas," and as one of *Food and Wine* magazines's 1995 "Top five barbecue joints in America," it's only because they hadn't made their way to Sealy yet.

As good as the meaty, outsized Pork Ribs are in Wharton, Hinze's in Sealy gets my vote for the best ribs in Texas (outside a friend's ranch down near Brownsville). The ribs are left to marinate overnight in a dry seasoning that includes garlic and chili powder – and this is the secret – brown sugar. Sugar, especially brown sugar, and pork always make a fine marriage, and when Carl slow-cooks them, an irresistible crust caramelizes on the ribs making them as close to perfection as I may ever taste. No trip through Sealy on my way back to Houston from Austin will be complete without a sackfull.

Carl says he uses the same sweet/savory dry rub on the pork butt and cooks it "along side the brisket for about twelve to fifteen hours."

Rosemary adds that they've only been serving the pork for about half as long as the other meats, but that she thinks it's "even better than beef." I find the pork at both locations is about as close to sublime as a pork butt is likely to get.

I've always considered Chicken the ultimate test of a barbecue master's skills. Is it juicy? Has the skin been seasoned well? Has it been cooked slowly enough for the sweet taste of smoke to flavor the meat to the bone? Yes. Yes. And yes!

"Everybody comments about the chicken," Rosemary says. "It's just so moist. It's cooked slow … and you have full flavor there." Carl agrees, "It's critical not to cook it too fast."

Like all other meats, it's basted regularly with the Hinze family "mop" – equal parts "oil, vinegar and cut-up lemons." The brisket still gets basted every couple of hours just like it did when they started out.

The dedication doesn't stop there. Both Hinze's Bar-B-Ques are busy before dawn as Chocolate, Lemon and (my favorite) Coconut Pies with what seem like miles of towering meringue with soft, golden peaks, and one of the chewiest pecan pies I've ever tasted, are prepared daily. Rosemary says they bake about thirty pies every morning except at Thanksgiving when they sell as many as five hundred pies the day before. (Pecan pie $9.95/Meringue $8.95).

There is no question that Hinzes consider barbecue the family business. W. C. says, "All seven kids have worked for us. Our daughter Arlene (Korenek) has a place called A&A Barbecue in Bay City. Three of our children work full time in Wharton, daughters Marlies (Sciba) and Lydia (Kubicek), who do the books, and our youngest Michael, who's there most of the time." Rosemary credits all three children with keeping a constant eye that W. C. and her high standards are always met.

"That's one thing I'm really proud of – how consistent we are. Michael in particular, just loves the business. I don't think he ever goes home. He just wants to make sure everything is done right!" Carl agrees, "I don't see how you can do it right if the owner is not there! You just can't. You have to love it to stay with it."

THE HOBBIT HOLE

1715 S. Shepherd
Houston, Texas 77019
713/528-3418

Type of Cuisine: American/Eclectic/Vegetarian
Bar: Beer and Wine
Dress: Casual
Entertainment: No
Payment: All Major Credit Cards
Entrée Range: $5.25-$10.95
Recommended Dishes:
Appetizers: Cheese Shrimp Rolls
Quesadillas (Chicken) with guacamole
Entrées: Sandwiches: T-BLT
Smaug's Delight
Grillado
Gandalf
South of the Border: Spinach Mushroom Enchiladas
Dessert: Key Lime Pie
Hours: Monday-Thursday, 11:00a.m.-9:30p.m.
Friday-Saturday, 11:00a.m.-11:00p.m.
Sunday, 11:30a.m.-9:00p.m.
Reservations: Accepted for larger parties

From day one, beaded, bell-bottomed vegetarians and carnivores alike have faithfully queued at the Hobbit Hole Café for sandwiches and cold, rich fresh fruit smoothies. The sandwiches were whopping two-fisted affairs teeming with "natural" ingredients on soft, freshly baked whole wheat bread, and the smoothies – simply puréed seasonal fruit and ice, sweetened with a little honey.

It was January, 1972, and brothers Raymond and Forrest Edmonds – barely a year apart in age – had recently graduated from the University of Texas. They patterned the Hobbit Hole after a popular late sixties Austin haunt – Mother Nature's Smoothie Shop. The older of the two, Raymond explains that "we just fell in love with the place." So, although he had a degree in finance, and Forrest in accounting, they set out to find the perfect location in their native Houston. This was a cozy, red brick, cottage-style house on South Shepherd built in 1917.

"It only cost us $8,000.00 to open up. We were 'a natural foods restaurant' – a sandwich shop really, with smoothies, fresh fruit juices and a few soups and salads. It was community seating; all ages 'from eight to eighty' I used to say, business professionals to artists."

"We started out Ok, but what really put us on the map was that three months after we opened, (artist) Peter Max had a show in Houston and we did a breakfast for him here. After that, business just exploded!" Once they hit their stride, they opened a little health food store upstairs on the second floor of the house.

What's changed? Plenty! I stopped back in recently for a Gandalf (my favorite sandwich), and to reacquaint myself with the Hobbit Hole. I was amazed to see how they had evolved in their twenty-six years. While they're not exactly serving pork rinds, they have expanded their once strictly vegetarian menu to include ten "South of the Border" dishes, grilled tuna steak, jerk chicken and (yikes!) burgers topped with a choice of cheese or bacon!

Raymond says that they beefed up their repertoire in the early eighties as an added incentive for vegetarians to dine with their "meat eating" friends. "Still, I think we're thought of as 'that sprouts restaurant!'"

From (fairly) recently added appetizers to desserts, there's a lot to recommend, but the Hobbit Hole still makes a sandwich like no one else. Nine of the original list of twelve sandwiches still exist. They are all named after inhabitants of the mythological Kingdom of Middle Earth from J. R. R. Tolkien's fantasy novel for children, *The Hobbit,* written in 1937. No longer sold for the almost-inconceivable price of 95¢ each, they are now wisely available in two sizes – the original size "classic," or the more-manageable "slim," prepared with two-thirds less ingredients and on a thinner slice of bread.

The Gandalf has always been Hobbit Hole's most successful creation. It is sliced avocado and mushrooms under a warm blanket of melted Monterey Jack cheese on whole wheat toasted bread. It is named for the wandering wizard and raconteur from *The Hobbit,* "who was responsible for so many lads and lasses going off into the Blue for mad adventures." (My idea of a mad adventure these days would be to add bacon to the Gandalf.)

Another favorite, the Far Downs, once offered with optional avocado, now combines a simply, but nicely seasoned egg salad, creamy guacamole and slices of tomatoes. As good as the egg salad and guacamole are, this strikes me as too much of a mushy thing. So I would order the Far Downs with just egg salad and go for Bilbo the Magnificent, another Hobbit Hole classic, that features the wonderful guacamole with sliced tomatoes and the pleasant crunch of cucumbers topped with a tangle of sprouts.

Raymond tells me of the new-fangled favorites, Smaug's Delight is the current #1 seller. In the old days Smaug's Delight was made with freshly churned cashew butter, but it is now constructed from neat layers of sliced mesquite smoked turkey breast, avocado and tomato, topped with melted cheese.

Always a sucker for a BLT, the T-BLT is especially good. The "T" is smoked turkey breast and the whole wheat bread – unless otherwise asked - is toasted.

Raymond tells me that their signature whole wheat bread is now baked to their specifications by Williams Bakery and not on the premises as it was when they had their health food store upstairs. They closed it in the early eighties. "No point in trying to compete with Whole Foods," he says. That space has been converted to another dining room and is also used for parties. (It has a little balcony and may be even more charming than the slightly-dark original seating area downstairs!) If the weather's good, there is an outdoor dining area behind the house.

Only two of the fifteen sandwiches are not made with whole wheat bread. A round, flat, rosemary-flavored Italian focaccia roll is used for the fabulous Grillado, a very recent addition. It is a nod to the nineties – crumbly goat cheese warmed between seasoned and grilled eggplant and zucchini.

A nice idea for a light lunch might be to order one of the pert, well dressed salads – either the Greek or the Caesar salad, and split a Grillado with your dining companion. The Quesadillas, one of six appetizers, is another good choice for this. They are excellent, more substantial than usual, with sweet grilled red and green peppers, blackened chicken (or tuna), and clearly made by someone who knows what a good quesadilla should taste like.

It is. The two women who have cooked for the Hobbit Hole since the early 80's, "when we finally put in a stove," Raymond says, are from Mexico and El Salvador, respectively. This also explains why the "South of the Border" dishes have the ring of authenticity. The best of those are the first two listed – Spinach and Mushroom Enchiladas and Chicken Enchiladas. The most unusual is the tabouli-stuffed Poblano Relleno. To my amazement, this is a great dish – a classic relleno preparation but stuffed with what amounts to warm, garlic flavored bulghur wheat, their version of tabouli. Most of the South of the Border dishes are accompanied by a generous portion of nutty, assertively-seasoned brown rice and good, still firm, black beans.

For a while, the Hobbit Hole had a Thai chef which explains the Americanized but Thai-inspired Cheese Shrimp Rolls. The thin, crispy cylinders are filled with cream cheese, chunks of shrimp and shredded carrots, and come with the appropriate sweet, red pepper-flecked dipping sauce.

The only real miscalculation on the menu is the Gazpacho – a cold, tomato-based soup that was unnecessarily harsh and bore no resemblance to the silky, Andalusian original recipe.

The burgers are made on fresh, sesame-sprinkled whole wheat buns. My favorite and the most distinctive was the smoky, perfectly-grilled Buffalo Burger. Raymond boasts that they were one of the first restaurants in town to make hamburgers with the leaner, more healthful buffalo meat, which wasn't that easy to get in the beginning. "We have a steady source now that deals with exotic game," he says.

Those looking for a more consequential meal might consider the thin, impeccably-fresh Grilled Tuna Steak, cooked-to-order, or the Jerk Chicken – an aggressively-seasoned, grilled, then sliced chicken breast.

Diners in need of a chocolate fix should go for the Dark Chocolate Mousse Cake, but the best dessert of all is the dense, Key Lime Pie which just happens to be low fat. Or you could be really good and finish with a helping of Fresh Fruit Salad. "We're kind of famous for it," Raymond says.

JOSEPHINE'S ITALIAN RISTORANTE

1209 Caroline (at Dallas)
Houston, Texas 77002
713/7599323

Type of Cuisine: Italian
Bar: Wine and Beer
Dress: Casual
Entertainment: On Occasion
Payment: All Major Credit Cards
Entrée Range: $7.95-$14.95
Recommended Dishes:
Appetizers: Stuffed Artichoke
Special Garlic Bread
Spinach Saltati
Sausage and Peppers
Mixed Italian Salad
Seafood Salad
Entrées: Pizza
Chicken Lasagna
Chicken Cappelletti ("Little Hats" filled with Chicken)
Veal Special
Desserts: Cannoli
Cookie Pudding Pie
Hours: Lunch: Monday-Friday, 11:00a.m.-5:00p.m.
Dinner: Monday-Thursday, 5:00p.m.-9:30p.m.
Friday-Saturday, 5:00p.m.-10:00p.m.
Reservations: Accepted

In *Italianamerican... The Scorsese Family Cookbook,* by Catherine Scorsese with Georgia Downard, film director (and son of Catherine Scorsese) Martin Scorsese comments that, "The Italians of my parents' generation are held together by the notion of the family. That is why the pasta sauce is so sacred to the Italian family."

There is scarcely an aspect of Josephine's Italian Ristorante that doesn't reflect the deep family roots of owners, Josephine and Johnny Storenski. The "Home Cooking" on the menu refers to the kind of old fashioned recipes that Josephine grew up eating around her grandmother's table with first cousins Damien, Vincent and Tony Mandola – all well known, successful restauranteurs in their own right.

"We opened (in 1988) serving Grandma's food," John explains, "old Sicilian food. Josephine is a very good cook. She learned from her mother, and her mother learned from her mother in the Old Country."

Josephine, or Jo Francis, as she's known by family and friends, says that from the moment they even thought about opening a restaurant, each member of their extended families has been supportive. "It was so touching. Each one of them. I mean, they couldn't do enough. Vincent would call me every day, 'Are you doing O.K.? Can I do something? Damien, naturally; cousin Rosie was so helpful and her son, John Carrabas, and you know Tony started us out!" John interrupts, "Yes. He's the one who found us the location. He was thinking about taking this one or the downtown location on West Gray and he said, 'Well, you know, I'll just go ahead and take West Gray. Would y'all like that one?'"

"At first we thought we'd open a deli since we had experience doing that," Josephine continues, "and then Tony and Damien came around and said, 'You know, I'll bet a good pasta and meatballs place would be just what people really want down here.' So, I went right to Mama and she came and helped with the old recipes. Tony stayed with us a good while and helped us with things I had no idea about...like quantities. Oh, it was wonderful. I didn't expect them to do those things, because naturally they already had their own places established."

John says, "What is interesting is that although they are all Mandolas and it was one grandma that a lot of these dishes came from, every family has their own unique way of cooking, preparing and presenting them."

For the first two years Josephine's served lunch exclusively. They began serving dinner by popular request in 1990. Lunch is served daily, cafeteria-style for the sake of expediency, but at dinner the red and white checkered tablecloths are graced with white candles stuck in Chianti bottles covered in months of melted wax. "Ò Solo Mio" plays on the sound system, and the diner is transported back to one's earliest memories of eating Italian food in America.

At closer inspection, the menu is not as nostalgic as the decor. Sure, there are meatballs and spaghetti, lasagne and eggplant Parmesan, but that's not what they do best.

Let's start right at the top of the list of appetizers. Standard garlic bread is raised a notch by the addition of freshly grated Romano cheese to olive oil, garlic and chopped parsley. After a brief tenure in the pizza oven, Josephine's Special Garlic Bread arrives bubbling hot and absolutely delicious. The melted cheese can be topped with sautéed mushrooms or marinera sauce. John says, "That's sort of my pride and joy. I love that garlic bread." He adds that some customers order the Spinach Saltati – barely-wilted fresh spinach sautéed just enough in olive oil with garlic to eat with the cheesey Special Garlic Bread.

The Sausage and Peppers is a mild, homemade, finely ground Italian sausage topped with a sauce of sweet peppers and garlic.

The Fried Calamari are tender with a crisp, well-seasoned dusting of flour and a little cornmeal. A dish of warm, chunky marinera sauce comes with it and it is exceptional – full of roughly cut onions, tomatoes, garlic, red pepper and plenty of chopped fresh herbs. The marinera sauce also goes well with the Fried Artichoke Hearts and, for dipping, it is my preference over the melted butter they serve with them.

My absolute favorite appetizer is the Stuffed Artichoke Frances. Named for Josephine's mother, Frances Corona, the freshly made stuffing tastes of good fresh herbs, cheese, and garlic. It is a messy affair, but well worth the trouble.

The Pizza is offered with the usual assortment of toppings and is available in three sizes: nine, twelve and sixteen inches. "A lot of people order them as an appetizer before their meal," John tells me. That's what I did and I thought the crust was terrific – thin, light and flavored with fresh rosemary, closer to focaccia than a traditional pizza crust.

A meal could be made of either Josephine's Mixed Italian Salad or the Italian Seafood Salad. The components of both were uniformly chopped, wonderfully fresh, and dressed with an Italian vinaigrette so remarkable that those who know it often buy it by the pint. John says, "We get a lot of comments on our salad dressing. It's been in the Mandola family for years and years."

One aspect that I am certain distinguishes Josephine's cooking from her grandmother's or even her mother's, is her ability to buy and use fresh herbs. John agrees, "That's the trick. You've got to have fresh stuff. We get all our herbs from an herb farm in Needville. We use lots of oregano, rosemary and lots of fresh basil."

There are three different Lasagnes to choose from: a traditional beef, the newly-popular vegetable, and the lasagne of my dreams, Chicken Lasagne.

Unique to Josephine's, it is neatly constructed, compact layers of sheets of pasta, chicken breasts sautéed "Italian style," as John says, in olive oil with mushrooms, garlic, parsley and oregano, and tomato sauce tinted pink by the addition of ricotta cheese. It can be topped with tomato sauce, but it makes an even finer marriage when covered with the ambrosial Alfredo sauce.

It is Josephine's most successful dish. John says, "People come from everywhere to get that. The Alfredo sauce is really extraordinary. We cook it the way they do in Rome, thick and rich."

The Chicken Cappelletti runs a close second in my affections. Listed under Pollo (chicken) and not pasta, these not so "little hats" are fresh squares of homemade pasta filled with finely minced chicken and proscuitto ham, flavored with fresh basil and a little curry powder, an unusual choice. It works well. Ten cappelletti are served with a pink tomato sauce thinned with a little cream.

The Veal Special is fabulous. The thinly sliced veal is sweet and tender, cloaked in a batter that is eggy, thin as intricate lace, and topped with a divine lemon infused butter cream sauce.

John says that "the Veal Special is a real popular dish. We've got a lot of people who come just for that!" It comes with a mound of linguine, and I ordered the Spinach Saltati (sautéed spinach) to accompany mine.

The heavier dishes on the menu are balanced by a substantial number of lighter "heart healthy" choices. "We added these to the menu in 1992, and that brought in a whole new wing of customers who watch their fat and cholesterol." John says the challenge, of course, was to keep the flavor and lose the fat from the recipes. I especially enjoyed the Pasta and Shrimp; briny, dark green capers contributed to the peppery pungency of the basil-fragrant tomato sauce.

Josephine's particular culinary gift may be in the area of desserts. She admits that she was the designated dessert maker for family gatherings and that most of these desserts are "just desserts that I've made forever at home." The classic ricotta and cream cheese filled Cannoli was perfect – studded with dark chocolate chips. But, the Cookie Pudding Pie, Josephine's invention, combines several of my favorite things – layers of chocolate pudding and cream cheese sweetened with powered sugar, all supported by a square of pecan cookie. Another winner, the Fudge Cake, is slathered with marshmallow cream when it comes out of the oven, then topped with gooey chocolate fudge icing.

KAM'S

4500-C Montrose Blvd.
Houston, Texas 77006
713/529-5057

Type of Cuisine: Chinese
Bar: Wine and Beer
Dress: Nice Casual
Entertainment: No
Payment: All Major Credit Cards
Entrée Range: $7.95-$13.95
Recommended Dishes:
Appetizers: Pan Fried Pork Dumplings
Steamed Vegetable Dumplings
Shrimp Toast
Barbecued Pork in Scallion Pancake
Cold Summer Rolls
Crab Meat Cream Cheese Rolls
Entrées: Soft Shell Crabs
Sweet and Sour Shrimp
Sesame Chicken
Manchurian Birdnest Beef
Ho Fan (Rice Noodles with Beef)
Singapore Vermicelli
Garlic Green Beans
Steamed Watercress
Hours: Monday-Thursday, 11:00a.m.-10:00p.m.
Friday, 11:00a.m.-11:00p.m.
Saturday, 5:00p.m.-11:00p.m.
Sunday, 5:00p.m.-10:00p.m.
Reservations: Accepted

There's a Chinese proverb that says, "If you want your dinner nicely cooked, don't offend the cook."

I wouldn't dream of it. I come to praise the cook and not offend him. He is the talented and versatile Quang Ho, chef and owner, along with sister and manager Kim Ho, and two others, of the delightful restaurant, Kam's on Montrose.

One of the many things that makes Kam's so special is the marriage of the subtle, restrained style of cooking of Quang's native Canton and the more aggressive, assertively seasoned specialties from the Western province of Szechuan.

One could easily make a meal of the appetizers. The Cantonese are famous for their dim sum or "heart's delight" sometimes eaten as a snack but often a meal composed of an assortment of, among other things, steamed or fried dumplings, spring rolls and shrimp toast. His are the best dumplings I have eaten outside of a restaurant specializing in dim sum. Prepared with impressive care, both the Panfried Pork Dumplings and the SteamedVegetable Dumplings were exceptional.

Before the dumplings arrive, an assortment of homemade sauces are placed on the table in incredibly charming little corked apothecary bottles so the diner can mix his/her own dipping sauce on the plate – a very nice touch. In one bottle is Chinese soy sauce; in another, sesame oil with a dried bay leaf inside; and in the third, rice vinegar flavored with an incendiary dried red chili. On the condiment tray is also a threatening little saucer of freshly chopped jalapeño, ginger, garlic, vinegar and salt. As wonderful as the green sauce is, I would also ask for the equally delicious, powerfully concentrated (again, homemade) red chile/garlic sauce.

The fantail Shrimp Toast is first rate, and the Barbecued Pork in Scallion Pancake is actually crisped pancake "pockets" stuffed with a little hoisin sauce, barbecued pork and scallion brushes peeking out the top of them. Two non-Chinese local favorite appetizers round out the list – Kam's Cold Summer Rolls and Crabmeat Cream Cheese Rolls, both excellent.

Next, I'd dive right into a plate of the seasonal, off-the-menu specialty of Soft Shell Crabs that I have been assured from now on will be a permanent fixture. The heavenly little creatures are hacked into bitesize pieces, fried quickly in vegetable oil and served with a scallion-flecked, dense, dark brown Szechuan sauce on the side for dipping. Another seafood highlight that it would not have occurred to me to order is the Sweet and Sour Shrimp – lightly battered whole shrimp, fried and drizzled with a mixture of sugar and vinegar. A sly variation on a familiar theme, the dish actually manages to be light, instead of the unspeakably cloying, gelatinous mess that we've all come to associate with anything "sweet and sour."

Listed under "Kam's Specialties," the Sesame Chicken and Orange Beef are both understandably big sellers, but the Manchurian Birdnest Beef was even more interesting – sautéed pieces of beef and leeks resting on a "nest" of fried vermicelli or rice stick noodles.

A symbol of longevity in the Chinese culture, the noodle dishes are given extra attention. One standout is Singapore Vermicelli, a Cantonese dish that made its way from Singapore to Southern China. It is a stirfry of shrimp, chicken and vegetables served with vermicelli that's flavored with the very un-Chinese spice of curry. Another noodle choice, and maybe my favorite beef dish, is Ho Fan – homemade, practically transparent rice noodles tossed with marinated beef strips and bean sprouts.

Fried rice is popular snack food in China and the Young Chow Fried Rice is especially toasty-tasting and chock full of goodies. Kim says the Vegetable Fried Rice is equally popular.

What we've come to recognize as dry sautéed or twice-cooked green beans are called Garlic Green Beans at Kam's and are as good any I've eaten in town. Two other vegetable highlights are the unusual Eggplant Julienne – a sauté of sweet, battered eggplant – or the seldom-seen, pepper-flavored Steamed Watercress topped with garlic sauce.

The only dessert offered is worth ordering. Called Kam's Original Coconut Freeze, it is homemade vanilla ice cream flavored with coconut and served in old fashioned sundae glasses garnished with lychee nuts and a sprig of fresh mint.

Kam's opened in 1988 and is definitely a neighborhood restaurant and a well kept secret. The small L-shaped grey and white interior seats only fifty-four and is elegantly spare with framed panels of silk and satin Chinese ceremonial robes decorating the walls.

KENNEALLY'S IRISH PUB

2111 S. Shepherd
Houston, Texas 77019
713/630-0486

Type of Cuisine: Pizza/Sandwiches
Bar: Full
Dress: Casual
Entertainment: Occasionally
Payment: All Major Credit Cards
Entrée Range: $3.95-$11.95
Recommended Dishes:
Appetizers: Potato Chips (Homemade)
Irish Nachos (Potato Skins)
Entrées: Pizza
Ham Sandwich
Hours: Monday-Friday, 3:00p.m.-2:00a.m.
Saturday-Sunday, 5:00p.m.-2:00a.m.
Reservations: Not Accepted

Before there were cigar bars, brew pubs, or even micro breweries, there was Kenneally's Irish Pub. Owner, John Flowers, tells me that when he opened Kenneally's in October of 1983, he wanted to serve his beer in pint glasses and that "the restaurant supplier said, 'pint glasses? How many do you need? One or two?' I said, 'No, we need like ten cases of them.' He said, 'We don't have that many in the state.' Now, everybody serves in pint glasses, whereas everyone used mugs before. So, we've changed the market a little."

Kenneally's was also one of the first to offer Guinness Stout on tap. "The first time we bought Guinness, people had no idea. What? Black beer? But, you know, I knew how to do it. The salesman didn't know how much I needed, how to plug it in, how to sell it or market it. And the distributor had no idea what it was."

Although this little neighborhood bar, named for his father-in-law, Patrick Kenneally, has enjoyed a steady, loyal following during its fourteen years, Flowers laughs, "It's amazing how many people drive by and they'll come in, you know, and get to talking, and say, 'I've been driving by this place for the last ten years and never stopped in.'"

I might have been one of those who was still just "driving by" if I hadn't been told by reliable food sources a couple of years ago that Kenneally's served the "best pizza in town."

Great pizza at a little neighborhood Irish pub? The concept is a little easier to grasp once you know that Flowers is from Chicago, a town where people eat well and where Irish and Italian immigrants hold equal culinary sway. "In Chicago, there'll be a pizza joint, like a dry cleaners here, on every corner." So in 1990, when Flowers decided to serve pizza at Kenneally's, he went back to Chicago to "learn how to do it right."

"They come from everywhere to have our pizza, especially on weekends. They come from all over...Clear Lake...The Woodlands."

He says, "The hardest part was making the dough." Well, they got it right. They are justifiably famous for their crust. It is a work of art; yeasty, crisp, and thin as a Carr's Water Biscuit. He says that a lot of people order the plain cheese pizza because they enjoy the unfettered flavor of the crust with just a little tomato sauce and the melted cheese. "But pepperoni is probably the number one seller."

The Shamrock Special runs a close second in the affection of regulars, he says. It sports fresh mushrooms, bell peppers, and the Irish part-crisped, salty little curly cues of corned beef. It is good, but my recipe for a great pizza from the selection of possible toppings is this: onions, jalapeños, double Italian sausage and half the allotted cheese. This is a fabulous pizza. Whichever toppings you choose, I recommend asking for half as much cheese as usual. The thin crust, particularly in the center of the pizza, doesn't stand up well to the weight of the cheese.

While you're waiting for your pizza and, if they're busy, there might be a wait, order a basket of the highly-addictive, homemade, hot, fresh-out-of-the-oil, Potato Chips. Another option is a plateful of Irish Nachos, just added to their short menu a year ago. Whole baking potatoes are sliced lengthwise, thin as a quarter with their skin still on, deep fried, loaded up with cheese, jalapeños, juicy nuggets of corned beef and "thrown in the pizza oven," as Flowers says. "I mean, it's a meal. It's a whole potato, you know."

The Cheeseburger is a nice manageable size and tastes of the grill, but the French Fries that come with it are exceptional – slivered wedges, cut on the bias, irregularly shaped, and perfectly fried.

Flowers says that they have always served sandwiches and believes that their success depends on the excellent quality of the ingredients he uses. He says the Turkey Sandwich is the biggest seller, but our waitress, Tina, suggested I try the ham and I'm glad she did.

As advertised on the menu, they are "honey baking" their own hams and it shows. "We buy a whole ham and bake it with brown sugar and molasses...like Mom did." I ordered a Ham Sandwich with the house "spicy mustard" on rye bread with onions and cheese and it arrived warm, the bread toasted, with Swiss cheese melted over a fistful of sweet, pink, razor-thin ribbons of ham. He says their secret weapon is the pale yellow horseradish-honey-based mustard made from scratch for them by "a lady in Winnetka, Illinois."

Kenneally's Irish Pub is a gutsy little neighborhood bar with a lot of character and great food. Flowers says, "People just feel kind of at home here. I can't explain it."

They recently had an Irish group called Seven Nations performing on their little stage. So, entertainment is booked sporadically.

THE KING BISCUIT PATIO CAFE

1606 White Oak Drive
Houston, Texas 77009
713/861-2328

Type of Cuisine: American/Burgers
Bar: Full
Dress: Casual
Entertainment: Thursday and Saturday nights
Payment: All Major Credit Cards
Entrée Range: $5.95-$14.95
Recommended Dishes:
Appetizers: Baked Stuffed Mushrooms
Quesadillas (Pulled Pork)
Entrées: Blackened Tuna
Snapper Filet
Chili Cheddar Jalapeño Burger
Philly Cheese Steak
Ed's Grilled Chicken
Thai Pasta Salad
Hours: Monday-Friday, 11:00a.m.-12:00a.m.
(Kitchen closes at 10:00p.m.)
Saturday, 12:00p.m.-2:00a.m. (Kitchen closes at 11:00p.m.)
(Closed Sunday)
Reservations: Accepted

Don't go to The King Biscuit Patio Cafe looking for biscuits or even a broadcast of the old radio show, The King Biscuit Flour Hour. Do go looking for fun, good food and what is sometimes one of the loveliest unfettered views of downtown Houston. That is, when as the surrounding trees lose their leaves.

"Uptown food with a downtown view" is how owners Rob and Kendra Fleming describe this charming converted 1927 Esso station nestled onto the side of one of the few hills around Houston on White Oak Drive in the Heights. If it wasn't for the view, The King Biscuit would feel exactly like a bar-restaurant in a beach community with its whimsical décor, ceiling fans, brightly colored walls, terrace tables shaded by umbrellas, and particularly, the kitchen's emphasis on fresh seafood. Rob says if he could rename the restaurant, he would call it El Pescado – the fish.

Their most popular dish and the one he's proudest of is the award-winning Bow Tie Blackened Tuna. A blackened and seared tuna filet rests on top of bow tie pasta that has been cooked then coated lightly in a mixture of spinach, mushrooms, fresh basil, garlic, chipotle chili paste, and finished off with a dash of heavy cream and cheddar cheese. It arrives surrounded by roasted seasonal vegetables and is a masterful presentation. It's easy to understand why the dish won first place

"Best Entrée" in the Great Taste of Houston 1995, although, the one day I tried it, the blackening spice was so hot it was scary. The dish reflects the kitchen's vigorous style and the owner's love of heat.

A tamer but equally good alternative is the Sunflower Seed Encrusted Snapper Filet. Fresh local red snapper is coated with ground sunflower seeds, well-seasoned and pan fried in canola oil to achieve the wonderful crisp texture, and topped with mango-flavored hollandaise sauce. The filets are placed on a bed of cous-cous.

Cous-cous (pronounced koos´-koos) is granular semolina or coarsely ground durum wheat and not very small pasta, as some people believe. It is a staple of North Africa and when flavored with saffron and cooked with lamb, onions and chick peas, is the national dish of Morocco. Rob says they chose it as an alternative to rice, and although I have always thought it seemed too much like soggy bread crumbs, it works well in the dish and does its job admirably absorbing the flavors of the fish and sauce.

Also good was the Honey Dijon Glazed Salmon Filet – seven ounces of salmon marinated briefly in honey Dijon mustard, as advertised, grilled and served over white rice cooked in chicken stock scented with fresh basil and studded with sunflower seeds.

While all of these dishes are commendably turned out of an apparently closet-sized kitchen, I would beat a path back to their door in a second for their Chili Cheddar Jalapeño Burger. The slightly searing burger is topped with sliced jalapeños, cheddar cheese and a ladle full of real Mexican chili made by Paula Renosa who presides over the kitchen during the day. My second favorite sandwich is Pennsylvania native Rob's own version of the Philly Cheese Steak.

What distinguishes it from the usual, he says, is that he grills both onions and green peppers and then seasons the thinly sliced strip steak with Worcestershire and a little of the blackening spices while it cooks, melts mozzarella over it and loads it all on a freshly baked kaiser roll. This is a great sandwich. But, so is Ed's Grilled Chicken.

Named after an old friend and ex-bartender who "just threw it together one day," the moist chicken breast is grilled and topped with (again!) sliced jalapeños, strips of good smoky bacon, melted jack cheese and an especially fresh-tasting sesame seed bun from local Ashcraft Bakery. I recommend asking for the delicious, but misnamed smoked jalapeño mayo to go with it. The mayo is actually seasoned with ancho chili paste made from sun drying poblano peppers rather than jalapeño peppers. Never mind, whatever they call it, you'll want some. All sandwiches and burgers come with skin-on French fries, available regular or spicy or the very homemade-tasting Poore Brothers potato chips.

My two favorite appetizers are the Baked Stuffed Mushrooms with highly seasoned bread crumbs and gooey mozzarella cheese, and the Quesadillas filled with a choice of vegetables, shrimp, chicken or beef. (Opt for the more unusual Pulled Pork Quesadillas.)

A whole pork butt is seasoned and roasted in the oven until it can be literally pulled off the bone. It goes particularly well with the accompanying mango pico de gallo and any of the more than forty beers they have on hand.

The Thai Pasta Salad is a recent addition to the menu. It is a sprightly mélange of penne pasta tossed with snow peas, sliced red onion, scallions, red and green bell peppers, in a peanut vinaigrette arranged on pieces of romaine lettuce with a sliced grilled chicken breast on top garnished with whole peanuts.

Soups are a big seller at King Biscuit and everybody's favorite appears to be the Chicken and Vegetable Soup, another specialty of Paula Renosa. Irregularly available as the soup of the day, it is filled with fresh tomatoes, zucchini, yellow squash, onions, rice and whole chunks of chicken.

Rob and Kendra opened King Biscuit Patio Cafe on January 2, 1993. A devotée of the blues, Rob says he named the restaurant after "the famous harmonica blues player, Sonny Boy Williamson, who died in the mid-sixties, and his band, The King Biscuit Entertainers from Helena, Arkansas, where they still commemorate the blues every year at a week-long festival called the King Biscuit Times Festival." Rob himself commemorates the blues by featuring a blues band every Saturday night in the bar area from 9:00 p.m. to 1:00 a.m. There is a jazz band from 9:00 p.m. to midnight on Thursday's (no cover charge).

Rob says the first five years have been largely "trial and error and I know it will just keep getting better." As it is, it's a dandy place to hang out. Rob agrees, "We don't have normal restaurant table turn. People come into our place, they eat, sit back, drink beer or sip their wine and enjoy the downtown view – sort of camp out."

"Yeah!" Kendra chimes in, "Hot food, cold drinks and cool people!"

KOREA GARDEN RESTAURANT

9501 Long Point Road
Houston, Texas 77055
713/468-2800

Type of Cuisine: Korean
Bar: Full
Dress: Casual
Entertainment: No
Payment: All Major Credit Cards
Entrée Range: $7.25-$21.50
Recommended Dishes:
  Appetizers: Kim Chee (Pickled Cabbage)
    Pan Fried Assorted Seafood and Scallions in Batter
      (Korean Pizza)
    Boiled Beef Dumpling
    Fresh Lean Raw Beef (Tartare Steak)
  Entrées: Dishes BBQ'ed on Grill in Middle of Table
    Bulgalbi (Short Ribs)
    Butgogi (Prime Rib)
    Hyumit Kui (Tongue)
    Mixed Rice with Seasoned Vegetables
    Stir Fried Squid with Vegetable and Hot Pepper
Hours: Lunch: Monday-Friday, 11:00a.m.-2:00p.m.
  Full Menu: Monday-Sunday, 11:00a.m.-10:00p.m.
Reservations: Accepted

The renowned Twentieth Century French restauranteur, Marcel Boulestin believed, "It is not really an exaggeration to say that peace and happiness begin, geographically, where garlic is used in cooking." If Boulestin were alive today, he might think that "peace and happiness begin, geographically," roughly near the corner of Long Point and Blalock in Spring Branch, the location of Korea Garden.

While the Korean culture has been heavily influenced by its neighbors to the north (China) and south (Japan), the style of cooking and combination of ingredients remain completely distinctive. Garlic, apparently enjoyed but never used in the Japanese kitchen, is a predominant flavor in the short list of ingredients used in varying degrees in Korean dishes; garlic, hot little red peppers, Asian chili powder (bright red in color with a sweet flavor closer to paprika than what we think of as chili powder), red chili paste, scallions, ginger, sesame (seeds and oil), rice vinegar, soy sauce and Asian fish sauce.

Twelve years ago inveterate restauranteur, Siwon Moon, designed Korea Gardens to resemble the exterior and interior of a Korean yangban house or nobleman's house. Originally the birch booths surrounded a garden in the middle of the "house" that never quite received enough sunlight to flourish.

This serenely handsome restaurant glommed on to the end of a small strip center seats 150 people including the private dining rooms with sliding screen partitions – an excellent choice for parties of eight or more. In October 1984 when he opened Korea Garden Moon's objective was, and still is, to introduce Houston to the joys of Korean cuisine in as attractive and comfortable an environment as possible. Indeed the "nobleman's" presence is felt in the graciousness of the atmosphere and the warmth and gentle sense of humor of its owner.

Any discussion of the Korean diet must begin with Kim Chee. This pickled vegetable is eaten at virtually every meal including breakfast and is considered a staple. Although there are many varieties of vegetables used in the making of kim chee (160 are featured in the Kim Chee Museum in Seoul) it is most commonly made from cabbage. Every fall when cabbage is harvested and is at its very sweetest, in every household in Korea it is still preserved with salt, garlic and chili and packed into huge earthenware jars to be eaten throughout the long, cold winter. Before you have even ordered, small dishes of kim chee are placed on the table to enjoy with your drinks at Korea Garden. Their version, made with bean sprouts, is addictively delicious and was an instant hit with all of my fellow diners.

Moon says although it's not uncommon for Koreans to drink scotch on the rocks with dinner, we prefer to order OB, the only Korean beer on the menu, and sake. Recently we tried soju, a clear, vodka-like, almost flavorless liquor served chilled in elegant little shot glasses, and found that it complimented the fiery richness of the food perfectly, straight through to the end of the meal. Unlike vodka, soju is only 24% alcohol. Unlike their Asian neighbors, among Koreans, tea is not that popular a drink and is often made with barley or ginseng.

In Korea, a meal is not usually staggered into courses of appetizers and then entrées. All dishes including the ever-popular soup are all served at once. So, it's not unusual to see as many as twenty dishes gracing the table at an average dinner. Many of these dishes are namuls- vegetable side dishes such as spinach, bean sprouts, cucumbers, white radishes and some form of sea vegetable, like laver, kelp or seaweed individually blanched and doused with either rice vinegar or sometimes sesame oil or seeds. The contrasting flavors of these little salads represent the ancient Asian principle of the five flavors: sweet, sour, hot, salty and bitter.

For a country surrounded by water on three sides, it's not surprising to find an abundance of seafood on a Korean menu. However, beef has become very popular and unlike in China and Japan, is actually preferred to chicken or pork. Deferring to Western custom, appetizers are listed on the menu, and the meal, unless otherwise specified, is brought in courses.

You'll be instantly won over if you start with one of Korea's national dishes, maybe the best thing on the menu – the third appetizer down listed as Pan Fried Assorted Seafood and Scallions in Batter. This is really a pancake of massive proportion teeming with goodies, brought to the table cut in wedges and still sizzling in its pan. It is sometimes known as Korean pizza for obvious reasons and is my very favorite appetizer followed closely by the first two pancakes offered. All three pancakes are meant to be eaten with chopsticks and dipped in a sauce of soy sauce, rice vinegar, fresh ginger, crushed toasted sesame seeds, chili powder and a pinch of sugar. This chojang or dipping sauce is also used to dip two of my other favorite appetizers – Boiled Beef Dumplings which are quite similar to the lightest version of Chinese steamed dumplings, and the more unique Fried Beef Dumplings which are crescent-shaped beef-filled fried pastries, peculiarly listed on the lunch menu as "mini egg rolls."

For those who eat steak tartare, the Fresh Lean Raw Beef served with a tangy Korean sauce was just that-absolute perfection in its freshness of ingredients and simplicity of presentation with an egg yolk on top and garnished with julienned slices of raw garlic, cucumber and Asian pear.

We also enjoyed the appetizer of Stir Fried Octopus on a Bed of Noodles, but would recommend the mollusk-minded save themselves for the powerfully-flavored Stir Fried Squid with Vegetable and Hot Pepper. The first dish on the menu under "Fries," this stir-fry is an excellent example of how in the Korean kitchen garlic is added near the end of the cooking process to, combined with the hot peppers, pack an extra wallop.

For the uninitiated diner, Moon feels that the most important dishes to try are the ones barbecued on the grill in the middle of the table. The best known are Bulgalbi, short ribs sliced thin and removed from the bone to cook quickly on the grill, and Bulgogi – prime rib. They are marinated overnight in a sauce of garlic, ginger, scallions, chili powder and soy sauce to which a little sugar has been added. The grill and exhaust fan are turned on while appetizers are being eaten. When the grill is hot enough, the meat (or squid) is put directly on the grill by the waitress then turned by the diner with chopsticks or a fork as it browns and the sauce and sugar caramelize and crust on the outside. When they're done, the crisped morsels are placed inside a piece of fresh romaine lettuce to which you have added a little soybean paste, topped with slivers of white radish, folded into a little bundle and eaten. Yum! Although I like both the bulgalbi and bulgogi, I have discovered that my favorite beef to barbecue is Tongue. Now, I happen to love tongue, but even the most daunted, non-tongue eaters have loved it prepared in this fashion and also preferred it to the other choices of beef. Of the other choices to barbecue, Moon's favorite is the Pork and I agree that it is wonderful and is marinated a bit differently from the beef in a bit of chili paste.

Koreans love soup and of the thirteen listed on the menu the two that are best known in Korea are the Meat Filled Dumpling Soup with a rich and flavorful broth, and the incendiary Hot Seasoned Beef Soup, usually served in the dog days of summer to cool the eater off with perspiration.

It's important to note that when there is a little jalapeño next to a dish on the menu, it is an indication that these dishes are "hot and extra spicy." They are not kidding, even by Texas standards. The Hot Seasoned Beef Soup is an excellent example. Crimson red with chili powder, one bite and your tongue dials the fire department. I'd still order it in a second and any other "hot and extra spicy" dishes because the heat, while eye-popping, doesn't mask the other dominant, complex and very wonderful flavors of the soup. This is unusual and quite a neat culinary trick!

Korean white rice, a short to medium grain rice that's a bit sticky when cooked, is served in little individual steel bowls with everything. However, I wouldn't miss the sheer pleasure of the palate-soothing Mixed Rice with Seasoned Vegetable in Hot Stone Bowl. This rice dish actually finishes cooking in the hot stone bowl at your table as the waitress stirs the raw egg and fresh vegetable into the rice – it works like a salve to the senses. Also remarkable for the clarity of its flavors is the Cold Noodle with Seasoned Vegetable.

The other stir fried dish listed under "Fries" that was terrific and not nearly as hot as the stir fried squid is Stir Fried Mixed Vegetable Beef and Noodles. The noodles are the clear, slippery cellophane noodles that are the perfect foil to the richness of the tender slices of beef and sauce.

Dessert is only eaten on very special occasions, so the meal is finished with the sweetest, coldest most refreshing sectioned orange you will ever eat.

As you will be enjoying this meal in Spring Branch rather than some distant province of Korea, you can probably blow with impunity, but you might want to keep the slurping and belching to a minimum.

LA FOGATA

11630 Southwest Freeway (at Wilcrest)
Houston, Texas 77036
281/575-8736

Type of Cuisine: Columbian
Bar: Wine and Beer
Dress: Casual
Entertainment: No
Payment: American Express, MasterCard, Visa
Entrée Range: $7.00-$14.00
Recommended Dishes:
Entrées: Calentado (Scrambled Eggs)
Bandeja Montañera (Mountain Tray)
Picada de Carne (Mixed Grill-Beef & Pork)
Churrasco
Pescado Frito (Fried Red Snapper)
Cameron al Ajillo (Garlic Shrimp)
Dessert: Tres Leches
Arequipe
Hours: Monday-Sunday, 11:00a.m.-8:30p.m.
Reservations: Accepted

Rustic is the word that springs to mind when I think of the food at La Fogata. The "Especialidades de la Comida Colombiana" as they're called on the menu, are hearty, stick-to-the-ribs stuff – full of flavor and meant to be cooked over una fogata (an open fire).

It is the style of cooking typical of the central coffee growing region of Colombia where owner Carolina Carmona and her family are from. Nephew Hector Carmona says about the fare at Houston's oldest and most highly-regarded Colombian restaurant, "We were always trying to make the food as home-made as possible." He adds that his father, Hernan Carmona, who cooks, still gets there at 7 every morning "to prep the vegetables and get ready for the day."

Corn, beans, pork and plantains are the cornerstones of this agrarian diet. Even the Empanadas distinguish themselves from their Latin American cousins' by being encased in a dough composed of coarsely ground corn. The crusty yellow turn-overs are filled with a thick, brown beef stew rich with whole chunks of beef shank and potatoes. Hector says, "We are kind of famous for our empanadas!" On my first visit, Hector's mother, Luz Villafane, insisted we try the empanadas and en-couraged us to spoon pique sauce into the pastries once we had taken a bite. She told us, "Some people like to squeeze lime on them, but I prefer the hot sauce." Pique is short for piquante and it's a sassy, cilantro-based sauce that is long on flavor and short on heat. In Colombia, this is called aji sauce and is made from the small, sharp, bright red aji pepper. At La Fogata, they're using jalapeños, but not much because, as one Colombian friend told me, "Our cuisine is not hot – certainly not by Mexican food standards."

La Fogata is best known for their Bandeja Montañera (literally "mountain tray"). The plate originated in Medellin as "bandeja paisa." (The Carmonas are from Pereira, the capital of Risaralda, one of the four "paisa" states.) The plate or "tray" is piled high with fluffy white rice, beans, a thin piece of marinated and grilled skirt steak, a fat-edged curl of scored and fried pork rind, a wedge of avocado, and a sweet brown ribbon of fried plantain – all topped with a fried egg. "All the foods on the Bandeja Montañera are accessible to people living in farms and ranches in the Andean mountains," Hector says.

Beans and rice, staples of this sturdy South American meal, come with everything. The long grain white rice is flavored simply by adding a whole scallion and lemon to the water while cooking, and the beans are gutsy and wonderful. Red kidney beans are cooked in a strong chicken broth seasoned with garlic, cumin and whole chunks of tomatoes, onions, green peppers and chewy pieces of pork.

The plantain is cut length-wise, fried and dusted with a little salt. It is delicious and also comes with everything.

Thin, crisp corn cakes – Arepas – are eaten instead of bread in both Colombia and Venezuela. The three basic types of arepa are all made from either fresh or dried corn. One is shaped in a ball. One is flattened and filled with white cheese – either panela or Mexican ranchero. (These are both called arepas de maiz.) And then there's one that's eaten with everything like a tortilla at La Fogata – the arepa de choclo. (I liked the arepa de maiz that was filled with cheese, but I think the arepa de choclo must be an acquired taste.)

In Colombia, hors d'oeuvres are called picadas, but at La Fogata it is a mixed grill (or fritanga) of assorted meats. The Picada de Carne (for two people) is a carnivore's delight – the perfect way to sample the maximum number of beef and pork dishes.

The platter sports paper-thin pieces of beef liver, skirt steak – both grilled – crispy disks of breaded filet of pork (chuleta de cerdo) and best of all, meaty chicharrones and Colombian sausage or chorizo with whole identifiable pieces of leg of pork and garlic. The platter is rounded out by arepas, beans, rice, a couple of empanadas and a mound of French fries.

Beef tongue is simmered for hours with tomatoes, onions and garlic for the classic Colombian preparation of Lengua

Sudada (literally "to sweat"). It's a wonderful dish, if you like tongue.

Luz Villafane's recommendation was the Churrasco. It is a sirloin steak about an inch thick and the same general acreage as the state of Wisconsin. The wooden platter it's served on barely contains this massive piece of meat, fork-tender and nicely-flavored from having been marinated overnight in an oil-based mixture of chopped garlic, onions and tomatoes.

Colombia boasts both a Caribbean and Pacific coastline, so it stands to reason that Colombians have an affinity for seafood. Red Snapper is as popular there as it is here. It was scored and fried skillfully at La Fogata (Pescado Frito). Another favorite, Camaron al Ajillo (garlic shrimp) was a classic Spanish casserole of shrimp in a parsley-flecked, garlicky butter sauce that screamed for crusty bread to absorb the leftover sauce. (But, I was reminded that they don't really eat bread.)

Two of the daily specials I sampled were superb. Mondongo (available Tuesday), another paisa regional specialty, is a tripe and pork stew that bears more resemblance to Spain's callos than a Mexican menudo. The Wednesday "especialidade" was an equally satisfying Costilla or Rib Soup that like the Mondongo also had a hearty deeply-flavored chicken broth base.

My favorite dish of all may have been Calentado listed under "Breakfast/Desayuno." Calentado means "warmed" or "to warm up leftovers" and although it can be ordered any time, Hector says, "It is my favorite breakfast." Rice, beans, chunks of chicharones and chorizo are scrambled with eggs.

Hector's mother confects a fine Trés Leches for dessert, or you might want to try the Colombian version of dulce de leche – Arequipe.

There is Mexican and American beer and California wine, but most of the regulars seemed to be drinking fresh fruit juice with their meal.

La Fogata is small and the service is pretty low-key, so don't go in a hurry.

LA JALISCIENCE TAQUERIA RESTAURANT AND BAR

1308 Montrose
Houston, Texas 77019
713/524-8676

Type of Cuisine: Mexican
Bar: Full
Dress: Casual
Entertainment: Live 9:00p.m.-1:00a.m. Friday and Saturday
Payment: All Major Credit Cards
Entrée Range: $2.00-$7.95
Recommended Dishes:
    Steak a la Mexicana
    Pollo Jaliscience
    Pollo Cilantro
    Breakfast: Huevos Rancheros
        Migas con Huevo
Hours: Sunday-Thursday, 10:00a.m.-3:00a.m.
    Friday-Saturday, 10:00a.m.-4:00a.m.
Reservations: Accepted

If you crave great Mexican food at two o'clock in the morning, I've got your place.

La Jaliscience is straight up my alley. It looks like a smalltown South Texas cafe. Envision lots of black and white tile, ceiling fans, walls covered with neon fixtures and authentic memorabilia, wooden booths upholstered in aqua Naugahyde and one fabulous jukebox.

Owner, Frida Marquez, believes that the unusually late hours and the extremely reasonable prices are what distinguishes her restaurant from others. "Also the food is good. It doesn't matter if you are inexpensive, if the food's no good."

She's right. A good impression is made instantly by a threatening little saucer of addictive, homemade pickled peppers, onions and carrots placed on the table to eat with warm, freshly made chips and hot sauce. That's "hot" as in temperature. "That's one of the things that makes a difference," Marquez says. "Anybody who makes salsa uses the same ingredients – tomatoes, onions, garlic. But we serve it the way it's supposed to be. Hot. That's why it's called 'hot sauce.'"

The margaritas passed our "straight up" test, that is, if the flavor of the cocktail withstands being shaken and strained into a glass, it's good.

Crusty, bobbin-shaped bolillos are used to make the Mexican sandwich, Torta. My choice of the possible fillings steak, ham, chicken, avocado or chorizo con huevo (scrambled sausage and eggs) is the steak. La Jaliscience's excellent beef fajitas are used in this messy, but immensely satisfying sandwich composed of lettuce, sliced avocadoes, tomatoes, onions and sour cream. Marquez says they are a big hit, especially at lunch. She adds, "My many vegetarian customers like the torta with just avocado."

The two most popular things on the menu are the Beef and Chicken Fajitas and the Burritos. The beef fajitas are way above average, probably because, unlike many places, they take the time and trouble to marinate them. The same is true of the Carne Asada (literally "flame-cooked meat") where the same marinated skirt steak is left whole and served with faultless guacamole, moist and flavorful Mexican rice and a cup of frijoles a la charra. The charros are the elegant horsemen of Mexico, so "a la charra" means in the style of the lady charro stewed with garlic, onions and serrano peppers and cilantro. The creamy refried beans benefit from the same wonderful flavors.

Marquez and I agree that our favorite beef dish is the Steak a la Mexicana. Here the fajita meat is diced and cooked quickly with cilantro, chopped tomatoes, onions and a generous measure of jalapeño peppers. She says, "Mostly Mexicans eat 'La Mexicana' because many people find it very hot." I did not.

Two other dishes that she says are popular almost exclusively with her Mexican customers are the tender Tacos made from Beef Tongue, and the Mexican Menudo. This rich soup of honeycomb tripe and hominy is made only on weekends (Saturday and Sunday). Apparently, both of these dishes are favorites of Willie Nelson's who makes a point of visiting whenever he's in town. "He usually just comes in by himself at two or three in the afternoon when nobody is around. He likes very, very authentic Mexican food. He is such a nice guy." Marquez says Tommy Tune and Cindy Lauper have also both been in and that the band, ZZ Top, are regulars.

My two favorite chicken dishes are Pollo Jaliscience and Pollo Cilantro. Both divine, they should be chosen because they are delicious and not because they are light. The Pollo Jaliscience is covered with a rich, brown blanket of finely-chopped mushrooms and the Pollo Cilantro has a heavenly sauce of sour cream, white wine and cilantro.

All of the dishes listed as Desayunos (breakfast) – Huevos Rancheros, Huevos con Chorizo and Migas con Huevo, to name a few, are offered all day and night.

The only dessert available was a wonderful dense, eggy Flan.

La Jaliscience (pronounced halees´seeinsay) according to Marquez, is the expression used for someone from the huge, central state of Jalisco, Mexico. "I am from Honduras, but when my husband, Jose, and I opened the restaurant in 1979 we named it after him." For the first two years it was little more than a very popular taco and burrito stand. "When we started out, the dining room was where the kitchen is now. We had five tables, but people lined up around the block for our burritos, especially." She says they are still the most popular items on the menu, "I don't know why. Maybe because they are big and cheap!" (I'm not really a burrito fan, but they are good.)

After a couple of years, they were able to take over the space next door, so although it doesn't feel it, the restaurant now seats up to two hundred in two separate rooms.

There is live entertainment Friday and Saturday nights roughly from about 9:00 p.m. to between 1:00 and 2:00 a.m. "I have blues, jazz, rock and roll, mostly local groups. Right now there is a South American band, Los del Sur, playing South American folk music."

Marquez now runs the restaurant singlehandedly with the assistance of daughter, Claudia, a student at Houston Community College. Claudia has encouraged her mother to expand the menu to include more healthful options. "Now my daughter, when we open the al fresco dining in the back, is going to add some vegetarian dishes to the menu, and some new plates. She is very health conscious. Besides, all the old favorites are going to stay with us."

LA MEXICANA

1018 Fairview
Houston, Texas 77006
713/521-0963

Type of Cuisine: Mexican
Bar: Full
Dress: Casual
Entertainment: No
Payment: All Major Credit Cards
Entrée Range: $6.50-$11.75
Recommended Dishes:
Entrées: Torta (Best in Town)
Tacos (a la carte)
Quesadilla
Napolitos (Cactus)
Chicharron en Salsa Verde (Pork Rinds in Green Salsa)
Milaneza de Res (Breaded Skirt Steak)
Weekend Specials: Chicharron (Fried Pork Rinds)
Barbacoa (Beef Cheek)
Carnitas (Pork)
Breakfast
Hours: Monday-Sunday, 7:00a.m.-11:00p.m.
Reservations: Accepted

With its thatched roof patio, tiled walls and a menu where Chicharron en Salsa Verde (pork skin in green sauce) shares equal billing with Flautas de Pollo, La Mexicana would fit as easily on a sunny street in Puerto Vallarta as it does on the corner of Fairview and Montrose.

La Mexicana began its life thirty years ago in a neighborhood that owner Eduardo Treviño says was predominantly Mexican "when my wife, America, and I bought it from the previous owners in 1982. It was quite well known in the Mexican community as a food market, but business was quiet in the beginning. After six or seven months, I said, 'I don't think we're going to be sending the kids to college with this kind of business.' So, we started making sandwiches – ham and cheese, tuna, chicken salad and everybody liked them, especially our triple decker. Then our customers said, 'We've had enough of your sandwiches, how about some fajitas?' Well, it was just about the time fajitas were becoming very popular in the city, so we said, 'Why not?' Let's try something different! We went out and bought a stove and a hot plate, and started making fajitas. Suddenly we got a little crowded and they wanted to sit but we didn't have any tables. So after about six months we decided to get rid of some of the shelves and I put three tables out. We set up the steam table where it is today at the front of the store and started selling beans, rice, homemade tortillas things that moved fast. People started stopping by in the morning, 'What do you have?' We made chorizo potatoes, ham and eggs and eggs Mexicana (scrambled with tomatoes, peppers and onions), and people would say 'Well, fix me up a couple of soft tacos.'

"Soon, there were people waiting for those three tables at breakfast and lunch. I said, 'Let's get rid of the other shelves, the canned goods and the beer coolers.' That's when the place changed. It was becoming a restaurant."

The transformation from food market to the panaderia (bakery)/restaurant it is today took seven years. For the first couple of years, they had no menu just what was written on the board on the wall. In fact, it's still there. The current menu has existed for five years and to my delight, is heavily populated with dishes that show greater regard for Treviño's heritage, the food he grew up eating and that old neighborhood, than pleasing the general public. Nothing is more thrilling than flagrant disregard of conventional restaurant wisdom.

Even the Fajitas a la Mexicana that he started with are more accurately an old-fashioned Carne Guisada (beef stew). "It is one of my favorites. The carne guisada is a dish my mother made everyday when we were little boys. It's a good piece of meat – skirt steak, but more tender, softer, juicier, different from most people's fajitas."

Ordered on its own or folded into a soft, warm taco, another guisada, the Guisado de Puerco is just as satisfying – tender forkfuls of pork cooked in a rich, red stew of tomatoes, chiles and onions.

Even the often pedestrian customary accompaniments, beans and rice, are unusually good. "Everybody who comes into my place says, 'Your beans and your rice just taste excellent.' I have customers who say, 'As soon as you taste the beans and they're good, than means the food is good.' And there's a secret to doing beans this way!" He assures me that unlike most Mexican restaurants, the secret ingredient doesn't include the use of lard and that they pride themselves on not using lard or any animal fat to cook with. He claims that it's still used by most Mexican restaurants. "But you don't have to use lard to give flavor to a meal. Even our chips are dry, not greasy."

The chips are dry, freshly made and arrive with a sassy saucer of salsa verde – a tomatillo-based sauce with just the right balance of cilantro, jalapeños and garlic. The first impression is good. There is no mistaking that before you've even seen the menu, you're in for a completely different Mexican dining experience.

Forego the standard order of nachos and instead choose from one of the list of no fewer than twenty-five à la carte items. I love this. It is possible to compose a virtual Mexican smörgasbord, perfect for those who can never quite get their combination platter right and don't mind either going without the wonderful beans and rice or paying a little extra to order them on the side.

Two things about this à la carte list fascinate me. The first is the Torta. I ordered this one without asking any questions and with no explanation given on the menu or anywhere else – a huge, absolutely delicious sandwich arrived. Given a choice of meats ham, pork, chicken, fajitas or my favorite, milaneza (breaded skirt steak) the sandwich is carefully composed layers of mayonnaise, guacamole, shredded lettuce and tomatoes, on a light, freshly made bolillo (Mexican roll). Apparently torta stands are common on street corners all over Mexico where occasionally beans and a fried egg are added to the already interesting concert of flavors and textures.

The second aspect of this part of the menu that appeals to me is the ability to order from a choice of ten different kinds of individual Tacos, making it possible to sample everything from guisado de puerco to the more adventurous beef tongue nestled in a soft, warm freshly made tortilla. An individual Quesadilla can be ordered and the Tamales are as you would expect – the genuine article.

Fans of Ceviche should not miss ordering theirs. Served as you would find it in Acapulco or Puerto Vallarta – in a sundae glass with a teaspoon – the impeccably fresh shrimp, octopus and firm white fish are marinated overnight and generously garnished with diced avocado, tomatoes, cilantro and onions.

Treviño is especially proud of La Mexicana's Molé. Along with the seafood specialities and some of their more complicated dishes, he says it is one of the things America prepares herself. Her rendition of this ancient black sauce has more than twenty-nine ingredients and is ladled over either enchiladas or a chicken breast.

A dish you're not likely to find elsewhere is Napolitos En Salsa Chipotle. Sliced, fleshy paddles of the prickly pear cactus are boiled then sautéed in a dense, rust colored, slightly pungent sauce of chipotle peppers (smoked jalapeños). The flavor and texture is a cross between green beans and okra. For the truly brave, I recommend both the Lengua Guisada (beef tongue stewed with onions, green peppers, tomato and garlic) and the Chicharron en Salsa Verde (pork rinds braised in the house green sauce).

I'll come clean right now and admit that among the weekend specials (available Fridays, Saturdays and Sundays) I have a weakness for the Chicherron sold by the pound at La Mexicana.

Made from the pork saddle so there is still substantial meat attached, these are not mere pork rinds, but the kind of "crackling" you would get yourself if you had roasted your own pork. Not something to make a habit of, but they sure are good.

Other weekend indulgences sold as specials or at the steam table to take home, are the fabulously tender, perfectly seasoned Carnitas. Fist-sized chunks of pork or beef are browned, braised for hours, then fried until crisp. This is serious Mexican soul food.

A favorite of the regularly listed entrées is the Milaneza De Res. A dish made popular in Northern Mexico by Italian immigrants, this adaptation of veal Milanese is skirt steak pounded wafer thin, lightly breaded and fried, served with papas fritas (French fries). It's not uncommon to ask for a fried egg on top. Which brings us to breakfast. Sunday is their busiest day.

Served between 7:00 a.m. and noon seven days a week, the breakfast menu is full of standard classics that were traditionally developed in Mexico at a time when the day began with one breakfast of pastry or maybe a tortilla and coffee, a desayuno, and was followed midmorning by an almuerzo – a meal of much more substance preparing the diner for the days work at hand. All reliably good, the most interesting to me is the Machacado con Huevo. Eggs are scrambled with machaca – salted and dried beef that was, in its day, as indispensable to the cowboys and ranchers in Northern Mexico, as beef jerky was to early Western American pioneers.

The panaderia (bakery) was added two years ago. "We wanted a traditional Mexican neighborhood bakery. People often stop in and buy bread in the morning on the way to their office or end their meal with a piece of pastry or cookie." I never leave without a piece of the Pastel de Queso – a flat, dense triangle of Mexican cheesecake.

LATINA CAFÉ & FOOD MARKET

1972 Fairview
Houston, Texas 77019
713/521-2611

Type of Cuisine: Cuban
Bar: Wine and Beer
Dress: Casual
Entertainment: No
Payment: All Major Credit Cards
Entrée Range: $7.00-$8.45
Recommended Dishes:
Appetizers: Tamal Cubana (Cuban Tamale)
Entrées: Steak Sandwich
Chicken Soup
Bistec de Palomilla (Steak)
Pierna de Puerco (Roast Pork)
Baked Chicken
Paella (check for availability)
Daily Specials
Hours: Monday-Thursday, 10:30a.m.-9:30p.m.
Friday-Saturday, 10:30a.m.-10:00p.m.
Sunday, 10:30a.m.-9:00p.m.
Reservations: Not Accepted

It is said that when Christopher Columbus discovered Cuba in October of 1492 that he thought it was "the most beautiful land that human eyes have ever seen."

Until I'm able to visit this tropical paradise and see it for myself, I suppose I'll have to be content with the knowledge that the sultry, authentic flavors of Cuba are available every day here in Houston as the balmy breezes blow near the corner of Hazard and Fairview.

Historically, the influences on Cuban cuisine are vast – Chinese, Portuguese, African and Indian with the emphatic culinary accent of Spain and Europe. The best of these cultures fuse to define a highly individual style of cooking and eating that is as robust and complex as it is deliberately simple.

Any discussion of Cuban food must begin with their beloved Frijoles Negros (black beans). They accompany every entrée at Latina Café and are always eaten with another staple, long grain white rice. More soup than side dish, these lush, darkly delicious black beans have been first cooked, and then added to a sofrito – the sauté of garlic, onions, chile and green peppers and seasoning in olive oil that is used as the fundamental base to most Cuban dishes – then cooked slowly again until the beans crack open.

The Caribbean/West Indian influence is felt in the choice of either twice-fried green or sweet, ripe Plantano (plantains) with all main dishes. Indigenous to the tropics, the plantain looks like our dessert banana, but isn't as sweet and is used more as a vegetable than a fruit in Cuban cooking. While I would normally gravitate towards the savory, instead of the sweet with my meal, the winner of the two, handsdown, is the fried sweet plantain, a tropical treat sumptuous and irresistible.

If you have the good fortune of going on Monday, Wednesday, or Friday, start the meal with a bowl of Chicken Soup. It is dense with chicken and vegetables with a rich, intensely-flavored broth, colored deep yellow by the addition of bijol – a mixture of cornflour, ground cumin and food coloring commonly used in Cuban cooking in place of the more expensive saffron.

The Entremese (appetizer) to absolutely not miss is the distinctively different Tamal Cubano (Cuban tamale). They are made from fresh ground corn, filled with minced, well-seasoned pork and glazed with mojo – a thin, white sauce made from garlic, vegetable oil and naranja agria (sour orange) – and served with the unintentionally whimsical garnish of boiled ham, a Kraft American cheese slice and sliced dill pickles.

Listed on the menu as an appetizer, the Pan con Bistec y Mariquitas (steak sandwich) is spectacularly good – thinly-sliced, pounded and marinaded top sirloin cooked on the grill with nearly translucent rounds of sweet onion, loaded onto a piece of warm, buttered Cuban bread and topped with a handful of shoestring potatoes. It comes with Mariquitas (banana chips), but the french fries have a delicious, old-fashioned quality and are worth ordering à la carte.

There are many dishes to recommend among the Platos Fuertes (main dishes). The Bistec de Palomilla (palomilla steak) is exactly the same thing as the steak sandwich with grilled onions minus the shoestring potatoes and the bread. As good as it is, pork gets a bigger and far better play in the Cuban kitchen. Both the Masas de Puerco Fritas (chunks of fried pork) and the Pierna de Puerco (roast pork) were exceptionally tender and juicy, but my favorite entrée may be the succulent, perfectly seasoned Baked Chicken.

While the Cubans can't lay claim to Paella (pronounced pyay´yuh), probably the defining dish of Spain, they love it just the same, and Latina Café's rendition, while quite different from any of the paellas I tried in Spain, is a masterful presentation. It must be ordered for a minimum of four people twenty-four hours in advance to give them a chance to assemble the great assortment of seafood; lobster, crab claws, shrimp and perch. In addition to the seafood, there are thin disks of chorizo (Spanish sausage), moist pieces of chicken breasts, green peas, scarlet ribbons of pimiento (more for color than flavor) and unexpected slivers of green olives cooked with all of that rice. For those who have tasted a truly authentic Spanish paella, the Cuban variety is quite different but equally delicious. Theirs is not cooked in the traditional wide shallow pan for which the dish is named and has a moister, soupier consistency. Another difference is that the rice is cooked through and not al denté as it is in Spain. Also, they use long grain rice instead of the short grain Spanish rice and again, bijol is used in place of saffron to color it vibrant yellow. Theirs is a lyrical piece of work the kind of dish a dinner party should be built around, and is perfectly complemented by both Spanish wines available the hearty red Sangre de Torro or the dry, crisp white Viña Sol. An even better idea might be to order it to go. While the fluorescent lighting and plastic tablecloths have a charm all their own during the day, they're a bit jarring at night.

Other Cuban classics are available as "Specials" on specific days. Those to look out for are Picadillo a la Criolla (Cuban/creole ground beef in tomato sauce available Tuesday), or Vaca Frita literally "fried beef" flank steak cooked, marinated then fried or sautéed in olive oil with onions until crisp, also available Tuesday. One of the Wednesday specials is the well-known Cuban dish, Ropa Vieja (which translated means "old clothes") shredded beef brisket in a tomato based sauce (and it tastes a lot better than any of my old clothes). Regulars flock to Latina Café on Friday to eat Arroz con Pollo ("rice with chicken"), actually a modified version of paella without the seafood.

The dessert of choice is a classic Flan – eggy, rich custard swimming in a pool of amber-colored, caramelized sugar.

For lovers of espresso, Cuban coffee is a memory that lingers sweetened with sugar, and served in tiny tacitas (demitasse cups). Café Cubano is the perfect way to end the meal.

LOS RANCHITOS

7687 Clarewood
Houston, Texas 77036
713/777-5703

Type of Cuisine: Salvadorean
Bar: Beer
Dress: Casual
Entertainment: No
Payment: Cash or Check Only
Entrée Range: $4.50-$6.95
Recommended Dishes:
 Appetizers: (Order as Appetizers)
  Pupusas (Cheese and Combination Pork and Cheese)
  Tamales (Chicken)
  Pastelitos
 Entrées: Consome de Apretadores
  Sopa de Mondongo
  Carne Asadas-Lomitos de Puerco (Pork, Beef)
  Mojarra Frita
 Dessert: Empanadas de Platano
  Platanos Fritos
  Tamales de Elote
Hours: Monday-Thursday, 10:00a.m.-9:30p.m.
 Friday-Sunday, 10:00a.m.-10:30p.m.
Reservations: Not Accepted

A recent wrong number to a Salvadorean businessman's office bore such exotic fruit that I owe him a debt of gratitude for spending a good fifteen minutes on the phone (with a total stranger) proudly sharing the names of his favorite Salvadorean restaurants and which dishes not to miss.

That's how I discovered Los Ranchitos. And what a find it is. This week, my food vocabulary expands to include Pupusas, Curtido and a Salvadorean seafood bisque-like soup fine enough to hold its own against any bowl of soup anywhere in this town.

Owner, Oscar Flores, who shares cooking duties at Los Ranchitos with his wife, Milagro, says he "learned about spices and the secrets of the kitchen" from his mother growing up in the small town of San Miguel in eastern El Salvador.
When ordering at Los Ranchitos bypass the "Apertivos" – the Coctel de Conchas, a "black clam" ceviche was so strong it was scary – and go straight for the fabulous "Lo Mas Tipico de la Comida Salvadoreña" (the most typical Salvadorean dishes). Pupusas are at the top of the list.

Sold on crisp pieces of banana leaves by street vendors on every corner in El Salvador, Flores says that "pupusas are our national dish." The handmade ground corn tortillas are smaller, but thicker than their Mexican cousins as they are not subjected to a tortilla press before they are browned on a dry, flat grill. Alone as "tortillas" they are not that interesting, but when filled with cheese, pork or both, they become pupusas – something to write home about.

The Pupusas de Queso con Loroco is the most common and the most popular. Flores uses a mixture of mozzarella and Farmer's cheese that he says best mimics the flavor and texture of the white, fresh cheese used in El Salvador. He mixes the cheeses with loroco – a tiny green flower grown seasonally and imported "from home," as he says. The pork filled pupusa is made with minced, fried pieces of pork cooked with tomatoes, onion, garlic and "our spices." The Queso Pupusa is great – a sort of Salvadorean grilled cheese sandwich – but the combination of the pork and cheese is even better. Order (at least) one per person, split them at the seams and fill them with Curtido, tart pickled cabbage with shredded carrots, onions seasoned with oregano and red pepper flakes.

Central American Tamales are large and steamed in emerald-green banana leaves. "Tamales are the hardest job because everything must be cooked separately," Flores says. The finely ground corn is formed by hand around thin wedges of sautéed potatoes, chickpeas and either ground pork or (my preference) shredded chicken. I liked them with a spoonful of the mild, but flavorful tomatoey salsa, notable for the judicious use of jalapeños. "Salvadoreans don't really like things too hot," Flores explains. The salsa is placed on the table once you are seated with a basket of Tajadas – curled, crisp ribbons of plantains cut lengthwise and fried golden brown.

The Pastelitos Salvadoreños are another must to sample. Small, half-moon shaped turnovers are filled with well-seasoned ground beef, potatoes and onions, encased in a mini-corn tortilla and fried. They are served with curtido that has been doused with a light, onion-flavored tomato sauce. Flores says to eat correctly, one must take a bite of the pastelito, then spoon curtido and the tomato sauce directly onto the little pastry.

My recommendation is to devise a "Combinado Tipico" (typical combination) of one pupusa, one pastelito and one tamale de pollo per customer as an appetizer. All three can be ordered individually á la carte. Consider all of these a prelude to the main event, the Consome de Apretadores (which comes with a cheese pupusa, by the way).

The Consome de Apretadores is made "al estilo 'la pema de Santa Rosa de Lima'" as it says on the menu. It is "in the style of" a childhood friend of Flores' mother from Santa Rosa de Lima whom he says "invented" the dish almost thirty years ago and still serves the definitive rendition at "the most popular restaurant in San Miguel."

It is neither consommé as we think of it, nor is it made with "apretadores," a sort of stone crab indigenous to the Pacific Ocean just south of San Miguel. This "very local soup," as Flores calls it, is pale satiny yellow. The deep-flavored broth is touched with cream and tinted yellow with ground annatto seeds. Meaty Gulf crabs – in lieu of the apretadores – bob happily in the white porcelain bowls with plump shrimp still in their soft (edible) shells and whole eggs that have been poached directly in the simmering soup. It is heaven. Eat it as they do in San Miguel – with a generous squeeze of lime and – like many of the Salvadorean dishes – with your hands (the shellfish, anyway!).

Flores claims Comsome de Apretadores is famous among Salvadoreans for its restorative powers after a long night out on the town. But my money's on Mondongo, the earthy, intensely-flavored tripe stew as an all-out cure for la cruda (a hangover) or anything else, for that matter.

"In every town in El Salvador – it doesn't matter how big or small is it – you will find somebody who sells Mondongo and nothing else," Flores explains. "But, you must go early. If you go around eleven o'clock, you will be told there is no more mondongo until the next day."

Comparable to, but even more complex than Mexican menudo, Sopa de Mondongo is full of (mostly) winter vegetables – pale green chayotes, chunks of cabbage, carrots, yuca, fresh corn and slender quarters of pipian (tiny, sweet Central-American grown zucchini). The distinctive, forcefully-concentrated flavor comes from a freshly-ground blend of what Flores refers to as "our spices" – black pepper, cumin, oregano, bay leaf, garlic, basil and always the brick-red, faintly smokey, whole annatto seeds. It is this fragrant mixture of spices that separates Salvadorean cooking from its neighbors.

The best among the listed "Carne Asadas" is the Lomito do Puerco. A succulent piece of pork loin is marinated in the traditional spices and Worcestershire Sauce and cooked quickly on the char broiler. The beef fajitas, prepared the same way, are almost as good. Both are covered with onions caramelized on the flat grill and come with refried pinto beans close enough to pass for the Mexican variety, and a mound of moist, white rice "cooked the way my mother taught me," says Flores, "sautéed first in a little oil and chicken base, then cooked in water flavored with finely shredded carrots."

Flores is especially proud of the Mojarra Frita, listed under Ricos Mariscos (seafood dishes). Sweet, white-fleshed tilapia farmed locally (near Sealy) is substituted for the

Salvadorean freshwater fish called Mojarra. The pound to pound-and-a-half whole fish is split, dry seasoned, refrigerated for about thirty minutes and deep fried to a flawless (greaseless) turn. It is meant to be eaten with your hands - crisp, edible, bones and all, with a simple spritz of lime. Flores tells me that his ten-year-old daughter, Lisa, cheerfully plucks the eyes from the fish with her dainty little fingers, gives them a little squeeze of lime, and eats them. Now that's adventurous!

The robust Regia was my favorite of the two Salvadorean beers available. It only comes in a quart-size bottle, so if you are not sharing, the Pilsener is a good second choice.

I save a final loving memory for dessert. All found back under "Lo Mas Tipico" on the menu, the Plantanos Fritos con Crema are thickly-cut plantains fried and served with sour cream thinned with buttermilk. Another Salvadorean specialty, Tamales de Elote, are sweet corn tamales cooked in corn husks also served "con crema." Or best of all, order an Empanada de Platano for everyone at the table. Mashed ripe plantains are molded around a sweet, snow-white paste of rice flour, milk and sugar flavored with a little cinnamon. It is a fine way to finish this very special meal.

LUPE TORTILLA'S RESTAURANT

318 Stafford (at Highway 6)
Houston, Texas 77079
281/496-7580

Type of Cuisine: Tex-Mex
Bar: Full
Dress: Casual
Entertainment: No
Payment: All Major Credit Cards Accepted
Entrée Range: $1.95-$17.95
Recommended Dishes:
- Soft Chicken Tacos
- Steak Lupe
- Fajitas-Beef and Chicken
- Three Pepper Steak
- Cilantro Jalapeno Chicken
- Chicken Lupe
- Chicken Little

Hours: Lunch: Monday-Friday, 11:00a.m.-2:00p.m.
Dinner: Sunday-Thursday, 5:30p.m.-8:30p.m.
Friday-Saturday, 5:30p.m.-9:30p.m.
Reservations: Not Accepted

Humorist Mark Twain's approach to diet was a simple one. "Eat what you like and let the food fight it out inside." He could have easily been talking about a rousing, ripsnorting meal at a TexMex restaurant and since the first one documented was the Old Borunda Cafe opened in 1887 in Marfa, Texas, maybe he was.

For years I've heard people talk about the restaurant "Lupe Tortilla's" and how wonderful it is. One of the many people singing its praises is a friend who lives in the area (Addicks Road/Highway 6) who has tried to get me to meet her there for lunch for at least two years. Now I share the same weakness for (or maybe lowgrade addiction to) Mexican food as most of my friends who have grown up in Texas, but I couldn't imagine why any reasonable person who was lucky enough to live in an area of Houston surrounded by Mexican restaurants of infinite variety would willingly get into their car and drive twenty-five minutes to eat even really great TexMex food...maybe it's the atmosphere...maybe it's the margaritas...

No. It's the food. The Soft Chicken Tacos alone are worth the drive . . . good enough to make even the most jaded TexMex devotee dance the fandango. When I asked the owners, Stan and Audrey Holt, why their food is so much better than the competition, they said it's because it's fresher than anyone else's, partially by necessity because the kitchen is minute, but mostly because their philosophy of serving great food is that it should be "cooked to order, when you order, even if it takes a little longer." This may be true, but it's more than that.

A truly gifted amateur cook, Stan has expanded the menu from the original eighteen items to fifty-five entrées, having added approximately five a year since they opened in 1983. Indeed the main menu covers all conceivable major points of interest on the TexMex culinary landscape: tacos, enchiladas, chalupas. In fact, there is almost nothing to indicate how incredibly special #29, the Soft Chicken Tacos, are except the suggestion that they are not what you think and that you should ask your waiter. No, they are much better than anything you could imagine; grilled shredded chicken breasts wrapped in impossibly large, thin, fresh, flour tortillas, surrounded by a light oniony, chicken stock-based ranchero sauce and baked in the oven to melt the aged Monterey Jack cheese. An adaptation of a dish Stan had tried at the old La Fogata in San Antonio, this is one for the books and makes a perfect case for that old cooking axiom that a dish is only as good as the sum of its parts. There are two tacos in an order, but as wonderful as they are, if you're dining with a fellow carnivore, I'd order the Steak Lupe on the "Mas Especiales" part of the menu and split the two dishes.

This is a half-pound fajita steak covered with chopped tomatoes, onion, cilantro, peppers, and a thin veil of melted cheese. This dish will bring tears to your eyes mostly because theirs is the definitive rendition of beef or chicken fajitas. An old favorite practically reinvented here, they are unusually tender and smokey with a pronounced flavor of lime. When I asked the Holts what makes them so special he answered cryptically, "It's the slope of the floor," explaining finally, that after the whole fajita steaks and chicken breasts are removed from the grill where they've been cooked, they rest briefly on a griddle before they are sliced to become fajitas, weighed or left whole to become Steak or Chicken Lupe, for instance, and in that brief time, because of the "slope of the floor," they are pushed up against the side of the griddle and forced to rest in and absorb each other's cooking juices; clearly a happy accident, but the truth may lie in an even happier one...the origin of the recipe.

On a trip to San Antonio to buy supplies, the Holts spent the afternoon at the United Meat Market buying fajita pans and when they asked the grandfather of the owner what he thought was the best way to make fajitas, he boasted that he had the "best recipe in the world," but that it was a secret. After five hours, the old man was sufficiently charmed by Audrey's petite stature and sweet nature to part with the recipe scribbled on a matchbook cover, handing it to her as they left.

The Fajitas are served with guacamole, grilled tomato wedges, poblano pepper strips, scallions lightly brushed with peanut oil and grilled instead of the traditional sliced onion and handsdown the lightest, thinnest, freshest-tasting flour tortillas in town rolled thin enough for the original and present tortilla maker, Alva Garcia, to "see her paycheck through." The beef fajitas are great, but I've never tasted a juicier, more succulent chicken fajita! So I recommend them equally.

Apart from the spectacular Steak Lupe where the fajita steak is left whole, another favorite is the Three Pepper Steak, a wonderful addition on the "mas" menu and the influence of twenty-one year old Judd Holt, a recent graduate of the Culinary Institute of America. He's also responsible for the first listing on that menu, the Cilantro Jalapeño Chicken, my second favorite treatment of a whole chicken breast...after the Chicken Lupe, that is.

The other chicken dish I love is the Green Chicken Enchilada made with green tomatillo sauce. Stan Holt feels that one of the best dishes on the menu is the one listed unfortunately as "Cheekin Leetle" in a controversial and (I think) somewhat misguided attempt at TexMex humor. It is a marinated chicken breast on a homemade corn tortilla covered with ranchero sauce and roasted poblano peppers and baked until the cheese melts.

A word of warning, some of the dishes are garnished with grilled serrano, jalapeño or habanero peppers which are wonderful in small doses but not to be eaten whole unless you're desperate to clear your sinuses and those of your ancestors'.

Whichever you choose, you might want to sooth the savaged taste buds with an order of heavenly, egg-rich Flan or maybe the Bunuelos, crisped to perfection, drizzled with honey, dusted with cinnamon and topped with a surprise scoop of vanilla ice cream.

This 1930's farmhouse is easily the most charming Mexican restaurant I've ever seen, especially if you're lucky enough to be seated in one of the original cozy little jewel-like rooms, two of which are small enough to fit only three or sometimes four small tables. Over the years, by necessity the little frame house has been virtually engulfed by decks and porches, some enclosed, some open. The restaurant now seats 149 at one time. The popularity of Lupe Tortilla's has grown to such an extent that the Holts say on Saturday night there can be as many as 175 people waiting in line when they open at 5:30 for dinner. After their fluctuating fortunes and some hard lessons learned in the restaurant business, they take nothing for granted, and say that this crowd is a thrilling sight and that they often encourage the kitchen crew, most of whom have been with them for as many as fourteen years, to come out to take a look at the assembled masses and tell them "it's because of what they do." The bar or "canteen" opens at 5:00 p.m. to serve those standing in line.

An attractive couple in their late 40's, the Holts apparently inspire a great deal of loyalty from both customers and employees; rare in a business that's known for its exceptionally high rate of turnover.

Since I'm not good at waiting, Audrey Holt says that it's quieter if you come for dinner Monday, Tuesday or Wednesday nights and for lunch after the early crowd has thinned out, between 1:00 and 2:00 pm. They say that the kitchen is too small to handle parties larger than eight.

LYNDON'S PIT BAR-B-Q

13165 Northwest Freeway
Houston, Texas 77040
713/690-2112

Type of Cuisine: Barbecue
Bar: Wine and Beer
Dress: Casual
Entertainment: No
Payment: All Major Credit Cards
Entrée Range: $3.75-$9.75
Recommended Dishes:
Weekend Specials: Pork Loin
Prime Rib
Regularly Available: Charcoaled Half-Chicken
Pulled Pork
Pork Ribs
Potato Salad
Coleslaw
Stuffed Jalapeños
Hours: Monday-Saturday, 11:00a.m.-9:00p.m.
Sunday, 12:00p.m.-6:00p.m.
Reservations: Accepted

How old were you when you knew what you wanted to be when you grew up? Do you remember the defining moment? Lyndon Maeker of Lyndon's Pit Bar-B-Q does.

"I participated in my first barbecue when I was ten years old. I still remember that day. It was my parents' 25th wedding anniversary. My dad had both his side and my mom's side of the family over. That was about eleven aunts and uncles with their spouses and kids. That's a lot of people.

"This was on the farm where I grew up about 15 miles east of Lubbock. They constructed a pit for the occasion – a rather crude device. My dad built a fire of mesquite roots and the root was actually bigger than the tree. The fire was separate from the pit and he would put the embers or coals beneath the meat. He cooked half a beef that day. I couldn't believe what was involved in the process. I was absolutely fascinated."

Fast forward some forty-seven plus years and this recent ex-oil field equipment executive has turned a family pastime into a thriving business. With the help of two of his three grown sons, Mark and Matt, Maeker opened Lyndon's in August of '97.

Maeker prefers the subtlety of hickory or pecan to mesquite now, and his equipment is light-years more sophisticated, but the result is an assortment of barbecue ever bit "as unique and delicious" as Maeker says he found the beef on that memorable day.

The weekend menu at Lyndon's features Prime Rib delicately smoked over pecan – an old specialty of Maeker's that he says he's cooked for twenty years or so at his annual barbecue for up to seventy-five of his closest friends. The prime rib is an elegant alternative to Lyndon's also-exceptional, long-smoked Beef Brisket.

Another weekend enticement – unless we can convince Maeker otherwise – is Pork Loin of juicy, eye-popping perfection. Maeker does not exaggerate when he boasts that "the pork loin is out of this world."

In an effort to not obscure the fine flavor of this excellent (and expensive) cut of meat, Maeker wisely seasons the pork – like the prime rib – with nothing more than salt and a liberal dose of black pepper. It then takes a turn in the pit with the prime rib over pecan wood. Here's an idea – sample the pork loin there and take a piece of prime rib home for sandwiches over the weekend.

Fans of Pulled Pork – the beloved barbecue favorite east of the Mississippi – happily, can enjoy Lyndon's any day of the week. "It is smoked…smoked…smoked… and unbelievably tender," explains Maeker. "We use a boneless pork shoulder butt and we cook it alongside the brisket over hickory all night. We remove it in the morning, wrap it in aluminum foil and put it back in the pit for a couple of hours to help break down the internal fat. When it's ordered, we literally 'pull' the meat off with a fork and knife." It is spectacular and should be eaten just as they do "back East" on a bun with tart, vinegar-based sauce – the "Carolina Sauce" – that Maeker has on hand for this purpose, and loads of coleslaw. The pulled pork is good enough to have won over some die-hard, beef-eating Texans. "They heard about if from friends and curiosity killed the cat!" Maeker laughs.

When asked what his favorite barbecued meat is, Maeker says, "I'm not going to hem haw around here. I like the chicken, and I like the pork loin. Those are my two favorites." It's hard to argue with the man. The chicken is fabulous. Called Charcoaled Half-Chicken to indicate that they are not heavily smoked, the succulent, golden-brown split fryers are fresh and never frozen. They are seasoned with garlic, salt and pepper, and put on the pit, "strictly pecan," as Maeker says, with the superb Pork Ribs that receive the identical treatment. "The secret is that you have to mop (the chicken) to keep it moist. I learned the hard way. My mop recipe is water-based with fresh onion, garlic and lemon. It becomes very much a flavoring medium." The meaty ribs emerge with a crisp, well-seasoned exterior.

The Sausage is a good, lightly-smoked, mostly pork

sausage that Maeker says, "Just rang a bell when I tried it. This Bohemian fellow is making it for me and it's the closest thing I've ever tasted to what my dad and uncles used to make on the farm after the first hard freeze."

The house barbecue sauce is a well-balanced, classic tomato-based sauce with whole, identifiable pieces of onion. As a thoughtful touch, glass Heinz ketchup bottles are half-filled with barbecue sauce and dept warm at the condiment station for diners to take to their tables.

Side dishes are prepared with particular loving care. In order of preference, the Coleslaw is ideal, crisp, cold, lightly-dressed and not-too-sweet. Maeker credits his sister with the superior Potato Salad recipe. "She gave it to me with her permission." It's skins-on potato salad enriched with sour cream and the standard mayonnaise and French's mustard with a welcome crunch of good dill pickle.

Maeker says he is particularly proud of his Beans. Similar to Mexican El Charro beans, the "Rio Grande" beans are a sultry mix of pinto beans sautéed with onions, garlic, cilantro, jalapeño and whole pieces of smoky bacon.

Stuffed Jalapeños are made with crisp, almost-sweet halves of fresh, seeded jalapeños filled with a creamy mixture of pimento cheese and cream cheese.

The Onion Rings are hand dipped in a nice, garlicky beer batter, "my son Matt's idea," Maeker claims. A warning: they are huge and a full order is enough to feed a large, very hungry family.

The creamy, jalapeño-flecked Spicy Corn – the most successful of the three advertised casseroles – is the perfect partner to pork or any of the barbecue, for that matter.

In spite of being located at the corner of a fairly characterless, spanking-new strip center (at Northwest Crossing), once you get inside, Lyndon's has all the requisite rustic charm of an old barn. Whether you eat in or take out, Lyndon's is worth a visit because, as Maeker says, "Like I tell my sons, 'you can't rush barbecue!' "

LYNN'S STEAKHOUSE

955-1/2 Dairy Ashford
Houston, Texas 77079
281/870-0807

Type of Cuisine: Steak/Continental
Bar: Full
Dress: Jacket Recommended
Entertainment: No
Payment: All Major Credit Cards
Entrée Range: $17.95-$31.95
Recommended Dishes:
Appetizers: Gumbo
Escargots
Écrevisse (Crawfish)
Goat Cheese Salad
Entrées: Veal Ribeye
Veal Chop
Rack of Lamb
T-Bone Steak
Hours: Lunch: Monday-Friday, 11:00a.m.-2:00p.m.
Dinner: Monday-Friday, 5:00p.m.-10:00p.m.
Saturday, 6:00p.m.-10:00p.m.
(Closed Sunday)
Reservations: Recommended

I came across the following tribute to gumbo in the *Historical Sketch Book and Guide to New Orleans and Environs* by William H. Coleman, published in 1885: "The great dish of New Orleans, and which it claims the honor of having invented is the GUMBO. There is no dish which at the same time so tickles the palate, satisfies the appetite, furnishes the body with nutriment sufficient to carry on the physical requirements, and costs so little as a Creole gumbo. It is a dinner in itself, being soup, pièce de résistance, entremet and vegetable in one. Healthy, not heating to the stomach and easy of digestion, it should grace every table."

I agree with Mr. Coleman. Especially if it's the particularly thick, densely-flavored, darkly delicious Gumbo served at Lynn's Steakhouse. Proprietor Lynn Foreman says they use the exact same recipe that her grandmother taught her many years ago in her native hometown of Abbeville, Louisiana, twenty-five miles south of Lafayette.

My three favorite gumbos in Houston are all found in fairly unlikely places – Maxim's, The Confederate House (available Fridays only) and now Lynn's. They all have one thing in common: a thick, earthy roux and lots of fresh seafood – shrimp, crabmeat and oysters.

The gumbo's given great competition on the menu by

two other hot starters – the Escargots and the Écrevisse (crawfish). The snails and the crawfish tails receive similar treatments: both are seasoned with an herb-garlic butter (and cayenne pepper in the case of the crawfish tails), tucked into a porcelain dish with little indentations and held captive under little individual domes of puff pastry (a word of warning – they both require a tremendous amount of cooling before they can be eaten).

The influence of the particularly affable Frenchman, Loic Carbonnier, wine steward and waiter of nine years, is felt, especially in the composition of the salads. We enjoyed the seasonally-available Caesar salad; the Hearts of Palm Salad with julienned strips of hearts of palm, radishes, cucumbers and carrots dressed with a puckery balsamic vinaigrette spiked with a little raspberry vinegar; and the fabulously-conceived Goat Cheese Salad – creamy, marinated disks of goat cheese melted under the broiler and slid on top of an already dressed mixture of field greens.

While it is possible to order a piece of fresh fish (usually either tuna or salmon filets) or a sweet, broiled Lobster Tail of heroic proportion from the distant shores of either Australia or New Zealand, this is after all a steak house and as John Wayne said to the cook in "The Man Who Shot Liberty Valence"..."Burn me a good thick one, Pete. Meat and potatoes."

The Duke would have loved this place. We found all of the steaks to be perfectly seasoned, cooked exactly to order and of impeccable quality, from the slightly gamey New Zealand Rack of Lamb – seven tender, tiny chops no bigger than your thumb – to the simple, unadorned T-bone of considerable acreage (24 ounces).

Although the hulking brute of a Veal Chop was wonderful, one of the best veal dishes in town may be the Veal Rib-Eye – really a tenderloin of veal – juicy, buttery-tender, precisely cooked and sauced to perfection with a port wine-flavored, mushroom-flecked cream sauce.

The à la carte vegetables is a question of rounding up the usual suspects: Asparagus with Hollandaise Sauce, huge Fried Onion Rings, crunchy bite-size morsels of French Fries with their skin on (both served with a dish of tangy red cocktail sauce) and my two favorites – Mushrooms sautéed simply in butter, red wine, salt and pepper; and the unimprovable Lyonnais Potatoes – new potatoes first steamed, then quartered and sautéed until crisp with garlic and sweet onions.

The Creamed Spinach Gratin that accompanies all entrées is a rare bonus, apparently a much-coveted recipe which beats hollow all other versions served in these parts.

Lynn Foreman opened Lynn's Steakhouse on October 11, 1985. The dining room which seats ninety people, has a rustic, romantic, old world charm with soft lighting and dark wood beams – a comfortable, cozy atmosphere that Lynn describes as "casual elegance." There is a private dining room that was added just last March that seats up to sixteen people, but the real gem is the tiny room off the bar called the "wine room" that seats only four people and is almost always reserved for lunch and dinner, but it doesn't hurt to ask.

There are two things that distinguish Lynn's Steakhouse from other restaurants; the first is the extraordinarily professional wait staff, many of whom are from the original Tony's. Lynn and her husband Bob, a retired Air Force pilot also from Southern Louisiana, have created a happy, civilized working environment and it really shows. The service is flawless. (How often can you say that?)

The second feature is the remarkable wine list. There are no fewer than seventeen hundred bottles, eight hundred and four wines and vintages to choose from, although there is an astonishingly comprehensive selection of California wines, about two-thirds of the list are serious estate wines of exceptional vintages from France, Italy, Spain and Germany. Nationally recognized, they have won the Award of Excellence from the esteemed "Wine Spectator" every year since 1990. Again, the influence of Loic Carbonnier is felt. He has helped expand and develop the wine list over the years and manages to be extremely knowledgeable, but never pompous. He is a huge asset to the place.

Finally, the desserts of particular note are a lovely, eggy Créme Brulée and the spectaculary good Bananas Foster (prepared in the kitchen and not at the table for insurance reasons). "Just what you want bananas Foster to be and never is," commented one diner. Instead of vanilla ice cream, rum and banana soup-like consistency, the bananas are practically candied, cloaked in crisped brown sugar and rum with a scoop of vanilla ice cream. Hmmmm...

MADRAS PAVILION

3910 Kirby Drive
Houston, Texas 77098
713/521-2617

Type of Cuisine: Indian
Bar: Wine and Beer
Dress: Casual
Entertainment: No
Payment: All Major Credit Cards
Prices: Buffet: Weekdays $6.95, Weekends $7.95
Entrées: $5.99-$9.99
Recommended Dishes:
Special Rava Masala Dosai (Filled Crepes)
Uthappam with Onion and Hot Chili (Indian Pizza)
Kadai Bhindi Curry (Okra and Tomato Curry)
Pongal (Rice and Mashed Lentils)
Special Vegetable Uppuma (Cream of Wheat and Vegetables)
Tamarind Rice
Madras Pavilion Special Coffee
Hours: Buffet: Monday-Friday, 11:30a.m.-3:15p.m.
Saturday-Sunday, 11:30a.m.-5:00p.m.
Dinner: Monday-Thursday, 5:00p.m.-9:30p.m.
Friday-Sunday, 5:00p.m.-10:00p.m.
Reservations: Accepted

A visit to Madras Pavilion is a little like Alice's excursion through the looking glass; things are not always as they seem. Curries have no curry as we know it, and at least one chutney bears more resemblance to Ninfa's green sauce than the jammy – preserved mangoes of the Major Grey variety.

I approached this Indian kosher vegetarian restaurant with trepidation. Could I enjoy an Indian meal without my beloved tandoori chicken or an order of koftas – the sausage-shaped, ginger flavored lamb meat balls? The answer is yes! What this Indian southern style of cooking lacks in meat products it more than makes up for in extraordinary diversity and a real kind of sophistication. There are seemingly no limitations placed on the kitchen by the restrictions of being either strictly vegetarian or kosher.

In order to sample the maximum number of dishes, I recommend either going with a group for dinner or – my first choice – for the buffet at lunch. The composition of the buffet changes daily. In one week there are more than one hundred different dishes featured. Two constants are considered staples of the southern Indian diet – Sambar and Rasam.

While they may look similar, Rasam – taken from the Sanskrit work for "broth" – is really a soup, and the diner is intended to leave the vegetables at the bottom and ladle the liquid off the top into your bowl. The rasam is always a spicy lentil vegetable mixture, but the flavor alternates subtly between Pineapple Rasam one day and Tomato Rasam the next.

Either a ramekin or bowl of Sambar is a must. It is souplike, but is used more as a sauce to moisten and flavor almost everything from Iddlies – the doughy white steamed rice and lentil patties – to the Vadas – fried, lentil-enriched donuts. Sambar is considered a major source of protein in Tamil Nadu – a southern state of India where the capital of Madras is located. It is at least one-third vegetarian. There it is eaten all day long, beginning at breakfast with Dosais – the thin crepes made of pureed lentils and rice. Rajan Radhakrishnam, who manages Madras Pavilion with Mahesh Shah, tells me, "You need expertise to make a sambar. Most of the Indians go to a southern Indian restaurant because of the sambar." It is a stew primarily of yellow split peas, diced vegetables – onions, potatoes, carrots – and seasoned with tamarind paste, roasted black mustard seeds and that astonishing cocktail of spices and seasonings that distinguishes this food from any other.

A visit to the buffet should also include a plateful of the highly-addictive Papadums. Also called Papad on the menu, the wafer-thin deep fried disks of dried split peas are made in the south without peppercorns or seeds of any kind. Like chips and dip at a Mexican restaurant, in the evening before the diner is even given a menu, the waiter brings a basket of papadums and two sauces they call chutneys. One is a Green Chutney – a sassy, incendiary little number of puréed cilantro, mint, jalapenos and a little lime. The other is a syrupy, deep scarlet Imli or tamarind chutney that manages to be both sweet and tart. Spoon some of each onto your plate and dip pieces of the papadums into them. At lunch you should take a sampling of them from the buffet back to your table in individual ramekins. The other two chutneys that you can expect to see are a mild, white Coconut Chutney and a more interesting pinkish puree of onion, red pepper and paprika called Onion Chutney. You might also want to try some of the piquant, homemade Lemon Pickles.

Along with the sambar, these are the five condiments served with almost everything and although I am ordinarily more than happy to gild the lily, I found the "lily" in this case to require little or no further embellishment. The flavors of most of the dishes are so intense that I recommend tasting everything before dipping or adding sauce to it.

When choosing from the buffet, consider sampling a little of each dish. A good rule of thumb is to let your eyeballs be your guide. It is fairly safe to assume that anything colored deep yellow or orange will be fiercely-seasoned and probably hot, while the more innocent-looking creamy white or cream of wheat mixtures should be spooned onto your plate next to them to counteract the heat of the other dishes. It is exactly the contrasting pleasures of sharp/spicy and smooth/mild that makes this cuisine so interesting.

Raita – a liquidy relish of yogurt with chopped tomatoes, cucumbers and mint – works as a welcome coolant. Either bring a dish from the buffet to share amongst your fellow diners, or at dinner, ask for a side order.

Once you are seated with your plates at lunch, a huge cylindrical Dosai – a crepe the size of a ski board and thin as a handkerchief – arrives for whole groups; smaller ones for individuals or smaller groups. The dosais are fresh out of the oven and are meant to be eaten immediately. A piece should be broken off and used to scoop up some of the accompanying Potato Masala – a savory mustard seed flavored mixture of potatoes, onions and chilis. If it is already filled with potato masala, fold a piece over the contents and eat with your fingers.

Of the twelve different possible dosais, my favorite is #12 Special Rava Masala Dosai. Lighter than the others and the texture of intricate lace, this dosai batter is airy with layers of ghee (clarified butter) and cream of wheat with the deep nutty aftertaste of fenugreek.

The dosai batter is transformed when various vegetables are added. It is then flattened and grilled. This is Uthappam and is also referred to on the menu as Indian Pizza. My absolute favorite is #3 with Onion and Hot Chili (jalapeños). Radhakrishman tells me that the tamer #5 Vegetable Uthappam with tomatoes, peas, carrots, chilis and onions is popular with families, but that the onion and chili studded version is "exactly the most favorite of any southern Indian."

Of the two most memorable dishes listed as curries, one actually has no curry in it at all. "Curry" is used both as a term for a style of cooking vegetables and for the explosively-flavorful mixture of spices called garom masala that falls somewhere between artistry and alchemy in the Indian kitchen. Pepper, cinnamon, cardamon and cloves in varying measurements are warmed before grinding to release their oils and maximize their flavors.

The dish I will return for over and over again is #7 Kadai Bhindi Curry – full-out, vibrantly-seasoned tender pods of okra first deep fried, then stewed with tomatoes, onions and the distinctive mustard seeds that are used in the south as a spice. A perfect way to eat the okra is Indian style – scooped with a piece of puffed fried bread made from curds and flour – the #5 listing under Indian breads – Batura.

Another favorite, #2 Channa Masala Curry is chick peas in a powerful-concentrated sauce that includes garlic, ginger and chili powder, and garam masala. It goes well with a soothing order of Pongal #7 – a creamy mixture of rice and mashed lentils – and like #8, the Special Vegetable Uppuma, a subtly-seasoned cream of wheat and vegetables – is a perfect antidote to the volcanic intensity of both of the curries mentioned.

Radhakrishnam is rightfully proud of all of their rice dishes. The #2 Vegetable Pullav is colored yellow from ground tumeric, chock full of vegetables, and was placed on the buffet garnished appealingly with sweet thin rings of caramelized onion.

The rice dish not to miss, though, is the #5 Tamarind Rice. The fragrant white basmati rice is tinted a deep red and the contrasting sweet/tart flavor of the rich tamarind fruit when combined with chilis creates a dish of explosive, eye-popping intensity.

Madras Pavilion serves both beer and wine. At lunch, ice water is the most traditional accompaniment, but I enjoy the puckery, palate-soothing Lassi – iced yogurt drink. Available in plain, sweet or salted – I like the salted. It recalls that old Southern custom of salting your glass of buttermilk.

The #5 Madras Special Payasam is sort of soupy rice pudding made with vermicelli noodles and ends this pleasant assault on your taste buds on a soothing note. (The Mango Favored Lassi might also serve this purpose for me.)

Coffee was introduced to India by the Arabs and southern Indians are big coffee drinkers. The Madras Pavilion Special Coffee is exceptional. It is a classic, strong filter coffee enriched with lots of hot milk and I highly recommend it any time of day.

On the counter by the door there are two separate bowls of fennel seeds – one sweetened, one savory. The small yellow, aromatic seeds are considered a natural breath freshener. I preferred the savory. Try a pinch as you leave.

Radhakrishnam boasts that Madras Pavilion is the only kosher Indian restaurant in town. The vegetarian part I understood. When I asked him, "Why kosher?" he said, "Well, I have a lot of Jewish friends, so why not?"

MISS SAIGON CAFÉ

5503 Kelvin
Houston, Texas 77005
713/942-0108

Type of Cuisine: Vietnamese
Bar: Wine and Beer
Dress: Casual
Entertainment: No
Payment: MasterCard and Visa
Entrée Range: $8.50-$13.95
Recommended Dishes:
    Appetizers: Vietnamese Egg Rolls
        Vegetarian Spring Rolls
        Fried Calamari
    Entrées: Char-Grilled Pork Sandwich
        Flambé Steak Cube
        Caramelized Salmon Claypot
        Vietnamese Crépe
    Dessert: Banana Flambé
        Banana and Coconut Bread Pudding
        Coconut Crème Brulée
Hours: Lunch: Monday-Friday, 11:00a.m.-3:00p.m.
    Dinner: Monday-Thursday, 5:00p.m.-9:00p.m.
        Friday, 5:00p.m.-9:30p.m.
        Saturday, 11:00a.m.-9:30p.m.
    (Closed Sunday)
Reservations: Accepted

Smoky grey and deep Tropicana rose-colored walls. Candlelight. Crisp, starched white tablecloths. A gentle mural covers the south wall in the style of Delacroix, the foremost painter of the French romantic movement. It is of Saigon, but it could be of Paris.

With an emphasis on the "café" part of the name, this elegant little jewel box of a restaurant began its life May 1997 as a Vietnamese sandwich shop – an improbable mission that has, by popular demand, metamorphosed into a full-fledged restaurant.

Dawn Huynh, who owns Miss Saigon Café with her two aunts, Thuy Huynh and Xuan Tran, explains, "From what I'd heard, 99% of the Caucasian market that had eaten a Vietnamese sandwich just loved it. But they didn't know about it unless they had a Vietnamese friend or colleague. So, we thought, 'That's what we'll do. We'll open a sort of Vietnamese deli in Rice Village, where there wasn't even a Vietnamese restaurant.'"

The original menu featured five sandwiches, one pork and shrimp Spring Roll, one classic Vietnamese Egg Roll,

Chicken Noodle Soup and eight Búns – bowls of vermicelli with assorted toppings.

Only two sandwiches remain and one in particular, the Char-grilled Pork, is a humdinger. Sweet, paper-thin slices of pork, char-grilled to caramelized perfection, are wedged between crisp pieces of crusty French baguette. Whole branches of cilantro and cool slivers of cucumber, fresh jalapeño and pickled carrots teeter precariously on top of the pork. (Expect to lose a few on the way to your mouth.) And this is the best part – the bread is slathered with homemade mayonnaise. Homemade mayonnaise, like French bread, is just one of the many gastronomic legacies of nearly one hundred years of colonization of Vietnam by the French.

This unusual and very delicious sandwich is available only at lunch. Think about either preceding or accompanying the sandwich with an order of tempura-fried wedges of Sweet Potatoes, listed as an appetizer.

East meets West again when lightly battered and fried pieces of Calamari are paired with Southwestern-style aioli – a garlic-based mayonnaise spiked with jalapeños and sweet smoky bits of ancho chiles.

Still, I wouldn't miss sampling Miss Saigon's exceptional Vietnamese Egg Rolls. Called Cha Gio, great pride is taken in the preparation of probably the national dish of Vietnam. They are teeming with fresh crabmeat, shrimp, chicken and pork. Golden-crisp cylinders are cut diagonally and, as always, meant to be swaddled in "table salad" – romaine lettuce with julienned pieces of cucumber, whole sprigs of mint, coriander and purple basil. Roll all this in as neat a bundle as can be managed and dip it in the citrusy, slightly pungent fish sauce called Nuoc Mam. (It actually works out better to spoon the sauce directly onto the egg roll to avoid spilling the contents.)

There are now four varieties of Spring Rolls, Miss Saigon's number one selling dish. The traditional pork and shrimp were good, but (surprise!) the Vegetarian Spring Rolls were even better. Packed with pieces of tofu sautéed with soy sauce and plenty of black pepper, Houston's only vegetarian spring rolls were conceived to accommodate their many vegetarian customers. The rice paper wrappers are especially thin and soft, and the spring rolls, clearly made-to-order.

Another notable improvement is the attending peanut sauce. Less cloying and over-bearing than its competitors, their peanut butter and hoisin-based sauce is thinned with coconut milk and enhanced by a generous dose of puréed red chiles and garlic.

The truly adventurous should consider an order of the refreshing and healthful Seaweed and Jelly Fish Salad. The completely flavorless jelly fish, much admired in Asia for its crunchy texture, takes on a life of its own when dressed with a tart vinaigrette of lime, ginger and garlic, and mixed with shredded carrots, daikon (white radish) and dark green ribbons of Japanese seaweed. A singular fresh shrimp is decoratively perched on top.

A light, but substantial, lunch could be made of an order of spring rolls followed by a large piping bowl of Hot and Sour Shrimp and Chicken Soup. The sour flavor is taken from a puckery paste of tamarind. Dawn's aunt, Xuan Tran, the source for most of the recipes used at Miss Saigon, adds that it is her favorite, but that in Vietnam it would be made with fresh tamarind and a whole fish instead of shrimp and chicken.

Another dish adapted to their environs is the Caramelized Salmon Claypot (available for dinner only). Traditionally made with either catfish or pork in Vietnam, Xuan chose what she believed to be the more appealing salmon filet as the vehicle for the nutty-sweet black pepper-flecked sauce. A heady fragrance is released at the table as the lid is removed from the little individual earthenware hot pots.

The most popular of Miss Saigon's entrées – the Spicy Lemon Grass Chicken – lives up to its advertised sass with whole pieces of aromatic, pleasantly acidic lemon grass and identifiable flecks of ground red chiles.

The distinctive flavor (and color) of the Curry – made with either chicken or shrimp – is achieved by blending curry powder from Thailand and a powerfully-concentrated curry paste from India. The result is divine; neither as sweet as a Thai curry nor as hot as an Indian curry. Like all the entrées, both curries come with a scoop of slightly-sticky, extra long grain (Vietnamese) rice topped with a tangle of fried leeks.

The Vietnamese Crépe, a popular favorite on street corners in Saigon, resembles an omelet but has no eggs. The crépe batter is made from a mixture of rice flour and coconut milk, and is tinted a golden-yellow from the addition of tumeric. The resulting dish is thin as a handkerchief and as delicate as lace folded over its weighty filling of sautéed shrimp, pork, onions, mushrooms and bean sprouts. As cumbersome as this may seem, this dish is also intended to be eaten by breaking off pieces and placing them with appropriate garnishes in lettuce, rolled and dipped in nuoc mam (fish sauce).

The best entrée of the bunch is the Flambé Steak Cube. One-inch squares of tender flank steak, "no thicker than your thumb," as Xuan says, are given added depth by the salty, intensely-flavored condiment – Maggi Sauce. A little sugar is added to caramelize the onions and steak, and the whole mess is doused with Jack Daniels and ignited (in the kitchen).

Depending on your tastes, any of the Bún (vermicelli dishes) are recommended. I lean toward the classic, (previously mentioned) char-grilled pork, but Dawn says she always recommends the combination egg roll and char-grilled pork. Whichever you choose, the hot ingredients are placed on top at room temperature, string-like rice noodles in a bowl and garnished with (guess what?) lettuce, bean sprouts, cucumbers, carrots and assorted fresh herbs.

Desserts are another area where the French clearly left their mark. When quizzed, Xuan quickly tells me that the ambrosial Coconut Créme Brulée is an authentic Vietnamese recipe, as is the heavenly Banana and Coconut Bread Pudding made with chunks of bananas and French bread, and served with both a coconut and caramel sauce. The Fried Banana is dipped in tempura batter and served with vanilla ice cream. But the best of all, Banana Flambé is flamed with rum and also served with a scoop of vanilla ice cream. It is a dead ringer for a classic Bananas Foster – a dish Xuan says she not only has never tasted, but has never even heard of!

There is a short list of California red or white wines available. The light, ale-like Saigon Beer is a good match for this meal.

Whatever time of year, it's a nice place to linger over a glass of thick, incredibly rich "Iced Vietnamese Café," as it says on the menu. Dawn agrees, "That's just what we had in mind!"

MOM'S KITCHEN

2620 Joanel
Houston, Texas 77027
713/622-7290

Type of Cuisine: American/Homestyle Cooking
Bar: No
Dress: Casual
Entertainment: No
Payment: Cash or Check Only
Price Range: $3.50-$6.25
Recommended Dishes:
Egg Salad Sandwich
Chicken Salad Sandwich
Natural Energy Sandwich (Vegetarian)
Spinach Salad
Lasagna (Thursday)
Dessert: Double Chocolate Brownie
Chocolate Chip Cookie
Hours: Monday-Friday, 11:00a.m.-3:00p.m.
Reservations: Not Accepted

The thing about Mom's Kitchen isn't just that their egg salad sandwich would pass a blind taste with your mom's. It's that it feels so much like home.

"I think the biggest compliment we were ever paid was when a little girl came in with her mother. She looked around and said, 'Mommy, does someone live here?'" tells Dot Dimiero who, with her daughter, Dana Aichler, comprises the self-described "Mom and Momette" team who own and run Mom's Kitchen.

These veterans in the lunch business are, in fact, accidental restauranteurs who are more comfortable discussing art and antiques than the simple fare that they've served to many of the same customers for sixteen years.

Aichler adds, "We probably know 75% of our customers by name – mostly women, who we have watched get married and have one, two, and three babies. They even bring their families in when they visit at Thanksgiving and Christmas."

Lines form at 11:00 a.m. Monday through Friday for the simple but real food circa 1965. The most popular sandwich – the Egg Salad Sandwich – is an absolute testimony to earlier times when the idea of freshly hard boiled eggs, chopped and mixed with mayonnaise and a little salt and pepper was as complicated as lunch ever needed to be. It is ideal either loaded onto soft whole wheat bread or embellished with sprouts, slices of avocado and rosy Roma tomatoes – or my personal favorite – topped with thin smoky ridges of crisp bacon.

Dimiero agrees, "For all the current hoopla about health, we sell a lot of bacon sandwiches – especially the BLT!" The bacon, lettuce and tomato is a classic – also served on whole wheat but with welcome added wedges of perfectly ripe avocado.

Another masterpiece of understatement, the Chicken Salad, is – as advertised – nothing more than snow-white chunks of chicken breast, chopped hard boiled eggs, celery and (oh yes!) salt and pepper. It is fine as a sandwich, a "salad plate" rimmed with sliced tomatoes and quarters of hard boiled eggs or spooned into a hollowed out tomato.

Another tea room favorite, Stuffed Celery, is an order of cold crisp celery hearts filled with Price's Pimiento Spread – the only thing not made from scratch at Mom's because both women felt they simply couldn't improve on Price's. Dimiero says that, "Mostly women eat that, but we have one man who comes in once a week and that's all he orders. That, and a cookie."

The cookies are superb. Baked every morning, they are soft, still a little warm, chewy and crisp around the edges. Aichler laughs that, "The oatmeal raisin recipe is the original one off the side of the Quaker Oats box (it's different, now!), and the chocolate chip is the one on the Toll House Chocolate Chip package!" Even more irresistible is what they call the Double Chocolate Brownie - gooey wedges of fudge pie.

Mom's may be known best of all for their Tortilla Soup. Dimiero shyly admits that, "It has become a bit of a specialty. We stew about 50 chickens everyday for both soups – the Chicken Noodle and the tortilla soup. We have a huge following of kids who come during holidays and the summertime just to eat the tortilla soup!" The chicken broth is richly concentrated and the soup is chockfull of shredded chicken, diced avocados and tomatoes, and creamy with softly dissolving tortillas and lots of melted Cheddar cheese. I loved it, but almost preferred the simple goodness of the same heady broth with chicken and fusilli pasta – their version of chicken noodle soup.

The practice of using fusilli pasta instead of more traditional noodles is a legacy of the original owners of Mom's Kitchen on West Alabama before it belonged to Aichler and Dimiero.

Dimiero explains, "This precious little Hungarian couple had this tiny restaurant where they used to serve soup, chicken paprikash, and goulash – dishes like that. We had another business in the same building hand-knitting sweaters and we used to go there for lunch. When we learned they were going to retire, we decided – sort of on a whim – to buy the business. So, we went from knitting sweaters one day to serving food the next."

The earliest customers were men who had gravitated to Mom's for the hearty Hungarian specialties, but they quickly phased those out in favor of "sandwiches, salads ... just basic lunch dishes that you might make in you own kitchen with a couple of soups, and always a hot daily special." They piped in classical music, began selling antiques – table accessories and knick-knacks, and hanging and selling their own oil and acrylic paintings. "That's our first love, really!" Aichler claims. After fourteen years the building sold and they moved to the present location on Joanel.

That little girl was at least partially right. "Someone does live (there)." Both mother and daughter have been there every day since they opened ... plus, the two women who have done the majority of the cooking since day one – Nettie Guillen and Rosie Rivas.

The fact that these four women have worked this closely for sixteen years explains their unique, decidedly low-tech method of taking and filling orders. Dimiero takes and repeats the orders to Giullen and Rivas who make sandwiches and hot plate specials at break-neck speed in the adjoining kitchen. Then Aichler rings it up. Nothing is ever written down. Everything is remembered. Aichler says, "Mother and I have our own system. When we try to change it, it doesn't work."

The hot specials are rib-sticking old timers such as King Ranch Chicken (Wednesday) and a very cheesy Lasagna (Thursday). Aichler believes that the secret to their success may be that "Nettie adds about twice as much cheese as any of the recipes call for!" Nicely seasoned Crispy or Soft Tacos – ground beef or shredded chicken – have become so popular, they are available daily.

The Polish Sausage Sandwich is dressed with mustard, tart sauerkraut and served on a po-boy roll – a holdover from the previous owners. Dimiero says that along with the Peanut Butter, Banana and Honey Sandwich originally intended for children, the Polish sausage sandwich is ordered almost exclusively by men. (Another interesting observation, "We sell a lot of egg salad to pregnant women. It's sort of a joke around here.")

Those craving something lighter than Polish sausage or egg salad should love the Spinach Salad made with the usual baby spinach leaves, chopped eggs, crumbled bacon, and sliced mushrooms, but served with puckery vinaigrette composed of lemon juice, a little vinegar, a very little oil, Dijon mustard and a bit of finely crumbled Bleu cheese. The Vegetable Salad is simple and light, little more than a tossed salad with good, fresh ingredients. And the Natural Energy Sandwich "added for our vegetarian customers," Aichler says, is better and more satisfying than mere salad between two slices of bread. (It is a good idea – if you're ordering this for health reasons – to substitute mozzarella or Swiss cheese for the misplaced American cheese that comes on it!)

Fresh Lemonade appears to be the drink of choice. "We sell a lot of that," Dimiero says. "They stand and squeeze two cases of lemons every morning to make that lemonade. It's pretty intense!"

Although they rarely get away, both mother and daughter agree, "It has been a great sixteen years. We have a great clientele. And we have such fun with each other. It's like a party every day!"

NAM

2727 Fondren #3A (at Westheimer)
Houston, Texas 77063
713/789-6688

Type of Cuisine: Vietnamese
Bar: Wine and Beer
Dress: Casual
Entertainment: No
Payment: American Express, MasterCard, Visa
Entrée Range: $5.95-$15.95
Recommended Dishes:
Appetizers: Butter Chicken Wings
Ravioli
Nam Crepe
Vietnamese Egg Roll
Entrées: Special Crunchy Noodle
Nam Special Chicken
Vietnamese Smoked Beef
Shrimp Simmered in Clay Pot
Salted Baked Crab (ask for soft shell)
Grilled Chicken Salad
Hours: Lunch: Monday-Saturday, 11:00a.m.-3:00p.m.
Dinner: Monday-Thursday, 11:00a.m.-10:00p.m.
Friday-Saturday, 11:00a.m.-11:00p.m.
Sunday, 5:00p.m.-10:00p.m.
Reservations: Accepted

"We don't make Chinese food. We don't make any Thai food. My restaurant makes the original Vietnamese food that they eat in Vietnam. And maybe a little bit from France," explains owner and Saigon native Toan C. Tran when asked what he thinks distinguishes Nam from other Vietnamese restaurants. "This is why I don't have too many items."

The menu is short only by Vietnamese restaurant standards. Tran says that many other restaurants serve Chinese and Thai dishes because the owner may be Chinese born in Vietnam. "But I am Vietnamese, so I cook Vietnamese food." He says that the menu is a short list of his favorite dishes and that most of the recipes originated with either his mother, his sister-in-law, who had a restaurant in Saigon, or – in the case of the highly-addictive butter-based sauce – straight out of a French cookbook.

This you definitely won't find in any other Vietnamese restaurant. What he calls "French butter sauce" on the menu is fabulous when spiked with red pepper flakes and teamed with shrimp (#6 Spicy Shrimp) or the fried crisp soft shell crabs (#E8 Salted Baked Crab), but best of all when paired with chicken wings listed as appetizer #A7 Butter Chicken Wings.

The word "dreamy" springs to mind here. Roll up your sleeves and tuck into a platter of meaty chicken wings and drumettes that have been first fried and then covered in this superb sauce that is French with an Asian accent; part butter, part garlic, a little sugar and a lot of onions – both scallions and yellow or white onions.

Other appetizers I fell for in a big way were #A3 Nam Crepe and #A5 Ravioli. Literally translated, "Banh Xéo" is called Nam Crepe or "sound pancake" because of the sizzling sound the crepe batter makes when poured into the hot pan. Tran says, "They also call it Vietnamese pizza, you know." It looks like an omelet to me. A simple batter is made of rice flour and boiling water and colored yellow by the addition of ground tumeric. It arrives golden brown and neatly folded over a delightful stir fry of baby shrimp, chicken breasts, onions and crunchy bean sprouts. I was a little surprised that pieces of the crepe with the contents are meant to be broken off, folded into pieces of romaine lettuce with branches of curly mint, cilantro and the spikey greenery that Tran calls "Spicy mint" and dipped in nuoc cham – fish sauce.

This seemed like a good time to ask Tran why so many Vietnamese dishes are eaten with what is known as table salad. "Because the Vietnamese people are very, very scared of getting fat. So they believe that eating their food with lettuce, and herbs like mint and cilantro kills the fat in the stomach and aids the digestion."

The result is that contrasting textures are a constant theme in Vietnamese cuisine. A perfect example is #A1 Vietnamese Egg Roll – finer and more delicate than the old Chinese rendition and also meant to be eaten with "table salad."

Tran tells me that #A5 Ravioli are sold off small carts on the street in Vietnam. "They pull right up in front of your house and ask, 'You want some ravioli?' If you say 'yes' they make them for you right there." I love this dish. Almost transparent rice noodles are folded like handkerchiefs over sweet, rich barbecued pork, and arrive on a plate with tangled mounds of boiled bean sprouts and chopped cilantro, cucumber and lettuce. Tran insists that they must be eaten by first spooning the wonderful salty/citrusy house fish sauce over them and then including in each bite some ravioli, some bean sprouts and some chopped "Vegetables." "To taste good, it needs to be eaten together," he says.

The #B1 Hot and Sour Shrimp Soup is chock full of vegetables – tomatoes, onion, celery and bean sprouts and sections of fresh pineapple. It has a chicken-based broth with the clean, tart taste of lemon.

Another dish that Tran says is popular with people who

are watching their diet is #C1 Grilled Chicken Salad. Salads are as revered in Vietnam as they are in America, and this one is exceptional. A fiery, crunchy mass of chopped cabbage, carrots and mint supports warm strips of grilled chicken breast and is dressed with a light, but assertively-seasoned vinaigrette. The salad comes surrounded by fried "chips" of rice paper. Some salad and chicken should be placed on individual chips and eaten like that, according to Tran.

If you don't order the butter chicken wings listed under "Vietnamese Specialties," you might try Tran's favorite recipient of the butter sauce – #E6 Spicy Shrimp. They are good, but I almost preferred #E12 Shrimp Simmered in a Clay Pot – a dish of hot, garlicy, eye-popping intensity.

The #E14 Charbroiled Catfish is a filet of catfish glazed with hot chili sauce and scored on the grill. It is wonderful and apparently wildly popular at lunch.

My favorite "Specialty" is #20 Special Crunchy Noodle. A nest of boiled, then crisply-fried egg noodles is topped with a slightly searing sauté of shrimp, tiny scallops, chicken, beef and vegetables.

The first listing under "Chicken" on the menu was practically fought over at our table. #E22 Nam Special Chicken is golden, marble-sized nuggets of chicken breasts, strewn with sesame seeds, flavored with ginger and garlic, and wreathed with tiny, bright green broccoli flowerettes.

The best of the beef dishes is #E33 Vietnamese Smoked Beef. Tran's technique for smoking the flank steak is to cook it quickly in a wok in very hot oil. "The smoke part comes from the big fire. The fire comes in the food and it smells of smoke right away."

It is a reflection of Tran's good nature and sweet disposition that long grain white rice arrives molded into a sleepy, smiling face instead of the standard butterfly. "The face on the rice is my idea. When I went back to my country in 1992, I asked my cousin to make me a mold of a face in wood. It's something a little elegant…a little nice. When you put the plate down, people smile and say 'Oh! It's a face!'"

A small mound of vermicelli shares the plate with most entrées and is an even better alternative to the white rice. Tran says he offers it as an option to rice by adding a little to the platter for the diner to sample.

A cold, sweet, sectioned orange is a fitting way to finish this feast, but if you have any room at all left, consider a Charbroiled Banana – a sort of Vietnamese banana split. An adaptation of a Vietnamese recipe, Tran says, "If we made it like they do in Vietnam, it would take half an hour, but we just put a banana on the grill for five, ten minutes. Then we cut it open and fill it with chopped peanuts and cashews, pour some condensed milk in there, and put some whipping cream on the top." This is pretty close to heaven.

The final temptation for me at Nam is a chilled mug of iced Vietnamese coffee made with little individual drip filters and sweetened condensed milk.

This restaurant is a beehive of lunch special activity in the middle of the day, but settles into quiet, candlelight elegance at night. Both beer and wine are served. We found that a California white Zinfadel went especially well with the powerfully-concentrated flavors of Nam's fare.

NEW YORK PIZZERIA

4870 Beechnut
Houston, Texas 77096
713/349-8787

Type of Cuisine: Italian
Bar: Wine and Beer
Dress: Casual
Entertainment: No
Payment: All Major Credit Cards
Entrée Range: $6.50-$8.95
Recommended Dishes:
Appetizers: Fried Calamari
Roasted Garlic Soup
Salads: Mediterranean Salad
Boccinni Salad
Entrées: Muffalatta
New York Pizza
Stromboli
Eggplant Parmesan
Lasagne
Dessert: Chocolate Cake
Canoli
Hours: Sunday-Thursday, 11:00a.m.-10:00p.m.
Friday-Saturday, 11:00a.m.-11:00p.m.
Reservations: Not Accepted

One bite of "cheese pie" and I'm transported. Frank Sinatra's on the juke box and there is the unmistakable flicker of fluorescent lights overhead. I could be enjoying "a slice" at John's on Bleeker Street in New York but I'm not. I'm in Meyerland at New York Pizzeria.

"New York pizza has the same deserved reputation as Texas barbecue," says chef and owner Anthony Russo. "You can eat pizza in every city in the world, but when you take your first bite of New York pizza, you know it's special."

It is the poster child for simple things done perfectly: a thin, crisp crust, the pleasant bite of freshly-made tomato sauce and a creamy, white veneer of soft, fresh mozzarella cheese. No toppings or peripheral frou-frou. Just "cheese pie" as it's known on the streets of New York.

"The trick is to use the finest possible ingredients and to make everything from scratch," Russo explains, a philosophy passed down from his grandfather, Guiseppe Russo, who still has a restaurant in Sicily. "My grandfather always says, 'When you make it yourself, you know it's good.'"

Happily, this idea applies not only to pizza, but also to the full array of pastas and the utterly irresistible, freshly-baked "Tuscasni" bread. Russo says customers practically swoon at the smell of bread baking in one of the two brick ovens imported from New York. (Another essential component of making authentic New York pizza).

Tuscani bread comes with everything that isn't bread already – sandwiches, pizza and calzones – and is served with a shallow dish of garlic sauce that consists of nothing more complicated than roughly-chopped garlic, parsley and basil in extra virgin olive oil. It is addictive. We found ourselves dipping everything in it, including the crisp, airy rings and tangled tentacles of Fried Calamari. (The calamari comes with it's own sauce - a basil-fragrant, deeply flavored marinara that appears in several guises on the menu.)

Two other worthwhile appetizers are Eggplant Rollatini and a soulful Roasted Garlic Soup. The soup is a hearty vegetable stock rich with whole leaves of spinach, chunks of tomatoes and (homemade) penne pasta. The Rollatini, one of Russo's favorites, is thinly sliced eggplant rolled around an herb and caper-filled breadcrumb dressing, then doused with marinara sauce. It was great, but eggplant fans should opt for one of the best Eggplant Parmesans I've ever tasted.

The secret is that he slices the eggplant very thin before salting and draining it of excess moisture (and bitterness). The slices are dipped in egg batter and baked. He then constructs alternating layers of crisp, very lightly coated and baked eggplant with fresh tomato sauce and gooey mozzarella cheese. What is often a heavy, oafish dish becomes light with the smoky rich flavor of eggplant. As an added bonus, the eggplant Parmesan is served on top of a generous mound of (also, homemade) spaghetti that has been tossed with tomato sauce.

When I rave about his Lasagna, Russo says it's not as g
as his mother's. (That must be some lasagna, because
spectacular.) It is a classic case of the whole being only
as the sum of its parts. Buttery, freshly-made sheet
ricotta and mozzarella cheese – both imported fro
Bakery in Little Italy – and an intense, power
trated meat sauce that he says he cooks for at le
the while adding red wine.

Di Paulo is also his source for the It
provolone cheese that he uses to assem
would be the envy of even Central Gr
(where the sandwich originated in 19
of work. Not only the exceptiona
nutty crunch of garlicky choppe
itself is what distinguishes his
the Tuscani bread is enriched
and again, mid-bake, with
and garlic.

The salads are composed of organic vegetables and the house dressing is a skillfully balanced vinaigrette (fine olive oil and 25-year-old Balsamic vinegar that he's also getting from Di Paulo). I had two favorites: the Mediterranean Salad, a festival of flavors and textures – Romaine lettuce with sliced cucumbers, red onions, sun-dried tomatoes, pine nuts and crumbled Gorgonzola cheese; and the Boccinni Salad that features slices rather than "small balls" (bocconcini) of Buffalo mozzarella and sun-dried tomatoes.

Back to the pizza. There are actually 21 different toppings to choose from for your "slice," medium-size (12 inches) or large pizza (16 inches), but I liked his pizza in it's purest form, maybe with just razor-thin disks of pepperoni sausage on top. A "slice" is a whopping 14 inches and is taken from a 28 inch pie the size of a small coffee table. (This would be ideal for a children's party!)

He also uses his fine pizza dough to excellent effect for the New York Calzone (stuffed with ricotta, cubed Canadian bacon and mozzarella), regular Calzone (with spinach, garlic and sliced tomatoes), and the Stromboli ("It is a Philadelphia favorite," Russo says, and it is stuffed with everything – tomato sauce, sausage, pepperoni, mushrooms, bell peppers and black olives.).

Among the four desserts both the Tiramisu and the Canolis were wonderful. (He's making the lady fingers for the tiramisu and the canoli shells himself). I loved the New York cheesecake – a dense, dryish classic that tastes like the real thing, and there's a fudgey chocolate cake that Russo says regularly attracts customers for a different kind of "slice."

New York Pizzeria offers an assortment of domestic and imported beer, but Italian wine, exclusively. (I enjoyed my Chianti, but wished it hadn't been served in a plastic water tumbler.)

Those who recognize the Russo name may remember
his parent's restaurant, Russo's Italian Restaurant in Galveston.
His family moved to Galveston from New York in 1978 and
e restaurant existed until 1996. In 1993, Anthony Russo
ened Café Anthony that became Russo's Café Anthony on
ntrose and Richmond. When his lease expired in October,
, he closed and moved his employees and staff to his new
rant, New York Pizzeria on Beechnut across from
land Plaza. His sister, Teresa Russo runs a location at
Vest (across from Willowbrook Mall), and there is an-
ew York Pizzeria that sells solely pizza, calzones and
s for pick-up or delivery near the Medical Center (at
Holcombe).

NIELSEN'S DELICATESSEN

4500 Richmond Avenue
Houston, Texas
713/963-8005
713/963-8006

Type of Cuisine: Deli with Danish Specialties
Bar: No
Dress: Casual
Entertainment: No
Payment: Cash and Checks Only
Prices: $3.50-$5.40
Recommended Dishes:
- Homemade Mayonnaise Spread
- Potato Salad
- Pasta Salad
- Deviled Eggs
- Liver Paste
- Roast Beef
- Chicken Salad
- Cheesecake

Hours: Monday-Sunday, 8:00a.m.-4:00p.m.
Reservations: Not Accepted

There is an old adage that says that a sandwich always tastes best when it's made by someone else. For me, as far back as memory serves, that someone else has been Nielsen's Delicatessen. As a child, there was no happier sight on Saturdays than to see my father come through the door with a crisp, white sack full of Nielsen's roast beef sandwiches for lunch.

Vita and Niels Nielsen came to Houston in 1952 to join their daughter, Ellen Andersen and her husband, Dick. They left behind three deli's and one butcher shop in Esbjerb, a small town on the western coast of Denmark. That spring they opened Nielsen's Delicatessen in Highland Village with the intention of introducing Houstonians to the elegant, artfully arranged, openfaced sandwiches known as smørrebrød (literally "buttered bread"). The dainty, neatly constructed works of art are meant to be eaten with a fork and knife and are still standard fare for a light lunch in Denmark.

These were the days of the massive, cartoonlike Dagwood sandwich. "They didn't go over very well," laughs Ellen Andersen who now, with her son Rick, owns and runs the Delicatessen. "For one thing, people didn't know how to eat them. The other thing was that the Health Department didn't want us to put them out on trays like we did in Denmark."

After a few months, the smørrebrød were phased out in favor of the good old, two-fisted, American-style deli sandwich. The composition may have changed, but fortunately the components have not, because the Nielsen's knew then what the family still knows now, that the secret to a good sandwich (or deli salad, for that matter) is that the whole is only as great as the sum of its parts.

At the heart of (almost) all that is good at Nielsen's is their homemade mayonnaise. I would be willing to wager that no other deli in town makes mayonnaise from scratch. Andersen says, "It is just the oldfashioned way, really. It takes a long time to make and it is always fresh. People still make their own mayonnaise back home, you know. We have customers who have been coming in for years to buy the plain mayonnaise to make their own crab salad."

In fact, my refrigerator is never without at least a pint of it. I use it as a base for any dips that require mayonnaise because as anyone knows who has tasted the real stuff it bears almost no resemblance to the store bought variety. I am also never without Nielsen's legendary spread. It is the homemade mayonnaise colored a bold yellow by the addition of what I've always guessed was a little French's mustard. The standard Nielsen sandwich is always made with the spread and it is the only way to go.

The choices of meat are corned beef, ham, pastrami, turkey and my favorite, roast beef. Andersen says that the #1 selling sandwich is turkey breast on whole wheat bread with Swiss cheese and spread "probably because we roast all our own turkeys." But the sandwich of my dreams is this: 3 1/2 ounces (a "regular") of transparently-thin rare roast beef, a wedge or two of liver paté, a slice of Danish Havarti, a slice of authentic Swiss cheese and Nielsen's spread on good, fresh pumpernickel bread.

First in the affections of most Danes, the Paté is actually "a typical Danish liver paste," according to Andersen. "In Scandinavia we eat it with homemade beets." The liver paste is heaven – finely ground and densely rich with eggs and cream, and has the unmistakable aftertaste of allspice and cloves.

Andersen says that the Pickled Beets, like the Red Cabbage, have always been popular with Scandinavians and Germans, but (after about forty-five years) are just starting to catch on with American customers. I think that they are both wonderful, and work perfectly as a contrast to the rich, mayonnaise-based salads that they are justly known for.

Starting with the Potato Salad – it is simply composed of roughly-chopped *hard boiled eggs, celery, onion,* homemade mayonnaise and good Idaho potatoes. It gets my vote for the best potato salad in town, to go with Nielsen's sandwiches or barbecue or just about anything. Andersen says that it is what she's proudest of – "strictly everything is made from scratch."

The Chicken Salad is another masterpiece of understatement. Take some home and scoop it onto fresh slices of juicy tomato for a fabulous lunch or have them load it between two slices of their excellent whole wheat bread with maybe a little lettuce and tomato. (The traditional Nielsen sandwich was never made with either lettuce or tomato, but they have recently made them available by popular request.)

The Pasta Salad also was added probably twenty years ago "when pasta started getting real popular," Andersen says. Green, white and orange-colored shells are dressed simply with mayonnaise, finely chopped scallions and fresh dill. As pasta salads go, it is also unrivaled in the city. "It's the dressing that does the trick," Andersen says. (She's right!)

Nielsen's should also be your source for old-fashioned, impeccably-deviled eggs for your next picnic. They are sold in immaculate little Dixie cups. The well-seasoned, mustardy mixture is piped back into the egg white halves and attractively garnished with a slice of pimento-stuffed green olive and a sprinkling of paprika.

Also sold in little individual Dixie cups are pairs of incendiary jalapeño halves piped with cream cheese. They may look harmless enough, but run for your lives; they will bring tears to your eyes. They are good, but not for the faint of palate.

Their pickles are classic kosher dills which they are happy to cut in wedges and put in a quart size container with some of their own juice to take home.

I always buy the Cole Slaw, although it is a bit creamier than I ordinarily like cole slaw to be.

The Beans listed under salads are good, sweet, tomatoey pork and beans with cubes of ham, apparently a classic Swedish dish.

Of the two soups, the regularly available Chicken and Rice is homey and comforting full of big chunks of chicken, rice, celery, carrots and leeks, in a lovely homemade stock.

Nielsen's may be most famous of all for their Cheesecake. Also not a Danish dish, Andersen says that her mother "got the recipe from one of the Houston ladies a long time ago. She got four or five recipes, tried them out and decided she liked this one the best." The rest, as they say, is history. Actual fist fights have almost broken out over which is the better, most authentic cheesecake – New York-style or Nielsen's. I don't know, but it is the standard by which I judge all others. The top and the bottom are dusted with finely ground graham crackers and in between is an ambrosial mixture of eggs, cream cheese and sour cream flavored with a little vanilla. Approach their cheesecake as an all-out splurge and take one home. (For almost thirty years they were made and sold in Pyrex dishes, then they switched to more convenient aluminum tins.) It is at its creamy, silky best when it is left out at least fifteen to thirty minutes to allow to soften before eating.

Nielsen's moved to the corner of Richmond and Mid Lane about thirteen years ago. As they have always been, they are open seven days a week. There are six bar stools to perch on while you eat your lunch, but I wouldn't try to go between eleven and one. They are always busy then. For orders $25.00 and over, they will deliver for $3.00 inside the Loop and $6.00 outside.

PAULIE'S

1834 Westheimer
Houston, Texas 77098
713/807-7271

Type of Cuisine: American/Eclectic/Vegetarian
Bar: No (You can bring your own wine.)
Dress: Casual
Entertainment: No
Payment: MasterCard and Visa
Price Range: $3.95-$8.95
Recommended Dishes:
  Sandwiches: Grilled Shrimp BLT
    Pork Tenderloin with Cajun Mustard
    Grilled Tuna with Wasabi Mayonnaise
    Grilled Portobello Mushroom & Red Pepper
  Salads: Spinach Salad
    Caesar Salad
  Pasta: Summer Spaghetti
    Conchiglie with Broccoli & Imported Parmesan
  Dessert: Shortbread Cookies
    Oatmeal Raisin Cookies
    Peanut Butter with Chocolate
    Chocolate Cake
Hours: Monday-Saturday, 11:00a.m.-8:00p.m.
  (Closed Sunday)
Reservations: Not Accepted

Kathy Craft Petronella is famous for her neckties. And her sunflowers. And her t-shirts. In fact, she's famous for all the shapes, colors and sizes of her shortbread cookies. Not just because the brightly-iced cookies are colorful little works of art, but because they taste so good.

She is a baker's baker who has arrived on this formula for the perfect cookie by combining two powerful culinary influences in her life – her Irish grandmother's shortbread recipe and her Italian (maternal) grandmother's pizzle recipe. This buttery-rich bit of perfection may be what she's best known for from her catering days (as Kathy Craft Cooks), but what will creep into my consciousness as (lunch) hunger pangs hit, is her Grilled Shrimp BLT – one of several exceptional sandwiches at Paulie's, Petronella's brand new lunch and early dinner spot on Westheimer.

Paulie's is named for co-owners (and co-chefs) Bernard and Kathy Craft Petronella's young, good-looking son, Paul, who takes orders at the counter. It has the bare floor and clean, uncluttered lines of a SoHo loft. The menu is a short list of spectacular sandwiches, salads, a couple of specialties from her catering menu and a handful of pasta dishes that Petronella says she and her husband grew up eating "and loved."

"My mother was Italian – actually born in Italy – and Bernard's parents were both Italian, he's half-Pizzatola and half-Petronella, so we tend to cook the kind of stuff our moms cooked." Apart from having inherited her mother's talent (and enthusiasm) for baking, Petronella also inherited her mother's slavish devotion to using the best, freshest ingredients available. "That's probably what I'm proudest of. Everybody knows it's possible to cut corners. But I'm a real stickler about good ingredients."

It shows. This is the anatomy of a great sandwich. Take one freshly-baked roll studded with toasty sesame seeds. Smear it with a little homemade mayonnaise. Top that with just the right amount of green leafy lettuce, a few ruby-red slices of Roma tomatoes, several crunchy strips of good, hickory smoked bacon, and finally, a half-dozen shrimp that have been first scored on the grill, then tossed quickly in a pan with butter and champagne enriched with a dash of cream. A little of the sauce is slathered on the top half of the warm roll for good measure. Petronella believes that the Grilled Shrimp BLT is a combination of almost everybody's favorite things which explains why it is Paulie's most popular sandwich.

Still, I would be regularly seduced by another fine effort, the Pork Tenderloin with Cajun Mustard. Trouble is taken to marinate (overnight) a pork tenderloin no bigger than your wrist in chopped onion, garlic and ginger with freshly squeezed lime juice and soy sauce. It's grilled for a moment, then finished in a hot oven. The result is a sandwich with rosy, sweet slices of pork offset nicely by the sharpness of horseradish and cayenne pepper flavored "Cajun mustard." A less dainty, but almost as good sandwich, the Plain Old Pork Chop, is a modified version of a favorite sandwich from Bernard Petronella's youth. Two pork chops are grilled to roseate perfection, bones removed, then wedged onto a soft white roll with lettuce, tomatoes and the Cajun mustard.

Son Paul's favorite is a masterful rendition of an old-fashioned club sandwich named Paulie's Club. A Pullman white bread with just a touch of sourdough is toasted, trimmed of its crust and layered with paper-thin slices of smoked turkey, ham, Swiss cheese, bacon, lettuce, tomato and (of course) homemade mayonnaise, all neatly assembled and impaled with frilly toothpicks.

The Chicken Salad Sandwich is an adaptation of the chicken salad that Butera's became known for. That's because Petronella developed the recipe and was responsible for opening the deli in the back of Butera's Grocery Store on Bissonnet in 1974. In 1979, she helped open the "original" Butera's Restaurant on Montrose before she went out on her own to launch her catering company in 1991.

The Chicken Salad is one for the books. It has the familiar crunch of chopped toasted pecans, celery and Kosher dill pickles, but this time Petronella's making it with grilled (instead of poached) chicken breasts only and just a hint of garlic.

The Grilled Tuna with Wasabi Mayonnaise is a fabulous sandwich for those looking for something a little lighter. A filet of tuna is brushed with chopped ginger and lime-flavored soy sauce before and just after its tenure on the grill. It's complemented perfectly by a dose of sinus-clearing wasabi (Japanese horse radish) tamed with mayonnaise.

To my surprise, two of the most satisfying sandwiches in Paulie's virtuoso repertoire contain no meat (or seafood) of any kind. The best was the Grilled Portobello Mushroom and Red Pepper that oozed with an unexpected layer of soft, warm goat cheese. The Grilled Vegetable Sandwich featured thick, meaty slices of eggplant and sweet red peppers that tasted of the grill. In fact, Petronella has a talent for grilling vegetables and they can be found in several guises on the menu – among them, wrapped in a tortilla, cut diagonally and served with a dipping sauce that's a sort of Southwestern pesto (the Vegetable Burritos). Or, consider ordering them on their own, fresh off the grill with a crumbling of good salty feta cheese over the top as the Grilled Vegetable Platter. (Petronella comes clean here and says she's a vegetarian. "Oh, I haven't eaten meat in about ten years.") Is that why they're so good?

Sandwiches come with a choice of good skins-on, vinaigrette based potato salad tarted up with pungent pitted Kalamata olives or even better – a handful of homemade focaccia chips, oven baked and crusty with freshly-grated Parmesan cheese, crisp thin rings of red onion, and a little garlic.

If I had to pick a favorite among the seven salads listed, it's a toss up between the Traditional Spinach Salad and the Caesar Salad. The Spinach Salad is exactly what you want it to be – tender leaves of baby spinach, wedges of hard boiled egg and Roma tomatoes, nearly-transparent rings of red onion, and a crumble of smoky bacon, all dressed with a creamy Dijon mustard-enriched vinaigrette. The Caesar Salad has an ideal sharpness – a reminder of what a Caesar salad is meant to be.

Both Petronellas use a light hand when re-creating their mothers' pasta dishes. The Summer Spaghetti has a graceful, but well-seasoned sauce made from oven-roasted Roma tomatoes and lots of fresh herbs. (Notice the herb garden out back.) The spaghetti is tossed with this tomato sauce, then served with thick rich rounds of smoky grilled eggplant resting on top.

Huge conch-shaped pasta shells are used to catch whole slivers of sautéed garlic and Parmesan cheese and barely-blanched broccoli flowerets for the Petronella's favorite – Conchiglie with Broccoli and Imported Parmesan. "Bernard and I both love this one. We eat it several times a week!" Petronella tells me. She adds that the pasta dishes are more popular for dinner than lunch and that since they don't have a liquor license – they're directly across the street from Lanier – some customers have been bringing in their own wine. (Note that they close at 8:00p.m.)

Back to dessert. All are recommended. The Chocolate Cake is fudgy and rich. The Cream Cheese Brownies are gooey and delicious. But the cookies are the best. The Oatmeal Raisin are chewy and moist, with the distinct aftertaste of cinnamon. The Peanut Butter Cookies are thick (also chewy) and half-dipped in milk chocolate. However, once you've tried the Shortbread Cookies, you won't want to leave without a dozen or so ($1.50 each).

The time of year and proximity of holidays dictates the design of the cookies (e.g. Father's Day – neckties; Fourth of July – stars and flags). There are 339 possibilities – that's how many cookie cutters she owns.

With an hour's notice, box lunches (for eight or more) are put together and tied up with a pretty red ribbon – a perfect idea for your next lunch meeting.

PETE'S FINE MEATS

5509 Richmond Avenue
Houston, Texas 77056
713/782-3470

Type of Cuisine: Barbecue/Delicatessen
Bar: No
Dress: Casual
Entertainment: No
Payment: All Major Credit Cards
Entrée Range: $2.69-$6.99
Recommended Dishes:
- Steak Hoagie
- Cheeseburger
- Barbecue: Ribs (Country, Spare and Beef)
  - Brisket
- Whole Suckling Pig
- Whole Cabritos

Hours: Monday-Saturday, 9:00a.m.-6:00p.m.
(Closed Sunday)
Reservations: Not Accepted

Looking for a suckling pig for your next luau? While I can't help you find poi, Pete's Fine Meats is your place for suckling pig or cabrito or the kind of barbecued beef brisket that inspired the legendary Cactus Pryor to proclaim: "It's common knowledge among the clergy that God invented beef briskets for Texans."

A native of Wharton, Texas, butcher Pete Ratcliffe Cruz says he married into the meat business in 1956 when he met his wife. Bringing with him quite a following from his successful shop in Fulshear, Texas, he opened Pete's Fine Meats at 5509 Richmond on October 15, 1969, with the exclusive purpose of selling only the finest available prime, choice beef, pork and lamb … "to handle nothing but the best."

"The first day I think we took in eighteen dollars – sold maybe some hamburger and some pork chops. Within six months we were up to sixty-five hundred dollars a week."

By 1974, business was good enough to buy the adjoining space and double the original nineteen foot wide store to thirty-eight feet. Five years later, Pete says they "took over the washateria and expanded to the present sixty-five feet and that's about as far as we can go."

In 1988, Pete set up a rotisserie in the back and went into the barbecue business – spit-roasting "ribs, chicken and one hundred briskets a week for people," basting them while they cooked with a sauce that he says is a recipe that originated in Pecos, Texas, and has been in his family, unaltered, for seventy-five years. He bottles and sells his sauce now in pint ($2.99), half gallon ($5.00) and gallon ($10.00) size containers and ships it all over the country, as far away as Hawaii.

In 1991, Pete made a final commitment to the glorious world of real pit-smoked barbecue by building huge pits in the back "so we could slow-smoke the meat the way we'd been wanting to," says son Michael, Pete's heir-apparent, who joined his father in the business straight out of high school.

The Barbecue is exceptional – turkey legs, brisket and several different kinds of ribs (country, spare and beef) all emerge from the pits blackened with smoke, but not burned. They're moist, tender and tasting pretty much the way our Texas ancestors, who've been barbecuing since the turn of the century, had in mind.

From the beginning, the barbecuing duties have been in the ample and extremely capable hands of general manager, Blake Kirksey, who's been with Pete for the better part of ten years.

All meats are first marinated for at least three days in a dry rub which they sell in plastic bags as "All Purpose Seasoning," then smoked over pecan wood in the time-honored fashion (in the case of the brisket, for as long as fourteen hours).

Although Pete says he's still proudest of the quality of choice meat they sell, he admits that both the barbecue brisket and ribs are pretty spectacular. "It's the time we take with it. We don't rush it." It shows.

What started out as a butcher shop/deli became a full-fledged destination for lunch about five years ago. They are now able to seat fifty people and Michael says, although they serve food all day, 9:00 a.m. to 6:00 p.m., they're often filled to capacity Tuesday through Friday between 11:30 a.m. and 2 p.m.

As good as the barbecue is, it may be surpassed by the Steak Hoagie – one of the best sandwiches I've ever eaten – tender slices of rib eye, New York strip and top sirloin, all seasoned with Pete's All-Purpose Seasoning, browned on the grill with thin caramelized slices of sweet onion and loaded onto a warm, fresh hoagie bun dressed with mayonnaise and lettuce with Swiss cheese melted over the whole juicy mess. Ask for it "all the way" and load up on napkins. Pete says that they've sold between seventy-five and eighty hoagies a day since they started making them six years ago.

Another winner hot-off-the-grill is a flawless, classically-made Cheeseburger. As Pete's nephew, grill chef Charlie Peña says, "People love them because they're made the old fashioned way"- well-seasoned lean ground round, seared on the grill, topped with a slice of American cheese and served on a buttered, toasted bun. Again, best ordered "all the way" with cool, shredded iceberg lettuce, sliced onion, tart slices of dill pickles and the regulation mayonnaise and mustard.

Pete says they've been making Po-boys for twenty years and they're good enough to give the famous Antone's "super" a run for its money; paper-thin slices of sweet ham, salami and provolone cheese with mayonnaise on a thin fresh baguette of French bread.

Paul La Chappell from Mamou, Louisiana, is the source for their Boudin. Another winner, it is seasoned to perfection – generously flecked with red and jalapeño pepper and spicy even in it's "mild" form.

There is a menu, but Blake Kirksey says they're happy to cook anything from the meat or seafood case to order for lunch or to take home.

The salads or side dishes need a bit more attention and aren't quite up to the very high standards set by the barbecue, boudin and other sandwiches. Michael says there's a plan to start offering French fries almost immediately.

Their Beef Jerky is outstanding – sirloin tips marinated in Pete's famous marinade, then hung in the smokehouse for eighteen hours until they're dried to the customary shoe-leather stage. For fans of Cracklin's, the famous snack food of ex-Presidents, they make their own; available between March and June, the skin is smoked, then they are cooked slow in what Blake says is an "all day process."

Suckling Pig is a great delicacy for those who haven't tasted it. While it's common to spot them roasting vertically at roadside stands in Ecuador, to find the very best, you might have to travel to the northern half of Spain's central plateau, to the little Castillian towns of Segovia or Arévalo where both suckling pig and cabrito are roasted in bakers' ovens. In China, they're prized, like Peking duck, for their crisp skin and served in stages much the same way. A little closer to home, Hawaiians cook suckling pigs for luaus in an imu oven; a huge hole lined with volcanic rocks is dug in the backyard and then filled with fresh bamboo leaves. The pig is placed in the imu pit, covered with more bamboo leaves, a tarp, some dirt and left to cook all night.

Unless you are up to this task, you might want to call Pete's Fine Meats and let them do the work. Their suckling pigs weigh between twenty-five and thirty pounds, will feed as many as twenty lucky people, and take at least three days to prepare – two to marinate the pig in dry seasoning and one day to slow smoke it over pecan wood at very low heat. Blake says he rubs it down every thirty minutes with a mixture of white vinegar and garlic powder. They need at least four or five days notice to prepare a suckling pig and charge about $110.00 for a thirty-five pound porker.

The Cabrito is cooked virtually the same way as the suckling pig. A twenty-pound cabrito costs about $85.00 cooked and feeds approximately fifteen people.

They are happy to marinate anything for customers who want to cook their meats themselves at home, and Pete says that hunting season is an especially busy time for them because they smoke freshly shot wild game for many of their customers . (They charge $1.25 per pound for this service).

My feeling is that the steak hoagie and the cheeseburger should be eaten there, fresh off the grill, but Michael says they do a brisk business with customers "who work late and don't feel like cooking. They call and we cook a steak and maybe a baked potato just before we know they're coming. We wrap it up well in aluminum foil so it can be eaten as soon as possible when they get home, still warm without having to reheat it."

P. F. CHANG'S CHINA BISTRO

4094 Westheimer
Houston, Texas 77027
713/627-7220

Type of Cuisine: Chinese/American
Bar: Full
Dress: Casual
Entertainment: No
Payment: All Major Credit Cards
Entrée Range: $6.95-$12.95
Recommended Dishes:
  Appetizers: Peking Ravioli (pan fried)
    Steamed Shrimp Dumplings
    Chang's Chicken in Soothing Lettuce Wrap
  Entrées: Beef a la Szechuan
    Crispy Honey Shrimp
    Orange Peel Beef
    DanDan Noodles
    Garlic Snap Peas
    Szechuan-Style Long Beans
    Spinach Sauteed with Garlic
Hours: Sunday-Thursday, 11:00a.m.-11:00p.m.
  Friday-Saturday, 11:00a.m.-12:00a.m.
Reservations: Not Accepted

I don't know about you, but when I hear the word "chain" associated with a restaurant my heart sinks a little; I immediately lower my expectations and brace myself for assembly line food and an atmosphere devoid of distinct personality. Happily, that is not the case with P. F. Chang's China Bistro. This is a big, fun, noisy, brand spanking-new restaurant that serves up some terrific Americanized-Chinese dishes in a lively, energetic setting.

I'm not sure I'd call it a bistro, though. When I think of a bistro what springs to mind is a cozy, neighborhood place, a steaming bowl of French onion soup and maybe a glass of the house Burgundy.

Never mind. Picture instead, the all glass and stone house perched on the side of a hill in the movie North by Northwest, but instead of facing Mount Rushmore, it's facing River Oaks Burger Joint. The house in the movie was strikingly-handsome – probably meant to look like a Frank Lloyd Wright design in those days – and so is P. F. Chang's, but a bistro, well..."cavernous dining hall" is more like it. I mean, the restaurant seats about two hundred people.

By its very loosest definition, French authority Patricia Wells says a bistro might be defined as "a place for good times with friends" and clearly P. F. Chang's is that. By 8:30 almost any night they're three-deep at the huge circular bar drinking martinis, one of the thirty-six wines available by the glass, and mai-tais with maraschino cherries and chunks of pineapple in them. (It is possible to avoid a wait by arriving before seven p.m. or after nine; at lunch – before noon or after one-thirty p.m.; or calling from home to have your name put on the list.)

The food itself is enhanced by the atmosphere and the high energy level. Those who are familiar with my column know that while I appreciate good cooking wherever I can find it – I'm a sucker for authenticity and, although I know they think it is, the menu at P. F. Chang's isn't any more authentically Chinese than the menu at Outback Steakhouse is Australian.

That's OK. There are a few dishes you might want to avoid, but the things they do well, they do extremely well.

They should, too. All of the recipes originated with Phillip Chang who, with his mother, owns both the illustrious Mandarin Restaurants in Los Angeles and San Francisco.

These are the dishes I'd come back for. Among the appetizers, the Peking Raviolis are exceptional. Better pan fried than steamed, these pork and vegetable-filled dumplings are better than most for two reasons, according to chef Bill Kirk – the secret marinade developed by Chang for the pork, and the wrapper is thinner and more delicate than usual. "It's just a wonton wrapper, but thinner than those you usually see, so you're getting less dumpling and more meat." The dipping sauce is a mixture of chili oil (they steep it themselves with fresh chilis), rice vinegar and soy sauce. The same, nearly translucent, wonton skins are used to make the equally good, lighter, steamed shrimp dumplings served with the ginger-infused dipping sauce.

Another excellent choice among the appetizers is the Chang's Chicken in Soothing Lettuce Wrap – minced chicken sautéed with finely-chopped water chestnuts and black fungus mushrooms, and seasoned with soy sauce, vinegar and a little sugar. It is meant to be spooned into cold, fresh cups of iceberg lettuce, folded like a burrito, and eaten with your hands. They have Traditional Spare Ribs – hung on a hook, cooked in the duck oven, then glazed with the house barbecue sauce, and the more interesting, but slightly dry, Northern Style Short Ribs. They are trimmed of fat, boiled until tender, boiled again in a marinade, dried well, deep fried and served with a little dish of Five Spice Salt and Pepper dip, an intensely-flavored blend of ground star anise, cinnamon, fennel, cloves and Szechuan peppercorns.

Kirk says both Hot and Sour and Wonton Soups sell especially well when the weather is cold, but when it warms up, customers lean towards any of the five huge California-style salads. I liked the idea of the Warm Duck Salad – nicely seasoned and roasted duck sliced and placed warm on a heaping mound of shredded red and green cabbage dressed with a soy-based vinaigrette.

The two unqualified winners listed under "Chang's Recommends" are the Beef a la Szechuan and the Crispy Honey Shrimp. Julienned slivers of beef are cooked twice with crunchy shards of celery, carrots and onion, and flavored with a powerfully-concentrated chili paste and sugar. It's one of Kirk's favorites. "The meat is cooked once to seal in the juices and then it is fried again to give it an almost beef jerky-like texture. It is hot. It is supposed to be – the flavor is intense. When you first eat it, you'll get the sweetness of the sugar, and then – wham! – the heat hits you! It's almost like two things happening in your mouth at once!"

In sharp, but pleasant contrast, the Crispy Honey Shrimp are plump shrimp lightly battered, fried, then barely glazed with a not-too-sweet sauce. They rest on crisp white threads of fried rice noodles that add further texture to the dish.

The ever popular Orange Peel Beef had wonderful flavor but was drier than we have come to expect. Kirk says that it is a hallmark of their dishes that they have noticeably less sauce than one might find in the same dish at their competitors'. "That's the difference. We dry sauté and try to get just enough sauce to adhere to the food – to bring out, but not hide the flavor of the food."

The Spicy Ground Chicken and Eggplant is good enough to make converts of anyone who thinks they don't like eggplant. Unlike the sweeter Chang's Spicy Chicken, it has the advertised fire of ground chilis and the deep, rich flavor of minced chicken, garlic and Japanese eggplant appealingly turned and cut on the bias.

However, if it is a choice between ground chicken dishes, opt first for the DanDan Noodles. I believe it is the best dish on the menu. I was convinced that they were making their own pasta, but Kirk says they are freshly-made for them in California and flown in daily. You can tell the difference. Spooned on top of a tangled nest of perfectly-cooked egg noodles is a silky, garlic and chili-spiked, light brown sauce of finely ground chicken breasts. The same noodles are featured on the lunch menu as DanDan Chicken Noodle Soup, and as Kirk says – "If you like the noodles, you'll love the soup."

On the minus side, I was disappointed to find both the Garlic Noodles and Singapore Noodles in desperate need of not necessarily hotter, but more complete seasoning, and Chang's Lemon Scallops may qualify as one of history's most misguided seafood dishes; the sauce tasted like it had been made with Country Time Lemonade.

All of the vegetables were wonderful, though, starting with nature's own sweet Sugar Snap Peas enhanced with a little garlic and flecks of red pepper. They are crunchy, sweet and are my preference over the delicious, more assertively-seasoned Szechuan-Style Long Beans (especially if you plan to order the Beef a la Szechuan or Spicy Chicken and Eggplant). Spinach lovers will enjoy the simple goodness of fresh Spinach Sautéed with Garlic.

The few desserts offered are being prepared by a local bakery. The best I tasted was the dense, flourless Chocolate Torte served on a plate divided by equal measures of raspberry coulis-puréed raspberry sauce and créme anglaise – a rich, custard sauce (both made by Kirk). They were about to add Turtle Cheesecake to the menu and were very excited about it.

The real surprise with the fortune cookie was that the cookie itself was thinner, crisper and fresher than I ever remember tasting. Kirk tells me, "Phillip Chang and I sat down one day and had a fortune cookie taste-off and decided which ones were the best. I think it has a wonderful flavor."

P. F. Chang's doesn't take reservations although it is possible to reserve what they call the Captain's Table nestled in the lively nook between the bar and the kitchen, seating up to eighteen people.

PHÔ CÔNG LY

2600 Travis (at McGowen)
Houston, Texas 77006
713/522-9694

Type of Cuisine: Vietnamese
Bar: Beer
Dress: Casual
Entertainment: No
Payment: Credit Cards Accepted
Entrée Range: $3.60-$4.00
Recommended Dishes:
    Phô Gà (Chicken Noodle Soup)
    Phô Tái Chin Nac (Steak and Brisket Noodle Soup)
Hours: Monday-Sunday, 7:00a.m.-7:30p.m.
Reservations: Not Accepted

10800-F Bellaire Blvd. (at Wilcrest)
Houston, Texas 77072
713/879-8185

Type of Cuisine: Vietnamese
Bar: Beer
Dress: Casual
Entertainment: No
Payment: Credit Cards Accepted
Entrée Range: $3.95-$5.05
Recommended Dishes:
    Appetizers: Spring Rolls
        Shredded Pork Rolls
        Fried Egg Rolls
    Entrées: Pork Rice Plate
        Vermicelli Bowl
Hours: Monday-Sunday, 8:00a.m.-9:30p.m.
Reservations: Not Accepted

The first thing you notice when glancing at the menu at Phô Công Ly at Travis and McGowen is the stunning absence of anything but Phô – Vietnamese noodle soup. But those familiar with it know that phô is more than a simple bowl of soup. Phô is a salve to the senses that soothes the soul, and fills the diner with an overwhelming sense of well being.

Pronounced "fa" like the musical note, the word "'phô" means specifically beef noodle soup," explains owner Binh Nguyen. "This dish originated in the northern part of Vietnam where the weather is colder than it is in the south." He tells me that it was originally sold by vendors who would push heavy carts laden with huge steaming stock pots heated over charcoal through the streets, and announce their contents by singing out, "Phô . . . Phô!"

"Later on, when phô became very popular, people set up noodle houses to serve beef noodle soup. Eventually, people began to use chicken and so then there was chicken noodle soup, phô gà. 'Gà' means chicken, you know."

"Phô" is now the generic term for Vietnamese noodle soup, the way the word "fajitas" is used to describe a manner of cooking rather than a cut of beef.

The rich, intensely concentrated broth is achieved by roasting shallots and ginger and adding them to vast, individual cauldrons of chicken and beef stock. Cloves, cinnamon and the hauntingly aromatic, star anise – the Chinese eight point pod that holds tiny seeds give the soup its distinctive flavor.

By ordering the large bowl of phô, the kitchen is able to serve the correct proportion of noodles to broth – one part noodles, four parts soup. The noodles are always rice noodles or vermicelli. Nguyen says that Phô Công Ly's noodles, made from rice flour, come from a supplier in Southern California fresh and not dried, and are really "no different from those you would find at a noodle house in Vietnam."

Although Nguyen hopes to simplify the menu a little, at Phô Công Ly there are more than twenty possible combinations of contents from which to choose. The way to go, particularly for the novice, is either #2 Phô Tái, Chín Nac with "eye round steak and well done brisket" or, my preference, #21 Phô Gà, chicken noodle soup. Another option is the newly added seafood phô where shrimp, squid and imitation crab are simmered in chicken broth. Beef meatballs are another possible addition, but are a little tougher than we're accustomed to from the addition of beef tendon to the ground meat. Included in the category of "Fortifying Combinations" is what they call "book" tripe, and the slightly rubbery, gelatinous aforementioned beef tendon just what it sounds like the tendon or "big muscle" of the cow.

There are still more decisions to make. There may be an insert inside the menu asking your preference... "Do you want nonfat broth? More chicken skin? Scallion Heads? Fatty Broth?" . . .things like that. Nguyen tells me that the ability to make these choices is unique to Phô Công Ly and that they are determined to serve phô to the diner "exactly the way you like it," as it says.

The first time, at least, you might try just ordering the way it is normally prepared (and on future visits adjusting the ingredients to better suit your tastes).

Whichever phô you choose, deep white ceramic bowls arrive piping hot and richly fragrant, covered in a vibrant, emerald green blanket of chopped scallions and cilantro. There are chopsticks and ceramic spoons on the table, but they are happy to supply silverware. You may notice that many of the Vietnamese use both chopsticks and spoons to eat the noodles, beef, and broth at the same time. Nguyen says he prefers to alternate between the chopsticks and the spoon.

Before your soup arrives, a plate of traditional accompaniments is placed on the table. Razor thin slices of fresh jalapeño peppers are topped with a tangle of bean sprouts under a nest of branches of sweet basil. The plate is rimmed with wedges of lime. There are three sauces on the table – the divinely pungent Vietnamese fish sauce, nuoc mam; sweet, brown hoisin sauce in a cafeteria-style squirt bottle; and the bright red chili-garlic sauce.

When I ask about the bean sprouts he says, "You can use bean sprouts if you prefer. People from the North never eat bean sprouts. It is considered that they dilute the taste and aroma of the phô." Then why have them? "Because in the South (of Vietnam) they eat everything with bean sprouts and we have many customers from the South." I agree with him. The bean sprouts add nothing.

About the three sauces . . . "I don't use any of them because the taste is supposed to be correct already. I used hoisin sauce when I was a boy because it made it sweeter, but when I grew up and ate with old people I stopped using it." To add heat to the phô, he says he prefers using fresh jalapeño to chili sauce "because that chili sauce has garlic in it and phô is never made with garlic."

I'm with him on these two points. I believe the delicate flavor and full impact of the soup is altered too radically by adding either chili or hoisin sauce, but I'm a sucker for the salty flavor of nuoc mam so although he doesn't recommend adding that either. "Our cook just never cooked with it!" I think a couple of drops add a subtle complexity.

Phô is quite filling, but they have dessert if you have room. Listed on the menu as "Chè, Homemade Puddings," my favorite was #5 Combination Bean Pudding. This is a tall, cafeteria-style glass layered decoratively with first white bean "pudding," red bean "pudding," then something that looks a lot like squiggly, green gummy worms (Nguyen says it is green-colored tapioca), crushed ice, all covered with coconut milk. It arrives with a teaspoon stuck into the glass and is meant to be stirred, then eaten. Why not? You don't want to follow the Zenlike purity of this meal with a banana split, do you?

The other Pho Công Ly that Nguyen owns in Houston is located at 10800-F Bellaire (at Wilcrest). As their kitchen is larger than the restaurant downtown, they are able to offer appetizers; the glorious Vietnamese spring rolls, shredded pork rolls and fried egg rolls. They also have "rice plates" – steamed rice with various toppings. My favorite was the one with a thin, moist, grilled pork chop and sweet, succulent morsels of roasted pork. Another winner was the "vermicelli bowl" with marinated prawns and pieces of the grilled pork that gave the noodles a lovely, smokey aftertaste.

Nguyen says that especially in the morning, it is common for the Vietnamese to drink the sweet/rich iced coffee with condensed milk with their phô, but I preferred the lemon iced tea jasmine tea flavored with lemon juice and lots of granulated sugar.

PIZZITOLA'S BAR-B-CUE

1703 Shepherd Drive
Houston, Texas 77007
713/227-2283

Type of Cuisine: Barbecue
Bar: Beer
Dress: Casual
Entertainment: No
Payment: All Major Credit Cards
Dinner Plate: $7.95-$8.95
Recommended Dishes:
Ribs
Brisket
Sausage
Chicken
Grilled Vegetables
Coleslaw
Potato Salad
Dessert: Coconut Cake
Banana Pudding
Hours: Monday-Friday, 11:00a.m.-8:00p.m.
Saturday, 11:00a.m-3:00p.m.
(Closed Sunday)
Reservations: Not Accepted

Jerry Pizzitola says he's not a "real barbecue man." He cites Jim Goode (of Goode Company Barbecue) as an example of a "real barbecue man." But, I say it takes one to know one.

Pizzitola says his idea of great barbecue when he was growing up was the open pit variety – a special feature of the kind of places his father used to take him when he was a child – Matt Garner's, Lockwood Barbecue, Green's on Almeda and especially, Shepherd Drive Barbecue to eat (proprietor) John Davis' brisket.

In 1981, Pizzitola was busy working at Regal Food, the family business, when he wandered into his beloved Shepherd Drive Barbecue for some brisket and their distinctive puckery, palate-awakening, bright orange barbecue sauce that goes so well with it. He noticed that something had changed. "Both John and his wife, Lela, had died and the family was running it." He says it took two years of aggressive wooing to convince their daughter, Lois Davis, to lease the property and pass the mantel to him.

He changed the name of the then 45 year-old institution to Pizzitola's Bar-B-Cue. He laughs that "maybe I should have called it Bubba's or something. People wander in asking for pizza or something Italian." He surrounded himself with a couple of real barbecue veterans, Christine Lewis who still runs his kitchen, and Carlton Gould from the venerable Otto's – both keys to his success, he says. "I count on them. The people who work for me have to be awake at all times. We cook right on the fire. I call that 'direct.' People ask 'how long do you smoke your brisket?' I tell 'em, 'I don't smoke 'em, I cook 'em."

His is juicy, buttery Brisket with just a ghost of the grill; smoky without being overwhelming. It passes the ultimate test – the lower lean, "tight" portion is as moist as the fattier, marbled upper cut. It is a work of art.

But so are the Ribs. Meaty, crisp-edged beauties with plenty of salt and pepper seared directly over the fire. "The ribs and the chicken are a family thing that started with my great grandmother Liuzza, my father's grandmother. She would take a number 3 washtub, put some wood in there, put a screen over it and cook ribs or chicken – always just seasoned with salt and pepper. That's how she cooked and how my dad taught me." At this point, he adds that Pizzitola's may be best-known for their ribs. "There are people who swear by the brisket or the chicken, but they all have the ribs; sometimes even as an appetizer." He says he likes them so much he named his company Spareribs Incorporated!

The Chicken's golden skin is studded with salt and coarsely ground pepper. The meat is juicy and tastes very faintly of hickory. ("I use hickory because that's what Mr. Davis used," Pizzitola says.) It is served on or uniquely, off-the-bone. "This started a couple of years after we opened as a favor to a regular customer who said, 'Pizz, I love your chicken, but I hate to eat it on the bone. Would you mind boning it for me?' I said, 'What, are you crazy?' But I'm looking at an empty restaurant at this point, so we took a half a chicken and removed the bones. The people at he next table said, 'Hey, I want that!' And pretty soon it caught on as a sort of off-the-menu specialty." After a couple of years he says he finally got "the nerve" to put it on the menu and charge a dollar for the service. He adds, "Me, I like the mess of eating it on the bone. That's one of the reasons I've always insisted on having cloth napkins at Pizzitola's. People always said I was crazy to do that, but there isn't a paper alive that's gonna remove that stuff from your hands!" (I have to tell you, I love that he does this. I wish everyone provided cloth napkins!) Anyone eating chicken (on the bone) or ribs is also treated to a hot towel at the end of the meal.

The Sausage is spectacular – taut-skinned, coarsely-ground, mostly beef Czech sausage with just enough pork to make it good and juicy. "It comes from Cistern close to Flatonia. The brand is V and V for Vinklarek and Vinklarek – a couple of brothers. It's the same sausage John Davis served, so together we've bought from these guys a total of twenty-five years."

The Potato Salad is a finely-chopped, mustardy-yellow, old-fashioned variety with lots of good crunch. I adore the Coleslaw – cold, very lightly dressed chopped cabbage seasoned with salt and a pinch of sugar. Period. The Beans are ranchero-style kidney beans tarted up with Rotel tomatoes.

The best surprise of all though, is the unusual offering of Grilled Vegetables.

Carrots, onions, bell peppers and tomatoes are grilled, roughly chopped and sautéed in a little olive oil. It's a heavenly-smoky, Texas-style ratatouille. Pizzitola says, "We started making that in '92 or '93. I had quit smoking and had gained about 100 pounds. So, I started working out and eating the gilled vegetables with some (white) rice over our skinless and boneless chicken breast and I lost the weight. Now, they're more popular than the coleslaw!"

Pizzitola's mother, Margaret Raley, has made his desserts for thirteen years. "I think I was buying pies from House of Pies, and Mother said, 'Jerry, would you like me to make some cake or some pudding?' I said, 'sure!' She's good at cooking everything, but especially desserts." The stand-outs delivered daily by Pizzitola's stepfather, Ed Raley – are an old-fashioned, made-from-scratch Banana Pudding and a Coconut Cake from your dreams – moist yellow cake with chunks of pineapple sandwiched between the layers, with a gooey white icing spiked with feathery coconut.

Pizzatola says, "This has been so much fun for me. When I started, I didn't know anything about the restaurant business and I'd heard about dealing with the public. But, so far I haven't met any public."

QUEEN OF SHEBA

5710 Bellaire Boulevard
Houston, Texas 77081
713/665-3009

Type of Cuisine: Ethiopian
Bar: Wine and Beer
Dress: Casual
Entertainment: No
Payment: All Major Credit Cards
Entrée Range: $3.40-$7.35
Recommended Dishes:
    Kitfo (Tartare Steak)
    Beyaynetu (Combination of Stews)
    Doro Wote (Chicken Stew)
    Lega Tibs (Beef with Jalapeños and Onions)
    Misser Wote (Red Lentil Stew)
    Yetsom Beyaynetu (Vegetable Combination)
Hours: Tuesday-Thursday, 11:00a.m.-10:00p.m.
    Friday: 11:00a.m.-11:00p.m.
    Saturday: 12:00p.m.-11:00p.m.
    Sunday: 12:00p.m.-10:00p.m.
    (Closed Monday)
Reservations: Not Accepted

The moment you enter Queen of Sheba you are at once seduced and enticed by the tantalizing aroma of exotic spices being toasted in a hot pan for berbere, the powerfully concentrated seasoning mixture that is at the heart of most Ethiopian dishes. Equal measure of ground cumin, coriander, ginger, cardamom, fenugreek, nutmeg, cinnamon and cloves release their fragrant oils and fill the air. They stimulate the appetite and announce to the diner that he or she is in for something quite special. Ethiopian cuisine may just be Houston's best kept culinary secret.

At Queen of Sheba there are no appetizers or desserts. The menu is short and highlights Ethiopia's most traditional dishes. Familiar meats and vegetables of always impeccable quality are prepared and served in unfamiliar ways with flavors so intense and so memorable that I am willing to bet you will become a regular. Food cravings are based on dishes as distinctive and fiercely seasoned as these.

There is an assortment of beer and wine to choose from, but you might want to try at least one glass of the tangy, mildly acerbic honey wine made on the premises, called Teg (pronounced "tudge").

Any explanation of Ethiopian dining must begin with Injera, the earth's most unusual bread. It is a spongy, slightly-fermented flat bread that in Ethiopia might be used in place of a tablecloth. Individual dishes would then be eaten communally, spooned directly onto the bread. Pieces of the soft, pliable bread are broken off with your right hand and used to scoop up bite-sized morsels of food, trying not to touch your fingers to either the food or your mouth directly. Although injera can be made with whole wheat flour, it is at its most authentic best when made with "teff" – a kind of cereal indigenous to Ethiopia. The grain is so tiny that if dropped on the floor it is "teff," the Armharic word for "lost."

At Queen of Sheba, most dishes arrive from the kitchen already ladled onto a platter covered with injera. If not, the dish should be spooned onto the bread before being eaten. The injera is served on a separate platter folded neatly into quarters and arranged overlapping like grayish-beige napkins.

Each diner places one whole round of injera on his or her plate and tears off small, manageable pieces with which to enfold a bite of food.

I sampled all thirteen dishes on the menu and there isn't one that doesn't deserve a ringing endorsement. My suggestion is to order the combination, #7 Beyaynetu. It is a well-balanced assortment of different wotes, or stews, that includes lamb, ground beef, a cubed beef stew and two vegetable wotes – a mustard-yellow chick pea stew and a mixture of the vegetables on hand enhanced with garlic. The presentation is a handsomely composed artist's palate of dishes in burnt orange, sunny yellow and chile powder red. Each dish has its own complex, distinct flavor.

Depending on the size of your party (or your appetite) I would include in your order #1Kitfo and #2 Doro Wote – Ethiopia's first and second best known dishes.

#1 Kitfo is Ethiopian tartare steak. Cool and elegant in its simplicity, the finest, leanest beef is minced, seasoned with berbere, lemon, finely chopped onions and garlic, and served mounded into a separate bowl. Put it on the injera before eating it and sprinkle it with the cayenne pepper based mixture that comes in the little saucer on the side. (The chopped tomato and onion garnish that comes with most dishes is especially good with the Kitfo).

#2 Doro Wote is a chicken stew that is also served in its own bowl. Ethiopia's second best-loved dish has a chicken leg and a whole, peeled hard boiled egg inside the bowl which should be broken up with the spoon before placing on the injera. More "stew" than chicken, this dish has a vivid, lingering taste.

Another favorite vegetable is #10 Misser Wote. Blindfolded, you might easily mistake this red lentil stew for a bowl of Texas chili; it is so similar in flavor and texture. Misser Wote is also the only Ethiopian dish that can be compared to anything I've eaten anywhere else.

Queen of Sheba is a small, unpretentious restaurant named for the biblical character, Makeda, Queen of Ethiopia. The enchanting story of how she came to marry Solomon, King of Israel, and establish the first royal line of the Kingdom of Sheba, is printed on the backside of the menu. It is one of only two Ethiopian restaurants in Houston and since its opening in 1982, has outlasted several. The secret to its success is the extraordinary cooking of chef and owner, Yewegnenh Cheho, and the genial presence in the dining room of younger brother, Seifu Cheho. They are proud of having received Marvin Zindler's Blue Ribbon Award in 1995.

Seifu Cheho knows that this food is foreign to his "American" customers and asks only that we come with an open mind . . . and an adventurous palate.

REGGAE HUT

4814 Almeda
Houston, Texas 77004
713/524-2905

Type of Cuisine: Jamaican
Bar: Wine and Beer
Dress: Casual
Entertainment: Live DJ, Friday, 8:00p.m.-11:00p.m.
Payment: Cash and Check
Entrée Range: $2.95-$11.00
Recommended Dishes:
Appetizers: Fried Plaintains
Patties (Best are Chicken and Beef)
Cocoa Bread
Entrées: Jerk Chicken
Curry Goat or Chicken
Oxtails
Garlic Crabs
Fried Rice
Hours: Monday-Saturday, 11:30a.m.-10:00p.m.
(Closed Sunday)
Reservations: Not Accepted

To fully appreciate the cooking of Jamaica and it's complexity, it's important to understand the rich ethnic diversity and history of the island.

" 'Out of many, one people,' that's our motto in Jamaica," explains Kingston native, chef Andrew Walker. "Jamaica is a combination of a lot of different ethnic groups and we take dishes from practically everyone. There is a vast population of Chinese, so we have experience with (Chinese cooking techniques) like stir fries. Another ethnic group is the (East) Indian population and they are, of course, experts in the field of curry – so they popularized that."

My favorite dish at Reggae Hut is probably Jamaica's best known export after Blue Mountain coffee and Bob Marley – Jerk Chicken. This technique of preserving or "jerking" meat dates back at least as far as the mid-eighteenth century to the Maroons, escaped ex-slaves who caught wild boar and preserved them by seasoning them heavily with salt, pepper and especially pimento. Walker continues, "Pimento is what you call allspice here. (Probably because it smells and tastes like a mixture of cinnamon, nutmeg and clove.) It grows on trees all over Jamaica and looks a little like whole black peppercorns, maybe a little bigger." In fact, Spanish explorers mistook the berries for peppercorns in the late fifteenth century and named the spice pimento. "This is what predominantly gives jerk seasoning its unique taste; it's a very big part of any jerk dish. I get it whole, of course, and grind it myself.

"The original way to cook jerk was on some kind of pit outside with the wood from the pimento tree, but we cook ours in the oven exclusively now. This takes a little from it, but not much."

I can't imagine improving on the already hauntingly aromatic, eye-popping perfection of the Jerk Chicken at Reggae Hut. The seasoning mixture "goes back to when I was a youth. At home, it was an everyday thing on a Saturday or Sunday afternoon to make up a batch of seasoning and get a couple of chickens."

The jerk seasoning is a paste that Walker says includes "onions, bell peppers, fresh thyme, escallions (scallions or green onions), garlic, pimento, clove, celery, a little vinegar, a tad of cooking oil and more Scotch bonnet peppers than we use in any other dish." (Scotch bonnet peppers are the lethal little lantern-shaped peppers that we call habañeras. Sometimes added simply for flavor, they are the source of heat in most Jamaican dishes.)

There are a thousand variations of jerk seasoning. Walker agrees, "We created an all-original seasoning here; this is one-of-a-kind. There may be people who do it their way, but this is how we do it at Reggae Hut." I think I'd eat a shoe if it was marinated and cooked in this seasoning. I was happy to hear that Walker and his two partners, Houstonians architect Kevin Bingham and Gary Mosley, are working on bottling this elixir as we speak.

The jerk chicken, while it's a memory that lingers, is just the beginning of what they do well.

Starting at the top, listed under appetizers and sides are Plantains, Beef or Vegetable Patties and Cocoa Bread. Plantain, the green banana that must be cooked to be eaten, is indigenous to the West Indies. Although Walker says, "We usually get plantains from South America, we choose (plantains) that are not overly ripe and not too green, so you get somewhat of a sweet taste. We deep fry them quickly on very high temperature so they don't absorb any oil and then pat them dry." You wouldn't know they are deep fried, it is done so skillfully. They are ambrosial; a little like bananas Foster without the ice cream.

The Patties are large crescent-shaped turnovers or what we might call empanadas in this part of the world. This is Jamaica's most popular fast food eaten almost like a hamburger there. At lunchtime in Kingston there might be a line around the block at a popular patty stand. At Reggae Hut, it is possible to choose beef, vegetable or chicken patties. The vegetable variety is good, but the ground beef and ground chicken are seasoned so intensely (and expertly) by resident baker, another

Kingston native, Carl Roden, that I wouldn't miss sampling either of them. Another must to try is Roden's Cocoa Bread. "It's called cocoa bread because in the old days it was made with coconut milk in it. I bake it twice a day." The sweet, fresh bread arrives warm in a pool of butter that has seeped out of the folds in the dough.

The first-listed entrée is Curry Goat, one of the national dishes of Jamaica. Walker says, "It is served at almost everybody's wedding. It's automatic. Curry goat is pretty much right there with the groom. It's a traditional dish." The curry goat and Curry Chicken undergo, whenever possible, a two day process of being seasoned heavily, left to marinate overnight, then cooked the next day. "The goat is chopped into tiny chunks, then seasoned with a mixture that includes a vast amount of garlic because it brings out the flavor in the goat meat and (Jamaican) curry powder." The secret is that "we burn the curry into the meat in a hot pan with very little oil for about fifteen minutes before we add any liquid. This brings out the flavor of the curry and seals it into the goat or chicken." The result is a dense, greenish yellow curry sauce that is intoxicating to smell and heaven to eat.

I found the Oxtails to be an earthy, heartwarming dish on a cold winter's day. Tiny one-inch sections of oxtail are seared in a pan to "remove most of the fat," as Walker says, "and to give them a brownish complexion. Then we sauté them or 'brown stew' them down with onions, bell peppers, garlic, thyme and other spices to form a gravy. Then we add potatoes and carrots and broad beans from the islands to thicken it without having to use flour or cornstarch; this gives body to the gravy." The Brown Stew Chicken is prepared similarly and is equally satisfying.

There is a depth of flavor and harmony to these dishes as much from the impeccable quality of the ingredients used as the time taken to prepare them.

Walker concedes that he doesn't eat as much meat as he used to, so his favorite dishes tend to be seafood. "My favorite is pretty much the Red Snapper – dry-seasoned, fried whole then served on the bone with a rich brown sauce, and I'm partial to the Ackee and Saltfish."

Ackee (pronounced a´ki) is a fruit that grows in Jamaica. It is inedible unless it is blanched first in hot water. "The dish itself is almost considered a vegetable. I grew up eating this dish; we had an ackee tree in my back yard, so I had access to it every day. It's a little hard to find here. We get some fresh ackee when it's in season (from Florida). It's really a sauté. We flake the saltfish and cook it with lots of vegetables – onions, peppers, garlic – then we add the ackee. It's a very unique dish.

I've never known quite how to describe it. It is an acquired taste. Once eaten you're either going to like it or hate it."

I love it. Ackee has the texture of custard or scrambled eggs, is cut in small pieces and acts as the perfect foil to the sharpness of the fish and vegetables. This is an off-the-menu special and is considered the national dish of Jamaica.

My other favorite seafood dish is one of the specialties of Harry Edwards, the last Jamaican to join the team – Garlic Crabs. Our own Gulf crabs are boiled, hacked in half, then treated to a sultry bath of butter, garlic, parsley and herbs.

Although the curries are probably best eaten with plain white rice, most entrées share the plate with a medley of fresh steamed vegetables that Walker calls Succotash that changes according to season, and the Jamaican staple Rice and Peas. While it is possible occasionally to get Gungo peas – small green peas similar in flavor to our blackeyed peas here, rice and peas is almost always made with red kidney beans. After the first fifteen minutes, the beans are enhanced by adding coconut milk, then the uncooked white rice is added near the end of the cooking process so the rice absorbs the wonderful, rich flavor of the beans.

There are three Fried Rice dishes available as entrées and they deserve special comment. There is shrimp, chicken or vegetable fried rice all chock full of goodies and toasted brown, with the welcome nutty flavor of mushroom soy sauce.

It says on the menu to "ask about ground provisions" so I did. Walker says, "This is a Caribbean expression for vegetables grown under the ground – yellow yams, sweet potatoes, things like that. At the moment, we're having a hard time finding yellow yams."

This almost amounts to a tragedy from my standpoint because the equally-difficult-to-find white yams are a featured ingredient in an irregularly-available dessert called Sweet Potato Pudding. I was less crazy for the more commonly available Bulla Cake, a dryish flat cake flavored with ginger.

The two "Thirst Quenchers" I'd opt for are either Red Stripe, a good Jamaican beer, or Ginger Beer, a nonalcoholic Jamaican soft drink with the assertive bite of fresh ginger.

There is also white wine, red wine, fruit smoothies, Peanut Butter Punch – a shake made with fresh peanuts, banana, coconut milk and ice – and a concoction called Irish Moss – a seaweed, tree sap-based tea that many consider to be an aphrodisiac.

The restaurant seats only 52 people. Smoking is permitted only at the few tables set up outside.

ROLAND'S SWISS PASTRY AND TEA ROOM

6504 Del Monte (off Voss)
Houston, Texas 77057
713/785-4294

Type of Cuisine: Swiss
Bar: Wine and Beer
Dress: Casual
Entertainment: No
Payment: MasterCard and Visa
Prices: $3.75-$8.95
Recommended Dishes:
- Bratwurst
- Liverwurst
- Meat Roll
- Bundnerteller (Air Dried Beef)
- Raclette
- Quiche
- Dessert: Truffles
  - Almond Cherry Cookies
  - Milk Chocolate Florentines

Hours: Monday, 9:00a.m.-5:00p.m.
Tuesday-Friday, 7:00a.m.-7:00p.m.
Saturday, 7:00a.m.-5:00p.m. (Deli-Bakery until 6:00p.m.)
(Closed Sunday)
Reservations: Not Accepted

A German friend of mine has the annoying habit of pointing out that one should always take responsibility for one's actions by saying, "Die wurst nach dem manne braten," which roughly translates to "Each man fries his own sausage."

I know what he means – "You made your bed, you must lie in it" – but what I'm always thinking when he says it, is that "wursts" or sausages are so significant in his native culture that even the simplest expression or admonition is wurst-related.

Fans of this 27-year-old institution may beat a path to their door for their picture-perfect, lattice-topped Linzertortes, Black Forest Cakes or even their classic Quiche Lorraines, but it's the wursts – the Bratwursts, Knackwursts and even Liverwursts – that I think makes Roland's such a special place to eat (or take out).

Elvira Schaefer, who with her husband, Gerhard, bought Roland's from Roland Lanz several years ago, says that their sausage is especially good (and authentic tasting) because they were lucky enough to discover a Swiss butcher shop in Denver that produces the real McCoy. "This was especially important with the bratwurst," she says. "Nobody makes good bratwurst in Houston." They are divine – pale, virtually fat-free sausages made from veal, subtly flavored with a little nutmeg, marjoram and mace. They are split and grilled or "fried" in a pan, hence the name "bratwurst" or "fry wurst." An order comes with sharp, yellowish-brown Dusseldorf mustard and a couple of slices of good, freshly-baked rye bread. The two other sausages featured on the menu are Wienerli – long, skinny, slightly-smoked frankfurters or hot dogs and the stubby, garlic-flavored Knackwurst – offered boiled cold, or my preference, split and grilled. All three are good, but the bratwurst is my favorite.

If the weather is cool, then warm, buttery Red Cabbage and fat, doughy homemade noodles, called Spätzle, are the ideal accompaniments. Or, if it's hot, a coarse-grain mustard Potato Salad made with skins-on new potatoes and an order of cold Red Cabbage go nicely with the wursts. All side dishes must be ordered á la carte.

Roland's Liverwurst Plate gives the diner a chance to sample two sublime patés, really – one "coarse" and one "fine." A third chunky-textured one called Hausmacher, is available by request. I loved all three, but the grayish medium-coarse lightly smoked Westphalian Liverwurst was the best of all. All are slathered on rye bread and garnished with the requisite onion slices, tomato and tart, crisp, tiny cornichons (pickles).

Bavarian smoked meats are well represented at Roland's. The Schaefers are importing several from Germany and Switzerland. The Black Forest Ham has an intense, nut-like flavor and is cut in delicate ribbons. It is comparable to Italian proscuitto. The less subtle, but equally good, Bauernschinken (farmer's ham) is served – if you request the smoked rather than cooked ham – on the Imported Ham Plate. Both hams, particularly the Bauernschinken, are still eaten as a traditional Vesper or mid-morning snack with Bauernbrot (farmer's bread) throughout the Black Forest region with a bracing glass of chilled fruit-flavored brandy like Kirschwasser (cherry) or Himbeergeist (raspberry).

The most distinctive of the imported meats is the air dried beef called Bundnerfleisch by Swiss-Germans or Viand de Grisons by Swiss-French. At Roland's it is listed under "Sandwiches" as Bündnerteller. It is exquisitely lean, Burgundy-red beef that is first marinated then, by law, cured at 1,500 meters or higher in small wooden huts with slatted sides in the Alps in the Canton of Frisons in Switzerland. It is always sliced paper-thin and eaten with cornichons and onions, but a dish called Raclette is the most luxurious accompaniment of all.

Raclette is cow's milk cheese similar to its cousin, Gruyere, with a nutty, smooth flavor and semi-firm texture. The word raclette is taken from the French verb "racler," to scrape, because in Switzerland the tops of huge wheels of raclette are exposed to heat over an open fire or sometimes an electric heater, then the melted layer is scraped onto the plate and served with boiled potatoes, bread, cornichons, onions and always, always a cold glass of white wine – Gewürztraminer or Dezaley, for instance. At Roland's the custom is simplified a bit by melting the raclette directly onto freshly-baked French bread. It makes a fine marriage with a plateful of Bündnerfleisch.

Listed as "Specialties," there are Toasts or hearty, open-faced sandwiches variously composed of ham, spinach, mushrooms, salami and a generous slice of melted Swiss cheese, probably Gruyere, and topped with a fried egg. The most interesting composition in this category is the Grilled Fleischkäse. The closest thing we have to this is a coarse, really good bologna. Sold at snack stands all over Bavaria as Leberkäse, the Fleischkäse is cut in thick slices, grilled in a pan and topped with sweet, caramelized onion and a fried egg.

Two other "Specialties" not to miss are as fine a traditional Quiche Lorraine as I've tasted in Houston and what's called a Meat Roll. Both give the kitchen a chance to show off its (savory) pastry-making skills. There are several types of Quiche to choose from, but the classic Lorraine made with good Swiss ham and cheese, I believe is the best. Elvira's favorite is the one made with grilled onions and bacon called Zwiebelkucken, which is not always available, but worth asking about. Roland's supplies quiches to Whole Foods Market.

The Meat Roll is finely minced ground beef seasoned well with onions, parsley and a little nutmeg, encased in buttery puff pastry and baked in the oven. For a little extra, they will melt Swiss cheese over the top, which is a fine idea unless you've ordered it "to go."

My favorite of the soups is the one Elvira tells me they most recently added – Lentil Soup. "People like that, especially in winter time. Gerhard is from the Black Forest and it is a Black Forest specialty to add Spätzle to the lentil soup and serve it with some wienerli on top. We have that on our special menu."

This menu is a list of monthly rotating daily-specials that includes Potato Pancakes with apple sauce (another favorite of Elvira), Stuffed Bell Peppers and a classically-prepared Wienerschnitzel. It was as thin and crisp as parchment, served with Farmer's Potatoes (what we call "German fries") and begged to be converted into Veal Holstein by the addition of a fried egg on top.

Pickled herring is definitely an acquired taste, but fans of Herring Salad will enjoy it at Roland's, made with slivers of

Granny Smith apples, onions, and sour cream seasoned with pickling spices, and garnished with sliced hard-boiled egg and rosettes of radishes. The most appealing (and unusual) of the salads is the Cervelat Salad. Elvira explains that Knackwursts are called "cervelats" in Switzerland. So slim, garlic-flavored sausages are sliced thin and mixed with onions, pickles and a silky, mustardy, homemade mayonnaise that she refers to as Swiss dressing. The shredded Swiss cheese on top is a nice touch.

The various breads and chocolate truffles are my favorite things from the bakery. The Hazelnut Coffeecake is heaven – an eggy bread, iced and swirled with cinnamon. Carrot cake is a Swiss classic, so it's not surprising that the Carrot Bread is excellent. And the Cheese Danish are about six inches in diameter – a massive, but worthwhile undertaking.

Among the cookies, I liked the iced vanilla, pretzel-shaped butter cookies and the chewy crescents that she calls Almond and Cherries. More candy than cookie, really, the Florentines are a specialty in Germany. The classic Florentine, made with almonds and dark chocolate is good, but the milk chocolate variety, gooey with caramel and imbedded with rich whole hazelnuts, is better.

A handful of homemade Truffles would make a delicious treat for anyone, including yourself. My favorites were the soft, powder-sugar coated rum flavored truffles or the creamy, milk chocolate ones.

Breakfast is served every morning from 7:00a.m. – 11:30a.m. and on Saturdays groups form to practice their German between 10:00a.m. and 12:00p.m. Lunch is served until 4:00p.m. Monday through Saturday. There is a limited choice of good German wines and 14 different imported beers to choose from.

No matter how hard you squint, you're not going to see the Matterhorn outside the window on this lonely little strip of Del Monte, but at Roland's you can still eat like it's out there.

SAWADEE THAI RESTAURANT

6719 Weslayan
Houston, Texas 77005
713/666-7872

Type of Cuisine: Thai
Bar: Wine and Beer
Dress: Casual
Entertainment: No
Payment: All Major Credit Cards
Entrée Range: $8.95-$13.95
Recommended Dishes:
Appetizers: Seafood Pancake
Soft Spring Rolls
Sawadee Chicken Wings
Entrées: Spicy Honey Pork
Chicken with Kaffir Lemon Leaves and Green Beans
Squid with Sweet Basil and Hot Peppers
Patt Thai
Eggplant with Sweet Basil and Garlic Sauce
Hours: Monday-Friday, 11:00a.m.-3:00p.m, 5:00p.m.-10:00p.m.
Saturday, 11:00a.m.-10:00p.m.
Sunday, 5:00p.m.-10:00p.m.
Reservations: Accepted for Larger Parties

Yut Teimchaiyatoom Heckler makes a fine ambassador for his native Thailand. Even his restaurant's name, "Sawadee," is a salutation of warmth. "It means, 'Hello. How are you?' Like 'Aloha.' It should be the first Thai word foreigners hear."

He is knowledgeable and proud of his culinary heritage. When I ask if maybe the Seafood Pancake – Sawadee's best appetizer – isn't a Korean dish, perhaps inspired by his wife, Kye, who is from Seoul, Yut explains that, "Thailand or Thai food is a crossroad of all Asian food. For instance, even Patt Thai is not a true Thai dish because Thai people don't make noodles. That comes from China. Curry comes from India. Satay is inspired by Malaysian food. We're a melting pot. What makes something Thai are the Thai ingredients." He points to the exotic, pink-stemmed galangal ginger and the divinely aromatic, guitar-shaped Kaffir lemon leaves as examples. "Even basil," he says. "The Vietnamese use it as a garnish. We incorporate that, we cook that to release the flavor of basil into the dish." In fact, two of my favorite dishes at Sawadee feature Kaffir lemon leaves and the fine marriage of sweet basil and hot peppers.

At the top of my list is Chicken with Kaffir Lemon Leaves and Green Beans. Tender snow white chunks of chicken breasts and green beans were the perfect foil for the sauce made by combining chili paste with the glossy, dark green Kaffir lemon leaves. Yut tells me that it is an especially expensive chili paste that supplies the lingering tingle.

However, among the chicken dishes, the most popular on the menu is the Stir Fried Chicken with Sweet Basil and Hot Peppers. "It's always the first dish that I recommend because it is a taste that suits most Americans, although I prefer to eat the Stir Fried Beef (with Sweet Basil and Hot Peppers). You know, in Thailand we eat a lot of beef, but in America, chicken is the meat of the time right now." As much as I enjoyed the chicken and the beef cooked this way, my favorite seafood dish at Sawadee (after the Seafood Pancake) is Squid with Sweet Basil and Hot Peppers. Small heavenly bodies of unbelievably tender Asian farm-raised baby squid curl gently around thin strips of red pepper and become perfect little vessels for the fragrant brown sauce.

I was less crazy about the other seafood dishes I sampled. I found the sauce for both the extremely popular Royal Shrimp and the Red Snapper with Triple Flavor Sauce to be a bit heavy going and better suited to something a little sturdier like the messy but delicious appetizer, Sawadee Chicken Wings.

Heckler is from the land-locked city of Korat in Issan, the Northeastern, mountainous region of Thailand. He says that seafood really isn't the kitchen's area of strength because he didn't grow up eating it and the preparation of it isn't as second nature to him, as for instance, beef or pork.

As evidence of this, the Spicy Honey Pork, a dish of Heckler's invention, is spectacularly good. It is a deceptively simple stir fry of the leanest possible tenderloin of pork cut into thin medallions and caramelized in a wok with squares of sweet, crunchy cabbage. Heckler says he added Spicy Honey Pork to the menu as a way to woo his many health-conscious customers "back to eating pork," but that he prefers the Garlic Pork with Mushrooms and Green Onion. "That's a traditional Thai dish that comes from my own neighborhood. I love the strong flavors of garlic and pork and the cooking technique is one I was raised with."

Another dish Heckler "grew up on" is Patt Thai. He says it is the best known dish to fans of Thai food and probably the most difficult one to prepare. That lovely familiar smoky flavor comes from combining two different widths of the delicate rice noodles "in the hottest wok in the kitchen."

"It requires some skill to cook the noodles quickly so that they achieve that nice, glazey look instead of being tough or burned." Still, he says that Patt Thai, although not originally Thai, is the standard by which most Thai kitchens are judged. Sawadee's is excellent.

My second favorite noodle dish – Raad-Naa – we ordered at Kye's suggestion. This time the wide rice noodle was pan fried with whole pieces of Chinese broccoli and was perfect when paired with beef.

Heckler says that many of his customers are vegetarian and while I may never acquire an affinity for tofu, the sautéed Eggplant with Sweet Basil and Garlic sauce is as satisfying a dish in both texture and taste as you're likely to find. Thick, meaty rounds of firm-fleshed Japanese eggplant are cooked with the peel still attached and hold up well to the garlicky, powerfully-concentrated sauce. An off-the-menu vegetable dish not to miss is the irregularly available Chive Flowers. Heckler notes that "there are a lot of vegetables that we encounter in Asia that we never see in American produce. For instance, the chive flower is the stalk of the chive. In America, you only utilize the leaves." The thin, green tangled mass with tiny yellow bulbs at the ends is sautéed simply and has a wonderful, almost peppery flavor.

My standard in Houston for the perfect soft spring roll has always been the Thai restaurant, Nit Noi, in the Rice Village. Sawadee's are every bit as good and Heckler comes by this talent naturally. His many regulars know that Nit Noi is owned by his mother, Alice. Maybe this accounts for what he refers to as his "quite reasonable palate. I trust my taste, you know."

Kye and Yut set out on their own in August of 1993. When they found the perfect location, they bought the building and renovated the space themselves. "I did all the demolition myself. I used to build houses and a friend of mine from those days who was a carpenter helped me. That's why my place is sort of rich with woodwork." He opened December 16, 1993. "We invited three hundred people to the grand opening; three hundred and fifty showed up!" They have been busy ever since. So busy in fact, that in April of '97 he expanded into the adjoining space.

No discussion of Sawadee would be complete without mentioning the absolutely mesmerizing reef tank in the main dining room. Heckler is especially proud of his ability to keep the very difficult hard coral alive. Exquisite, exotic fish from the Red Sea fill the tank and all perform a particular function. "It attracts a lot of people. All the exotic marine life dealers in Houston have been here."

He says that the original idea, before it became a hobby, was to "try to get things to harmonize. It's the Oriental, or mostly Chinese concept of Feng Shui – the placement of objects that's both pleasing to the eye and good for the mind."

SEOUL GARDEN

9446 Long Point
Houston, Texas 77055
713/935-9696

Type of Cuisine: Korean
Bar: Full Bar
Dress: Casual
Entertainment: No
Payment: American Express, MasterCard, Visa
Entrée Range: $9.95-$14.95
Recommended Dishes:
  Appetizers: Goon Mahndoo (Pan Fried Dumplings)
    Haemool Pahjun (Scallion and Seafood Pancake)
    Yook Hwae (Seasoned Raw Beef)
  Entrées: Korean Barbecue:
    Gahlbee (Short Ribs)
    Hyumit Goo-e (Tongue)
    Dwae-Ji Bod Gogee (Sliced Pork)
    Nahkgee Bakum (Stir Fried Octopus)
Hours: Monday-Sunday, 11:00a.m.-10:30p.m.
Reservations: Accepted for larger parties

At first glance, Seoul Garden might easily be mistaken for a Japanese restaurant. There are tranquil water wheels, delicate rice paper paneled walls … a familiar, gracious serenity. There are Japanese dishes on the menu. There is even a sushi bar.

But, though they happily borrow the best from their Japanese neighbors to the south, what draws me like a magnet to the Korean table are the extremes of flavors and textures; the Asian principle of the five flavors – sweet, sour, hot, salty and bitter – gone berserk. It looks harmless enough, but Korean cooking is a wolf in a sheep's clothing.

Tony Yang, who helps run Seoul Garden with his parents Ton Kap and Chun Chimi Yang, believes that "what distinguishes Korean food from other types of ethnic cooking is the simplicity of ingredients, but more importantly, the intensity of flavors. Korean foods are very spicy." As example, he cites the blistering beef noodle soup, Yook Gae Jahng.

Colored crimson-red from cochijang, a puréed red pepper and rice flour mixture, Yang says that a Korean friend regularly brings "a group of Americans from his office who just love this soup. They have a name for it. They call it 'atomic soup,' because it is so spicy." The heat of the soup is meant to be tempered by taking alternating bites of soothing, slightly-sticky, medium to short grain rice scooped into little individual bowls. Soup accompanies virtually every meal in Korea (including breakfast), and if you're looking for a tamer alternative to the "atomic soup," try the Dhuk Mahndoo Gook – pork-filled dumplings in a wonderful beef broth.

Neither soup is listed under "Soups" in English. Yang concedes that the menu desperately needs to be reorganized (and clarified). Part of the confusion stems from the fact that Korean meals are not traditionally served in stages. Including the vast assortment of panchan (side dishes) or namuls (blanched and seasoned vegetables), there might be as many as twenty dishes on the table at once.

If you find this a little overwhelming, as I do, they are happy to stagger the meal into courses.

The three dishes I would recommend starting with are found on the "À la Carte" page rather than "Appetizers." Goon Mahndoo are crescent-shaped, pan-fried Korean dumplings. The scallion and seafood pancake – Haemool Panjun, sometimes referred to as "Korean pizza" – is a must to try. Both the dumplings and the pancake are eaten with chojang – an all-purpose dipping sauce of soy sauce, a little sugar, crushed sesame seeds, sesame oil, ground chili peppers, and rice wine vinegar in ginger meant to be spooned onto your plate.

Anyone who's game for raw beef should sample the Korean version of steak tartare – Yook Hwae – another good way to start the meal. A mound of lean, ice-cold, freshly cut beef arrives flavored simply with an egg yolk, a little sesame oil, and ultra-thin julienned pieces of cucumber, Asian pear and garlic – lots of garlic.

A stranger to the Japanese kitchen, garlic is not merely used in Korea, it's celebrated. Whole, peeled, raw garlic cloves are often nibbled like peanuts with cocktails.

Stir-fried octopus and vegetables in Spicy Sauce, Nahkgee Bokum is a dish of volcanic intensity. It features the devil's own chiles – both jalapeños and incendiary little red Thais or cayennes, and heavy doses of garlic are added last to the sot, a Korean wok, for extra impact. The resulting dish is strictly Korean, but the technique is a legacy of China, Korea's neighbor to the north.

It seems we have Genghis Khan and his Mongol hordes to thank for introducing not only their love of beef, but their distinctive method of cooking it, to the 13th Century Korea. This is Korean barbecue called Kui, and it is the main event at Seoul Garden.

Beef, for instance, is cut in delicate ribbons and marinated overnight in sweetened soy sauce, garlic (of course), ginger, scallions and the fiery, orange-red Korean chili powder. It is then cooked by the wait staff on a grill in the middle of the table. Beef short ribs are most commonly used for maximum flavor and although the Joomookuck Gahlbee (short ribs off the bone) may be more manageable, I prefer Gahlbee where some meat is left clinging to the stubby little bones. Yang maintains that the Dwae-Ji Bod Gogee – sliced pork in spicy sauce – has even more flavor than the beef. He may be right. The pork marinade is a little sweeter and a little more robust. But for me, it's a three-way tie with the Hyumit Goo-e. OK … it's beef tongue and it's fabulous. Keep an open mind here. Sliced razor-thin, it takes to the marinade and grill like a duck to water.

The Korean method of eating the barbecue is to place the pieces of cooked meat in cold, fresh leaves of romaine lettuce with shreds of white radish and a little soy bean paste. It should then be folded and eaten with your hands. Yang says they are happy to supply these garnishes but in their place at Seoul Garden they serve a sort of "Western-style salad with very Eastern ingredients." The salad is composed of romaine lettuce, cucumbers, scallions and slivers of onions, but the vinaigrette has soy sauce, red pepper flakes, vinegar and the nutty aftertaste of sesame oil.

Best of all, for contrast to the richness of the beef or pork, is the assortment of namuls, often as many as eight little vegetable side dishes placed on the table before the barbecue even arrives.

The bright, clean, almost astringent quality of both the watercress and the bean sprouts – both simply blanched and dressed with a little sesame oil – serve this purpose perfectly.

Kim Chee is the best known of these little side dishes. Although Kim Chee can be made with almost any vegetable, the one that Koreans eat with breakfast, lunch and dinner is made with Chinese cabbage. It's scarlet-red with chiles and has a pungent but pleasing flavor.

Yang tells me Koreans typically drink Scotch on the rocks throughout the meal, but I prefer the combination of Korean beer, OB (stands for Oriental Brewing) and the chilled clear, flavorless vodka-like, soju, served neat in little shot glasses.

The Korean dining experience ends on a perfect note – with a cold, sweet sectioned orange.

THE SUNDANCE GRILL

222 Jennings Island
Seabrook, Texas 77586
281/474-2248

Type of Cuisine: American/Seafood
Bar: Full
Dress: Casual
Entertainment: Lunch and Dinner Friday, Saturday and Sunday
Payment: All Major Credit Cards
Entrée Range: $9.95-$22.95
Recommended Dishes:
Appetizers: "Hanzee's" Cakes (Crab Cakes)
Boiled Shrimp
"Bahama Mama's Shrimp" (Fried Shrimp)
Gumbo
Entrées: Mixed Seafood Grill
Trout Meliniere
Steak au Poivre
Lousiana Swamp Chicken
Hours: Monday-Thursday, 11:00a.m.-10:00p.m.
Friday-Saturday, 11:00a.m.-11:00p.m.
Sunday, Brunch 10:00a.m.-3:00p.m., Dinner 3:00p.m.-10:00p.m.
Reservations: Accepted

Hans Mair knows a good thing when he sees it. Standing in the club room of the venerable old Regatta Inn at the Seabrook Shipyard in the shadow of the Kemah Bridge, he says he took one look out of the huge windows, saw the sun "dance" on the water and thought, "What a perfect setting – the ideal place to enjoy fine American-style food in a relaxed, European atmosphere!" He set out to transform the wonderful, but tired, forty-year old restaurant into a place where diners could come seven days a week from 11:00 a.m. to 10:00 or 11:00 p.m. (Friday and Saturday nights) and tuck into anything from a cheeseburger and fries to Steak au Poivre and a bottle of Burgundy.

The Sundance Grill offers a welcome alternative to what Mair refers to as "cholesterol alley." They buy the best possible, freshest seafood and grill it, hence the name. The menu can only be described as regionally eclectic with an emphasis on Southern California-style dishes. It is a short, comprehensive menu that celebrates local bounty like our beloved Gulf shrimp, crab meat, red snapper (and when available, as specials – tuna, swordfish, flounder and oysters) and delicacies from distant shores like salmon – served grilled and topped with a snappy avocado, citrusy salsa; New Zealand mussels (cultured in Canada) – steamed in beer, garlic and fresh herbs; and grilled scallops from New England that make an appearance several places on the menu.

The appetizers include such old seaside friends as Crab Cakes and "Boilt" Shrimp but with a vibrant, distinctive variation on the traditional treatment. Called "Hanzee's" Cakes, the sautéed crab cakes are a mixture of fresh poached salmon and crab meat, lightly bound together and served with a heavenly Choron sauce – a tomato-tinged béarnaise sauce named for the French chef who created it. The boiled or "Sea Isle" shrimp were cool, plump and served with a puckery, tomato-based relish called Jamaica Island sauce. Another favorite appetizer is the Bahama Mama's Shrimp – one of the only fried dishes on the menu apart from French fries. They are coconut-flecked, thinly battered, quickly fried and served with an appealing sweet/spicy pineapple relish. Mair says that the Cozumel Cyclone (the seafood tamales) are popular. I thought they were good, but found the filling a bit dry to my taste.

All the portions are generous and the salads are no exception; from the Oriental Chicken Salad with cucumber salsa tossed with a jazzy Japanese vinaigrette to the excellent Caesar salad – great on its own, or as the Capri salad topped with grilled warm strips of either chicken breast, scallops or shrimp. The Seabrook Shipyard Gumbo is chock full of seafood and good enough to meet the approval of even the pickiest gumbo aficionados. However, the day I tried the Crawfish Bisque, I found the consistency a bit heavy-going.

The list of sandwiches includes long-standing favorites, prepared with the chef's individual spin, such as Grilled Chicken Breast with Roasted Peppers, avocado and melted jack cheese, and the Sundance Po-boy served open face with grilled or fried shrimp, homemade roasted red pepper mayo and fries.

By ordering the Sundance Mixed Grill, it is possible to sample an assortment of unadorned, gently grilled shrimp, scallops, snapper and salmon, served with a selection of house salsas. The Scampi (sautéed in a traditional butter, lemon, garlic sauce) were especially good, and Trout Meuniére was just added to the menu "by popular demand," Mair says. All seafood entrées are accompanied by a simple, but flavorful rice pilaf and crisply steamed, seasonal vegetables.

In the red meat genre, the Pepper Steak, another recent addition to the menu, was exceptionally good – excellent tournados of beef tenderloin impaled with fresh peppercorns and served with a pepper-lashed, cognac spiked sauce garnished with grilled chunks of Idaho potatoes.

Mair says they change the menu every few months and for instance, will add duck and maybe venison in the fall when the weather cools. All of October they celebrate Octoberfest by serving an assortment of German beers and German regional favorites like rouladen, weiner schnitzel, and wursts with sauerkraut, roast potatoes, red cabbage and potato pancakes. These dishes are second-nature to this transplanted Austrian who moved to Houston first in 1965. He also plans to have a German band on weekends.

As first chef, then general manager of Vargo's since the fall of 1970, Mair leased the Regatta Inn in March of 1995. It was a celebrated old watering hole and haunt of great local and visiting international sailors who docked their boats during local regattas at the shipyard and astronauts like Alan Shephard and Wally Schirra in the early days of NASA in the 70's. Aware of its history and charmed by its warm, clubby atmosphere, he decided to change it as little as possible. One huge difference is that the sloping lawn with families of ducks paddling by outside the window has become a large multi-tiered deck with white plastic tables and chairs and colorful red and blue Cinzano umbrellas. Mair says they are the most popular tables in the restaurant, particularly at sunset and in the evenings. On Friday nights, outdoor diners enjoy a bit of cool jazz while the steel drums of Trinidad inspire spontaneous limbo contests and dancing Saturday and Sunday nights.

There is also a swimming pool where they offer full service for anyone who wants to eat and swim at the same time. While almost anything goes around the pool, Mair insists that there be no bare feet and swimsuits in the other outdoor dining areas. There is a dock, so the Sundance Grill is approachable by either car or boat.

One recent development has been the purchase of vintage cognacs and fine cigars. Long considered an oasis of civilization, the restaurant was originally opened by legendary yachtsmen, brothers Albert and Ernest Fay, to serve fellow sailors and friends. They would approve.

SUPER STEAK AND MORE

2826 Kirby Drive
Houston, Texas 77098
713/523-3200

Type of Cuisine: American/Eclectic
Bar: No (You may bring your own wine.)
Dress: Casual
Entertainment: No
Payment: All Major Credit Cards
Entrée Range: $3.25-$16.95
Recommended Dishes:
- Buffalo Wings (Mild or Hot)
- Crawfish Étoufée
- Cajun Fried Cornish Game Hen
- Fried Potatoes
- Cajun Rice
- Sautéed Spinach
- Imperial Rolls
- Philly Cheese Steak
- Filet Mignon
- Shrimp Scampi
- Pizza
- Dessert: Pies

Hours: Monday-Thursday, 1:00a.m.-10:00p.m.
Friday-Saturday, 11:00a.m-10:30p.m.
Sunday, 1:00p.m.-10:00p.m.
Reservations: Not Accepted

Here's your dilemma. It's Wednesday night. It's raining. And it's dinnertime. Two kids want pizza. One wants a hamburger. Your husband feels like a steak, and seafood – maybe shrimp – is what you had in mind. Who ya gonna call? Super Steak and More.

There is something for everyone at Joe and Tanya Ng's tiny, brightly-lit place. Joe tells me that business at his restaurant is now about equally divided between delivery (by one of his three full-time drivers, "Four, if you include me," he adds), call-in and pick-up, or eat-in at one of the four tables. I mean, this place is small.

I must have driven by Super Steak and More a hundred times without realizing that the "and More" in the name meant such goodies as disparate as duck a l'orange and crawfish étoufée. I imagined that it was a Philly cheese steak sandwich kind of place and although he does construct a perfectly-delightful Philly cheese steak on a homemade, freshly-baked hoagie roll with all the trimmings, what I have developed is an out-and-out craving for their Crawfish Étoufée.

Served over white rice, it is bright orange and full of

flavor with the lingering tingle of cayenne pepper. Joe cooks sweet, meaty crawfish in white wine first "to remove the fishy taste and smell that crawfish sometimes has," he says. This is the real thing.

Where did a nice Vietnamese guy learn to cook like a genuine Cajun? From four years apprenticeship at Bilello's in Thibodeaux, Louisiana, where he attended Nicholl's State University in the early seventies on an athletic scholarship. "I started our as a busboy my second year at Nicholl's and worked my way up to being assistant to the owner, Sam Bilello."

Another dish that screams with authenticity is a down-and-dirty Cajun Rice. It is almost equal measures white rice, minced beef and chicken livers, fiercely-seasoned with sage, thyme, garlic and a little cayenne pepper. (It is interesting that the filling for the thin, crisp-skinned egg rolls called Imperial Rolls – also listed as a side dish – is similarly-seasoned.)

My idea of a wonderful meal might include the Cajun Rice, an order of Sautéed Spinach – which like all of the vegetables at Super Steak is purchased fresh every morning – and a Cajun Fried Cornish Game Hen or maybe some Buffalo Wings. Both the dainty hens and the Buffalo wings, particularly the "mild" ones, benefit from the same fine treatment. They are fried quickly (and greaselessly) in vegetable oil then liberally doused with Joe's lively dry seasoning mix. The "hot" Buffalo wings are dripping in a fiery, lip-smacking mixture of butter and vinegary hot sauce.

A fairly recent addition to the menu, Shrimp Scampi is grilled instead of sautéed with the usual finely chopped garlic, parsley and white wine, but with a little fresh cilantro for a nice Southwestern accent. (This might be a good time to mention that if a glass of wine sounds good with this, bring your own wine and glasses because although Super Steak doesn't have a liquor license, Joe and Tanya are happy for people to bring their own wine, beer or something stronger.)

I'm not sure that I agree, but Joe believes steaks are what he does best. He says his ribeye – available in three sizes (12, 9 or 7 ounces) – outsells everything else on the menu. But, apart from the Philly Cheese Steak which I love, and an excellent char-broiled hamburger, I believe his most super steak is the juicy, fork-tender Filet Mignon.

Joe says the secret to the popularity of his steaks is that he buys the meat "fresh everyday, never frozen," and the Super Steak Super Sauce, a teriyaki-tasting concoction that he's in the process of marketing. Steaks are brushed with the "secret sauce," char-broiled very simply and served with a little side helping of the sauce.

Do not miss ordering the Fried Potatoes, even if you split

them among your fellow diners. My heart does a little dance when I see a restaurant that seats a maximum of sixteen people go to the trouble of frying wedges of actual, skin-on Idaho potatoes instead of using a frozen "industry product." A steak dinner could be rounded out nicely by a side of Whole Mushrooms slathered with "secret sauce" and grilled.

"My mushrooms are famous," Joe says. He adds that they are a favorite among a variety of toppings for his pizza when sliced and cooked quickly on the grill. He is not making the pizza dough from scratch, but it's still a pretty darn good pizza. (One friend told me that her kids prefer Super Steak's pizza to Domino's.) The most popular appears to be the one with five toppings – which features an all-beef homemade Italian sausage. "It's another recipe I picked up from Bilello's, but I make it with beef instead of pork," Joe says.

The best surprise of all if that Super Steak and More turns out a fabulous Duck a l'Orange with a little notice (preferably 48 hours). "That I learned from my grandma. She had a big, very famous restaurant in Saigon." His technique involves retrieving the duck mid-bake from the oven, marinating it for a good three hours in freshly squeezed orange juice and returning it to the oven until cooks to a crisp, fatless turn. Very nice. He serves it with a nutty, fragrant mixture of wild and jasmine rice and two vegetables all for $25.00 (enough for three people).

I was tipped off about the duck a l'orange and when I asked what other tricks he had up his sleeve he said, "Oh, I can do almost anything. Roast beef. Lamb. I did a whole lobster dinner for a favorite customer's birthday party the other night!"

Tanya does most of the cooking these days and among her many talents is a fine hand at pastry, particularly baking Pies – cherry, peach or apple. They are old-fashioned pies with flaky, buttery crusts that were especially good warmed and topped with a scoop of vanilla ice cream. I've heard rumors that her Sweet Potato Pie – a specialty at Thanksgiving or Christmas (or by special order) – is spectacular.

T-BONE TOM'S MEAT MARKET AND STEAKHOUSE RESTAURANT

707 Highway 146
Kemah, Texas 77565
281/334-2133

Type of Cuisine: Barbecue
Bar: Wine and Beer
Dress: Casual
Entertainment: No
Payment: All Major Credit Cards
Prices: Lunch Specials $4.99
Steaks-Ribeye(12oz) $10.99
Barbeque Plates $7.99
Recommended Dishes:
BBQ Chicken
Sausage
Ribs
Hours: Monday-Thursday, 9:00a.m.-9:30p.m.
Friday-Saturday, 9:00a.m.-10:00p.m.
Lunch Specials, 11:00a.m.-2:00p.m.
(Closed Sunday)
Reservations: Not Accepted

During a lull in a business meeting in New York a few years ago, a New Yorker who was headed to Texas tapped me on the shoulder, leaned way back and in a conspiratorial whisper asked, "Who has the best barbecue in Houston? Goode Company? Otto's?" I replied that I knew a place in Kemah, Texas that beats both of them. A place called T-Bone Tom's.

"It's the stuff that dreams are made of," to borrow a line from the *Maltese Falcon*. In fact, one of the late owner's, Tom Fitzmorris', favorite stories is about a Chicago businessman who, on a visit to the area, developed such an affinity for his brisket and ribs, that he called from Chicago to say that he had been dreaming of his barbecue for six months and would it be possible to ship as much as, say, eighty pounds to Chicago for his birthday party? "We froze it and shipped it overnight. I know the freight cost more than the barbecue." My only question was, "Why no sausage?"

The Sausage alone beats hollow all competitors in these parts. The recipe goes back two generations to Fitzmorris' father, John Fitzmorris, a butcher and corner store grocer from Covington, Louisiana, just across the causeway from New Orleans. He had it for fifty years before he gave it to him. It is perfect – scented with a little nutmeg, piquantly seasoned with just the right mixture of mustard seed and garlic, and both cayenne and lots of black pepper. It's spicy without being hot, juicy and moist without being fatty; smoked and scored on what Fitzmorris called the pit of his dreams, a barbecue pit he purchased in Grand Prairie, Texas, seventeen years ago that replaced the brick pit his father had been using.

Tom's family moved from Covington to Dallas in 1953, when Tom was nine, in order for his mother to attend nursing school. They moved to La Porte, Texas, a year later. He said his father so missed the conviviality of having his neighborhood corner store and gas pump, that he wasn't truly happy again until 1968 when he took over his friend's place, Ben's Meat Market. After two or three years, he finally got around to changing the name to Kemah Meat Market and Grocery Store. They sold meat retail, groceries and barbecue to go. In 1973, his father became ill and called upon son Tom to take over the business. An industrial salesman at the time, Fitzmorris had no desire initially to follow in his father's footsteps. He took to it like a duck to water. Tagged "T-Bone" by his brother when he took over the business, Fitzmorris greeted everyone from the King of Norway to local plumbers with a friendly, "Howdy Nabor!" as it says under the caricature of him on the front door.

Necessity being the mother of invention, they only started serving food in 1983 to construction workers who were building the Kemah Bridge with the encouragement of Nathan "Blu" Griffin, who had been recently unemployed by Hurricane Alicia's untimely removal of the roof from the Kemah Cattle Company, a local steakhouse. Blu apparently had a great way with steaks.

They set up three picnic tables and started serving steaks and blue plate specials to the workers for lunch. The daily specials were a huge success and thirteen years later the restaurant, which now seats 135 people, thanks to the additional room in 1988, is jammed at lunch with people tucking into Chicken Fried Steak (Monday), Beef Tips and Noodles (Tuesday), Smothered Pork Chops (Wednesday), Fried Chicken (Thursday), and catfish (Friday). A banker in La Porte eats lunch there five days a week. Still, nothing on the menu compares to the barbecue.

Not only is the homemade sausage exceptional, but the Pork Ribs are meaty, smoky and tender. The Chicken, which may be my favorite, is split in half, dry-seasoned and lovingly cooked to bronzed, juicy perfection over oak, and the brisket is melt-in-your-mouth delicious. As good cold as it is hot, the chicken makes a perfect picnic or boating dish. The barbecue sauce is tomato-based and fairly tart with the addition of both white vinegar and lemon juice and while I prefer my own homemade variety, it perfectly complements the sweet, wood-smoked flavor of Tom's barbecue. Although, the highest compliment paid to any barbecue is that it is good enough to be eaten with no embellishment whatsoever, and his is.

The Coleslaw, finely diced green and white cabbage leaves, is good – neither too creamy nor too sweet – but the Potato Salad is exemplary – mayonnaise-based with a creamy, smooth texture and great potatoey flavor with tiny, crunchy flecks of celery and green onions.

If you have room, all three meringue-topped Pies – lemon, coconut and chocolate – are fabulous.

The restaurant is full of local color – from the actual characters who hang out there, to the caricatures of them which line the wall of the original room and continue to the second barn-like, beamed room. All of the caricatures and a huge mural of Fitzmorris's father are painted by local artist Stuart "S. J." Stout. Both rooms are warmed by the addition of authentic memorabilia.

Tom also collects exotic birds and has them caged in the front and to the side of the restaurant, so don't be surprised if you find yourself serenaded by a brace of cockatoos as you leave.

A family tradition has been continued as the torch was recently passed from "T-Bone" Tom Fitzmorris to his son, Timothy David and daughter, Glena.

TAJ MAHAL

8328 Gulf Freeway (at S. Bellfort)
Houston, Texas 77017
713/649-2818

Type of Cuisine: Indian
Bar: Full Bar
Dress: Casual
Entertainment: No
Payment: All Major Credit Cards
Entrée Range: $5.95 – $12.95
Recommended Dishes:
    Appetizers: All Tandoori Dishes
        Seekh Kabab (Lamb)
        Tandoori Prawns
        Keema Naan (Naan-Bread with Lamb)
    Entrées: Chicken Makhni
        Lamb Shahi Korma
        Malai Kofta (Vegetable Dumplings)
        Koali Daal (Black Lentils)
Hours: Lunch: Tuesday-Friday, 11:00a.m.-2:00p.m.
        Saturday-Sunday, 12:00p.m.-2:30p.m.
    Dinner: Sunday-Thursday, 6:00p.m.-10:00p.m.
        Friday-Saturday, 6:00p.m.-10:30p.m.
Reservations: Accepted for Larger Parties

Houston's first opportunity to sample red-dyed tandoori chicken or layered leaf-shaped breads was quite likely at the nearly twenty-year-old Taj Mahal.

This Northern Indian style of cooking was introduced to Houston by psychiatrist Dr. Babu Draksharams, who – although from the southern subtropical city of Hyderabad – thought tandoori cooked poultry, lamb and breads were the least foreign of the Indian culinary exports (after curry, maybe). Still, in those days the wait staff had to include a full time "designated explainer," nephew Babu Nisankarao tells me.

Nisankarao, who manages Taj Mahal with the help of another uncle, Rao Draksharams, says that they are so known for the tandoori dishes now, that there are many regulars who, without even having to ask, are served "the usual" week after week.

The most popular of "the usual" dishes appears to be the Taj Mahal Tandoori Mixed Grill and a side order of the creamed spinach dish, Saag Paneer. What they're getting are whole pieces of tandoori chicken; Boti Kabab – chunks of lean lamb, red and crusty with paprika (ask for medium rare); Chicken Tikka – large boneless pieces of unbelievably tender chicken; and (one of my favorites) the spicy, six inch sausage-shaped minced Lamb Seekh Kabab.

The natural juices of all meats are instantly sealed into whatever is skewered and lowered into the molten-hot tandoor (a whole chicken cooks in ten minutes). But I believe it is the ancient technique of marinating the chicken, lamb and seafood (often overnight) in yoghurt flavored with onions, garlic and the mixture of toasted and ground Indian seasonings called garam masala (literally, "hot spices") that renders these foods uniquely succulent.

All are recommended. But I've recently come to see this process as a vehicle to get to the really good stuff – Chicken Makhni. Rightfully referred to sometimes as "velvet butter chicken," still-pink strips of tandoori chicken luxuriate in a downright ambrosial sauce comprised of puréed fresh tomatoes, ghee (clarified butter), cream and bright green flecks of freshly chopped coriander. The delicately-perfumed basmati rice with finely shredded orange peel and almonds that accompanies all curries is ideal.

A perfect meal could be constructed by preceding the Chicken Makhni (and rice) with orders of lamb Seekh Kababs and Tandoori Prawns to split among fellow diners as appetizers. The prawns require little embellishment other than a liberal dose of lemon juice to make them perfect. These two tandoori specials come with an order of Naan, the best of the eight available tandoori breads.

This leavened bread fashioned from flour and eggs, is slapped onto the wall of the tandoor where it cooks side-by-side with the chicken. If you stray from the naan, try the scallion and herb strewn Onion Kulcha. Maybe instead of the Seekh Kabab, you might want to start your meal with an order of Keema Naan – warm, doughy layers "stuffed," as is says in the menu (or really mixed), with minced ground lamb.

Nisankarao tells me that another whole group of regulars return for the Chicken Tikka Masala. The sauce is similar to, but sharper than, the satiny Chicken Makhni. It's made with boneless chunks of dry-roasted chicken tikka rather than the superior tandoori chicken.

Of the lamb curries, the first-listed Rogan Josh ("the original lamb curry," as Nisankarao says) is richly flavored and tinted red from chilies and lots of fresh paprika. It's good, but it lacks the sweet subtlety and grace of the mace-scented Lamb Shahi Korma.

The velvety texture of the sauce is achieved by braising ("korma") the pieces of lamb in cream and almonds. Shahi means "royal," and this dish that dates back hundreds of years to Persia is truly fit for a king.

Any time the menu says something is "considered spicy" – call the fire department – they're not kidding. My third favorite lamb curry, the Lamb Vindloo, is a good example. This dark brown, body-heating curry is not for sissies. Nisankarao says that it's his favorite "because we Indians like the spicier dishes." I pointed out that we Texans do, too, and he said that it's not the heat from the chili peppers or the powder, but the intensity of flavors from the complex mixture of garlic and spices that he believes are alien to the average Western palate.

A glass of Lassi (whipped yoghurt either sweetened with puréed mango or "salted") or Raita (yogurt with uniformly diced cucumbers, onions and mint) serve as useful antidotes to the heat.

Consider accompanying the mixed Tandoori Grill or any of the individual Tandoori dishes with Vegetable Biryana – an elaborately-layered casserole of vegetables and fragrant basmati rice partially colored yellow by drizzling saffron-scented milk over the top before steaming it in a low oven.

Add chicken, and the exquisite biryana makes a fine centerpiece of a meal. This menu might be rounded out by ordering one (or several) of my favorite vegetables. Malai Kofta is at the top of my list. The firm dumplings are made from a puréed mixture of vegetables and Indian cheese and are simmered with green peas in an outrageously lush, aromatic sauce of tomatoes, butter and cream. The more aggressively-seasoned Kaali Daal is divine. The black lentils are cooked in the leftover heat from the tandoor in a light cream sauce that tastes of tumeric and ginger.

The Saag Paneer is Taj Mahal's most popular, and from my standpoint, the least interesting vegetable dish. It is fresh spinach creamed with paneer – a sort of soft curd homemade Indian cheese similar to Italian ricotta. I have nothing against it, it just lacks the impact of the Malai Kofta, the Kaali Daal, or even the fiercely-seasoned stewed chick peas, Channa Masala.

A soupy rice pudding confection called Kheer comes with the set meals, but unless you're nursing an ulcer, the freshly made mango ice cream, Mango Kulfee, is an even better choice.

There is a short list of wines available, but I wouldn't miss sampling the Indian Kingfisher Beer, "Most Thrilling Chilled!" as the label says. The warm, wafer-thin Papadums are northern Indian-style – studded with black pepper. They should be dipped in the (green) mint and jalapeno chutney and the syrupy (red) tamarind sauce once you've spooned a little of each onto your plate.

The daily buffet draws an enthusiastic crowd from downtown and the nearby University of Houston. I've visited mostly at night when it is considerably quieter, and it is possible to be lulled into a deep trance between courses by sitar music playing in the background.

TAMPICO

2113 Airline Drive
Houston, Texas 77019
713/862-8425

Type of Cuisine: Mexican
Bar: Full
Dress: Casual
Entertainment: No
Payment: All Major Credit Cards
Entrée Range: $2.95-$10.95
Recommended Dishes:
Appetizers: Queso Flameado
Molcajete with Avocados
Entrées: Snapper a la Plancha with Shrimp and Al Mojo Sauce
Seafood Parillada
Fried Snapper (Mexican Style)
Stuffed Crab
Enchiladas (Cheese)
Hours: Sunday-Thursday, 10:30a.m.-10:00p.m.
Friday-Saturday, 10:30a.m.-12:00a.m.
Reservations: Not Accepted

A commonly-heard complaint among food writers in this town is that for a city virtually on the Gulf of Mexico, it's hard to find good seafood in Houston. It's not. You just have to know where to look for it.

For the moment, I would direct all inquiries to the half-mile strip of Airline Drive across from the Farmer's Market. It has become a colorful, sort of multi-cultural restaurant row featuring (among other things) a diner, a couple of Chinese restaurants and Tampico – home of the fabulous Snapper a la Plancha.

A whole red snapper is yanked form the ice where it's on display, scored with a knife, dry-seasoned with owner Juan Gonzalez's secret seasoning mix, and cooked in butter on a flat grill or "a la plancha." It arrives in all its splendor on a bed of grilled onions and green peppers as much for flavor as to prevent the fish from sticking to the hot plate. For total seafood bliss, ask one of Houston's best and most enthusiastic waiters, Mike Martinez, to surround the fish with a half-dozen or so of the huge shrimp that are also grilled "a la plancha" with their spiny pink shells on.

There is a quartet of spectacular sauces to choose from that the kitchen is happy to spoon on top or serve on the side. My favorite to accompany the snapper and shrimp is the al mojo de ajo or just "al mojo" on the menu. "Wet with garlic" or "a shower of garlic" is how Nicki Gonzalez, manager and daughter of owners Juan and Alma, describes the sauce.

She tells me that the al mojo, like many of the recipes at Tampico, originated with her father's mother (and Nicki's namesake) Maria Nicolasa Gonzalez in the eastern coastal town of Tampico. It is a style of Mexican cooking that has become known as Tampiqueño.

The presence of more garlic that one ordinarily finds in the Mexican kitchen is evidence of Nicki's Spanish heritage. "My grandmother's generation was the first in Mexico (from Spain)" where, as Spanish writer Julio Camba once said, "Spanish cooking is thick with garlic and religion."

Al mojo is made with butter and onions, green peppers, sliced mushrooms and whole chewy cloves of garlic caramelized in their skins. Endless variations of the sauce are possible. For instance, the butter can be replaced with olive oil, or everything but the garlic can be eliminated (my personal choice) so it becomes a simple garlic butter sauce.

The snapper "a la Plancha" listed under "Fish Platters" is served with either excellent French fries or Shrimp Fried Rice.

So, what's a nice bowl of shrimp fried rice doing in a place like this? Nicki explains that all their Asian neighbors on Airline Drive serve fish with shrimp fried rice so they thought they should, too. Add minced chicken and Polish Kielbasa sausage and it becomes the Special Fried Rice. Best of all, ask for "hot fried rice" and they'll add chopped fresh jalapeño to it.

Any combination of seafood available can be devised for a Seafood Parillada. The "parillada" is the sizzling hot plate that it arrives on. Nicki says her favorite combo is red snapper, shrimp and some scallops. I might add some baby octopus which seemed to take particularly well to the grill. Nicki says she likes the idea of asking for three of the main sauces – Ranchero, Al Mojo, and the aptly named A La Diabla – to be brought on the side.

On one visit, our waiter Mike cooked smaller, shelled shrimp in the almost brown chipotle chili-flavored A La Diabla sauce for us as an appetizer and the dish brought tears to my eyes. First, because it was so good and second, because it was so hot. Both Mike and Nicki referred to this as "Mike's Special."

Another sauce that Mike made for us is an off-the-menu specialty called Molcajete. Named for the three-legged basalt mortar and pestle that it's made in, this heavenly sauce is an earthy, coarsely ground mixture of grilled tomatoes, onions and jalapeño peppers. When avocado is added it becomes the city's most irresistible sauce (of any kind) to eat with crisp warm chips.

Nicki says when diners are not in the mood for something grilled, she recommends Fried Red Snapper. "But fried like we eat it in Mexico with no breading. Just cut in steaks and thrown into hot oil. We serve that with lots of fresh limes." Mike adds that in Mexico they would call this chicharrones. I call it simply delicious.

The Stuffed Crab are worth a sample. The stuffing is a garlicky, finely minced mixture bound by a combination of corn meal and cracker meal. Nicki says they are also happy to stuff the jumbo shrimp. But the winner of the off-the-menu sweepstakes is the Brochetas. Shrimp the size of your thumb are folded around a piece of Chihuahua cheese, a sliver of jalapeño, wrapped in slices of good, smoky bacon, and grilled.

Whole Maine Lobster are split and grilled a la plancha on weekends (from Thursday through Sunday). Nicki says that regular customers from Central America and the Dominican Republic call ahead for Tostones – deep-fried slices of plantains – to eat with their lobster.

For starters, the Queso Flameado with either chorizo (Mexican sausage) or shrimp is the best of the dishes that Nicki calls "Mexican food," which seem to have been added to the menu as an afterthought to appeal to a wider audience. Apart from the very good cheese enchiladas, it's best to concentrate on seafood here.

A sundae glass of Ceviche made with firm, white Mahi-Mahi is an ideal way to start the meal. Given a little notice, bartender, Honduran native Chilo Figueroa, is happy to make "Chilo's Special" – a "cocktail" of finely diced onions, tomatoes, cilantro, shrimp and springy Canadian surf clams all marinated in the clean, bright flavor of lime. It is perfect.

A wedge of dense, eggy Flan is a nice way to end the meal.

Margaritas made from freshly-squeezed lime juice are lightly carbonated with Topo Chico – Mexican mineral water.

So, slide into a lemon-yellow formica booth, admire the shocking pink and baby blue neon reflecting off the gleaming white tiled walls and above all – don't rush dinner. Everything is made from scratch.

TAQUERIA CANCUN

227 Gessner Drive
Houston Texas 77080
713/932-9566

8111 South Gessner
Houston, Texas 77036
713/773-1777

9957 Long Point Road
Houston, Texas 77055
713/932-6533

1725 Wirt Road
Houston, Texas 77055
713/932-8800

Type of Cuisine: Mexican
Bar: Beer
Dress: Casual
Entertainment: No
Payment: MasterCard and Visa
Entrée Range: $2.95-$6.25
Recommended Dishes:
- Cocktel Camarones (Shrimp Cocktail)
- Platillos de Camarones a la Plancha (Grilled Shrimp)
- Quesadilla de Camarones (Shrimp)
- Tacos de Camarones (Shrimp)
- Best Beef Enchiladas
- Caldo Pollo (Chicken Soup)
- Caldo Res (Beef Soup)
- Best Menudo

Hours: **Long Point**: Monday-Sunday, 24 hours
Gessner Drive, S. Gessner and **Wirt Road:**
Monday-Thursday, 8:00a.m.-2:00a.m.
Friday-Sunday, 24 hours
Reservations: Not Accepted

At last count there were one hundred and nineteen taquerias in the Greater Houston area. What makes Taqueria Cancun so special? Everything.

First of all, it's been around longer than most (12 years) and second, it's owned by Hong Kong native, William Wong. What does Wong know about Mexican Food? It turns out – a lot. He loves it and it shows. Let's start with the admirable attention to detail. A small lidded jar of freshly chopped jalapeños, a plate of chopped onions and cilantro and not one, but three different sauces grace each table: one for the chips and two in cafeteria-style squirt bottles to squeeze onto your tacos.

Wong named his taqueria for a place he thinks "is pretty close to paradise," and in keeping with the Cancun theme, shrimp is the specialty of the house.

"I think we were pretty much the first ones to have Shrimp Tacos," Wong says confidently. "It's the taco that makes the taqueria, you know." The shrimp tacos are fabulous, but so are the Shrimp Quesadillas or just the filling for both as a "platillo" on its own – the Camarones a la Plancha – grilled shrimp.

It is the #1 listing under "Cancun Especialidades." Plump, scarlet-hued shrimp are stir fried with tomatoes, onions and lots of garlic. The orange-red tint comes from the sweet, almost fruit-flavored ancho chile. "This is our sazon – the special sauce that we come up with for the shrimp," Wong tells me. The "we" includes head cook, Satu Ramirez from Guerrero, Mexico.

"I'm really lucky. He's a great cook and he's been with me almost from the beginning." But then, I understand that most of the people who work for Wong have been with him from the beginning.

A close second in my affection is a classic Mexican Cocktel Camarones (shrimp cocktail) which arrives in a tall sundae glass with a teaspoon imbedded in its depths. What must be at least half a pound of meaty, medium-sized shrimp languish in a thick tomato sauce spiked with Tabasco®, Worcestershire Sauce© and lime juice. It is topped with pico de gallo and huge pieces of diced avocado. It is everything you want it to be – cold and refreshing. Judging by the number of people who order it for breakfast – clearly possesses some restorative powers.

Another "Especialidad" that deserves special comment is the #5 Caldo Camarones Grande (shrimp soup). This leads us into another area where Taqueria Cancun excels – soups. "We go the extra mile on the soup," Wong tells me. It's almost impossible to say which I like best. The Caldo Pollo (chicken soup) would be my first choice to nurse back to health if I were sick.

The "double broth," as Wong calls it, has a rich taste of chicken and is teeming with chunks of chicken and vegetables – whole pieces of potatoes, cabbage, chayote, carrots, sweet, barely-cooked corn on the cob, celery and calabaza – the pumpkin-like squash.

The same cast of characters fares equally well in the Caldo Res (beef soup), but this time the intense meaty flavor is extracted from boiling a beef shank. Both soups are popular, the portions are huge and an incredible bargain at $3.95 for the large bowl.

The Caldo Camarones is marginally more ($6.25) and worth every cent. The heavy broth tastes of the sea and the smoky, bell-shaped cascabel chile that gives it a reddish hue. "It is our biggest seller probably because people like the spiciness of it. Plus, they are getting a lot of shrimp."

Best of all is the Menudo. Blood-red and thicker than most, if it is true that menudo cures what ails you – his is intense enough to cure what ailed your ancestors. Wong laughs and says that it runs a close second as the "breakfast of champions" to the Cocktel Camarones on Saturday and Sunday mornings. The powerfully-concentrated soup is distinguished by Wong's technique of boiling both beef and pig's feet for three to four hours before adding the tripe and hominy. The extra gelatin from the bones gives Taqueria Cancun's menudo an unusually dense richness.

Wong says the Beef Enchiladas are the most popular dish on the menu and it's easy to understand why. I'll go out on a limb here and say that I don't think you'll taste a better beef enchilada in this town. "It's our secret sauce. I think that's the big difference," Wong says. "We use our homemade beef broth and then we blend some chile cascabel." He also uses his exceptionally tender and well-flavored fajita meat as a filling instead of ground beef.

The Beef Fajitas are marinated overnight in garlic, soy sauce and lime juice. They are good, but the Pechuga Pollo (sliced chicken breasts) may be even better. Also marinated overnight, they are cooked quickly on the grill with thin slices of onion and tomatoes.

The third dish listed under Cancun Platillo after fajitas and pechugas is Carnitas. Wong's method of tenderizing and seasoning the cubed, sweet pork butt is to marinate it for a few hours in milk mixed with cumin, paprika, garlic, salt and pepper – a trick he says he picked up from a chef in Mexico City. The pork is then dried well, seasoned a second time, and fried until crisp on the outside. The result is nothing short of spectacular.

Milanesa is the Latin adaptation of the Italian dish, veal Milanese. It is always made with beef (instead of veal) and at Taqueria Cancun they use beef side skirt that they marinade, then bread with fine fresh crumbs from bolillo – the soft, oval rolls used to make the Mexican sandwich, torta. Once again, theirs is my favorite rendition of this dish. Don't be surprised that it arrives cut in bite-size pieces. Wong says, "We used to serve it whole, but customers would ask us to cut it up for them. So that's what we do." As good as the rice and refried beans are that accompany all "Platillos," I think the Papas or fried potatoes go even better with the Milanesa. I like the idea that by adding 75 cents to your order you can get any combination of two meats on your "platillo."

TASCA KITCHEN AND WINE BAR

908 Congress
Houston, Texas 77002
713/225-9100

Type of Cuisine: Spanish
Bar: Full
Dress: Casual
Entertainment: Jazz Quartet Wednesday-Saturday 8:00p.m.-12:00a.m.
Payment: All Major Credit Cards
Tapas Range: $2.00-$5.00
Entrée Range: $14.00-$23.00
Recommended Dishes:
Tapas: Roasted Bone Marrow
Snail Ravioli with Anchovie Butter
Jamón Serrano Blackfoot
Crispy Fried Squid
Morcilla Spanish Sausage
Chorizo Sausage with Torres Brandy
Appetizers: Hackberry Lump Crabcake
Entrées: Grilled Airline Chicken Breast
Dry-Aged Grilled Beef Tenderloin
Chilean Sea Bass
Dried Mexican Chili Crusted Ahi Tuna
Desserts: Peach Chiffon Cobbler (seasonal)
Single Batch Bourbon Praline Cheesecake
Hours: Monday-Thursday, 11:00a.m.-11:00p.m.
Friday-Saturday, Full Menu 11:00a.m.-12:00a.m.,
Tapas until 2:00a.m.
(Closed Sunday)
Reservations: Accepted

Say "tasca" to a Spaniard and there is an instant image of a boisterous tavern, a bar laden with plates and a floor covered with shrimp shells, bread crusts and tiny napkins. This is where tapas are found.

What you will find at the Tasca near the corner of Congress and Travis is a fabulous-looking new restaurant, snappy, well-informed service, soft candlelight, a little jazz or swing broadcast through a perfect sound system and several dishes – considered actual delicacies – a combination of which you're not likely to find under any other single roof in the world.

Let's start with the Suckling Pig (currently a weekend special on Thursday, Friday and Saturday, unless I can convince them otherwise). I am helpless in the face of a heaving portion of sweet, pale pink meat under a dome of crisp, fat-edged crackling. Surround it with oven roasted vegetables – fennel, onions, carrots and maybe tomatoes – add a ladleful of one of the city's best, creamiest, most irresistable mashed potatoes and you have nothing short of a feast.

"Princeps obsoniorum," the "prince of victuals," is what Nineteenth Century British writer Charles Lamb called suckling pig in a little essay he wrote on the subject. How did we get so lucky?

Charles Clark, who owns Tasca with partners Grant Cooper and Rasheed Rafaey, recently returned from a nine month apprenticeship in Marbella, Spain, and roasting suckling pig is just one of the many things he learned. A talented young chef from Dequincy, Louisiana, "where everyone is in love with food from birth," he says, developed the original menu and was the chef at Dacapo's when they first opened. He was wooed away by an American couple who offered him a job as chef of their restaurant in Marbella.

What he brings back to the table is an unabashed appreciation of the bold, unpretentious techniques of Spanish/European cooking and the other glories of the Spanish culinary life, namely ham, sausage and cheese.

The most exceptional of these is listed quite simply smack-dab in the center of the "Spanish" tapas as Jamón Serrano Blackfoot. Comparable to, but with a richer, more intense flavor than proscuitto, it's Italian cousin, the "pata negra" (black hoofed) Serrano ("mountain") jamón is a rarity in these parts.

Clark, himself, appears tableside to carve the velvety, burgandy-red ribbons from a jamón – hooves removed, impaled and secured on a stand. Eat it with pieces of crusty, freshly baked, baguette-style bread and maybe a few shards of salty, well-aged Queso Manchego and you're off to a good start here.

The superb house Sangria makes an excellent apertif. It is fruity and refreshing – flavored (unexpectedly) with rum, Grand Marnier and lots of fresh fruit. It is made with either red or white wine and I recommend both.

Still, I craved the earthy, oak-flavored Spanish red wine Muga Riserva, or Lorinon Rioja – two of more than forty wines available by the glass – with the Spanish sausages and some of the other tapas.

Spanish Chorizo and Morcilla (blood sausage) are impossible to import from Spain and are being purchased from a source in California. The chorizo is flavored with garlic and pimenton – a sweet Spanish paprika. Clark is searing the sausage in a pan with Torres Brandy. The Morcilla, on the other hand, requires little more than warming to release its seductive, rich flavor.

Wedges of dense Spanish Potato Omelette are an ideal accompaniment to the sausage. It is, in fact, a tortilla, but Clark has not called it that on the menu to avoid confusion with its

Mexican namesake. Apart from their shape, they have nothing in common other than being derived from the same Latin word, "torte" or "round cake." Whether served warm or, more often, room temperature, it is a staple of even the most primitive offering of tapas.

I have only one thing to say about the Crispy Fried Squid. More! Technically a serving of tapas should be no more than a nibble or two, so Clark is absolutely correct in keeping the portions tiny, but you might consider asking for double (or triple) orders of the fried squid. He's bathing baby squid in buttermilk then coating it with cornmeal – a tip of the culinary hat to his native roots. The fiery dipping sauce is composed of sambal, an Asian ground chile condiment whipped into a little crème fraiche.

Roasted Bone Marrow with Parsley Salad and Sea Salt, listed as an "American" tapa, is the jewel in the crown of an already very interesting (and highly individual) menu. This dish alone would entice me regularly to Tasca even if they never roasted another suckling pig. Three beef bones, crusty and oozing with marrow, are assembled like Stonehenge on a thick square metal plate. A small pillar of sea salt is in one corner (you won't need it!) and a rosy, razor thin tangle of red onion and chopped parsley in the other. A grilled piece of sourdough bread is wedged between the bones. If they still haven't gotten marrow spoons in, a knife is the handiest utensil to remove the marrow and spread it on the toasted bread. Clark says he didn't expect "to sell one bone marrow in twenty visits, but I sell out every night. Like I always say, 'Don't underestimate Houston clientele!'"

The Snail Ravioli with Anchovy Butter is another memorable "American" tapa. A dish of Clark's invention, it is an inspired pairing of freshly made pasta filled with a finely chopped sauté of snails, garlic, shallots and a little parsley, then drizzled with butter, browned and nutty, flavored with anchovies. (Again, you might want to double up on the very small portion here. We fought over this one!)

Not wanting to overwhelm the kitchen initially, the dinner menu is a short, well-thought out selection of standard-sized appetizers ("Preludes") and entrées.

The Hackberry Lump Crabcake is the highlight of the "Preludes." The almost all crabmeat crabcake is very lightly bound with a little freshly made sweet cornbread, chopped scallions, roasted onions and peppers, and poised on top of luscious red square of creamy, well-seasoned polenta studded with plump, barbecued crawfish. The remoulade sauce zigzagged over the top is Zatarain's Cajun Mustard enriched with fat rendered from smoked ham hocks. (Hackberry is the closest Gulf inlet to Dequincy, Louisiana, where Clark says he used to go crabbing as a child.)

All "Main Course" choices that I sampled were skillfully executed and beautifully presented. It's really a question of what you feel like eating. The Grilled Airline Chicken Breast merited superlatives at our table for its flavor and succulence, if not for its potentially off-putting name – a reference to the wing bones being left in tact and extended – an "airline" cut.

Beef eaters should love the Grilled Beef Tenderloin. Fork-tender, well-aged beef is enhanced by a deep-flavored sauce of green peppercorns and a reduction of Rioja wine and beef stock. The steak is capped by a couple of ravioli filled with a purple-veined blue cheese called Cabrales, considered the true aristocrat of Spanish cheeses.

A chunk of Chilean Sea Bass the size (and shape) of a baseball is treated to a sauce of brown butter flavored with earthy, matchstick-size shreds of porcini mushrooms. The Chile Crusted Ahi Tuna is cut the same way as the sea bass and seared with a crisp exterior of incendiary ground ancho chiles. The accompanying mashed potatoes serve as a soothing balm to the heat of the dish. Braised leeks and bok choy (Chinese cabbage), as well as a few grilled vegetables, round out these very generous plates.

Apart from the suckling pig, keep an eye peeled for Paella as a special (or by special request). Taught by those who know, Clark's is an impeccable reading of a classic Andalusian style paella. Prepared with a rich, heady broth, it is golden-yellow with saffron and chockfull of the earth's treasures – seafood, chunks of chicken and welcome disks of both morcilla and chorizo sausages.

Desserts and all freshly baked goods are the province of Greg Dickson. The Single Batch Bourbon Praline Cheesecake is a thing of great beauty, but the Peach Chiffon Cobbler is an absolute must as long as peaches are in season. Order one "for the table" and dive into the huge white porcelain bowl filled with crusty, warm torn pieces of chewy chiffon/angel food cake topped with peach-flavored whipped cream and jammy slices of fresh Texas peaches.

A fitting finish to a fabulous meal at a dandy of a new restaurant. I'll tell you. I think these guys are onto something here.

TEXAS BORDERS BAR AND GRILL

19910 Park Row (I-10 at Fry Road)
Katy, Texas 77084
281/578-8785

Type of Cuisine: American/Burgers
Bar: Full
Dress: Casual
Entertainment: No
Payment: All Major Credit Cards
Entrée Range: $4.25-$9.95
Recommended Dishes:
Appetizers: Loaded Fries
Buffalo Wings
Stuffed Jalapeño
Cajun Fried Onion Rings
Entrées: Hickory Burger
Colossal Texas Club Sandwich
Quesadillas (Shrimp or Bacon and Mushroom)
Hours: Sunday-Thursday, 11:00a.m.-10:00p.m.
Friday-Saturday, 11:00a.m.-2:00a.m.
(Kitchen closes at 11:00p.m.)
Reservations: Not Accepted

Epicure Laureate and famous food writer, M.F.K. Fisher maintained that "almost every person has something secret he likes to eat." What guilty pleasures do you crave? If it's French Fries, hot gooey Quesadillas, or Onion Rings good enough to put all others' to shame – I've got your place.

What I love most about Texas Borders is that young owners, Kellie and Mark Messer, decided when they opened this self-described Mom and Pop operation to take these simple pleasures and just do them better than anyone else. "And especially," Kellie adds, "to serve them in a really fun, friendly, family-oriented place."

They've succeeded on all counts. It's a cross between a rowdy sports bar with a great jukebox and terrific food, and a place where parents sit comfortably by the window sipping Screwgies – the Dreamsicle-like frozen screwdriver – watching their children play in the huge sandbox outside.

The name, Texas Borders, is taken from the Messers' desire to cover all major points of interest on the Texas culinary landscape, incorporating favorite dishes from the bordering states and Mexico with an emphasis on "heat."

A sort of Chilis-on-steroids, the fare at Texas Borders is fresh, fresh, fresh, and made-to-order. Let's start with the Onion Rings – worth the drive alone, wherever you live.

Medium fat slices of sweet onion are hand-dipped-to-order in a peerless batter lightened with beer and seasoned liberally with paprika, cayenne pepper, and garlic salt. (It's important to note that 99% of the time you order onion rings elsewhere you're getting a frozen, pre-fab product.) "Yes. You know, there are actually people cooking in our kitchen," points out Messer, alluding to this practice. They are served with a portion of good, homemade ranch-style dressing made with bona fide buttermilk.

In fact, all dressings are made from scratch. (It's such a simple thing, but it makes such a huge difference. I wish all restaurants were in the habit of doing this.)

Other favorite options among the "Southwest Texas Starters" are the Stuffed Jalapeño (also clearly house-made) crammed with shrimp, crab and catfish – and the unusual Fried Jalapeños.

As your average jalapeño-happy Texan, I don't remember seeing this particular preparation. Pickled, medium-hot jalapeños are split, seeded, cut in strips, dipped in the house batter, and deep fried. They come with a hot bowl of diced tomato and chili-flecked chili con queso for dipping.

The guiltiest pleasures of all may be the Loaded Fries. They are recommended for sharing, although the Messers tell me there are customers who come in to eat that alone. "It's our answer to the big baked potato," Kellie says, "but it's really more like a pie." The Loaded Fries are constructed in layers – flawless, golden French fries are topped with the sinus-clearing Borders Spicy Chili (highly recommended), and crumbled bacon. Next comes a generous blanket of shredded Cheddar cheese. A trip into the salamander makes it a glorious, gooey mess that's then finished off with a spoonful of sour cream and chopped scallions.

The Buffalo wings, called Drums-n-Flappers at Texas Borders, are notable for their extraordinary size and choice of degrees of heat: mild, hot, explosive, and (by request) nuclear – made with habanera peppers. Mark adds, "They are jumbo party wings, really Texas-size, and they are one of our biggest sellers." Again, the blue cheese dressing that accompanies the wings is freshly-made and chunky with lots of authentic Wisconsin blue cheese.

The Messers say that the Quesadillas are wildly popular. It's easy to see why. A whopping ten-inch flour tortilla is studded with lots of sautéed onions, peppers and a choice of the standard beef or chicken fajitas or even better – Shrimp or Bacon and Mushroom. The shrimp are plump and flavorful, sautéed in "Cajun spices," and the bacon and mushroom quesadilla is so packed with chopped mushrooms and crumbled bacon, it's brown. Quesadillas are made "for the kiddos – under 12 or over 65," with smooth peanut butter and grape jelly.

The Chips-n-Salsa are particularly good. The chips are highly-addictive – warm, thin and crisp – and the salsa (also served warm) is hot and smoky from the extra step of roasting the jalapeños before pulverizing them.

Under "Gumbo, Chili, and Soup" it's a toss-up between the gumbo and the chili, both hot enough to wake the dead. Kellie is from New Orleans and the gumbo called Jo's South Louisiana Spicy Gumbo is named for her mother, Jo Ellen. "It's been her gumbo recipe all her life. Gumbo means something different to so many people. But, in our family the chicken and andouille sausage is your seasoning." Moss green from heavy doses of filé, it's made in the time-honored fashion – simmered for hours. "It takes such a long time to cook it. When the weather cools, it's hard to keep it in stock," Mark adds.

The Chili recipe is courtesy of Mark's father, a native Houstonian. Mark says, "It's an all-beef chili made the old fashioned way. My dad used to say, 'Texans don't eat beans in their chili.'" So, his heartburn-inducing rendition is made without beans but with identifiable pieces of red pepper flakes and chopped jalapeños.

It's great alone or ladled on top of the Chili Cheese Burger from Paradise. Kellie comments, "Burgers are probably our specialty. They are our biggest seller." Why not? They are flawless. Either the chili cheese burger or my favorite, the Hickory Burger. Cattleman's Smoky Barbecue Sauce is basted on, then actually seared into the hamburger meat on the flat top grill. It's topped with thick, crisp bacon, then Cheddar cheese is melted over the top. As good as the French fries are, consider substituting onion rings. The accompanying Cole Slaw is ideal – medium dry, crisp, cold and not too sweet.

Sandwiches are another area where the kitchen excels. A classic Philly cheese steak speaks with a Texas accent when made with hefty pieces of beef fajitas. This is the Fajita Steak Sandwich.

Suitable for sharing (or saving half for a separate meal), the Colossal Texas Club Sandwich is just that – a huge, but neatly constructed sandwich of sweet ham, strips of hot chicken fajita meat, bacon, shredded Cheddar cheese, lettuce, tomatoes, pickles and onions all enveloped by a twelve-inch whole wheat tortilla – a virtual symphony of flavors and textures. The Colossal Club is given some competition by the off-the-menu Ozark Wrap. More a "fold" than a "wrap," the tortilla in this case contains warm chicken tenders, Cheddar cheese, lettuce, tomatoes, onion and pickles, and as an added bonus the heavenly (homemade, of course) honey mustard dressing. Another great sandwich.

The Messers say that the Seafood Poboys are popular.

The one I sampled – the catfish – was impressive – made with an enormous filet of sweet, farm-raised catfish lightly cloaked in the wonderful house batter and fried.

The dessert menu varies but the one constant appears to be a lovely, old fashioned Strawberry Shortcake. The "shortcake" is actually a big biscuit made from Bisquick©, split and topped with Blue Bell© vanilla ice cream, warmed strawberries laced with sugar and Grand Marnier, and a generous dollop of freshly whipped cream.

The Messers' philosophy appears to be my own, that "anything worth doing, is worth doing well." Don't you agree?

TEXCHICK

712 1/2 Fairview
Houston, Texas 77006
713/528-4708

Type of Cuisine: Puerto Rican
Bar: No
Dress: Casual
Entertainment: No
Payment: Cash or Check Only
Entrée Range: $2.50-$7.50
Recommended Dishes:
 Bacon Cheese Burger
 Carne Frita (Pork)
 Mofongo Biftec
 Chuleta (Pork Chop)
Hours: Monday-Friday, 11:00a.m.-6:00p.m.
 Saturday, 11:00a.m.-4:00p.m.
 (Closed Sunday)
Reservations: Not Accepted

This tiny, pale blue wood and red brick building is nearly dwarfed by two old houses on either side. If you blink, you miss it. But, you'd be missing out on one of the finest old-fashioned cheeseburgers in town and sampling, as the words etched onto the window say, "Equisitos Platos Puertorrigueños" – exquisite Puerto Rican plates.

Why is one of Houston's only Puerto Rican restaurants called "TexChick?" And why are they almost as famous for their cheeseburgers and homemade onion rings as they are for their Mofongo and Carne Frita?

Here's the story ... Teodoro and Carmen Gonzales moved from Camuy, Puerto Rico, to Miami in 1952. They were transferred to Houston in 1959 by Teodoro's employer, Clark Aluminum. In 1967, when another transfer seemed imminent, he left Clark Aluminum to work at Walgreens on Westheimer (in the Montrose area where Blockbuster Video is now located). Teodoro managed the lunch counter for three years and when Walgreens threatened to move him to another store out of the neighborhood where they had settled, he decided that this food business couldn't be all that difficult and began looking around for a little restaurant of his own. He found TexChick (on Montrose where Big Frank's is now), a fried chicken/hamburger stand that a guy from Reno, Oklahoma, was ready to sell. He added a couple of Mexican plates to the menu – tacos and cheese or beef enchiladas – and there he remained from 1970 until 1983, perfecting his onion ring batter ("a big secret," he says) and his hamburger making technique.

"There were no tables, just orders to go, and I delivered in those days." Although his little business thrived, he closed it down, picked up and moved back to Camuy about an hour and fifteen minutes northeast of San Juan near the beach. They opened a Puerto Rican TexChick there, and if you find the name perplexing, imagine how odd the people in Camuy, Puerto Rico, thought it was since they specialized in neither chicken, nor Texan food.

This is where Carmen began cooking the kind of dishes she had always cooked at home, most of the same dishes that are listed on the menu as "Our Famous Puerto Rican Plates." "The place was huge (compared to the present space especially!) twelve tables and a big lunch counter," Teodoro says.

After six months, they decided to move back to Houston, leaving the Puerto Rican TexChick in the hands of Teodoro's older brother.

"When I came back, I looked around and I saw that so many fast food places had opened – JackInTheBox, Wendy's, MacDonald's – and I thought, 'This isn't going to work.' I had trained myself to cook Puerto Rican food. So, I looked for a small place to get started. I really just intended to sell orders to go, like I had before, but I made space for a couple of tables. That's how I started. I began calling friends, then I added more tables." There are four tables now and TexChick seats a maximum of fourteen people. "We still get a lot of calls for orders to go, but I don't deliver anymore!"

Since then, the cooking duties have been divided equally between Carmen and Teodoro. "We both cook everything. When I'm busy cooking one thing, she cooks the other. Mostly she does the cooking in the morning." This is the consummate Mom and Pop operation. When I ask him about having seen others working in the small kitchen, he says "Sometimes people come by, one or two friends, they see us in a jam and they help us."

There is an actual menu although you may have to ask for it. Most of the dishes available are written on a chalk board. On the front of the red laminated menu are the "American-Mexican" dishes. Skip the Mexican dishes altogether and start with the Steak Sandwich. This is lightly-breaded hamburger meat dressed and garnished like a regular burger. I was surprised at how much I liked it, but not as much as their flawless, classic American bacon cheeseburger.

Not a big sloppy number, but a neat, perfectly constructed drugstore hamburger from my youth, with just the right amount of shredded iceberg lettuce, tomato, dill pickle slices, French's© Mustard, two crossed pieces of crisp, smoky bacon and melted

American cheese with just the tiniest bit of nearly translucent rings of grilled onion for flavor.

When I ask what makes his hamburger so great, he says "Fresh meat and good nature." The burgers come alone, so Teodoro says that most people order French fries or onion rings to go with them.

"We sell a lot of Onion rings because we make them fresh. I can't tell you about the batter, that's a no no, but I will say that I used to watch these guys at Walgreen's and I thought, 'Why buy them premade when I can make them better myself?'"

I'm not mad for the onion rings. I think the same "secret" batter fares better on either the aforementioned steak sandwich or the Biftec (Empanado) one of the two ways they prepare steak topping the list of Puerto Rican dishes on the flip side of the menu. The other way is Biftec (Encebollado) where the same tenderized cut of top round steak of heroic proportion is cooked on the grill and smothered with onions. While the flavor is commendable, the beef has an unappetizing grey pallor, so of the two, I prefer the breaded version. Chicken fried steak fans especially will enjoy it.

For those unfamiliar with Puerto Rican food, here's a primer of the other "Famous Puerto Rican Plates." PastelArroz Habichuelo are similar to Mexican or Venezuelan tamales but the dough is made of ground plantains (green bananas) and yellow or white taro (instead of cornmeal), and they are cooked in banana leaves in place of corn husks. Pastales are time consuming to make and are mostly considered a holiday dish. Teodoro sighs, "We made about ninety dozen of these at Christmas, so we're taking a little break now." (Try them, if they have them when you visit.)

Arroz con Ganduras is considered a staple in most Puerto Rican households. It is white rice cooked with seasoned pigeon peas, usually eaten as a side dish.

Carne Guisada is beef stew small cubes of chuck roast cooked with carrots, potatoes and seasoned with a sofrito – a blended mixture of cilantro, onion, garlic and bell peppers that is used as the starting point for most Puerto Rican recipes. Although it is not listed, Pollo Guisado (stewed chicken) is also usually available.

Chuleta is a pork chop that has been deep fried (in vegetable oil), dry-seasoned with an all-purpose seasoning mixture called "adobo" – salt, black pepper, garlic powder, oregano and tumeric – then finished on the grill. Like all of the entrée dishes, it is served with a choice of white or yellow rice (choose yellow), richly-flavored stewed pinto beans and tostones.

Tostones are twice deep-fried pieces of green plantain

and are considered the French fry of Puerto Rico. In fact, I'd order them instead of French fries if you're eating a burger.

The one fish dish is Bacalao y Vianda. This is salt cod, hugely popular in Puerto Rico, soaked and boiled to remove all salt, then cooked with onions and tomatoes. (This is definitely an acquired taste. I haven't quite acquired it yet!)

This leads me to my two favorite dishes that, apart from their superior burgers, make TexChick worth a visit. The first is Carne Frita succulent nuggets of pork dry-seasoned, deep fried, seasoned again, then finished in a skillet with razor-thin slices of sweet onion. "Seasoning it twice is what makes the meat taste so good," Teodoro says. If this is what you're ordering, you must eat it with mofongo.

Mofongo. I even like the sound of this dish. Probably African in origin, step up to the yellow formica counter and watch either Teodoro or Carmen deep fry the wedges of green plantain and then pummel them with fresh garlic and barely detectable fried pork rind in a Puerto Rican pelon – mortar and pestle. It is then turned out onto the plate, the size and shape of a softball molded by the bottom of the pelon. Ordered on its own or to accompany Carne Frita, Biftec, or anything else, I wouldn't miss trying the most seductive of Puerto Rican national dishes.

The only sauce is an incendiary, emerald-green little number that is little more than puréed jalapeño peppers. Use with caution. A couple of drops and your tongue dials the fire department.

The one dessert is Flan – the firm, eggy variety which Teodoro says Carmen makes every morning.

TexChick serves no liquor and only takes cash. "Checks, too," Teodoro says, "If I put them in the freezer and nothing melts."

When I ask him if he ever wishes he had more space, he says, "I thought about having a bigger place, but I'd rather stay small and make quality food." Does he ever think about changing the name? "Puerto Ricans, who make up about 60% of my business, think it should have a Puerto Rican name, but it's the name I started with here, people know me by it, and besides, I've been lucky with it."

THAI GOURMET

6324 Richmond Avenue
Houston, Texas 77057
713/780-7955

Type of Cuisine: Thai
Bar: Wine and Beer
Dress: Casual
Entertainment: No
Payment: All Major Credit Cards
Entrée Range: $6.50-$12.95
Recommended Dishes:
Appetizers: Stuffed Eggplant
Crispy Rice
Gourmet Dumplings
Grilled Calamari
Fried Soft Shell Crab
Entrées: Crystal Noodle Salad
Pad Thai
Drunken Noodles
Basil Beef
Garlic Pork
Garlic Okra
Crispy Duck
Dessert: Fried Bananas with Coconut Ice Cream
Hours: Lunch: Monday-Friday, 11:30a.m.-2:30p.m.
Dinner: Monday-Thursday, 5:00p.m.-9:30p.m.
Friday, 5:00p.m.-10:30p.m.
Saturday, 11:00a.m.-10:30p.m.
(Closed Sunday)
Reservations: Accepted

Sanuk, an all-purpose Thai word for unfettered joy or pleasure, is the only way to describe the emotion behind the bold, bright flavors of Thai Gourmet.

"I love to cook!" says co-chef and co-owner, Watana "Toon" Phumswarng. "I learned from my mom and my sisters. They are all good cooks. Thai food is very special and all of my family is from Bangkok in the middle of Thailand." This is important, she says, because their style of cooking incorporated the finest traditions of each region. "Not too sour and not too hot. In the southern part of Thailand, the people eat (food) very, very hot."

"More authentically Thai" was the goal of Phumswarng, her husband and co-chef, Thussayu, and three partners Ubol Brennamen, Toolsin Kristanuwat and Phayoa Chansiri, when they devised the menu of Thai Gourmet which opened in December of '95.

In fact, outside of Thailand, several favorite dishes are not likely to be found anywhere but Thai Gourmet. Stuffed Eggplant is at the top of my list. Chicken is marinated, ground, then molded onto a thin cylinder of Japanese eggplant. It is dipped in seasoned flour and deep fried crispy brown. "Literally, melt-in-your-mouth" is how a fellow diner aptly described #11 of fourteen appetizers. Phumswarng agrees, "I love it very much! When I was young, my grandmom used to make this dish for us. Eggplant in Thailand is different, smaller and bright green. Very pretty!"

It is rivaled in my affections by the unusual Thai Gourmet Crispy Rice. Puffy, irregularly-shaped rice "cakes" are made by prying the bottom layer of white, long grain rice from the pot and deep frying it. A sweet, silky yellow-orange mixture of finely minced chicken, shrimp, garlic, peanuts and red onions enriched with coconut milk is meant to be spooned onto the wafers of crispy rice.

I wouldn't miss the elegant simplicity of tender Calamari steaks sliced thin lengthwise, dusted with salt and pepper and scored on the grill. It's best dunked into my favorite of the Thai chili dipping sauces, Nam Pla Prik. It is emerald-green, tart with lime juice, a little pungent Nam Pla (fish sauce), garlic and fiery Thai Bird chilies. Phumswarng says, "Thai people love to drink beer with Grilled Calamari and green hot sauce!" (She recommends their only Thai beer, Singha.)

Another appetizer, Fried Soft Shell Crab, is presented in a novel and appealing way. Almost everybody's favorite part of the crustacean, the crunchy legs, are served with a sweet white chunk of meat from the body still attached. They are very lightly battered and flawlessly fried.

Juicy, thin skinned Dumplings distinguish themselves from their Chinese origins by being strewn with flecks of garlic browned in a little oil. Try them alone, or dip them in the thick, dark brown soy sauce flavored with sugar, vinegar and garlic.

Cream cheese-filled Spicy Cheese Rolls are strictly an American invention. "We don't eat too much cheese in Thailand," Phumswarng says, but Thai Gourmet's – spiked with Thai chilies, shredded carrots and finely minced scallions – are especially good.

The Fresh Spring Rolls are in keeping with the notion of being "more authentically Thai." Do no expect them to resemble the dainty, transparent-skinned Vietnamese fresh spring rolls that have become so familiar. These are different. "Thai style," with a thicker, paper-like "wrapper" that you'll either love or hate. The filling includes bean sprouts, cucumbers, crabmeat and lop cheung – the wonderful, wine-flavored Chinese sausage.

Lemon grass, Kaffir lime leaves, cilantro, lime juice and the salty, pleasant tang of the finest grade of fish sauce all give Hot and Sour Shrimp Soup its distinctive, exquisite flavor. Pharmswarng tells me a complete Thai meal would always include a soup and the vibrant, contrasting flavors and textures of a Thai salad.

Two of the best salads are the Crystal Noodle Salad – a substantial, but light composition of chicken, shrimp, crisp vegetables and clear rice noodles – and the puckery, palate-awakening Calamari Salad dressed with lime-juice, garlic and plenty of red pepper flakes.

"Kin Khao!" ("Eat Rice!") are the words used in Thailand to invite friends to dinner. The rice dish that would regularly entice me to supper is the Spicy Fried Rice with the lingering impact of fragrant basil and a healthy dose of garlic.

Phumswarng says that noodle dishes (like the two I'm about to recommend) are usually considered a meal unto themselves and are never eaten in conjunction with rice.

A simpler version of Pad Thai – the stir-fried rice noodle dish – is hawked on busy street corners in Bangkok, but I cannot imagine improving upon the remarkable creamy recipe that originated with Phumswarng's mother. Add shrimp to the moist, already-rich mixture of chicken, eggs and bean sprouts, and it's perfect!

The wider rice noodles are used to make the divinely smoky Drunken Noodles, so named, according to Phumswarng, because "when Thai people drink, they love to eat something tasty and spicy." Given a choice of combining the noodles with chicken, pork, beef, or shrimp, this deeply satisfying dish is best when teamed with beef because basil and beef make such a fine marriage.

For this reason, my preference among the beef dishes is the Basil Beef. Flank steak is rendered almost delicate when first marinated in oil with salt and pepper, then sautéed with onions, bell peppers, mushrooms, garlic and aromatic sweet basil.

Phumswarng believes Thai Gourmet is best known of all for its curries. Of the three varieties of Thai curries – red (with chilies), yellow (with tumeric) or green (with herbs) – my favorite is the Green Curry Chicken. It is pale green and velvety-smooth with coconut milk, but watch for the bite of whole slices of small, slightly-searing green serrano peppers.

This is a good time to mention that most dishes should be ordered "medium" when asked, "How hot?" "Hot" obliterates all subtlety from the dishes and "mild" lacks the unique complexity of flavors that this cooking is noted for.

Garlic lovers will enjoy Garlic Pork. Thin slices of lean

pork tenderloin are marinated in garlic, cilantro and white pepper, then stir-fried briskly over the usual high heat so the white flecks of garlic adhere to the pork. It is a superb dish and is spooned on top of crunchy, stir-fried vegetables.

Another favorite, Crispy Duck, manages to be perfectly crisp but not even a little dry as is so often the case. "The key is not to pick a skinny duck," she says. It is sliced and also placed on top of a stir-fried mixture of baby snow peas, broccoli, mushrooms, onions and napa cabbage.

The Thai Gourmet Garlic Okra tops my list as one of the best vegetable dishes in town. If you even think you don't like okra, you need to try this one! Tiny, tender pieces of baby okra are chewy and black-rimmed from being cooked very quickly with a lot of garlic.

"All stir-fries start with garlic," Phumswarng says. So the second best, Stir-Fried Pakana, is pungent Chinese broccoli sautéed simply in a little oil with garlic.

For the customer's convenience, the Triple Spicy Fish is red snapper served off-the-bone although they are happy to fry the whole fish for those who ask. The filet is very lightly floured, and expertly fried, then napped with a speckled green sauce fragrant with Kaffir lime leaves and lashed with serrano peppers and red pepper flakes. "We love our fish in Thailand, you know." Phumswarng added, "This is a dish my mother made at home." The same extraordinary sauce – "Chef's Special Chili Sauce" – is offered with the entrée, Tasty Soft Shell Crab.

Reserve some appetite for Fried Bananas – crunchy fried wedges of bananas piled in a banana split dish with a scoop of homemade coconut ice cream drizzled with honey. Heaven.

THAI HOUSE

5704 Fondren
Houston, Texas 77036
713/7892666

Type of Cuisine: Thai
Bar: Wine and Beer
Dress: Casual
Entertainment: No
Payment: All Major Credit Cards
Entrée Range: $7.95-$11.95
Recommended Dishes:
Appetizers: Thai Appetizer Tray
Hoi-Jo (Fried Seafood/Vegetable Dumpling)
Koong Nao (Fried Shrimp)
Glass Noodles (Vermicelli with Seafood)
Tiger Cry (Barbecued Flank Steak)
Entrées: Red Snapper (Filleted)
Crisp Shrimp
Soft Shell Crab
Chicken Curry with Avocado
Soft Rice Noodles with Chinese Broccoli
Hours: Tuesday-Saturday, 11:30a.m.-10:00p.m.
Sunday, 5:00p.m.-10:00p.m.
(Closed Monday)
Reservations: Accepted

All the subtlety and the bright, contrasting flavors of the Thai kitchen are masterfully prepared and beautifully presented at another favorite Thai restaurant, Thai House. When asked what distinguishes her cooking from others', chef and owner, Tao Boonchoo explains that she learned her unique style by apprenticing in New York City in the kitchen of an Upper East Side favorite, Bangkok House.

Sandwiched between Star Karaoke and Old Galveston Fans just across the railroad tracks on Fondren, the decor is strictly converted early 1970's strip center, but the atmosphere is serene and welcoming – starched, white tablecloths and napkins with candlelight. If you're lucky, Max Supakul, who has been with Tao for eight years (that's dog years in the fickle world of wait service!), will take your order.

Singha, the only Thai beer Max tells us they are currently able to import, goes especially well with both the delicate and the more aggressively-seasoned dishes.

Another note – although they are happy to provide chopsticks, it is Thai custom to use a fork and spoon to eat.

Starting with the appetizers, what you won't find are soft spring rolls (they're Vietnamese). What you will find that you won't see on any other Thai menu in Houston, according to

Tao is Hoi Jo (A3) – a finely-ground mixture of shrimp, crabmeat and vegetables gently encased in a very delicate bean curd skin, steamed and then deep fried. This is a celebratory dish from Tao's native town of Prad, Thailand, about four hours east of Bangkok. "Only Thai House has Hoi Jo. In Thailand, we make it for special occasions, like wedding parties." There are eight bitesize bundles to an order and they are meant to be eaten with the gingery, sweet plum sauce, but I prefer the tart, lingering tingle of any one of the house hot sauces.

Another appetizer I don't remember seeing elsewhere is Koong Nao (A4) – outsized specimens of whole shrimp wrapped in an eggroll skin and deep fried. Tao explains that, "'Nao' means 'winter'. This is why we roll the shrimp in a 'blanket,' but I leave the tail out." If you order the Thai Appetizer Tray (A9), you get to sample both of these little delicacies along with the more predictable, but stellar renditions of beef satay skewered barbecued beef, always served with peanut sauce and cucumber salad and Thai spring rolls, smaller and more delicate than their Chinese neighbor's.

It is a characteristic of Thai restaurants to have especially long menus and, although I am confident that whichever dish you choose you will be delighted with, this is the menu I would order if I was entertaining a (large!) group at Thai House.

Also listed as appetizers, start with both the glass noodles, Yum Woon Sen (A5) – transparent bean thread vermicelli lightly tossed with a sauté of impeccably fresh seafood and pork, barely coated with a light sauce of onions, chilies and lime garnished with chopped peanuts – and an order of Tiger Cry (A10) – flank steak that has been massaged with cilantro then barbecued until it tastes just a little smoky. It is rare, exceptionally tender, sliced and served with my favorite Thai dipping sauce on the side that's "hot enough to make a tiger cry," says Tao. It is a mixture of crushed garlic, chilies (both jalapeño and Thai bird'seye), in a lime-based sauce with just a hint of the pungent nam pla (literally "fish water").

Tiger Cry is one of the few beef dishes I recommend because the kitchen's area of expertise is clearly seafood. Tao explains that her native Prad is known for its excellent seafood, but thinks that, "Houston has the best seafood and fish."

A stickler for quality, Tao says that the exceptional house specialty, Pla Lad Prik (H6) is only available when she thinks the red snapper is perfect. Fortunately, that is most of the time. Shimmering slabs of luminously fresh filets of red snapper are fried, then lightly-coated with what Tao calls the Thai House special picante sauce – a well-balanced, typically Thai sauce with the contrasting flavors of sweet (from palm sugar, a coconut flavored solid sugar), sour (from the citrusy, tamarind pods) and heat (from the devil's own chilies). This is a memorable dish.

A close second in my affections is the crispy jumbo shrimp, Koong GraPow (H8). Huge, succulent shrimp are dipped in egg and half and half, then dusted in baking flour, quickly fried and treated to a powerfully-concentrated dark brown sauce of garlic, fragrant sweet basil, and jalapeño peppers flavored with a little oyster sauce.

The sauce was altogether poetic and our waiter, Max, was right when he suggested that what little sauce was left on the platter might go well with the Deep Fried Soft Shell Crabs (H9). Another house specialty, the small, meaty crabs Tao says she imports from Japan, are lightly coated and deep fried. A little white wine is poured onto the hot platter around the crab as they arrive at the table "to bring out the flavor." They are served with a little sauce of puréed red chilies and garlic. (But I recommend asking for more of the sauce from the crispy shrimp!)

A tamer and more health conscious alternative to any of the above, PoTak (H7) – another house specialty – is sweet scallops, mussels, and shrimp steamed in a delicate white wine and ginger sauce. The heady perfume of ginger is released at the table as you open the "decorative foil swan."

If you never much cottoned to squid before, give Pla Muok GraTiem Prik Thai (F12) a try. Another highly addictive sauce compliments squid rendered so tender through skillful preparation and extraordinary freshness that it is practically unrecognizable.

Near the southern border that Thailand shares with Malaysia, there are many Muslims, which explains the presence and name of my favorite curry at Thai House Gai Masaman ("Muslim") (C9) – pieces of chicken breast and slices of avocado are in a silky curry sauce enriched with coconut milk and peanuts. The sauce is heaven – bright and intense without being too sweet.

In the noodle genre, forego the usual order of PadThai and try Pad SiYu (N3). The more interesting soft rice noodles are sautéed with slightly bitter, wonderful branches of Chinese broccoli and a choice of beef, chicken or pork.

There is a short list of vegetables and the one I recommend most is Pad RuomMit (V1) – assorted seasonal vegetables sautéed simply with a little oyster sauce.

Sticky rice is always a perfect way to finish a Thai meal, but even better, try the soothing off-the-menu Kanom Tuy, if available. It is an ambrosial little saucer of steamed coconut custard.

THAI RACHA

10085 Long Point (at Gessner)
Houston, Texas 77055
713/464-7607

Type of Cuisine: Thai
Bar: No
Dress: Casual
Entertainment: No
Payment: Cash Only
Entrée Range: $3.85-$5.99
Recommended Dishes:
Appetizers: Fresh Spring Rolls
Egg Rolls
Entrées: Tom Ka Soup
Kee Mow Chicken
Garlic Beef
Pad Thai (Chicken)
Pad See Ew (Beef)
Red Curry Chicken
Dessert: Sweet Rice with Custard
Hours: Monday-Saturday, 10:00a.m.-10:00p.m.
(Closed Sunday)
Reservations: Not Accepted

"'Racha' means "King,'" says owner Paul Nimsiri proudly. "The King of Thailand is like the father of the Thai people. I believe it is a blessing to have the name and that it will bring prosperity to the business." It already has. Thai Racha is a runaway success judging by the midday crush of people at this converted Kentucky Fried Chicken location.

The idea is great Thai food fast. Faster (in most cases) than you can get a hamburger and an order of French fries these days. "I'd had the idea for a long time," Nimsiri explains. "I wanted something that would fit the style of people over here."

Nimsiri says that when he moved from Bangkok to Houston to open Thai Racha in 1995, even his family questioned the concept. "They said, 'How are you going to do it? Are you going to serve everything in Styrofoam© containers? Why don't you have a plate and silverware like other Thai restaurants?' But, I like to do something different. I especially like the idea of customers using the drive-through. I think this makes us unique."

Business now is about equally divided among several options – drive-through, order-in/take-out and eat-in. Those eating-in place an order at the counter, pay (cash only) and take a seat. When your order is ready, it is served to you (in

Styrofoam© containers) on a tray. (My choice is call-in, pick-up, take-home!)

The menu is a short list of "really typical" Thai dishes, as Nimsiri says. "I wanted to keep it simple and maintain the quality," he adds. Does this taste like fast food? No.

Beginning with the trio of appetizers – the rice paper wrapped Fresh Spring Rolls have the customary clean, bright flavor and welcome crunch. I especially liked the accompanying dipping sauce – a sweet brown reduction of soy sauce, nam pla (fish sauce), rice vinegar and sugar.

Not quite as healthful but just as good, Nimsiri's favorite, the Egg Rolls, are crisply fried with a flaky, almost-delicate exterior and a juicy filling of ground pork and chicken, transparent glass noodles and slivers of carrots and onions.

Thai Toast, the third-listed appetizer, is a popular snack food in Thailand. Triangles of white bread are covered with a well-seasoned mound of marinated minced chicken and deep fried. They are wonderful and one of the few dishes featured at Thai Racha that- along with the noodle dishes – "takes a few minutes longer to cook. They just can't be rushed."

Any of these appetizers would make a fine meal when paired with a bowl of one of the three deeply satisfying Thai soups. "Tom" is Thai for "soup" and while I enjoyed the rich broth and whole pieces of napa cabbage in the simple Vegetable Chicken Soup, both the Tom Yum and Tom Ka Chicken soups are something to write home about.

In Thailand, there is a saying, "One will be sanctioned or condemned by one's Tom Yum." The Asian principle of contrasting flavors – sweet, salty, hot, and sour – is well represented in Thai Racha's Tom Yum Chicken Soup, which features slices of mushrooms and large white pieces of chicken breast rather than shrimp as it would be in Bangkok. (Nimsiri says that he has almost eliminated seafood from the menu in an effort to keep his prices as moderate as possible.) Pink Siamese ginger, ka or kalanga, is the dominant flavor of the equally-good (and almost as celebrated) Tom Ka Chicken Soup. The tartness of kaffir lime leaves, lemongrass and freshly-squeezed lime juice is tamed by satiny-rich coconut milk.

Salads are notable for their simplicity – iceberg lettuce, wedges of tomatoes, decoratively-cut pieces of cucumber and carrot, either alone or topped with sliced chicken breast (my choice) or beef. They are dressed with an appealing, puckery vinaigrette of lime juice and nam pla with a tiny pinch of sugar and no oil.

Both excellent, the Pad Thai and the Pad See Ew would pass a blind taste with any served in a more formal setting in town. Like everything else on the menu, both rice noodle dishes are prepared with a choice of chicken, beef or tofu (vegetarian). I liked the Pad Thai with chicken, but preferred beef for the Pad See Ew, a more robust stir-fry of rice noodles with broccoli and a healthy dose of soy sauce, called "see ew."

A Rice Bowl is a generous portion (in either small or large) of slightly-sticky steamed long grain rice topped with a choice of chicken, beef or tofu prepared several different ways: Garlic Beef or Chicken, Jalapeño Beef or Chicken, or my absolute favorite – Kee Mow Beef or Chicken. (All also made with tofu instead of meat.)

"'Kee Mow,' literally translated means 'drunk' in Thailand because people who like to drink like dishes to be very tasty and very spicy. But, it is also the name of a type of chili paste that we bring with us from Thailand because you don't have this type of chili here." It is a dish of eye-popping, wake-the-dead intensity. The best is the Kee Mow Chicken made from coarsely-ground chicken stir-fried with plenty of garlic, mint, onion, basil and the identifiable flecks of red chiles (the Kee Mow paste).

I wasn't at all surprised to hear that Kee Mow Tofu was the favorite among vegetarians at Thai Racha. Of the vegetarian options, I liked the Mixed Vegetable Tofu with mostly crunchy, soy-seasoned vegetables – Napa cabbage, bean sprouts, broccoli, carrots, onions and bamboo shoots – and just a few spongy triangles of browned tofu.

The only seafood on the menu are baby shrimp used for the Shrimp Fried Rice. Chicken and shrimp is the best combination fried rice – "Like pad Thai, always eaten as a 'single dish,'" Nimsiri says. (In Thailand, street vendors who sell fried rice as a light meal or snack would offer it with a fried egg on top.)

Those familiar with the three shades and varying strengths of Thai curries – yellow, green and red – will notice that Nimsiri has chosen to serve only red curry at Thai Racha. "It is the spiciest – made from ground red chili paste – and most popular among Thai people," he says. The Red Curry Chicken is ambrosial – velvety-rich coconut milk spiked heavily with pungent red curry paste from Thailand. It is a soup-like curry with long reedy slivers of bamboo shoots and huge chunks of delicately-poached white chicken breasts. Steamed rice is served on the side. The curry can be poured over the rice or a little rice added to the curry, as you wish.

A soothing finale to this fast food feast, the Sticky Rice with egg custard, is superb. Both the grayish egg custard and sticky (glutinous) rice are steamed, then drizzled with a little coconut milk.

THAI SEAFOOD

17926 Highway 3 (at NASA Road 1)
Webster, Texas 77598
281/338-8712

Type of Cuisine: Seafood/Thai
Bar: Wine and Beer
Dress: Casual
Entertainment: No
Payment: All Major Credit Cards
Entrée Range: $9.99-$14.99
Recommended Dishes:
Appetizers: Combination Satae
Grilled Shrimp in Lime Sauce
Entrées: Seafood Combo Curry
Seafood Combo in Panaeng Curry
Tiger Cry
Pad Ga Pad (Chicken with Basil and Chiles)
Pad Thai Goong
Dessert: Thai Custard
Hours: Tuesday-Thursday, 11:00a.m.-3:00p.m., 5:00p.m.-10:00p.m.
Friday-Saturday, 11:00a.m.-3:00p.m., 5:00p.m.-11:00p.m.
Sunday, 11:30a.m.-9:00p.m.
(Closed Monday)
Reservations: Accepted

Until recently the great attraction of Thai food has been lost on me. I found that it lacked the subtlety of Vietnamese cooking and the infinite variety of Chinese cuisine. There was a certain sameness to the dishes. Too many were either cloyingly sweet or blistering hot. That was before I'd eaten at Thai Seafood. When I asked Visuth Sophonsiwont, the manager of the restaurant, what it is that distinguished its food from the multitude of other Thai restaurants, he said that it's because their style of cooking is simply more authentically Thai than most other restaurants he has sampled in Houston. He believes that if it's not 100%, then it is at least 90% the genuine article, a better average than the majority of local Thai restaurants which he considers tailored to American tastes. "I want to show American people exactly what real Thai food tastes like."

Visuth (pronounced Vee'-soo) is joined in this effort by his older brother and chef, Juk (pronounced "Chuck") and sister Nantarat, who owns the restaurant, but still lives in their native Bangkok and only visits once a year. A trained pastry chef himself, Visuth came to Houston in 1980 and worked at the Warwick, the (then) Remington and Four Seasons Hotels. Juk says he has cooked since he was a child, and began cooking professionally at their family restaurant in Bangkok straight out of University. In 1982, Juk was the chef at Thai Tastes in

Washington, D.C., but returned to Thailand to work again at the family restaurant. He says he left again because he couldn't stand the traffic in Bangkok. The three siblings opened Thai Seafood in November of 1993, in the unlikely location of Webster, Texas, in the corner of a strip center just where Highway 3 meets NASA Road 1 because, Visuth says, "There were too many Thai restaurants in Houston" and virtually none in that area.

Although there is a preponderance of seafood, the menu offers many of the same dishes you'll find at other Thai restaurants, only better. My favorite appetizers are the tart and refreshing Grilled Shrimp with Lime Sauce served chilled like a salad with sliced red onions, scallions, cilantro and garlic dressed with lime juice, the cream cheese and crabmeat filled Spring Solls, the fresh mint Spring Rolls; or the Satae. One of the best known Thai dishes, "satae," is actually a gift from their southern neighbors, Malaysia. I recommend ordering the Combination Satae. That way it's possible to sample pork, chicken, shrimp and beef – marinated separately, threaded onto bamboo skewers and grilled. The pieces of meat and shrimp are always meant to be first removed from their skewers (not always an easy task), dipped in the traditional peanut sauce made form crushed roasted peanuts, and eaten with the crisp, sweet, contrasting flavors of Thai cucumber salad.

Thailand is situated midway between China and India, and while many of their cooking techniques are Chinese in origin, they have India to thank for the popularity of curry in their cuisine. They use many of the same ingredients that Indians use for curry – tumeric, cumin, coriander and star anise – but they use them in a uniquely Thai way. There is at least one curry served with each complete meal in Thailand. My two favorite curries happen also to be the two best seafood dishes on the menu. The first, the Seafood Combo Curry is also a favorite of both Visuth and Juk. Not only is the mixture of seafood wonderful – crabmeat, shrimp, huge meaty sea scallops, New Zealand mussels still clinging to their shells, and squid – but also the sauce is extraordinary. While it is called a "curry" on the menu, the clearest presence in the powerfully-concentrated sauce is sweet basil, one of the staples of Thai cooking. My other favorite is also a combination of seafood, but this time with a Panaeng Curry. Like a velvet dress with spiked heels, this red curry has the assertive bite of ground Thai bird's eye chiles laced with ambrosial coconut milk and manages to be neither too hot nor too sweet. I'm sure they are happy to omit squid from either dish, but it is especially good here – unusually tender and smoky tasting.

As a departure from seafood, the dish called Tiger Cry is

worth a visit alone – a lean, perfect piece of beef tenderloin is marinated in Thai herbs, seared on a grill, sliced and placed, still warm, over shredded white cabbage and carrots so the juices drip down, flavor and wilt the salad. It is served with an electrifying sauce of lime juice, garlic, cilantro with a healthy measure of nam pla – Thai fish sauce, literally translated "fish water," that is as important to Thai cooking as its Vietnamese cousin, nuoc nam, is to them.

The Chicken Basil is excellent and is a perfect example of an herb being used as a vegetable in the Thai kitchen. There is also a generous studding of the incendiary scarlet Thai Bird's Eye chiles which add both color and heat to this intensely-flavored dish. (I'd stay away from these little red devils unless you haven't had a good cry in awhile.)

Hawked on practically every city street corner and in every village market in Thailand, the fried noodle stir-fry, Pad Thai, is as close as it gets to a national dish. In Thailand, the translucent rice noodles are soaked rather than boiled before the cooking process continues. According to Visuth, its wonderful, distinctly smoky flavor is achieved by first heating a small amount of vegetable oil in a pan until very hot and adding a little water just at the same time as the meat and noodles are added creating a small fire and a lot of smoke in the pan that's extinguished as the food is sautéed.

That toasty flavor is achieved in the preparation of the Combination Fried Rice. "Kin kao" or "eat rice" are the simple words used in Thailand to extend an invitation to dine well, and if either the combination fried rice or the soon-to-go-on-the-menu Thai Basil Fried Rice, were being offered, I'd come running. Highly seasoned with red chili paste and chock full of shrimp and tender forkfuls of pork and chicken, the combination rice is almost a meal in itself and closer to what we know as jambalaya in this part of the world than a traditional fried rice. The other excellent, but tamer, alternative is Thai basil fried rice perfumed with basil and served with a fried egg on top.

For dessert, the sweet glutinous rice offered with either Thai Custard or Mango serves as a salve to the savaged (but happy) taste buds. There is also as assortment of Smoothies to choose form made from freshly-squeezed juices.

Thai Seafood serves seventy people and does not allow smoking. The décor is welcoming, but sadly, the service leaves a lot to be desired. Visuth says that he is there most of the time, but one particular Friday night he was not, and the dining room was a rudderless ship with seemingly no one in charge. Their standards for the food are so high, I can only hope that they aspire to match them with truly professional service.

THIS IS IT

207 West Gray (at Taft)
Houston, Texas 77002
713/659-1608

Type of Cuisine: American/Southern Homestyle
Bar: No
Dress: Casual
Entertainment: No
Payment: All Major Credit Cards
Dinners: $6.50
Recommended Dishes:
Entrées: Barbecued Rib Ends
Oxtails
Baked Chicken
Great Southern-Style Vegetables
Dessert: All Cakes
Peach Cobbler
Breakfast: Pancakes
Grits
Ham
Biscuits
Hours: Breakfast: Monday-Sunday, 6:30a.m.-10:00a.m.
Lunch/Dinner: Monday-Thursday, 11:00a.m.-8:00p.m.
Friday-Saturday, 11:00a.m.-10:00p.m.
Sunday, 11:00a.m.-6:00p.m.
Reservations: Not Accepted

In 1959, when Frank and Mattie Jones were shown the little house at 1003 Andrews in the heart of the Fourth Ward, Mattie knew the search was over, "This is It!" she said. They knocked down walls, converted the garage into a kitchen and started a business that has become an institution in this town... "Soul Food at it's best" as it says on the takeout menu. This is not an exaggeration!

They were at that location until 1983 when they moved to 239 West Gray (at Taft). After twelve years, Frank Jones' grandson, Craig Joseph, and his wife Georgette, bought the property to build the present location at 207 West Gray, and moved in April 1995.

Although Mattie's gone, eighty-three-year-old Frank is still cooking (incredibly all night long from 5:30 in the evening until 10:00 the next morning) virtually the same menu that he has cooked for thirty-nine years (minus stuffed bell peppers and baked stuffed rock cornish game hens) with the assistance now of either Gladys Jackson or Craig Joseph.

Craig is a forty-year-old firefighter who says he and his wife of ten years, Georgette, thirty-five, an administrative secretary when they met, got involved because he couldn't bear to see the "business and everything his grandparents had put into it be sold to a stranger." Georgette tells me, "Craig was known as 'Cafe' or 'Cafe Craig' by all the kids because as a child he spent so much time at the restaurant in a bassinet, or propped up in a car seat at the cash register just like our son was!"

When he's not fighting fires, a job Craig says after eighteen years he "still loves and is able to do because of (his) grandfather's presence at the restaurant," he joins Georgette who pretty much runs the show. His mother is "mostly retired," but still makes an appearance when she's needed. Apart from Georgette's world-renowned peach cobbler, Craig credits his wife with how attractively the new location is decorated, and appreciates her guiding hand in all other aspects of operating the business. For her part, she firmly believes that they "have the best soul food in Houston. It's kind of rare to find a place where you can get a plate of food without having to worry about adding more salt or pepper...it's just perfect."

Craig agrees. "The secret to our success is how we season our food. Like my grandfather says, 'It's the seasoning!'" This is a task Frank Jones takes so seriously that he insists only he or Craig "do (their) own seasoning. Don't let anyone else do it."

They're right. The food is well-seasoned when it's meant to be seasoned, during the cooking process and not afterwards at the table.

This is homemade soul food to make any Southerner's heart sing. Go helpless with hunger, the portions are huge and you'll want to eat every bite. Georgette says, "Most people say they'd prefer a nap to going back to work" after tucking into, for instance, three generous slabs of what may be the best Meat Loaf in town (available Monday, Thursday and Saturday). Craig believes "it's the fresh chopped garlic that brings out the flavor in the beef," and the tomato sauce is especially good, although he says he prefers the creamy, fall-off-the-bone tender Turkey Wings (a special Tuesday, Thursday and Saturday).

Georgette's favorite dish is BBQ Rib Ends, meaty chunks of pork, the brisket end of the rib, barely attached to the bone, full of flavor and cooked until they've absorbed the sweet-hot barbecue sauce (fortunately, available every day).

I agree with Georgette, they're terrific, but my favorite dish is the one that Craig believes "made This Is It" – Oxtails – something Georgette says she had "never ever heard of before she met Craig." They are actually sliced beef tails browned, then braised to deeply delicious perfection with lots of chopped onions, garlic, bell pepper and celery. Craig says they are good enough to convert the uninitiated (or even the squeamish)! "I guarantee that if I let you try 'em, you're gonna want oxtails!

They're on the steam table in the same place every day." I think he believes there'd be a revolt if they weren't. Frank Jones told me they go through "300 pounds of oxtails a day. When we opened in 1959, I used to slice 'em myself and sold 'em for 89 cents a plate." (They're $6.50 now and come with a choice of three vegetables and the heavenly cornbread muffins.)

I recommend a heaping plate of the oxtails with their dense, rich brown gravy spooned over white rice, cabbage, seasoned with small chunks of good smoky bacon, and given more texture than usual by the addition of the darker, coarser outer leaves, and maybe the green beans cooked according to well-founded Southern tradition. (Not al denté!)

Of course, you could play it safe and go with the buttery, golden-crusted Baked Chicken or the classic Pepper Steak (Tuesdays, Fridays and Sundays). Both are wonderful.

Dessert is a must – not only Georgette's Peach Cobbler, but also a selection of unimproveable lushly moist cakes, all baked on the premises.

This Is It is open for breakfast seven days a week from 6:30 a.m. to 10:00 a.m. and is the only meal not served cafeteria-style. Everything is cooked-to-order and right on the mark from the well- seasoned Grits served with a little pool of butter floating on the top, to the perennial favorite, Pancakes. All eggs come with a choice of grilled pork chops, bacon, two kinds of sausage (pan or Chappel Hill Country), or slices of sweet, baked ham that found their way between two butter-soaked layers of a flaky biscuit on my plate.

When I asked the Josephs if they ever offer Chicken and Dumplings (something I momentarily mistook for chitterlings, a daily special, on the steam table) they said "occasionally," but that they are happy to prepare them for parties of ten or more with at least a day's notice.

This Is It may be the perfect source for Fried Turkey (available with 48 hours notice). My friends in Louisiana tell me that the tradition of frying turkeys began in the summer at crawfish boils in the country and not, as you would imagine, during the holidays, as the same kind of equipment is required for both tasks. I recommend ordering one for your next picnic, country or city outing!

TIO PEPE

5213 Cedar Street
Bellaire, Texas 77401
713/667-4409

Type of Cuisine: Spanish
Bar: Full
Dress: Casual
Entertainment: Flamenco Wednesday and Thursday 8:30p.m.
Guitar and Singer Friday and Saturday 7:30p.m.
Payment: All Major Credit Cards
Entrée Range: $8.95-$12.95
Recommended Dishes:
Appetizers: Tapas Variadas
Camarones al Ajo (Garlic Shrimp)
Chorizo
Croquetas de Pollo (Chicken Croquettes)
Tortilla Espanola (Spanish Omelet)
Entrées: Paella
Lamb Shanks (Special)
Zarzuela de Mariscos (Spanish Bouillabaisse)
Merluza a la Vasca (Basque Style Hake)
Hours: Lunch: Monday-Friday, 11:00a.m.-2:30p.m.
Dinner: Monday-Friday, 5:30p.m.-10:30p.m.
Saturday, 5:30p.m.-10:00p.m.
Sunday, 12:00p.m.-10:00p.m.
Reservations: Accepted

With a history as rich and textured as a Moorish tapestry, Spanish food and its regional specialties are brought to us in all their splendor seven days a week by Renaissance man, restauranteur Carlos Roda at his restaurant, Tio Pepe, in the city of Bellaire.

The menu represents all major points of interest on the Spanish culinary landscape from Gazpacho Andaluz (chilled tomato soup) to Paella, the glorious saffron-scented rice dish named for the pan in which it's prepared.

Carlos Roda took over Vittorio's Italian Restaurant near the corner of Rice Boulevard and Kirby in March of 1978 to open the first Tio Pepe with the sole objective of introducing Houston to the straightforward simplicity and exuberance of authentically prepared dishes from his native Spain. Tio Pepe was at this location for four years until 1982, when he relocated briefly to Westbury Square, and then made his final move in July, 1985, to Cedar Street between Bellaire Boulevard and Bissonnet. Carlos and his four partners renovated what had been Arno's Italian Restaurant to look typically Spanish, with white stucco walls and Moorish arches dividing the little dining areas. Most of his patrons are regulars. The restaurant has a cozy, neighborhood feel to it. From the beginning at the first Tio Pepe, Carlos has played guitar on Friday and Saturday nights and for the flamenco dancers who perform at 8:30 p.m. for about half an hour on Wednesday and Thursday nights. (Carlos recommends making a reservation and coming early on those nights to eat before the entertainment begins.) In addition to composing much of his own music, Carlos began writing fiction in 1970 and his first novel, "Walter and the Space Traveler" was published in 1995. It is science fiction, and now he says he's busy working on a western about the 1849 gold rush.

The menu has changed little in eighteen years except for the Castilian influence of current part-owner and chef, Manuel Martinez. He is from León, the ancient kingdom north of Madrid known as the "zona de los asados," the zone of roasts, because of their special talent for roasting local lamb and suckling pig and their ability to make especially good chorizo (Spanish sausage). It is fitting, therefore, that both freshly-made Chorizo and Roasted Lamb Shanks, a weekly special, are featured on the menu.

Fabada, a favorite dish from Asturia, the bitterly cold northwestern part of Spain, is a richly satisfying bean stew similar to the French cassoulet. It is enhanced with generous chunks of Serrano ham and chorizo and although it is listed as a soup, one could easily make a meal of it.

Another soup, Sopa de Ajo (garlic soup), is centuries old and is famous for its restorative powers after a late night out on the town. Of Castilian origin, the recipe varies from region to region, but three of the main ingredients – garlic, bread and olive oil – are constants in the Spanish kitchen. Whether it is "al ajo," usually meaning whole cloves or, "al ajillo" (chopped), garlic is the one constant in the Spanish kitchen as styles of cooking vary form region to region.

Along with paella, Gazpacho is one of the most universally familiar of all Spanish dishes. Made at Tio Pepe "with love and a desire for authenticity" according to Carlos, his is a faithful recreation of an Andalusian (southern) dish that predates the Romans in Spain. In its purest form, it's a sort of liquid salad composed of tomatoes, bell peppers, cucumbers, onions, celery, garlic (of course), olive oil, vinegar and day-old bread soaked in water and squeezed dry that gives it its wonderful thick texture. The ingredients are painstakingly pulverized, originally with a mortar and pestle and now in a food processor or blender, and served chilled. Although it is eaten in the winter as well, it is considered a nourishing, thirst-quenching staple in the summer months in Spain.

You may want to begin your evening by ordering a pitcher of Sangria. "Sangria" is Spanish for "bleeding," as the main ingredient is red wine sweetened with sugar, spiked with triple sec, brandy, rum and club soda, with pieces of apples and oranges floating among the ice cubes. It is fruity and refreshing, complements this intensely-flavored food well, and is far stronger than it tastes. If sangria isn't your cup of tea, my two favorite Spanish wines, Marques de Riscal and Marques de Caceres, have the depth of flavor and body to stand up admirably to this emphatically-seasoned, lusty style of cooking.

All of the tapas (appetizers) are excellent and are perfect to share among the table with your sangria, from the number one seller Camarones al Ajo (garlic shrimp), to the Croquetas de Pollo – crunchy little deep fried pillows (croquettes) of ground chicken. Carlos' favorite is the Tapas Variadas, a combination of Serrano-style ham, manchego cheese and small sautéed disks of chorizo meant to be eaten with bread. I would also order a Tortilla Española as an appetizer. It is not listed on the dinner menu at all, but can be found under the lunch specials as "Spanish omelette." This tortilla has nothing in common with its Mexican cousin except the Latin word "torte," meaning round cake. It is an omelette made with browned slices of potato (and sometimes onion) and is eaten occasionally hot for breakfast, but usually cut in wedges or small squares and served at room temperature as a snack or as an appetizer with drinks. According to legend, the tortilla dates back at least four hundred years and was invented by a peasant to feed a hungry king.

Paella (pronounced py-ay'-yuh) as a recipe, originated in Valencia on the eastern coast of Spain only two centuries ago – a fairly recent development considering that rice has been a staple of the Iberian diet since the 9th century when the Arabs introduced it into the province of Valencia on land formerly irrigated by the Romans. Purists maintain that the only true paella is made outdoors over an open fire of vine cuttings no larger than the exact circumference of the width of the wide shallow pan known as a "paella." The ingredients vary from province to province using the seafood, game, or vegetables that are indigenous to the area, but it is always made with short grain Spanish rice, an intensely-flavored broth and saffron – the exotic, wildly expensive spice of Arab origin used to both flavor and color the rice golden yellow.

There are three varieties of paella to choose from at Tio Pepe; Valenciana with chicken and rice; Marinera with seafood and rice; and my personal favorite, the first listed simply on the menu as Paella with chicken, seafood and pork. They are happy to add chorizo for those who want it (I do!) or lobster which adds considerably to the price of the dish. It is moist, full of flavor, and an accurate recollection of the genuine article. As it takes at least thirty minutes for the rice to absorb the flavorful stock, you might order it at the same time as your sangria and tapas. Paella can also be prepared "to go."

As proud as Carlos is of the paella, he says his favorite entrée after the lamb shanks, is Zarzuela de Mariscos – an earthy mixture of shellfish and seafood cooked in a vibrant tomato-based sauce and served in a shallow earthenware casserole. This Catalonian specialty should be eaten like bouillabaisse – first, by removing all shells from the lobster, clams and mussels and then adding a little saffron rice to the dish as you go along.

Another favorite of both Carlos' and mine is the Merluza a la Vasca. Merluza is Spain's most popular fish – hake, a white fish with a flaky texture and a buttery, delicate flavor. "A la Vasca" means in the Basques style with butter, olive oil, garlic, onions, fish stock and lots of shellfish served in its own casserole, like the zarzuela, and eaten much the same way.

Flan (caramel custard) is practically the national dessert of Spain and while it's very good at Tio Pepe, the very un-Spanish citrusy Bread Pudding was even better.

Carlos' old friend Vittorio convinced him when he opened Tio Pepe that he must offer some choices other than Spanish food, so there is a list of dishes under "continental cuisine" on the menu that includes, among other things, steaks and a couple of Italian pasta dishes. I heard such raves about the Spaghetti with Meat Sauce that I had to try it and it was fabulous. Italian/Bolognese with a Spanish accent!

TOMMY'S PATIO CAFE

2555 Bay Area Boulevard
Houston, Texas 77058
281/480-2221

Type of Cuisine: American/Eclectic
Bar: Full
Dress: Casual
Entertainment: Live Music Wednesday 5:30p.m.-8:30p.m.
Friday-Saturday 7:30p.m.-11:00p.m.
Payment: All Major Credit Cards
Entrée Range: $10.95 – $19.95
Recommended Dishes:
Appetizers: Crab Cakes
Oysters Rockefeller
Oysters Bienville
Oysters Zanelli
Good Daily Specials
Shrimp Remoulade
Entrées: Herbed Salmon
Blackened Tuna Etouffé
Seasonal Vegetable Plate (Grilled)
Hours: Monday-Thursday, 11:00a.m.-10:00p.m.
Friday, 11:00a.m.-11:00p.m.
Saturday, 4:00p.m.-11:00p.m.
Sunday, 12:00p.m.-10:00p.m.
Reservations: Accepted

Tom Tollett has quite a fan club. Loyal devotées enthusiastically describe his restaurant in Clear Lake as "the nicest restaurant in the area." They rave about the atmosphere, the warmly professional greeting by general manager, Bill Nix, when they arrive for dinner, the soothing dark woods, and the crisply starched off-white tablecloths and napkins, but especially, the food. I just had to go see what the shouting was about.

At first glance, the menu looks like a case of rounding up the usual suspects: Stuffed Jalapeños (did somebody pass a law requiring restaurants to serve these?), Fried Crabfingers, Gumbo and stuffed or unstuffed Fried Shrimp, but at closer inspection, wedged between these perennial favorites, are Escargots cloaked in fresh spinach leaves and baked in shallot butter, a grilled or steamed Vegetable Plate groaning with an artful arrangement of seasonal vegetables which can include sautéed corn off the cob and a cheesy, garlicy spinach soufflé, and one of the best salmon dishes I've tasted recently, the Herbed Salmon. It is a dry-seasoned and seared filet of salmon placed warm on top of seven or eight kinds of baby greens barely wilted with a little olive oil and chicken broth, and topped with a roasted shallot vinaigrette. The dish doesn't just sound good, it's perfectly executed. Like the excellent Blackened Tuna Étouffée, it's served medium rare (still pink on the inside) the way it should be (unless otherwise requested).

This is what I think distinguishes Tommy's from his competitors. It's his ability to combine classic dishes and time-honored techniques learned from his early apprenticeship at one of the original Don's in Lafayette, Louisiana, with the most current and best food trends. For instance, a tangy Creole mustard-based Shrimp Remoulade is perched on top of a mountain of no fewer than fourteen exotic greens most of which are unpronounceable. (He says you get a free salad if you can name *ten* of them!)

My favorite dish may be the Crab Cakes. Mostly crabmeat, they are cooked to a turn and arrive floating on a crouton in a pool of beurre blanc – a classic French reduction of butter, shallots and white wine – and topped off with a few shards of fresh imported parmesan cheese. Heaven. My second choice of the hot appetizers is the Oysters Rockefeller, Bienville, and Zannelli (with garlic butter and parmesan cheese) which can be ordered individually or my favorite way, a mixture of all three.

A native of Baton Rouge, Tollett says the Oysters Rockefeller recipe has forty different ingredients and that he learned how to make the dish twenty-five years ago working along side Peepee, an elderly Cajun woman at Don's. "In 1974, when I started working at Don's, she was probably in her late seventies and had already been working at the restaurant for forty-five years. Many of the recipes I use now are derived from Peepee. The things she taught me to do are all very traditional. I've sort of stayed with the same concept, not only always using the freshest ingredients, but using old traditional methods in how we cook them. Today we use more reductions. Back then we used roux for everthing which made much hardier sauces. We want to make the sauces lighter now. Although she barely spoke English, she generously passed on many of the big secrets to me. She was a super influence in my life."

From Lafayette he joined some friends in Clear Lake in 1976 and after a brief stint as executive chef of Lakewood Yacht Club, he worked in a dual capacity as both chef and host for four years at Jimmy Walker's when it was in its heyday. Shortly after the neighboring Flying Dutchman opened in 1981, he was hired to work there as chef. His proudest accomplishment in his thirteen years at the Flying Dutchman and the adjoining Brass Parrot is the initiation of what he calls the "fresh seafood program."

As incredible as it seems, Tollett says, "In those days, no one was serving fresh seafood, it was all frozen. After six months at the Flying Dutchman, I started buying local seafood – tuna, flounder, redfish, snapper or drum, whatever was available. I'd buy it fresh either off the docks or from dealers who were really handling only the best. Crabmeat was the biggest thing. They had all been using frozen crabmeat. In Louisiana, you didn't know any different. You only bought fresh seafood and only when it was in season. That's one of the reasons our menu at Tommy's is the way it is. We change from crawfish to crabmeat as the season changes. That just makes sense to me. We'll have crab until January and then I'll change to crawfish." (For instance, those fabulous crab cakes will become crawfish cakes as one season gives way to the next.) Tollett says that seafood is purchased fresh every morning and that he doesn't even own a freezer.

This dogged devotion to freshness coupled with the inspired ingenuity of chef Mark Baumgartner, makes an excellent case for trying one of the many daily specials. A recent soup of the day, Roasted Snapper Bisque, was a heady concoction of sweet corn, red snapper and heavy cream sparked by the unexpected addition of liquid crab boil for added heat. Tollett claims that specials account for as much as 40% of their business. On a recent visit, he had bought live Soft Shell Crabs and offered them as a special one night topped with lump crabmeat and artichoke hollandaise, and sautéed on a bed of fresh spinach (Florentine) the next. Tollett says the other chefs working with Baumgartner in the kitchen are all students at various culinary institutes and that the specials "give the chefs a chance to use not only the freshest seasonal ingredients, but in the most creative ways, sometimes composing a dish they've been thinking about all week." Enthusiasm appears to be the order of the day at Tommy's. The service is excellent. Tollett believes, "They enjoy working here because they know we're so enthusiastic about what we're doing."

Bread lovers, this is your place. Served warm with sweet whipped butter, the Italian Country Loaf is baked twice a day fresh for lunch, then for dinner. It has developed such a following that they have to bake extra to keep up with the demand for those who want to buy whole loaves to take home. As good as it is, I'd leave room for dessert.

The two very best are Homemade Cinnamon Ice Cream, either served on its own or accompanying Carrot Cake, and the sensational deep dish Sweet Potato-Pecan Pie with a buttery shortbread crust offered room temperature with a spoonful of whipping cream or warmed with a scoop of vanilla ice cream.

The entertainment on Wednesdays (5:30 p.m.–8:00 p.m.) and Saturday nights (7:30 p.m.–11:00 p.m.) is especially good, and adds alot to the atmosphere, and deserves special comment.

This is an entirely different kind of dining experience for the area. After watching the crowds come and go on weekends and seasonally at the Flying Dutchman, he says he "wanted to have a local restaurant that would be supported year round, a casual place where people could come in comfortable attire, however they wanted to come, and eat great food at a reasonable price. I wanted to do something the local people would appreciate." Apparently he succeeded.

TOMOKAZU

6690 Southwest Freeway (at Hillcroft)
Houston, Texas 77074
281/334-9898

Type of Cuisine: Japanese
Bar: Wine and Beer
Dress: Casual
Entertainment: No
Payment: All Major Credit Cards
Entrée Range: $5.50-$11.95
Recommended Dishes:
All Sushi: especially, Crazy Maki
Crawfish Maki
Spider Maki
Appetizers: Tomokazu Platter
Beef Sashimi
Ika Teriyaki (Grilled Squid)
Seaweed Salad
Age Siumai (Dumplings)
Harumaki (Spring Rolls)
Dessert: Banana Tempura
Hours: Monday-Thursday, 11:00a.m.-11:00p.m.
Friday, 11:00a.m.-12:00p.m.
Saturday, 12:00a.m.-12:00p.m.
Sunday, 4:00p.m.-11:00p.m.
Reservations: Accepted

"Irasshaimase!" The word "welcome" washes like a wave across Tomokazu from owner Martina Yang, to the wait staff, to the sushi chefs when you enter. It feels great to be there. That's part of Yang's plan. "I want customers to feel at home; to feel welcome like they are our friends. To me, that's at least as important as the quality of the food."

I'm happy to report that the "quality of the food" (and service) is excellent. Tomokazu is a welcome, fresh face on the local sushi scene.

As the thermometer begins to clear 90°, sushi, sashimi and even the delicate, barely-cooked Japanese dishes, are the ideal antidote to the summer heat.

Those who eat sushi and sashimi will find their usual favorites, impeccably-fresh and well prepared with improvements in some cases. For instance, the California Roll is made without mayonnaise and with a choice of the standard imitation crab ($6.50 or $7.50 for "in/out") or fresh Alaskan King Crab ($15.95). There are especially good renditions of the popular newfangled, nontraditional, Americanized rolls (or makis) like Crazy Maki, Crawfish Maki and Spider Maki.

The Crazy Maki is a colorful kaleidoscope composed of

sushi rice, shrimp tempura and "very spicy tuna." Hold the wasabi. They're not kidding about the "very spicy" part. It is hot, even by Texas standards and absolutely delicious. The Crawfish Maki is another winner, and according to Yang, even more popular as a hand roll "because the soft shell crawfish is left whole."

The winner for me in the non-raw sweepstakes is the Spider Maki made with light, exquisitely-fried soft shells crabs. Crisp, brown legs gangle out from the neatly rolled and cut maki looking every bit like the "spider" that someone was reminded of when they named this new favorite "spider" maki. (Any of these maki's are an ideal choice for the novice or anyone who's squeamish about eating raw fish.)

The Japanese believe that the best way to cook a fish is not to. In keeping with this notion, purists should enjoy the fresh Conch at Tomokazu. It is best when eaten raw, sliced simply as sashimi. Yang says that her source for this unusual treat is a friend in Rhode Island who picks the best conch for her right off the boats as they come in, and sends them down to her directly.

Not a sushi eater? There are more than thirty-two other reasons to eat at Tomokazu, all listed as appetizers.

Starting at the very top, the Beef Sashimi is lean, "raw" beef sliced razor-thin and fanned out on the plate decoratively with almost transparent slices of lemon. It tastes vaguely smoky because it has been first seasoned, then grilled momentarily, so technically it's just very rare and not raw. The cold, crunchy, slightly-nutty flavor of Seaweed Salad goes especially well with Beef Sashimi.

Shiny, dark green strips of Wakame – the highly nutritious curly leafed Japanese seaweed has a pleasant, mild flavor, a wonderful texture and was pronounced "delicious" by my twelve-year-old niece. So, I would encourage anyone to give it a try.

Yang says that her favorite appetizer isn't even listed on the menu. Ika Teriyaki is Japanese – squid basted with rich, brown teriyaki sauce, scored on the grill, then cut into rings.

The Tomokazu Platter is a substantial offering of six of the kitchen's most successful appetizers. The assortment includes flawless Shrimp Tempura; Yakitori – glazed, skewered chunks of chicken breasts and scallions; marinated, fried Chicken Wings that are so good Yang says that she has one customer who orders them by the dozen; Beef Rolls (known at other restaurants as "negima") are rib eye steak rolled around scallions and shredded carrots, brushed with teriyaki sauce and grilled; spring rolls listed elsewhere on the menu as Harumaki – the elegantly simple Japanese version filled with crabmeat and carrot enclosed in a thin, crisp spring roll skin and served with a puckery, lemon-based dipping sauce; and last but not least, Siumai.

Age Siumai are the delicate little party-hat-shaped dumplings that I adore. The two types of dumplings regularly available at Japanese restaurants are filled with roughly the same mixture of finely ground pork and shrimp, but shaped and cooked so differently that each has a distinctive flavor all its own.

I highly recommend all of the aforementioned, and they can be ordered individually if the platter sounds like too much of an undertaking.

One appetizer I didn't try, that Yang says is a big seller, is the Stuffed Mushrooms. The mushrooms are stuffed with a mixture of ground shrimp and crab meat, dipped in tempura batter and deep fried. Sounds great, and I don't remember seeing them on any other Japanese menus in town.

Yang gives a lot of credit to Tomokazu's head sushi chef, Gary Yeung. She praises not only his skill at choosing the best, freshest fish, but also his incredible flexibility as a chef. Like Burger King, their motto could easily be, "Have it your way!" because they have a casual, made-to-order policy with many regular customers. "He can do anything. If we have the ingredients, he's happy to do it. We have one customer who comes in, she says, 'I'm so bored. I always get the same hand roll.' So, we took her favorite hand roll, dipped the whole thing in tempura batter, and then deep fried it. It turned out really nice. She loved it! Now, every time she comes in, she orders it."

What a novel, delicious sounding idea! Yang is quick to point out that this works best if the contents of the hand roll are already cooked rather than raw. For instance, Unagi, the sublime smoked, then grilled eel was used because it was the customer's favorite, but I can think of lots of fabulous options...soft shell crawfish, shrimp or even crab meat!

Tempura cloaked, Deep Fried Ice Cream is a fine way to end the meal. But my idea of heaven is Banana Tempura – crisp, bitesized nuggets of fried banana are placed still warm around a scoop of vanilla or mango ice cream.

UGO'S ITALIAN GRILL

8800 Katy Freeway, Suite 109
Houston, Texas 77024
713/365-0101

Type of Cuisine: Italian
Bar: Wine and Beer
Dress: Casual
Entertainment: No
Payment: All Major Credit Cards
Entrée Range: $6.95-$11.95
Recommended Dishes:
Appetizers: Calamaretti Fritti
Chele di Granchio di Pomodoro (Crab Fingers)
Funghi Portobello alla Griglia (Grilled Portobello)
Entrées: Pizza: Pepperoni
Sausage and Pepper
Lasagne
Cannelloni
Porcini Ravioli
Pollo in Umido con Penne
Pollo alla Francese
Dessert: Bomba
Strawberry White Chocolate Cheesecake
Chocolate and Italian Cream Cake
Hours: Monday-Thursday, 11:00a.m.-10:00p.m.
Friday, 11:00a.m.-11:00p.m.
Saturday, 4:00p.m.-11:00p.m.
Sunday, 12:00p.m.-9:00p.m.
Reservations: Accepted

"Real Italian food – good, fast and at a reasonable price," sounds like a tall order, but this is how owners Marty Vogt and Pat Lindsey characterize the year-old Ugo's Italian Grill. I'm happy to say that they have succeeded on all counts.

While some dishes are better than others, Ugo's – named for Lindsey's Italian maternal grandfather – combines some of the considerable pleasures of Lindsey's restaurant, Enzo's in Clear Lake, and Mario's Flying Pizza (the one on Highway 146 in Seabrook) owned by Vogt.

Both men credit talented Sicilian chef Vincenzo Floridia with the fine quality and authenticity of many of the recipes. Another secret to their success is a commitment to using the freshest, best possible ingredients for the simple, homey dishes on Ugo's short menu.

For instance, huge crab fingers the size of your thumb are rendered almost sweet when sautéed with freshly diced tomatoes, garlic, white wine, homemade chicken broth and a little of the hearty, well-seasoned house marinera sauce. "It's the crab!" Lindsey claims, "The trick is to sauté it quickly and to let the flavor of the crab come through!"

As good as the Chele di Granchio al Pomodoro (crab fingers) are, the ethereal Calamaretti Fritti is just one of several "bests" to be found at Ugo's. The rings of calamari are unusually tender, but the key is the buttermilk batter that just barely covers them. There is marinera sauce for dipping, but anything more than a little squeeze of lemon is too much.

Another fine choice, meaty Portobello Mushrooms are marinated quickly in vinaigrette then cooked on the grill. They are served on greens with sweet strips of roasted red bell peppers.

The same flame-roasted red bell peppers are puréed with a little heavy cream, garlic, and basil for the velvety, bright-orange soup – Crema di Pepperoni Dolci. The Insalata di Cesare (Caesar salad), made with tender young hearts of Romaine lettuce, has a rich, eggy dressing with enough garlic to keep Dracula at bay.

Whichever appetizer you sample, do not miss ordering at least a small pizza to split among fellow diners at the table. It is fabulous. The crust is excellent – light and crisp and, although there are the standard assortment of toppings to choose from, it's hard to improve upon the simple perfection of a well-crafted pepperoni pizza. "It is the universal favorite," as Vogt says. (Another "best.")

There are three Ugo's Signature Pizzas. The Sausage and Pepper runs a close second to the pepperoni in my affections. Juicy, fennel-flavored Italian sausage made exclusively for Ugo's (and Enzo'a and Mario's) is the star of this show. It is sautéed in olive oil with garlic, peppers and onions, spooned onto the crust and sprinkled with a very little shredded mozzarella and a lot more briny, fresh feta cheese.

This superb sausage is wisely used as the centerpiece of what gets my vote as Houston's best plate of Lasagne. In a classic case of "the whole is only as great as the sum of its parts," the lasagne at Ugo's is made with excellent Bolognese sauce, a tiny bit of ricotta, fine imported mozzarella, thin layers of minced sausage and – this is the important part – paper-thin sheets of delicate homemade pasta. Heaven. Happily, it is available for your next gathering at the incredibly reasonable price of $34.99 for a half pan (enough for ten people) or $64.99 for a full pan (which feeds as many as twenty).

The fragile, melt-in-your-mouth sheets of homemade pasta are cut into squares and folded around a subtle filling of minced beef, chicken, spinach, onions, blanketed in tomato sauce, and mozzarella cheese and baked for a refined classic Cannelloni – my second favorite pasta dish on the menu.

Those seeking something a little lighter should go for the Porcini Ravioli. A signature dish of Lindsey's invention, sizable triangles of fresh pasta are filled with an intense purée of porcini mushrooms and tossed in olive oil with sliced mushrooms, julienned pieces of sun-dried tomatoes and finally, topped with a crumbling of fresh feta.

Among the pastas not made from scratch, Bucatini, a sturdy spaghetti with a hole in the center, stands up well to the luscious basil-flecked, cream-based sauce with plump sea scallops and shrimp.

In a joint decision to keep Ugo's menu as simple (and reasonable) as possible, there are no beef or veal dishes. There are, however, six preparations of chicken breasts to consider on the "Chicken Menu." The best is the highlighted Pollo in Umido Con Penne.

The "humid" chicken is strips of white chicken breasts in a gutsy tomato sauce seasoned with lots of fresh rosemary, basil, sage, thyme and garlic, supported by a bed of penne pasta. A nice, hearty dish.

The Pollo alla Francese gets points for technique. An exceptionally moist chicken breast is cloaked in the same light buttermilk batter as the calamari and sautéed in a little butter, chicken broth, white wine and lemon. "The trick is to keep it real simple," Lindsey adds, "and not use too much lemon!" The chicken shares the plate with a side of Spaghetti Marinera. Vegetables really are not featured at Ugo's, but Lindsey says they are happy to sauté some spinach for anyone who asks. (The Pollo alla Francese is a good candidate for this.)

There is a short fine selection of (very) well-priced Italian wines. Ugo's Italian Grill is built a bit more for speed than for comfort. So don't expect tons of atmosphere or candlelight on the tables. Nevertheless, I am touched by the expert service and the amount of effort that is put into the food.

At least three desserts were down-right sublime and all are made in-house. (You have no idea how unusual this is these days!) The Bomba Mascarpone is a memory that lingers. It is alternating layers of chocolate and hazelnut-flavored mascarpone cheese all topped off with French pastry cream. The Strawberry White Chocolate Cheesecake is a very close second. Fresh strawberries are baked and wedged between spoonfuls of cream cheese lightened with melted white chocolate. The bottom graham cracker crust is divine, but so is the thin layer of toasted almonds on top. Finally, moist Italian lady fingers are used around the perimeter to support multiple tiers of Chocolate and Italian Cream Cake. All of these cakes can also be purchased whole for $25.00 each.

VAN LOC VIETNAMESE AND CHINESE RESTAURANT

3010 Milam
Houston, Texas 77006
713/528-6441

Type of Cuisine: Vietnamese/Chinese
Bar: Wine and Beer
Dress: Casual
Entertainment: No
Payment: American Express, MasterCard, Visa
Entrée Range: $3.95-$15.00
Recommended Dishes:
Appetizers: Imperial Rolls (fried)
Spring Rolls
Summer Delight Salad
Entrées: Fried Flour Cake with Egg
Special Thin Vermicelli with Charcoal Broiled Pork
Filet Mignon Chunk Steak with Lettuce and Onion
Salted Fried Squid "Vietnamese Style"
Tofu in Hot Chili and Lemon Grass
Hours: Sunday-Thursday, 9:00a.m.-11:30p.m.
Friday-Saturday, 9:00a.m.-12:30a.m.
Reservations: Not Accepted

Houstonian Jacob Johnson grew up in the restaurant business. "My father opened his first restaurant, the old Main Street Grill, here in Houston in 1927. I'm sure he's laughing at me now because I never intended to follow him into the business!"

He probably wouldn't have either if he hadn't married Kim Phan. "It was about a year after Kim and I were married. My mother-in-law was working down the street at Mai's. She said 'Let's open a restaurant.' I said, 'Well, all you need is a building.' So, we bought this one and opened Van Loc on August 22, 1984."

"It's been a family deal from day one – my wife, her two younger sisters, a few cousins, her dad, and of course, Mama, my chief cook. Nothing goes out of the kitchen unless she knows about it."

Wow. This means the nearly two hundred recipes on Van Loc's Vietnamese/Chinese menu all originated with "Mama." A daunting assortment of dishes that range from the pristine perfection of a citrusy Summer Delight Salad (#167) to the intense, earthy flavors of Short Spare Ribs cooked in Fish Sauce (#107).

My favorite dish of all hadn't even made it to the ever-expanding menu, although I was assured that it would. Fried

Flour Cake with Egg topped the list of daily specials scrawled on a black board. Johnson was surprised that I liked it so much. "Normally just Vietnamese customers eat that." If that's true, it's only because, as my grandmother used to say, "They just don't know what's good."

This dish is so wonderful that I insisted on ordering it on all subsequent visits, in addition to the many other specialties we had left to sample. Rice flour, made from whole grain rice, scallions, a little pork and whole eggs are mixed together and actually steamed rather than fried. It arrives before you a good six inches in diameter with crisped, curled edges of egg white and a dipping sauce of sweetened soy sauce. I think of this as Vietnamese comfort food.

Let's start with the appetizers. Van Loc owns bragging rights to some of the best "rolls" in the business, whether you opt for Spring Rolls (#1) or Imperial Rolls (#3). Johnson says that's because, "We don't make them ahead of time and let them dry out the way other people do. There are two women in the kitchen whose sole job it is to make spring rolls as they're ordered. So they are always fresh, soft and moist."

They are picture perfect. Orange and white striped bodies of shrimp show attractively through transluscent, tightly-packed rice paper. "I get these shrimp from Taiwan because Gulf shrimp are just white when they're cooked, and I think these look better!"

I usually find the accompanying peanut sauce too cloying and heavy for what amounts to salad in a gossamer thin wrapper, but Van Loc's is exceptional and made in such secrecy that Johnson tells me, "Mama arrives early in the morning to make the sauce when nobody is here to see what she's doing."

The fried Vietnamese egg rolls, Imperial Rolls (#3), are an impeccable reading of what is considered the national dish of Vietnam. They are hot, parchment crisp, and fried to order. Veterans of Vietnamese cuisine know that they are meant to be nestled in a piece of lettuce with sprigs of coriander, sweet basil, and mint, folded, and dipped in nuoc cham – the pert, garlicky, lime juice based sauce that tastes of the sea and is indispensable to the Vietnamese table as salt and pepper is in the West.

It is just this contrast of flavors and textures that makes a Vietnamese meal so distinctive; the cold, the hot, the soft, the crisp, the sweet and the salty. The Bún or Vermicelli dishes exemplify these qualities. These northern Vietnamese specialties are Van Loc's most popular dishes. Whether you opt for pork (my choice), beef (the #1 favorite of the Vietnamese) or chicken, crisp lean ribbons of meat are smoky and sweet from being charcoal broiled and are supported by a nest of thin rice or vermicelli noodles and topped with a tangle of crunchy fried onions. Each serving is rimmed by slivers of cucumber, carrots, mint and coriander, and each bite is meant to be constructed on a piece of lettuce, or rice paper if you order #73, the platter – apparently more popular at dinner – or a bowlful, #47. Warning – this dish is highly addictive. Johnson tells me that he has one couple who've been coming "four or five times a week for fourteen years, since we opened and ordering the same thing – #73 Charcoal Broiled Pork and Vermicelli." Although, he adds, "Most Americans order it with chicken. But, I'm a meat eater."

He says his favorite dish of all is #117 Filet Mignon with Lettuce and Tomato – a combination of flavors so remarkable that I can barely describe it without getting in the car and driving over there to eat it. Tender chunks of beef tenderloin are stir fried rare with whole, sweet nutty cloves of garlic and pieces of browned scallions. The whole divine mixture is then spooned onto a platter of lettuce, thick, juicy beefsteak tomatoes and topped with nearly-transparent rings of white onion. The hot contents of the wok, juices and all, wilts and flavors the onions, tomatoes, and lettuce making it a platter that returns to the kitchen clean. It is served with a superfluous shallow saucer of freshly squeezed lemon juice flavored with salt and pepper for dipping, but why trifle with perfection?

The lemon/salt/pepper dipping sauce does come in handy with the crisp-skinned, mahogany-brown Roasted Quail (#164). A popular pastime in Vietnam is to eat these delectable little birds by hand as a snack and wash them down with a cold lager of beer under a shady tree.

Another uniquely Vietnamese dish I loved was Short Spare Ribs cooked in fish sauce (#107). This tastes a lot better than it sounds. Pork ribs are hacked into tiny one inch pieces then caramelized quickly with brown sugar, onions, garlic, and seasoned, rather than "cooked in" nuoc mam, the savory Vietnamese sauce made from fermented tiny anchovies that makes Vietnamese cooking so memorable.

The real standout among the many seafood offerings was the Salted Fried Squid (#153). At Kim Johnson's suggestion, I asked for it "Vietnamese style," and I am glad I did. Curled bodies of baby squid are lightly coated in rice flour, deep fried, then wok-seared with slices of jalapeno peppers, whole garlic cloves and scallion pieces. Another winner.

The aforementioned Summer Delight (#167) or Seafood Delight (#168) would satisfy anyone looking for a light, but fiercely-flavored lunch (or dinner). Since it's hot in Vietnam and they are keen on salads, I was surprised when Johnson said they just added them to the menu in the last couple of years by popular demand of American customers. The array of seafood in both salads includes jelly fish, but not so you'd notice. It adds an interesting texture and almost no flavor at all, so don't be put off by it.

I never miss ordering the slightly bitter Chinese Broccoli with Oyster Sauce so I was delighted to see that on the menu. Van Loc has a lot of vegetarian customers and Kim actually coaxed me into ordering a tofu dish equally popular, she said, with vegetarians and non-vegetarians – Fried Tofu in Hot Chili and Lemon Grass (#182). It was great. Bronzed squares of tofu acted as perfect little sponges absorbing the spicy, red pepper-flecked, aromatic sauce. (I did notice that there is a chicken dish prepared with the exact same sauce for the tofu phobic – #96.)

The Phô (pronounce "fa") or beef noodle soup (#15) is as fine as you're likely to find anywhere. The broth is well-flavored and deeply satisfying, the rice noodles appropriately al denté, and the slices of beef, trimmed of all fat and cooked medium rare. It is the national soup of Vietnam and always considered a meal in itself, as popular for breakfast as any other time of the day.

What does "Van Loc" mean? Johnson laughs and says, "Some say it means 'much luck,' and some say it doesn't mean much of anything." To their many devoted fans, both Asian and American, it means "reliably great food."

THE VILLAGE BREWERY AND RESTAURANT

2415 Dunstan
Houston, Texas 77005
713/524-4677

Type of Cuisine: American/Eclectic
Bar: Full
Dress: Casual
Entertainment: Orchid Lounge next door
Payment: All Major Credit Cards Accepted
Entrée Range: $8.95-$16.95
Recommended Dishes:
Appetizers: Crabmeat Stuffed Portabello Mushrooms
Fried Calamari
Chicken Wings
Caesar Salad
Entrées: Stuffed Filet Mignon
Bone-In-Ribeye
Cedar Plank Pork Chops
Seared Beef over Capellini
Cheese Ravioli
Dessert: All Cakes
Hours: Tuesday-Wednesday, 11:00a.m.-12:00a.m.
(Kitchen until 11:00p.m.)
Thursday, 11:00a.m.-2:00a.m. (Kitchen until 12:00a.m.)
Friday-Saturday, 11:00a.m.-4:00a.m. (Kitchen until 12:00a.m.)
Sunday, 11:00a.m.-10:00p.m.
(Closed Monday)
Reservations: Accepted

Manly food with finesse is how I'd describe the menu since Jim Florence took over The Village Brewery and Restaurant in May 1997. The oldest among eight existing brew pubs in the Greater Houston Area has fine hamburgers, a few surprises, and a humdinger of a chef in young Adam Gonzalez.

Gonzalez says that when he sat down with Florence, general manager Marcus Caldwell and brewmaster Max Miyamoto to restructure the menu, their objective was to improve the quality of the existing burgers and best-selling appetizers, and incorporate beer into the preparation of some new dishes (and accompanying sauces) whenever possible. "There's no question that's what makes our menu special," Gonzalez says.

"Max Miyamoto helped me a lot to understand which beers would go best with which dishes. Also, the beers (like Houston Wheat) that we use in our cooking are unhopped beers. The advantage of having a brewery here is that we can pull some of the wort – raw beer flavor – our before it hits the hopping stage. What Max taught me was that the more hopped beer boils, the more bitterness comes out."

The precedent for cooking with beer dates back at least as far as "Le Guide Culinaire," written in 1903 by the lauded father of French cuisine, Auguste Escoffier. I like to think that he would smile warmly that among the chicken wings and the expertly-fried calamari is Crabmeat Stuffed Portabello Mushrooms with Beer Blanc Sauce.

It is a successful adaptation of a classic French sauce, beurre blanc ("white butter"), where beer is added to a reduction of vinegar, white wine and chopped shallots before cold pieces of butter are whisked in.

Meaty portabello mushrooms are marinated overnight in balsamic vinegar, red wine, rosemary, garlic, salt and fresh cracked pepper, stacked in a pan, baked in the oven, then scored on the grill. The stuffing is composed of fresh lump crabmeat, garlic and scallions. A little mozzarella cheese is melted over the top. The plate is drizzled with warm beer blanc sauce, then garnished with a perky black bean relish – black beans tossed with cool, crunchy pico de gallo.

It is impressive. But so is the Stuffed Filet Mignon with Beernaise Sauce. Gonzalez tells me that he invented the dish during his tenure as the evening sous chef at the now-defunct Moose Café. He assembles the dish "like a Napoleon," he says, in layers, starting by splitting an eight ounce filet mignon (of spectacular quality, I might add) in half, grilling it to order, stuffing it with a sauté of chopped garlic and parsley flavored chopped portabello and domestic mushrooms lightly bound with Japanese bread crumbs. The top half of the filet is then napped with a tart tarragon (and beer) flavored béarnaise sauce. The Stuffed Filet Mignon – like all eight entrées – comes with good, old-fashioned garlic mashed potatoes, and a seasonal vegetable, but I think the thin, golden pommes frites-style French fries – are an even better match with the filet. (The best idea of all is to ask for a little extra "beernaise" sauce on the side and dip you French fries in them as they do in France!)

The garlic mashed potatoes did go well with the succulent one-inch thick Cedar Plank Pork Chops. Sweet, pink chops are cut from a roll of sixteen when ordered, dusted with Cajun seasoning, seared quickly on the flat top, then finished in a hot oven on a cedar plank, which imparts a subtle, smoky flavor to the meat. The wort from another house beer, a rich malt Hampton Brown Ale, is used to flavor an otherwise-classic Espagnole sauce – a red wine, shallot and garlic-based sauce. On this particular occasion, the seasonal vegetable was green beans sautéed with a little garlic in oil.

The Bone-In-Ribeye with wild mushroom stout sauce is testimony to how good a simple ribeye can be. "Oh, man.

That's one of my favorites!" Gonzalez says. A ten ounce bone-in-ribeye is seasoned with salt and pepper exclusively, and marked quickly on the grill. "My theory is, when the quality of meat is this good, it's a mistake to disguise it!" Gonzalez adds.

Working backwards on the menu, the two pastas I sampled were both superb – unbelievably rich, but well worth abandoning your diet for. The Cheese Ravioli are made from scratch. Huge, floppy ravioli tinted pink and flavored with tomato purée, are filled with a mixture of feta, chevre (goat cheese) and Parmesan cheese. The dish is constructed in layers with first a thin base of tomato concassé (crushed tomato), then whole leaves of barely wilted spinach, chunky strips of portabello mushrooms, and finally the ravioli topped with a satiny, parsley-flecked Alfredo Sauce.

The Seared Beef over Capellini runs a very close second to the ravioli. Bite-sized bits of filet mignon are seasoned, seared quickly in a pan, then tossed with delicate capellini in a sauce made from rosemary-seasoned, oven-dried Roma tomatoes (even better than sun-dried) enriched with a little heavy cream. A basket of warm, homemade bread precedes all entrées, salads and pastas. A little of the Brewery's own Amber Owl, a darkish ale, is used to flavor both the bread and the molasses-laced creamed butter that comes with it. A nice touch. Olive oil is added to the bread dough for the crisp, well-flavored crusts of the house pizzas cooked in a clay-bottomed pizza oven.

In spite of all the other fine features of the new menu, "We still sell a lot, a lot of Hamburgers," Gonzalez says. Jim Florence adds that he believes, "We have the best hamburgers in town." It is a great burger. It is no surprise that the meat is excellent and as an added bonus, they are using talented local baker, Sheila Partin's superior sourdough buns. (I especially like that anything that is not made on the premises is being purchased from the best possible resources.) Hamburger eaters have a choice of either skinny, completely addictive French fries, or the wonderful puffy, slightly oily, beer-battered onion rings.

Other appetizers worth ordering – apart form the crabmeat stuffed portabello mushrooms – are sassy cayenne pepper-covered Chicken Wings (served with good, chunky homemade Bleu cheese dressing for dipping) and Fried Calamari. Trouble is taken to tenderize the sometimes rubbery calamari by letting them rest in buttermilk seasoned with black pepper for a day.

The best choice all to precede one of the hearty entrées may just be the Caesar Salad. The dressing is one of the best in town – not too creamy and tart with the ideal balance of the usual ingredients, crisp croutons fashioned from their home-made bread, and welcome threads of freshly-shredded Parmesan cheese.

Do not miss dessert – even if you share among fellow diners. All three cakes were memorable, magnificently moist and gooey, and garnished with a generous scoop of Amy's fabulous Mexican vanilla ice cream. It's a difficult choice for a favorite among the Cinnamon Chocolate, Italian Cream or "Hummingbird" (similar to Italian Cream but studded with chopped pecans and flavored with cinnamon). They are not making these cakes, but someone very talented is.

The short wine list consists of mostly American (and a few Italian) wines, but after all, this is a brew pub and customers are encouraged to try one of the selections of "hand-crafted beers." As you might expect, they complement the food well.

Jim Florence also owns the adjoining Orchid Lounge, and since he opened the nightclub in November 1997, he's gained an (unofficial) reputation as the local Sultan of Swing.

Lounge and swing music is featured, particularly on weekends when Florence is bringing in bands such as the Austin-based Mr. Fabulous and Casino Royale and Big Bad Voodoo Daddy from Los Angeles.

WEST GRAY CAFE

415 West Gray
Houston, Texas 77019
713/528-2887

Type of Cuisine: American/Homestyle Cooking
Bar: Full
Dress: Casual
Entertainment: No
Payment: All Major Credit Cards
Entrée Range: $3.75-$8.95
Recommended Dishes:
  Entrees: Chicken Fried Steak
    Fried Chicken
    Liver and Onions
    Great Southern Style Vegetables
    Chicken and Dumplings
    Blue Plate Specials
  Breakfast: Pancakes
    Sausage
    Biscuits and Gravy
Hours: Monday-Friday, 5:30a.m.-9:00p.m., Buffet, 11:00a.m.-2:00p.m.
  Saturday, 6:30a.m.-3:00p.m.
  Sunday, 6:30a.m.-3:00p.m., Brunch, 10:00a.m.-2:30p.m.
Reservations: Accepted

"Welcome to the house!" says Mathew Smith as he warmly greets one of his many regular customers to West Gray Cafe. "The house" was built in the early twentieth century in the East Montrose area of West Gray, and Smith says he knew the moment he and his two partners, Karen Lucas and James Kidds, saw it almost a year ago that it was "the perfect place for our little homey-like restaurant. We wanted to make everything simple a cozy, neighborhood atmosphere where everybody felt comfortable. I wanted to get back to basics – something different – fresh food, fresh vegetables cooked in a homestyle way plain, simple and without the grease."

The West Gray Cafe opened its doors for business on February 1, 1996, and has been serving the kind of food most of us Texans grew up eating; Meatloaf (Mondays), Chicken and Dumplings (Wednesdays and everyday for dinner) and a Chicken Fried Steak that would gladden the heart of any cowboy.

Like most everything on the menu, Bay City native Smith says their Chicken Fried Steak is "done the old fashioned way the way my mother used to make it." One minor difference is the quality of the meat. "We use a U.S. Choice eight ounce ribeye that we cut ourselves." This lovely piece of meat is then subjected to the usual abuse – hammered into submission and arrives perfectly cloaked in a layer of crisp batter under a rich warm blanket of cream gravy.

On the other hand, I'd probably do the Texas two-step the length of West Gray for their flawless Fried Chicken. It is made in the time-honored tradition – seasoned, floured in a paper bag and deep fried. Smith admits, "It's pretty popular. We go through a couple of cases on Tuesday when it's a special."

My third favorite dish is West Gray's superior version of Liver and Onions (available Wednesdays and for dinner Monday through Friday). Smith swears that they don't do anything special to it. "We just season it up, bread it (with flour) and sauté it with onions." It's buttery-tender, thinly sliced calves liver in a rich brown gravy of pan-caramelized onions.

Any of these three dishes go well with the house Mashed Potatoes and the excellent, seasonally available Mustard Greens and Cabbage. In another little twist on the standard preparation, Smith says they use the trimmings from ribeye steak instead of pork to season the vegetables and it works well. "A lot of people are trying to get away from pork, so I decided to use beef instead. We just brown off the trimmings, drain the grease out of the pan, add a pinch of fresh garlic, a little onion, salt, pepper, then the mustard greens or cabbage, and always a pinch of sugar to take out the bitterness."

Of the daily blue plate specials, there's something to recommend every single day. On Monday, those who like Meatloaf will love West Gray's. A generous slab of meat, seasoned well with sautéed vegetables is then topped with their distinctive Creole sauce – a blend of garlic, celery, sliced onions and bell peppers in a dense tomato sauce. Smith says the meatloaf is their second biggest seller (of the daily specials) after chicken and dumplings.

On Tuesdays, go for the Baked Spare Ribs. They are braised in a two day process; dry seasoned and browned in the oven one day, then covered with chopped vegetables and cooked in a low oven for three to four hours until the vegetables dissolve, nature makes it's own wonderful gravy from pan juices and the meat falls off the bone.

On Wednesdays, who would want to choose between Chicken and Dumplings, meaty Short Ribs (prepared the same way as the spare ribs) and Liver and Onions? They are justly known for their chicken and dumplings. Huge chunks of chicken are surrounded by flat dumplings that have been cooked in the chicken stock and allowed to rest for an hour to absorb the flavors.

Thanksgiving comes every Thursday, as Turkey and Dressing outsells such old friends as Salmon Croquettes and Beef

Tips. Don't miss ordering the Yams (Tuesday, Thursday and Friday) to go with it. Kimberly, our waitress, insisted we try them and she was right – they were divine.

Smothered Steak tops the list on Fridays. Rather than use hamburger meat, eight ounces of inside round steak are pounded out, lightly breaded, deep fried, covered with bell peppers and onions and baked in the oven. An order of white rice goes well with the rich brown gravy. My Friday favorite is the Gumbo with a roux the color of deep mahogany, it is full of shrimp, crawfish tails and crab claws added at the last minute. Smith says they sell about six gallons on Fridays. "It's an old family recipe. My secret is that I don't use the tomatoes, just the juice for flavor from canned stewed tomatoes. I got the idea from my mom years ago when she used to make tomatoes and dumplings. It's a drop dumpling that you put in tomatoes and just stew it down. It's an excellent item that most people haven't had. I'm about to add it to the menu."

Friday night features all you can eat seafood for $9.95 from 6:00 p.m. to 10:00 p.m. Catfish breaded with yellow cornmeal shares the bill with large, tail on, crackermeal-coated Fried Shrimp and by popular demand, Fried Chicken. Some appetite should be reserved for Smith's Home Baked Pies – apple, coconut fudge with pecans and my personal favorite, pecan pie made even richer than usual by the addition of heavy cream.

West Gray Cafe opens for breakfast well before the crack of dawn seven days a week. Light, perfect Pancakes and spicy Pan Sausage are outsold daily, according to Smith, by the freshly made Buttermilk Biscuits and Cream Gravy. The West Gray Special is a bargain at $4.95 – 3 eggs (any style), 1 sausage patty, a bowl of country gravy, grits or hashbrowns and a choice of toast or biscuits. Breakfast is served every day until 3:00 p.m.

Mathew Smith and Karen Lucas are there sixteen hours a day, seven days a week. Smith refers to Lucas as "one of the finest, hardest working ladies I've ever known." When Kidds, a silent partner, and Smith decided to go into the restaurant business, Smith says he worked hard to recruit Lucas who had worked as a waitress and supervised the dining room of the Avenue Grill for twenty-six years.

West Gray Cafe, unlike most blue platetype places, has full bar service and has just started what they call the "Early Bird Special" where such house specials as chicken and dumplings, liver and onions, fried or baked chicken are $4.95, ribeye $5.95, all served with a choice of two vegetables and the dessert of the day from 4:00 p.m. to 7:00 p.m. Monday through Friday. All of these entrees are offered after 7:00 p.m. (unless they have run out) for slightly more money.

WHAT'S COOKIN'

Farm Road 518
Kemah, Texas
281/334-3610

Type of Cuisine: German
Bar: Full
Dress: Casual
Entertainment: Yes
Payment: All Major Credit Cards
Entrée Range: $8.00 -$18.95
Recommended Dishes:
Appetizers: Goulash Soup
Sausage Samplers
Fling Wings (Buffalo Wings)
Baked Brie
Entrées: Schlachtplatte (Mixed Sausages and Pork Chops)
Sauerkraut
Red Cabbage
Spatzle (Dumplings)
Potato Pancake
Rouladen (Beef)
Weinerschnitzel
Hours: Monday-Thursday, 11:00a.m.-11:00p.m.
Friday, 11:00a.m.-12:00a.m.
Saturday, Brunch: 8:00a.m.-3:00p.m., Dinner: 2:00p.m.-12:00a.m.
Sunday, Brunch: 8:00a.m.-3:00p.m., Dinner: 2:00p.m-.11:00p.m
Reservations: Accepted

Don't be put off by the dimly lit, partially obscured sign or the gravel road that runs between an abandoned school bus and an auto paint shop … you're in deep Kemah. When the crunch of the gravel under your tires stops and the dust clears, what's before you in the disguise of a 1970's fern bar is the home of some of the best German (Alsation/Swabian) cooking this side of Bavaria.

Transplanted Hungarian, Christine Garbo, opened What's Cookin' over eight years ago. At that time, Garbo was a great local cook so known for her hospitality that her friends would appear at her door on any given evening and simply ask … "What's cookin'?" So she bought 2.12 acres on FM 518 between Kemah and League City and went about transforming a former beauty salon into a restaurant where her friends could gather, and she could serve the kind of food that was closest to her heart.

This is one Garbo who doesn't "vont to be alone." What's Cookin' has a gemütich (cozy) neighborhood feel. Locals come in regularly to hang out in the bar, schmooze, drink for hours, maybe watch a football game on TV and just order appetizers.

Among the most popular is the warm, gooey individual Baked Brie served with a crispy baguette, sweet red grapes, sliced d'Anjou pear and red Delicious apple. Other big sellers are the best Fling Wings or buffalo wings in town, Fried Calamari, the Sausage Sampler and a classic and very credible version of Escargots.

Although billed as a "European-style" restaurant, what I long for and what's worth the trip are the German/Hungarian specialties.

Start with the Goulasch Soup to warm the cockles; a rich broth flavored intensely with sweet Hungarian paprika and marjoram, actually a favorite midnight snack of Bavarians served in individual pewter casserole-porringers in crowded Munich beer halls.

There are a couple of ways to try the assorted sausages. My husband and I always order two Sausage Samplers, listed as an appetizer; grilled and sliced bratwurst, knockwurst, wienerwurst and Italian sausage served with sauerkraut and sautéed until caramelized red onions and bell peppers. To cover all the bases, we add side orders of Red Cabbage, a Potato Pancake and another Swabian specialty, Spätzle (pronounced shpet-zal) – tiny dumplings made from flecks of noodle dough. Or you could order the Schlachtplatte – a more traditional presentation, where the wursts are whole and accompanied by a sweet, smoked grilled pork chop. Of course, sauerkraut is essential.

This is Sauerkraut to make my German soul sing! I defy anyone to taste this buttery, densely-flavored version of this much-maligned dish and not be won over! The same can be said for the Red Cabbage, and the spätzle is a must to try. Perfect on their own with a little butter and parsley rather than with the mushroom gravy. The Potato Pancake should be ordered to share; browned crisp on the outside, a whopping eight inches in diameter, it's more onion than batter and served with applesauce.

The Rouladen is another excellent choice – round steak, sliced thin and braised for hours in stock with carrots and onions.

Now a word about the Weinerschnitzel. The preparation of this "schnitzel" or "sliced cutlet of veal" originated in Milan. Prepared incorrectly, it's a disaster! Prepared properly, as it is here, pounded to perfect tenderness and lightly breaded, it's a bit of heaven requiring no further embellishment of a sauce of any kind.

On weekends, brunch is served between 11:00a.m. and 3:00p.m. and on Sunday there is a jazz brunch. The menu is fairly traditional but perfectly executed. The highlights are the outstanding Pancakes just added to the menu, the requisite, but faultless, Eggs Benedict and Kemah Town Fry – eggs, cheese and oysters baked until crispy on top. The only weak link was the coffee.

There is a short, well-priced wine list, but this is food that cries out for a crisp, cold mug of beer and since they scan the globe, with 215 to choose from (expanding to 250 in the spring when they add the "pub" in the back) that's the overwhelming accompaniment of choice. If your are a martini drinker, start your evening with one of the smoothest martinis I've encountered anywhere.

This is pretty robust fare, let's face it, better suited to the climate of Bavaria, but since we live in the tropics, I wouldn't wait for the next cold front to try these hearty and wonderfully satisfying German classics.

So, as they say in Germany, "Gut essen, Gut trinken" – "Good eating, Good drinking!"

ZYDECO LOUISIANA DINER

1119 Pease at San Jacinto
Houston, Texas 77002
713/759-2001

Type of Cuisine: Cajun/Seafood
Bar: No
Dress: Casual
Entertainment: No
Payment: All Major Credit Cards
Entrée Range: $5.95-$7.25
Recommended Dishes:
Boiled Crawfish (Available February-May)
Red Beans and Rice
Crawfish Bisque
Crawfish Etouffé
Gumbo
Oyster Po Boy
Hours: Lunch, Monday-Friday, 11:00a.m.-2:00p.m.
Dinner, Tuesday-Friday, 4:30p.m.-9:30p.m.
(during crawfish season, February-May)
(Closed Saturday and Sunday)
Reservations: Not Accepted

In France they are called "écrevisse"; in China, "lung har chay." Whether you call them crayfish, crawfish, crawdaddies or mud bugs (my personal favorite), these glorious crustaceans are at the absolute peak of their season now and I can't think of a better place to tuck into a heaping mound of them than the Zydeco Louisiana Diner.

Put on some old jeans, roll up those sleeves and make a beeline for the "Miss Zydeco Famous Crawfish Boils" any Tuesday, Thursday or Friday night during crawfish season, roughly between February and May.

Zydeco manages to combine two absolutely essential elements that make peeling and eating these delicious but messy little monsters worth the trouble – the superior quality of their crawfish and a genuine knack for seasoning them right and cooking them to perfection.

Co-owner and Louisiana native, Martin Venable, admits that in the last seven years they have featured fresh boiled crawfish during the season. "We have kind of established ourselves as having really good crawfish." He says it's all in the timing. The crawfish must be cooked just the right amount of time and served immediately. "Plus, we pay a little bit more for our crawfish." He says he's getting these lovely outsized specimens from a farm near Eunice, Louisiana, "deep in Cajun country."

The crawfish are seasoned in the traditional two-step process of first boiling them in water flavored with lots of onion, bay leaves, garlic, celery, bell peppers and crab boil, and then topping them with a sassy, lip-smacking blend of spices that includes granulated lemon, garlic, paprika, cayenne pepper and enough salt to retain a small wading pool.

As a little experiment, we ordered a couple of pounds with the standard "top seasoning" and a couple of pounds without, and I found that each has its merits. I happen to love the strong, complementary flavors of the seasoning, but an argument could be made for foregoing the second seasoning process, allowing the rich, sweet flavor of the crawfish to shine through. They are happy to prepare them either way. Red-skinned new potatoes and pieces of corn on the cob colored crimson from being plunged into the same fiercely seasoned water as the crawfish, must (and should) be ordered separately.

Stuffed Jalapeños, available exclusively at dinner, are the only non-Cajun presence on the menu. They are delicious – hot without being painful and stuffed with lots of fresh lump crab meat mixed with cream cheese and a little fresh parsley, coated lightly with buttermilk batter and fried (like all other fried items) in Lou Ana cottonseed oil. When I asked Venable if they were making the stuffed jalapeños themselves (few restaurants do) he said, "Oh yes, of course! We don't even own a freezer...or a microwave oven, by the way."

I love to hear this. It means that everything is fresh! fresh! fresh! – including the exceptional, freshly-cut Onion Rings which benefit from the same Tabasco®-spiked buttermilk batter as the jalapeños.

As I work my way down the menu, the Red Beans and Rice are earthy and authentic tasting enough to provoke a fullfledged flashback to late night meals in my best friend's kitchen in New Orleans during visits when I was growing up. The rich, creamy texture of the beans is punctuated by a generous portion of good, smoky sausage.

The Crawfish Bisque runs a close second in my affections. Considered the test of a great cook in Louisiana, those familiar with it know that crawfish bisque is anything but a traditional French bisque or cream soup. Venable considers it a "soupyish stew," and says that the secret to both the bisque and his heavenly Crawfish Étouffée is the fat of the crawfish. "You know, you can buy crawfish fat in stores in Louisiana," he says, but here he must rely on using the freshly-peeled crawfish with the orange fat from the heads and the tops of the tails still intact.

The Gumbo has a dark, intense flavor similar to the bisque but a little thinner. "The region that I was brought up in, a real dark roux is always what was made around the house. Also, the key to any gumbo is the meat you put in it." The Seafood

Gumbo is crowded with shrimp, crab meat and okra, but I tend to agree with Venable when he says that, "It's hard to beat the Chicken and Sausage Gumbo. That smoked sausage just adds so much flavor to it." All soups come with a choice of crackers or a welcome square of the sweet, moist, almost cake-like Cornbread. Venable says his cornbread has such a following that "people stop in just to get a piece of cornbread...sometimes even to eat with meals they get from somewhere else."

As we ate crawfish at dinner, we were also surrounded by people eating Po-boys – available filled with a choice of fried shrimp, oysters, catfish or roast beef. The Oyster Loaf, as they're known in New Orleans, compares favorably with any I remember having in my youth and meets all the most important requirements: plump, impeccably fried oysters, and good, crusty, freshly-baked bread, hollowed out, buttered, then spread with what Venable calls their "po boy sauce" – a pinkish blend of mayonnaise, catsup, Worcestershire, lemon juice and a little horseradish. (This sauce is also served with the stuffed jalapeños.) Order them as they do in the Big Easy, "fully dressed" with cool, shredded iceberg lettuce and tomato.

There are now two Zydecos; a newer one called Louisiana Joint on Travis and the original Zydeco Louisiana Diner on the corner of Pease at San Jacinto.

Primarily because of their locations, both restaurants serve lunch exclusively (cafeteria style), except during crawfish season. For three nights a week, February through May, the Zydeco Louisiana Diner serves crawfish and other specialties from 4:30 p.m. until 9:30 p.m. (They are marginally cheaper on Tuesday nights.)

One of my favorite dishes from the steam table at lunch is happily available every day – Baked Chicken. Again, Venable says, "The big key to the chicken is using fresh, not frozen, whole chickens that we cut up ourselves. They are dry-seasoned with a sweet/savory blend of paprika, chili powder, garlic powder and brown sugar, and baked until crisp around the edges, but still moist and juicy inside."

The Jambalaya is the sort that inspires music, "Jambalaya, crawfish pie, filé gumbo...." Currently available at night and on Tuesdays and Fridays at lunch, it is colored a rich, deep brown and has a generous studding of whole chunks of chicken and sausage.

The homemade Mississippi Mud pie is a soothing, welcome antidote to all the spicy food.

At night, I recommend Dixie's Blackened Voodoo Beer as the smooth, dark ale of choice to chase those crawfish down.

Mainstream Choices

AMÉRICAS
1800 Post Oak Blvd.
Houston, Texas 77056
713/961-1492
Type of Cuisine: North, Central and South American
Bar: Full
Dress: Nice Casual
Entertainment: No
Payment: All Major Credit Cards
Entrée Range: $10.00-$18.00
Recommended Dishes:
Appetizers: Taquito de Codorniz (Quail)
Pato Chino-Latino (Duck Taco)
Tiritas-Calamari
Ensalada "César" Original
Entrées: Pargo "Americas" (Red Snapper)
Coneja en Nogada (Loin of Rabbit)
Churrasco Chico (Beef Tenderloin)
Hours: Lunch: Monday-Friday, 11:00a.m.-2:30p.m.
Dinner: Monday-Thursday, 5:00p.m.-10:00p.m.
Friday-Saturday, 5:00p.m.-11:00p.m.
(Closed Sunday)
Reservations: Accepted

ANTHONY'S
4007 Westheimer
Houston, Texas 77027
713/961-0552
Type of Cuisine: Italian/Eclectic
Bar: Full
Dress: Jacket Suggested
Entertainment: No
Payment: All Major Credit Cards
Entrée Range: $13.95-$28.00
Recommended Dishes:
Appetizers: Duck Pillows
Risotto
Seared Scallops
Salads: Arugula, Watercress and Radicchio with Stilton
Anthony's Homestyle Salad
Entrées: Pepper Crusted Tuna
Hearth Roasted Duckling
Grilled Veal Chops
Hours: Lunch: Monday-Friday, 11:30a.m.-2:00p.m.
Dinner: Monday, 5:30p.m.-10:00p.m.
Tuesday-Thursday, 5:30p.m.-11:00p.m.
Friday-Saturday, 5:30p.m.-11:30p.m.
(Closed Sunday)

BRENNAN'S OF HOUSTON
3300 Smith
Houston, Texas 77006
713/522-9711
Type of Cuisine: Creole
Bar: Full
Dress: Jacket Required
Entertainment: Jazz band and singer at Brunch Saturday and Sunday
Payment: All Major Credit Cards
Entrée Range: $22.00-$28.00
Recommended Dishes:
Brunch: Eggs Hussard
Eggs Rockefeller
Tournedos Rossini and Eggs
Appetizers: Turtle Soup
Chevre Cheese Fallen Soufflé Salad
Hudson Valley Foie Gras and Duck Boudin
Entrées: Louisiana Pecan Crusted Fish
Gulf of Mexico Crabcakes
Dessert: White Chocolate Bread Pudding
Creole Bread Pudding Soufflé
Hours: Brunch: Saturday, 11:00a.m.-1:30p.m.
Sunday, 10:00a.m.-2:30p.m.
Dinner: Sunday-Wednesday, 5:45p.m.-9:00p.m.
Thursday-Saturday, 5:45p.m.-10:00p.m.
Reservations: Accepted

BRENNER'S STEAK HOUSE
10911 Katy Freeway
Houston, Texas 77079
713/465-2901
Type of Cuisine: Steak
Bar: Full
Dress: Jacket Suggested
Entertainment: No
Payment: All Major Credit Cards
Entrée Range: $14.95-$32.95
Recommended Dishes:
Appetizers: House Salad with Roquefort Dressing
Garlic Bread
Entrées: Filet Mignon (ask for "au jus")
German Fries
Dessert: Apple Streudel
Hours: Lunch: Tuesday-Friday, 11:30a.m.-2:00p.m.
Dinner: Monday-Saturday, 5:30p.m.-10:00p.m.
Sunday, 12:00p.m.-10:00p.m.
Reservations: Accepted

CADILLAC BAR
1802 Shepherd
Houston, Texas 77007
713/862-2020

Type of Cuisine: Mexican
Bar: Full
Dress: Casual
Entertainment: No
Payment: All Major Credit Cards
Entrée Range: $6.95-$15.95
Recommended Dishes:
Appetizers: Nachos
Queso Flameado Chorizo
Entrées: Cabrito al Pastor (Baby Goat)
Fajita Relleno Dinner
Quail
Hours: Monday-Sunday, 11:00a.m.-10:30p.m.
Reservations: Accepted

CAFÉ ANNIE
1728 Post Oak Blvd.
Houston, Texas
713/840-1111

Type of Cuisine: Continental
Bar: Full
Dress: Nice Casual
Entertainment: No
Payment: All Major Credit Cards
Entrée Range: $22.00-$34.00
Recommended Dishes: (Seasonal Menu)
Appetizers: Seared Salmon Foie Gras
Gulf Coast Crab Meat Tostada
Enchilada of Rabbit with Red Chile Mole
Roasted Quail with House Made Duck Sausage
Watercress Salad with Pears and Roquefort
Entrées: Texas Farm Raised Redfish with Barbacoa Pork Tamale
Wood Grilled Lamb Rib Chops with Black Oaxacan Mole
Wood Grilled Heavy Aged Ribeye Steak
Dessert: Vanilla Bean Crème Brulee
Warm Chocolate Cake with Cappuccino Meringue
Toasted Poundcake with Vanilla Ice Cream
Hours: Monday-Thursday, 11:30a.m.-2:00p.m., 6:30p.m.-10:00p.m.
Friday, 11:30a.m.-2:00p.m., 6:30p.m.-10:30p.m.
Saturday, 6:00p.m.-10:30p.m.
(Closed Sunday)
Reservations: Accepted

THE CAPITAL GRILLE
5365 Westheimer
Houston, Texas 77056
713/623-4600
Type of Cuisine: Steaks
Bar: Full
Dress: Nice Casual
Entertainment: No
Payment: All Major Credit Cards
Entrée Range: $15.95-$27.95
Recommended Dishes:
Appetizers: Clams on the Half Shell
Pan-Fried Calamari
Salads: Beefsteak Tomato and Onion
Spinach Salad with Warm Bacon Dressing
Cottage Fries and Onion Rings
Entrées: Sliced Steak
The Grille's Signature Veal Chop
Filet Mignon
Great Sides: Roasted Seasonal Mushrooms
Creamed Spinach
Sam's Mashed Potatoes
Dessert: Créme Brulée
Key Lime Pie
Cheese Cake
Hours: Sunday-Thursday, 5:00p.m.-10:00p.m.
Friday-Saturday, 5:00p.m.-11:00p.m.
Reservations: Accepted

CAFÉ CASPIAN
2730 Hillcroft
Houston, Texas 77057
713/266-4900
Type of Cuisine: Persian
Bar: Full
Dress: Casual
Entertainment: No
Payment: All Major Credit Cards
Entrée Range: $8.95-$12.95
Recommended Dishes:
Appetizers: Caspian Special (Samplings of best of the menu)
Kashk-E Bademjam (Eggplant Dip)
Mast-O Mooseer
Borani Esfenaj (Spinach Dip)
Cottlet (Meat Patties)
Shirazi Salad (Persian Salad)
Entrées: Lamb Shank
Beef Chenjeh (Skewered Filet Mignon and Shrimp)
Chicken Chenjeh (Skewered Chicken)
Chelo Kabob (Ground Beef Kabobs)
Hours: Sunday-Thursday, 11:00a.m.-10:00p.m.
Friday-Saturday, 11:00a.m.-11:00p.m.
Reservations: Accepted

CONFEDERATE HOUSE
2925 Weslayan
Houston, Texas 77027
713/622-1936
Type of Cuisine: American/Southern Homestyle
Bar: Full
Dress: Jacket Suggested
Entertainment: Singer, Piano Monday-Saturday, 6:30p.m.-10:00p.m.
Payment: All Major Credit Cards
Entrée Range: $12.00-$29.50
Recommended Dishes:
Appetizers: Seafood Gumbo (Friday Only)
Hickory Smoked Shrimp
Salads: Tomato Aspic with Shrimp
Wilhemina Salad
Confederate Salad
Entrées: Chicken Fried Steak
Fried Shrimp
Soft Shell Crabs
Lamb Chops
Venison
Dessert: Pecan Ball
Hours: Lunch: Monday-Friday, 11:30a.m.-2:30p.m.
Dinner: Monday-Saturday, 6:00p.m.-10:00p.m.
(Closed Sunday)
Reservations: Accepted

DAMIAN'S
3011 Smith
Houston, Texas
713/522-0439
Type of Cuisine: Italian
Bar: Full
Dress: Casual
Entertainment: No
Payment: American Express, MasterCard and Visa
Entrée Range: $10.95-$26.95
Recommended Dishes:
Appetizers: Insalata Narparst
Antipasto Misto
Fritto Misto
Gnocchi Verdi
Sausage and Peppers
Entrées: Rigatoni Amatriciana
Fedilini al Buongustaio
Lamb Chops Arno
Costolette alla Griglia
Pesce Spada alla Livornese
Shrimp Damian
Hours: Monday-Thursday, 11:00a.m.-2:00p.m., 5:30p.m.-10:00p.m.
Friday, 11:00a.m.-2:00p.m., 5:30p.m.-11:00p.m.
Saturday, 5:00p.m.-11:00p.m.
(Closed Sunday)
Reservations: Accepted

GOODE CO. SEAFOOD
2621 Westpark
Houston, Texas 77098
713/523-7154
Type of Cuisine: Texas Seafood
Bar: Full
Dress: Casual
Entertainment: No
Payment: All Major Credit Cards
Entrée Range: $8.95-$15.95
Recommended Dishes:
Appetizers: Fried Pie
Campechana de Mariscos (Mexican Seafood Cocktail)
Boiled Crawfish (Seasonal)
Entrées: Texas Redfish Mesquite Dinner
Gulf Red Snapper Mesquite Dinner
Etouffée
Dessert: Pecan Pie
Hours: Sunday-Thursday, 11:00a.m.-10:00p.m.
Friday-Saturday, 11:00a.m.-11:00p.m.
Reservations: Not Accepted

GUGENHEIM'S DELICATESSEN
1708 Post Oak Blvd.
Houston, Texas 77056
713/622-2773
Type of Cuisine: New York Deli
Bar: Wine and Beer
Dress: Casual
Entertainment: No
Payment: All Major Credit Cards, No Checks
Sandwiches: $3.99-$8.99
Recommended Dishes:
Corned Beef, Pastrami, Tongue
Russian Dressing
Sauerkraut, Coleslaw, Potato Salad
Chopped Liver
Dessert: New York Cheesecake
Heavenly Hash Brownie
Hours: Monday-Thursday, 10:00a.m.-9:00p.m.
Friday, 10:00a.m.-10:00p.m.
Saturday, 9:00a.m.-10:00p.m.
Sunday, 9:00a.m.-9:00p.m.
Reservations: Not Accepted

HUNAN
1800 Post Oak Blvd.
Houston, Texas 77057
713/965-0808
Type of Cuisine: Chinese
Bar: Full
Dress: Jacket Suggested
Entertainment: No
Payment: All Major Credit Cards
Entrée Range: $4.95-$46.00
Recommended Dishes:
Appetizers: Diced Boneless Squab Packages
Shrimp Toast
Honey Crispy Walnuts
Entrées: Return of the Phoenix (Chicken)
Scallops and Prawn, Huang's Style
Hunan Beef
Spicy Crispy Whole Fish
Subgum Lo Mein
Tangy Spicy Green Beans
Hours: Lunch: Monday-Thursday, 11:30a.m.-3:00p.m.
Friday-Sunday, 12:00p.m.-3:00p.m.
Dinner: Monday-Thursday, 11:30p.m.-10:30p.m.
Friday-Saturday, 12:00p.m.-11:30p.m.
Sunday, 12:00p.m.-10:30p.m.
Reservations: Accepted

LA MORA CUCINA TOSCANA
912 Lovett Blvd.
Houston, Texas 77006
713/522-7412
Type of Cuisine: Northern Italian
Bar: Full
Dress: Jacket Suggested
Entertainment: No
Payment: All Major Credit Cards
Entrée Range: $10.95-$22.95
Recommended Dishes:
Appetizers: Antipasto Misto
Carciofi Fritti (Fried Artichokes)
Calamari e Gamberetti Fritti (Calamari and Shrimp)
Portabello alla Griglia (Grilled Portabello Mushrooms)
Radicchio Ripieni alla Griglia (Grilled Radicchio)
Entrées: Tortelli al Burro e Salvia
(Pasta Stuffed with Spinach and Ricotta)
Pollo Arrosto (Roasted Chicken)
Arista di Maiale (Roasted Pork)
Costoletto di Vitello (Veal Chop)
Dessert: Tiramisu
Hours: Lunch: Monday-Friday, 11:30a.m.-2:00p.m.
Dinner: Monday-Thursday, 6:00p.m.-10:00p.m.
Friday-Saturday, 5:30p.m.-11:00p.m.
(Closed Sunday)
Reservations: Accepted

LA RÉSERVE
Omni Hotel, 4 Riverway
Houston, Texas 77056
713/871-8181
Type of Cuisine: Continental
Bar: Full
Dress: Jacket Required, Tie Optional
Entertainment: Piano in the Lobby
Payment: All Major Credit Cards
Entrée Range: $19.95-$26.95
Recommended Dishes:
Appetizers: "Tasting Menu" (subject to change)
Roquefort, Fig and Walnut Terrine
Shrimp and Crab Tian
Foie Gras
Entrées: Braised Lamb Shank
Sesame Crusted Crab Cakes
Tuna "Filet Mignon" Steak
Hours: Monday-Thursday, 6:30p.m.-10:30p.m.
Friday-Saturday, 6:00p.m.-10:30p.m.
(Closed Sunday)
Reservations: Accepted

MARK'S
1658 Westheimer
Houston, Texas 77006
713/523-3800
Type of Cuisine: Continental
Bar: Full
Dress: Nice Casual
Entertainment: No
Payment: All Major Credit Cards
Entrée Range: $15.75-$26.00
Recommended Dishes: (Seasonal Menu)
Appetizers: Terrine of Eggplant, Sun Dried Tomatoes, Zucchini and Roasted Peppers
Grilled Medallion of Quail and Foie Gras
Roasted Atlantic Salmon
Mark's Caesar Salad
Entrées: Scented Backstrap of Lamb
Hearth Roasted Maple Leaf Duck
Hearth Roasted Chicken
Grilled Tuna Medallions
Desserts: Raspberry Shortbread Tart
Chef's Banana Cream Pie
Chocolate Cake with Mexican Vanilla Ice Cream
Hours: Monday-Thursday, 11:00a.m.-2:00p.m., 6:00p.m.-11:00p.m.
Friday, 11:00a.m.-2:00p.m., 5:30p.m.-12:00a.m.
Saturday, 5:00p.m.-12:00a.m.
Sunday, 6:00p.m.-10:00p.m.
Reservations: Accepted

MAXIM'S
3755 Richmond Ave.
Houston, Texas 77046
713/877-8899
Type of Cuisine: French/Creole
Bar: Full
Dress: Jacket Required
Entertainment: Piano Monday-Saturday 5:00p.m.-closing
Payment: All Major Credit Cards
Entrée Range: $16.75-$38.00
Recommended Dishes:
Appetizers: Tomatoes Priscilla (with Crabmeat)
Seafood Gumbo
Schlumberger Salad
Entrées: Snapper Charlie Belle
Snapper Excelsior
Veal à la Holstein
Lamb Chops
Pommes Soufflés
Asparagus with Hollandaise Sauce
Hours: Lunch: Monday-Friday, 11:00a.m.-2:00p.m.
Dinner: Monday-Friday, 11:00a.m.-10:00p.m.
Saturday, 5:00p.m.-11:00p.m.
(Closed Sunday)
Reservations: Accepted

NINO'S ITALIAN RESTAURANT
2817 W. Dallas
Houston, Texas 77019
713/522-5120
Type of Cuisine: Italian
Bar: Full
Dress: Nice Casual
Entertainment: No
Payment: American Express, MasterCard, Visa
Entrée Range: $8.75-$21.95
Recommended Dishes:
Appetizers: Antipasto Misto
Carciofo Ripieno
Calamari Fritti
Entrées: Stracci – Pasta Rags
Pollo Arrosto
Veal Vincent
Scampi alla Griglia
Hours: Monday-Thursday, 11:30a.m.-2:30p.m., 5:30p.m.-10:00p.m.
Friday, 11:30a.m.-2:30p.m., 5:30p.m.-11:00p.m.
Saturday, 5:30p.m.-11:00p.m.
(Closed Sunday)
Reservations: Accepted

NIT NOI THAI RESTAURANT
2462 Bolsover
Houston, Texas 77005
713/524-8114

6395 Woodway
Houston, Texas 77057
713/789-1711
Type of Cuisine: Thai
Bar: Wine and Beer
Dress: Casual
Entertainment: No
Payment: All Major Credit Cards
Entrée Range: $6.95-$12.95
Recommended Dishes:
Appetizers: Soft Spring Rolls
Thai Noodle Soup (Chicken)
Entrées: Patt Thai Korat (Flat Rice Noodles)
Thai Fried Rice
Yum-Woon-Sen (Clear Noodle Salad)
Egg Foo Yong
Chicken Curry
Spicy Beef
Squid Thai Style
Vegetable Delight
Green Beans with Kafir Lemon Leaves
Hours: **Bolsover:** Monday-Friday, 11:00a.m.-3:00p.m
5:00p.m.-10:00p.m.
Saturday, 11:00a.m.-10:00p.m.
Sunday, 5:00p.m.-9:00p.m.
Woodway: Monday-Saturday, 11:00a.m.-3:00p.m.
5:00p.m.-10:00p.m.
Sunday, 11:00a.m.-2:00p.m., 5:00p.m.-9:00p.m.
Reservations: Accepted for Larger Groups

OUISIE'S TABLE
3939 San Felipe Road
Houston, Texas 77027
713/528-2264
Type of Cuisine: Continental
Bar: Full
Dress: Nice Casual
Entertainment: No
Payment: All Major Credit Cards
Entrée Range: $14.00-$27.00
Recommended Dishes:
Appetizers: Ouisie's Spud & Smoked Salmon
House Pate
Grilled Asparagus (Seasonal)
Crabcake
Spinach Salad
The Stilton Salad
Entrées: Fresh Softshell Crab with Sauce Charon
Shrimp and Cheese Grits
Seared Double Thick Pork Chop
Chicken Run Over by a Truck
Hours: Lunch: Tuesday-Friday, 11:20a.m.-2:30p.m.
"Little Bites"-Appetizers only:
Tuesday-Saturday, 2:30p.m.-5:30p.m.
Dinner: Tuesday- Thursday, 5:30p.m.-10:00p.m.
Friday-Saturday, 5:30p.m.-11:00p.m.
(Closed Sunday and Monday)
Reservations: Accepted

PALM RESTAURANT
6100 Westheimer
Houston, Texas 77057
713/977-2544
Type of Cuisine: Steaks/Continental
Bar: Full
Dress: Nice Casual
Entertainment: No
Payment: All Major Credit Cards
Entrée Range: $14.00-$35.00
Recommended Dishes:
Appetizers: Clams on the Half Shell
Clams Casino
Chopped Tomato/Onion Salad with Roquefort Dressing
Pimento and Anchovies
Entrées: Jumbo Maine Lobsters
Rib Eye
Veal Chop
Linguine with White Clam Sauce
Sides: Creamed Spinach
Half and Half: Cottage Fries and Fried Onions
Hours: Monday-Thursday, 11:30a.m.-10:30p.m.
Friday, 11:30a.m.-11:30p.m.; Saturday, 5:00p.m.-11:00p.m.
Sunday, 5:00p.m.-9:30p.m.
Reservations: Accepted

PAPPAS BROS. STEAKHOUSE
5839 Westheimer
Houston, Texas 77057
713/917-0090
Type of Cuisine: Steaks/American
Bar: Full
Dress: Nice Casual
Entertainment: Piano Monday-Saturday 7:00p.m. -10:00p.m.
Payment: American Express, MasterCard, Visa
Entrée Range: $18.95-$32.95
Recommended Dishes:
Appetizers: Bacon-Wrapped Scallops
Shrimp Remoulade
Fried Oysters
Turtle Gumbo
Lettuce Wedge Salad
Entrées: All Steaks, especially Porterhouse Steak
Veal Chop
Roasted Wild Mushrooms
Skillet Potatoes
Dessert: Pecan Pie
Hours: Monday-Thursday, 5:00p.m.-10:00p.m.
Friday-Saturday, 5:00p.m.-11:00p.m.
(Closed Sunday)
Reservations: Accepted

PAVANI
7320 Southwest Freeway, #104
Houston, Texas 77074
713/272-8259
Type of Cuisine: Indian
Bar: Wine and Beer
Dress: Casual
Entertainment: No
Payment: All Major Credit Cards
Entrée Range: $6.95-$13.95
Recommended Dishes:
Appetizers: Vegetable Pakora Sampler
Ginger Chicken
Chili Chicken
Uthappam (Bread)
Masala Dosa (Crepe with Vegetable Curry)
Entrées: Pavani Mixed Grill
Tandoori Chicken
Boti Kabab (Lamb)
Lamb Masala Curry
Hours: Lunch Buffet: Tuesday-Friday, 11:00a.m.-2:00p.m.
Saturday-Sunday, 11:00a.m.-3:00p.m.
Dinner: Tuesday-Sunday, 11:00a.m.-10:00p.m.
(Closed Monday)
Reservations: Accepted

REDWOOD GRILL
4611 Montrose
Houston, Texas 77006
713/523-4611
Type of Cuisine: Continental
Bar: Full
Dress: Nice Casual
Entertainment: No
Payment: All Major Credit Cards
Entrée Range: $10.95-$22.50
Recommended Dishes:
Appetizers: Buttermilk Fried Calamari
Shelly's Quesadilla
Melissa's Famous Nantucket Blue Spinach Salad
Entrées: Asian Seared Tuna
Rainbow Trout Meuniere
Grilled Ancho Porkchop
Braised Colorado Lamb Shanks
Hours: Monday-Thursday, 11:00a.m.-2:30p.m., 6:00p.m.-10:00p.m.
Friday, 11:00a.m.-2:30p.m., 6:00p.m.-11:00p.m.
Saturday, 6:00p.m.-11:00p.m.
Sunday, 6:00p.m.-9:00p.m.
Reservations: Accepted

RUGGLES GRILL
903 Westheimer
Houston, Texas 77006
713/524-3839
Type of Cuisine: American/Eclectic
Bar: Full
Dress: Casual
Entertainment: At Adjoining Maxi and Jake's Wednesday-Saturday 9:30p.m.-1:30a.m.
Payment: All Major Credit Cards
Entrée Range: $9.95-$17.95
Recommended Dishes:
Appetizers: Sautéed Gulf Crab Cake
Salads: Ruggles Salad
Warm Baked Texas Goat Cheese Salad
Soups: Corn Chowder
Spicy Red Snapper and Crab Chowder
Entrées: Seasonal Vegetable Plate
Grilled Veal Liver
Black Pepper Pasta
Hours: Lunch: Tuesday-Saturday, 11:30a.m.-2:00p.m.
Sunday, 11:00a.m.-2:30p.m.
Dinner: Tuesday-Thursday, 5:30p.m.-11:00p.m.
Friday-Saturday, 5:30p.m.-12:00a.m.
Sunday, 5:30p.m.-10:00p.m.
(Closed Monday)
Reservations: Accepted

RUTH'S CHRIS STEAK HOUSE
6213 Richmond Ave.
Houston, Texas 77057
713/789-2333

Type of Cuisine: Steaks
Bar: Full
Dress: Nice Casual
Entertainment: No
Payment: All Major Credit Cards
Entrée Range: $17.50-$29.50
Recommended Dishes:
Appetizers: Barbecued Shrimp
Shrimp Remoulade
Spinach Salad with Warm Bacon Dressing
Entrées: All Steaks Especially Filet Mignon
Lamb Chop
Sides: Creamed Spinach
Lyonnaise Potatoes
Shoestring Potatoes
Hours: Monday-Saturday, 5:00p.m.-11:00p.m.
Sunday, 5:00p.m.-10:00p.m.
Reservations: Recommended

SABINE
1915 Westheimer
Houston, Texas 77098
713/529-7190

Type of Cuisine: Contemporary Southern
Bar: Full
Dress: Nice Casual
Entertainment: No
Payment: All Major Credit Cards
Entrée Range: $14.00-$25.00
Recommended Dishes: (Seasonal Menu)
Appetizers: Quail Leg Confit & Watercress Salad
Rabideaux's Pork Sausage & Baby White Lima Bean Salad
Fried Green Tomatoes with Lump Crab Remoulade
Entrées: Seared Tuna with Lady Cream Pea Salad
Braised Lamb Shank with Tasso Spiked Red Cabbage
Smoked Meatloaf with Foie Gras
Desserts: Cobbler of Strawberry and Rhubarb
Ginger Ice Cream
Hours: Tuesday-Thursday, 11:30a.m.-2:00p.m., 5:30p.m.-10:00p.m.
Friday, 11:30a.m.-2:00p.m., 5:30p.m.-11:00p.m.
Saturday, 5:30p.m.-11:00p.m.
Sunday, 11:30a.m.-2:00p.m., 5:30p.m.-9:30p.m.
(Closed Monday)
Reservations: Accepted

TOMMY MANDOLA'S GULF COAST KITCHEN
1962 West Gray
Houston, Texas
713/528-3474
Type of Cuisine: Seafood/Cajun/Italian
Bar: Full
Dress: Casual
Entertainment: No
Payment: All Major Credit Cards
Entrée Range: $9.95-$19.95
Recommended Dishes:
Appetizers: Ceviche
Oysters Damian
Gried Green Tomatoes
Mama's Gumbo
Coon Ass Coleslaw
Entrées: Mama's Shrimp and Crabmeat Spaghetti
Blackened Snapper in Lime Butter
Hours: Monday-Thursday, 11:00a.m.-10:00p.m.
Friday-Saturday, 11:00a.m.-11:00p.m.
Sunday, 5:00p.m.-9:00p.m.
Reservations: Accepted

TONY'S RESTAURANT
1801 Post Oak Blvd.
Houston, Texas 77056
713/622-6778
Type of Cuisine: Italian
Bar: Full
Dress: Nice Casual
Entertainment: No
Payment: All Major Credit Cards
Entrée Range: $25.00-$39.00
Recommended Dishes:
Appetizers: Caramelli
Tuna Tartare 'Susman'
Lobster Bisque
Foie Gras Bellissima
Entrées: Braised Short Ribs
Osso Buco Con Risotto Milanese
Roast Duck 'Lampone' with Raspberry Sauce
Whole Red Snapper
Desserts: Chilled Honeydew Melon Consommé
Chocolate Casiss and Texas Pecan Torte
Spiced Riesling Poached Pear
Hours: Monday-Thursday, 6:00p.m.-11:00p.m.
Friday-Saturday, 6:00p.m.-12:00a.m.
(Closed Sunday)
Reservations: Accepted